The Cambrian

and

General Advertiser for the Principality of Wales

1804-1930

The Cambrian,

AND

GENERAL WEEKLY ADVERTISER FOR THE PRINCIPALITY OF WALES.

PRINTED AND PUBLISHED BY T. JENKINS, SWANSEA, GLAMORGANSHIRE.

No. 1.] SATURDAY, JANUARY 28, 1804. [PRICE SIXPENCE.

TO THE PUBLIC.

COLLIERIES AND ESTATE, SOUTH-WALES. TO BE SOLD OR LET,

GLAMORGANSHIRE. TO BE LET,

SWANSEA. TO BE LET,

AT a MEETING of the MERCHANTS and SHIP-OWNERS, held in the TOWN-HALL, in SWANSEA,

DUTY ON PROFITS.

TIMBER AND DEAL-YARD, SWANSEA. THOMAS and LASCELLES

FELL PARKER,

BEAUTIES OF WALES.

THE CAMBRIAN ITINERARY;

ANNALS of PUBLIC ECONOMY.

THE ARTIST's ASSISTANT;

THE HISTORY of the CIVIL WARS of GRANADA;

ELEMENTS of ENGLISH GRAMMAR;

VALUABLE SCHOOL BOOKS.

ARITHMETIC,

AN IMPROVED METHOD OF BOOK-KEEPING,

HOTTENTOTS.

THE EVANGELICAL MAGAZINE,

NEWTON'S RESTORATIVE TOOTH POWDER.

The first edition.

The Cambrian

and

General Advertiser for the Principality of Wales

1804-1930

GLYNDEN TROLLOPE

with contributions by

GLENYS BRIDGES, SANDRA THOMAS
and DR. R. D. REES

Glynden Trollope 28.01.04.

2003

First Impression: November 2003

Published in 2003 by
Glynden Trollope
Shenstone Hill, Berkhamsted, HP4 2PA

A CIP catalogue for this book is
available from the British Library.

ISBN 0-9545074-0-1

Printed and bound in Wales by
Dinefwr Press Ltd.
Rawlings Road, Llandybie
Carmarthenshire SA18 3YD

Dedicated to a very dear son
Stephen
who died in July 2002

Acknowledgements

Many years ago my friend Professor David Farmer introduced me to the British Newspaper Library in Collingdale, North London, where I developed a fascination for Swansea's newspapers and *The Cambrian* in particular. It seemed a good idea to publish a book commemorating the bi-centenary of the newspaper's launch.

Professors David Farmer and Emrys Jones; Emyr Nicholas and Eddie John, of Dinefwr Press, and my wife Val and daughter Kate have all given me a great deal of encouragement and helpful advice, for which I am very grateful.

I would like to thank Ron Humphreys, my wife's cousin, for his kind help in obtaining indispensable photocopies of the *Cambrian* editions used in compiling this book and Julie Attree Director of MIND in Dacorum – a native of Swansea – and, chairperson Fran Deschampneufs. Thanks are also due to the British Newspaper Library, the National Library of Wales, the City and County of Swansea's Library and Information Service and Museum; the County Archive Service, Morgans Hotel, Susan Beckley, Bernice Cardey, Marilyn Jones, Gill Lewis, Bernard Morris, Hilary Thomas, Adrian Bailey, Swansea Council for Voluntary Service; Roy Noble, who has readily accepted an invitation to launch the book; others who help through various charities and organisations and those who respond after the book has 'gone to press'.

Two important papers are included as Appendices. The County Archivist, Swansea and Glenys Bridges and Sandra Thomas have kindly given me permission to use an extract from "The Report of the County Archivist, 1 April 1993 – 31 March 1994" (Appendix 1). R. D. Rees' paper, "Glamorgan Newspapers under the Stamp Acts, Morgannwg III (1959), pp. 61-94" (Appendix 2), is included by kind permission of Glamorgan History Society. My efforts and those of the Society to contact R. D. Rees have been unsuccessful.

I extend my thanks to: Martin K. Ewens of Ewens Graphic Design for the cover design. – The National Library of Wales and the City and County of Swansea Library and Information Service and Swansea Museum Service: Swansea Museum Collection respectively for allowing me to reproduce several front pages of *The Cambrian*, the photograph of The Cambrian Office and the print, 'A View of Cameron's Wharf, Swansea, c. 1847' by William Butler. – Swansea Museum Service: Swansea Museum Collection for permitting me to include the print of Butler's The Cambrian Office, Wind-street Swansea 1849. – Mrs Methuen-Campbell for the photograph of Penrice Castle – Mr. Michael Eddershaw for his photographs and Mrs Monica Phillips for the loan of a booklet, published for Swansea Corporation in 1902 and containing the advertisement for Swansea Empire and Weaver's. Many of the images are taken from my photographs and 19th century prints which I own. I apologise for any unintentional infringements.

The responsibility for the book's contents rests with me. I have tried to spot and eliminate my mistakes but, unless readers check editions, they will not be able to tell whether errors in the extracts are mine or those of the *Cambrian*'s compositors! It should be noted that the spelling of some words has changed over the last two centuries.

Berkhamsted, 2003. Glynden Trollope.

Contents

Foreword

PROFESSOR DAVID FARMER

The year 2004 is the bi-centenary of *The Cambrian* – the first English language newspaper to be published in Wales. It is apposite, therefore, that Glynden Trollope's fascinating collection of extracts, papers, illustrations and comments relating to the paper should be published at this time.

As will be seen, most of the book is made up of extracts from *The Cambrian* taken at two yearly intervals beginning with its launch in 1804 until 1904. These are followed by three further sections which focus respectively on editions published in 1914, 1924 and the final edition in 1930, after which *The Cambrian* merged with *The Herald of Wales*. In his Introduction Trollope explains the basis and limitations of his selections, though he need not be concerned about this aspect. Publications of all kinds about history involve difficult choices, especially when there are 6,204 editions from which to choose. The purpose of the book is to provide the reader with a 'glimpse' of *The Cambrian*'s style, content and format at stages during the one hundred and twenty-six years of its life. The material which has been chosen, meets the criteria admirably. Furthermore the papers by Bridges and Thomas, and that by Rees provide the reader with interesting background material.

Overall there is much to be commended in this book which will appeal to those familiar with *The Cambrian* and to newcomers alike. Certainly it provides the reader with an intriguing insight into a period of significant economic and social change; and the role of a newspaper in charting these changes. It should also stimulate further ideas regarding access to and the use of the superb newspaper archive resources in Swansea, Aberystwyth and London.

Finally, it is a pleasure to note that, apart from retailing costs, MIND in Dacorum and other charities which sell this edition will receive all the proceeds. Production and related costs have been met through supporters of the venture.

Swansea
October 2003

The Cambrian Office – early 20th century.

The site of the Cambrian Office – early 21st century.

Introduction

GLYNDEN TROLLOPE

This book celebrates the 200th anniversary of the first edition of *The Cambrian* or GENERAL ADVERTISER FOR THE PRINCIPALITY OF WALES. Between 1810 and 1812 the conjunction "or" replaced "and" in the title until c.1850. In 1846 the emblem of Britannia was printed on the top right, and the three feathers, with an inset harp, on the top left hand sides of the first page. Previously this order was reversed and from c.1848 the emblems were not displayed. *The Cambrian* was Wales' first newspaper, launched from 58 Wind Street, Swansea, on January 28th 1804. By the mid-nineteenth century it was renamed *The Cambrian* AND GENERAL ADVERTISER FOR SWANSEA AND THE PRINCIPALITY OF WALES. Published weekly, the secondary title emphasised the importance placed on advertisements from the outset. Its list of agents covered all the Welsh counties as well as many English cities, including Hereford, Bath, Bristol, Birmingham and Gloucester and several towns such as Ledbury, Frome and Shepton Mallett.

Reprinting 600 extracts for this book was difficult so hopefully, in future, the editions will become available through an electronic retrieval system. My extracts are taken at two yearly intervals covering a century from 1804 until 1904 and from editions in 1914, 1924 and 1930. At this stage *The Cambrian*'s life as a separate newspaper ended and it was absorbed as a minor partner within *The Herald of Wales*. The images in the book are either from *The Cambrian* or relate to its era.

Very little has been written about *The Cambrian* and this book is not a history or critique of the newspaper. However, two important papers are acknowledged and included as Appendices. In his paper, Appendix 2, R. D. Rees wrote that:

> "the best sources of information are the editions." and "A complete reading of the files, would give a very full social history of the times; the accounts are, therefore, highly selective, and cannot pretend to analyse all aspects of the paper . . . A large amount of material remains undescribed."

I share this view; there were 6,204 editions of *The Cambrian*! Fortunately, many people have been able to refer to these since they were deposited in the various archives; and professional and amateur historians alike find that the archives are veritable gold mines of local information. As part of a national programme the editions of *The Cambrian* and many other local newspapers are being preserved on micro fiche film for future generations; and an excellent index, currently covering 1840 to 1870, can be consulted for a reasonable fee at Swansea's Central Library. This source is especially useful in researching family history.

One of my aims is to give an impression of the development of a 19th and early 20th century weekly newspaper in Wales; and the extracts shed some light on social, economic and journalistic developments over a period of 126 years. The extracts raise a wide range of issues, some of which are referred to in this introduction and in the Appendices. The influences of editors, owners and changing technology are especially worthy of consideration together with the effects on a weekly journal when, subsequently, competing daily and other weekly newspapers were launched.

There is a bias in the selection of extracts towards items of local interest although in the earlier editions these are sparse and the emphasis is very dependent on the content of informative advertisements. During the first part of the 19th century, the pages of *The Cambrian* were dominated by pieces, often reprinted from other journals, dealing with international and national issues. These included long parliamentary, agricultural, commercial, and industrial reports. All these items were important for *The Cambrian*'s early readership – the nobility, clergy and gentry. The synopses in Appendix 3 give some indication of the newspaper's overall contents and the changes which occurred during its lifetime; these are also illustrated by the images of the first and final editions.

Even towards the end of the 19th century a wide coverage of world news formed an important part of the newspaper. Local news content, however, increased gradually throughout the late 19th and early 20th centuries; and *The Cambrian*'s final edition in 1930 was essentially one full of Swansea and south-west Wales news. As standards of literacy improved *The Cambrian* catered for an evolving and much wider readership. The price of the newspaper's early editions was an expensive 6d. rising to 7d. which could only be afforded by the elite; subsequently the price was reduced steadily to 1d. as economic and social circumstances changed and the readership expanded.

Initially *The Cambrian* did not face significant competition but as Rees explained:

> "After 1855 many more papers came out and daily papers began."

In 1861 the *Cambrian Daily Leader* was launched in Swansea and the owners of *The Cambrian* promptly objected to the use of the word "Cambrian" in its title. This was changed to the *Cambria Daily Leader* and a leading article from that newspaper dated 24th May 1861 is included in Appendix 3.2. Subsequently, publication of the *Leader* lapsed. It was relaunched in 1881 but it was later absorbed by the *Daily Post* whose management also published *The Herald of Wales*. The *Post* eventually became the *South Wales Evening Post*; so there are contemporary links with *The Cambrian*.

As can be seen from the images of front pages and R. D. Rees' paper, the format of *The Cambrian* changed significantly over its lifetime. At first, *The Cambrian* had four and sometimes six pages, each containing five columns. By 1836 it had eight columns per page. From 1860 there were eight pages but by 1892 the number of columns had been reduced to seven. Prominent headlines were not used until the later years of the *Cambrian*'s life; in earlier editions there was often little or no separation between items.

From time to time editors of *The Cambrian* showed interest in the newspaper's past. On 26th June 1896 there was an important piece entitled "Swansea through 'Cambrian Spectacles' – Interesting Nineteenth Century Facts", by Historicus Junior:

> "There are few things more interesting than the history of one's town particularly that portion of it associated with our early days. Swansea's veterans are rarely more delighted than when recounting memories of the past, or describing their connection, however slight it may be, with events which have shaped the development and history of the town.

There are few living among us who remember the first few years of the present century, but I will endeavour, through *The Cambrian* spectacles to present to old and young a true newspaper record of the town:

'Youth longs, and Manhood strives, but Age remembers.
Sits by the raked-up ashes of the past;
Spreads its thin hands above the whitening embers,
Which warm its creeping life-blood till the last.'

A well known gentleman said to me the other day, 'The most valuable thing in the Royal Institution of South Wales is *The Cambrian* file. What better record could we have of the town's commercial, social and, religious and municipal progress? That record I shall present to the readers of *The Cambrian* in the course of a series of articles. I have pondered over the files of the old paper from its first number. The result is that I shall be able to present my readers interesting, readable and instructive articles, especially to Swanseaites bred and born."

This was the first of a long series of articles and on 29 February 1904 another feature was published, as part of a series, entitled, "Echoes of the Past. – Interesting Extracts from 'The Cambrian' of 1805". Such series would be well worth reprinting. There was also a brief reference to *The Cambrian*'s 100th birthday:

"By the time this issue is in print, the hundred years will have elapsed ere the first number of the 'Cambrian', was taken up from the press on January 28th 1804, in the height of the Napoleonic struggle. Since then Welsh Journalism has grown to what is possibly today its maximum limit, and it is a sign of the times that the first newspaper published in Wales was in English throughout – and the tongue of the Sassenach has never lost the start it obtained then. In South Wales indeed Anglicising influences are fast obliterating the sense of distinct nationality – commerce and industries, the great welders of nations all the world over, have permanently broken down and absorbed all barriers and distinctions of race. Yet there is the consolation the reflection affords, that in journalism, as in so many other things, Swansea enterprise led the way!"

Time has not diminished the pride felt by Swansea people for a very special town and city.

The language of *The Cambrian* merits special mention. In a late 19th century reference to the newspaper's use of language, Historicus Junior commented that:

"It made its bow to the public in a well-written, dignified editorial, containing, however, much of the extravagance and floridity of language which marked the generality of newspapers of those days."

The first leading article in 1804 included, for example, ". . . before that august tribunal which is ultimately to fix its destiny . . ." and "we entreat attention while we concisely develope the innotives on which our pretensions to approbation and favour are granted." Elsewhere, words and phrases like "precipitrosy" are used and advertisers hoped that "by unwearied assuidity and constant attention, to merit a continuation of their (i.e. the customers) favours." There are examples of how the use of language has changed over the years. "Brought to bed" is used to describe confinement and there are phrases like, "The house is delightfully situated on an *eminence*" and "There is a good hit of fruit in the orchards."

Many more examples of change in the use of language are to be found in the extracts and the editions.

The development of transport was a continuing theme. Initially, sea and horse drawn services were in the ascendancy. Names and types of ships and carriages were to be found in the text. Timetables were published and there was evidence of intense competition. This was reflected in advertisements for coach journeys and there were instances of drivers racing each other, often recklessly; ignoring bridges by fording rivers, to obtain custom. Road tolls, with their infamous gates, were expensive and contentious; and there were controversies about the development of canals. The perils of travelling by sea and coach were recorded as well as the increasing threat to horse drawn coach firms through the planning and building of railways. Proposals for railway developments were outlined, including an 88-mile track, parallel to the sea, from Llanelly to Sharpness. Editions of *The Cambrian* often contained an array of railway timetables which referred to lines and stations long since closed. Despite the introduction of railways, horse drawn transport was an essential but diminishing part of the transport network, until, the internal combustion engine was invented. Soon after this era dawned a lorry driver was prosecuted for driving at 18 mph when the speed limit was 12 mph.

It is remarkable how many of the controversies reported by *The Cambrian* have a contemporary resonance. Plans for Swansea's infra-structure and various civic controversies were often covered and 'Letters to the Editor' featured regularly from the earliest of editions. Articles referred to the extension of the Mumbles railway, the development of tramways, absconding tax collectors and the excessive salary paid to the harbour master. Many proposals for major projects which did not materialise were included. In the 19th century, consideration was given to the feasibility of constructing a barrage across the river Tawe. There was a vigorous debate about the most suitable location for a safe harbour in the Bristol channel; possible sites included Swansea, Mumbles and Lundy. Towns, including Swansea, campaigned to be included on main railway lines and there was great concern about the inconvenience and costly disruption when Swansea's New Cut bridge jammed after allowing shipping to pass.

Developments in industry and trade can be traced, including dock building programmes. Details of arrivals and departures of ships and their owners, cargoes and ports of call were recorded. Ship-wrecks were reported along with references to the feats of life-boat crews under sail. In 1914 *The Cambrian* recorded that there were 92 vessels in Swansea's docks – 50 steam and 42 sailing vessels and there were references to transatlantic and southern hemisphere sea voyages for emigrants and details of passenger and freight services between Bristol Channel, West Coast and Irish ports. Access to Somerset, Devon and Cornwall was much swifter during *The Cambrian*'s lifetime than it is at the beginning of the 21st century!

Major economic and social changes can be observed, not least through analysis of advertisements. In this context descriptions of properties, long since destroyed by the blitz or development can be found, including Worcester House which overlooked Swansea's Strand and The Plas, Thomas of Lan's home; Thomas was a pioneer in providing Swansea's open spaces and his bust is to be found in Victoria Park near the Patti Pavilion. The readership of *The Cambrian* changed significantly during its lifetime. In the nineteenth century it published class conscious visiting lists from the resorts, births, marriages and deaths of the elite, descriptions of fashions and accounts of upper class fancy dress parties giving the names of the guests and their residences. Even in 1900 an incredible amount of space was devoted to an account of a local 'society' wedding, including details of all the presents and the donors.

In the early editions of *The Cambrian*, most references to education applied to the upper classes. Advertisements for schools and colleges were focussed on the sons and daughters of the gentry and featured the classics, university entrance, music and dancing. But as the industrial revolution gathered momentum the managing class recognised that its interests lay with educating the lower classes to operate its factories. Science and engineering were seen as especially important. The foundation of the Royal Institution of South Wales and the Tradesmens' and Mechanics' Institute were promoted as well as the establishment of schools, the Technical College and the University College of Swansea. Early movements to educate the children of the poor were reported, although there was concern about:

> "Servants being taught things that would unfit them for the discharge of the duties of their respective situations, the working classes being taken out their proper sphere of life; there being none left to perform the manual services in society."

The Cambrian contained verbatim accounts of court hearings giving details of crimes and accidents, floggings and executions. Its columns also charted the changes in punishment which took place and there was a debate on whether the death penalty should be abolished.

Other themes included the change from candle power to gas and then electricity; the transition from sail to steam and improved systems of navigation and communication. The histories of the theatre, music halls and cinema were recorded. Advances in medicine were followed and there was an incredible array of advertisements for proprietary medicines guaranteed to cure all medical conditions! Religious issues and news were also widely reported and there were many biographies of local dignitaries.

Throughout its period *The Cambrian* had specialist columns; some endured and others changed periodically. The titles included *The Cambrian* leading article and the London "Posts" columns. POETRY OR POET'S CORNER appeared in most editions. FOREIGN INTELLIGENCE was a regular feature and POSTSCRIPT was used to include late news. The importance of science and engineering was reflected in the columns SCIENTIFIC NOTICES and SCIENTIFIC INTELLIGENCE. There were references in 1822 to the use of Congreve rockets for whaling, the domestic telegraph and a bread machine. In 1830 compressed air was proposed as a substitute for steam and the importance of chemistry was stressed. INTERESTING NOTICES in 1844 marvelled at the "Extraordinary Production of Ice in a Red Hot Crucible" and a forthcoming meeting of the British Association for the Advancement of Science was mentioned. LITERARY AND SCIENTIFIC in 1852 referred to photographic developments but most of the snippets were anything but scientific and hardly literary. WELSH INTELLIGENCE covered items, written in English, from the Welsh shires. LITERATURE &C in 1854 included the following piece – "A Pretty Face. He who marries a pretty face only is like a buyer of cheap furniture – the varnish will not endure the fire-side blaze." There were columns entitled VARIETIES or LITERARY VARIETIES which could provide material, suitably adapted, for many an after dinner speech.

Agriculture and Trade, General Intelligence and Portfolio columns were featured and in 1896 Thoughts of Thinkers included – "it is not what others think of you which signifies, but that which you think of yourself. It matters little whether the world regards you through rose-coloured glass, but much whether you look through rose-coloured glass at the world." Chips of News contained snippets like "Mr. Reeves, butcher, Harrietsham near Maidstone, was passing over a level crossing at Lanham, when he stumbled and fell. Before he could recover himself he was run over by a train and cut to pieces." Our Pulpit summarized a long series of sermons by eminent preachers and Something for Young People contained poetry and children's stories. Sports and Pastimes appeared at the end of the 19th century and Chess and Draughts were also featured. Y Congl Cymreig was also a later initiative; in 1896 this column included the poem "Dydd yr Etholiad" and articles entitled "Llofion" and "Lecshwn". But relatively few items in the Welsh language were published. "The Cambrian" Magazine included, 'A Page for Old and Young' with a column entitled 'The Children's Corner', "conducted by Uncle Robin." In the 20th century the columns Our Post Bag and Post Bag were introduced.

These are just some of the themes and features which have attracted my attention; there are many more to be discovered in the extracts and the editions.

As I explained at the beginning of this introduction, relatively little has been written about *The Cambrian*. Perhaps this celebratory publication will encourage others to write about our local newspapers. As well as books, a series of essays and dissertations would add to our appreciation of 19th and early 20th century local journalism.

28th. January 1804.

To The Public

On the first appearance of a New Paper before that august tribunal which is ultimately to fix its destiny, *Custom,* exacts a disclosure of its claim to notice: obedient to her mandate, we entreat attention while we concisely develope the innotives on which our pretensions to approbation and favour are grounded.

The utility of Newspapers is too obvious to require a single comment; yet not withstanding their great increase of late years, particularly Provincial journals, the Principality of Wales has, till now, been denied one of those perles of refinement, instruction and amusement when in no part of the kingdom could the necessity for such an establishment more strongly exist. Its numerously enlightened inhabitants have thus been subjected to various inconveniences from the same cause, the importance of the trade of Wales, its valuable resources, and commercial enterprise, are at this time imperfectly known. These considerations gave birth to THE CAMBRIAN.

Our design is not merely to multiply the channels of general knowledge: we have formed expectations of a more elevated nature; and ardently hope to be instrumental in rendering service to the Principality lastingly beneficial. We, therefore *again* earnestly invite all who can estimate the means of promoting the best advantages of Wales, by the improvement of Agriculture, expansion of Trade or otherwise, to transmit their suggestions, (post-paid) and THE CAMBRIAN shall be the medium of dissemination.

It will moreover be our stand to convey early and authentic details of every interesting transaction at home and abroad: we shall faithfully record the proceedings of the Legislature, and all important decisions of the Law Courts: the prices of London Markets; all fluctuations of the Public Funds shall be correctly stated . . .

Independence and Impartiality shall be our basis – *Truth* our guide. We will never sacrifice at the shrine of *Party* . . .

Glamorganshire

TO BE LET
from Lady Day *next*

The Capital MANSION of BIRCHGROVE, with or without the adjacent FARM and LANDS, situate within five miles of the Town of Swansea, and very accessible from the two Turnpike Roads which pass near it. – The House is modern, and its situation, comfort and convenience, are strong recommendations.

For particulars apply by letter (post-paid) to Mr Levi Jones, Swansea.

———

On Thursday night and Friday morning last we experienced a tremendous gale of wind, which exceeded in fury any thing of the kind within recollection. The tide being out, the shipping received but trifling injury. Some vessels ran ashore at Mumbles, which have since been got off with inconsiderable damage. The streets of the town exhibited a distressing spectacle at the dawn of Friday, being covered with tiles, slates &c, scarcely a house having escaped uninjured, several chimnies were blown down, but providentially no lives were lost. It would greatly exceed the limits of a newspaper to particularise the mischief produced by the devastating element: we have received accounts from various quarters of Wales, and the neighbouring counties, of its melancholy effects – many cottages have been destroyed, houses and other buildings unroofed, ricks dispersed, large timber trees torn up by the roots. But amidst the general ravages, it will be extremely gratifying to the feeling mind to know there have only been one or two instances of persons having perished. Here as in other ports, the storm was preceded by an uncommon agitation of the sea, which seemed to indicate a surprising concussion of nature . . .

———

USEFUL NOTICE

Strengthening of Ships – A patent has been recently granted for the invention of a method to strengthen ships or other floating vessels. The use of this invention is, to preserve life and property, by making a ship much stronger than on the common construction; so that should she, by stress of weather, be driven on shore, she will keep upright, and be better able to resist danger, which is effected by laying a keel on each side of the middle line, distant from it, including the thickness thereof, one sixth of the average breadth at loading draft of water, or a little more or less, according to the fullness or sharpness of the ship. The patentee observes, that a ship thus secured from straining, is more likely not to work her plank loose, which often occasions foundering; and if, by stress of weather, she is unavoidably driven ashore, she has the advantage of ships on the common construction, as they, lying on their edge, easily roll by the agitation of the sea, and strike against the ground and when left by the tide, are often bulged by the over-hanging weight; but ships on this construction, having one third of their breadth to stand on, will neither roll, nor be likely to bulge; and if, from the declevity of the ground, another ship should overset, this will not, having two thirds of the weight to counteract it: therefore, as the preservation of lives and property at sea is of great importance, the above invention is certainly entitled to notice. The patentee requires only a small compensation per ton to allow any ship-builder the benefit of it.

———

LONDON

The invasion of this country by the French has for some time been the general topic of conversation, and various rumours are continually afloat on the subject. That the preparations of our implacable and designing enemy for the enterprise are of immense magnitude, we readily believe; but we have the satisfaction to know, at the same time, that our countervailing efforts are fully proportionate to the danger we have to encounter. It is the opinion of many that the attempt will speedily be made, while others believe it is postponed till the spring. We would by no means, however, encourage any imprudent confidence or relaxation in our exertions to guard against the impending attack. All we would wish to do is, to caution our countrymen against premature and needless alarm; to prepare and strengthen their minds against the moment of real danger; but not to harrass and perplex their imaginations with confused and exaggerated accounts that have little or no foundation in fact.

It is surmised that the French have it in contemplation to send a strong squadron from Brest with troops to the East Indies, in the hope of disturbing our tranquillity in that quarter. Government, it is understood, have intimated their suspicions on this subject to Admiral Cornwallis, who is now blockading Brest . . .

We know not whether the enemy have at last ventured to send their whole force to sea, or only a part of it, but they seem to have taken advantage of our ships being blown off the coast by the late gales. – Our squadron has for these three or four days been forced to return to the Downs. About noon yesterday a heavy firing was heard at Deal in a S.S.E. direction and continued when the post set out.

——◇——

At a MEETING of the MERCHANTS and SHIP-OWNERS, held in the TOWN-HALL, in SWANSEA on Saturday, Nov. 5, 1803.

WILLIAM JONES, *in the Chair:*

A letter having been received from Major General Gascoyne, approving the idea of providing four light FIELD-PIECES for the defence of the HARBOUR and COAST, (as recommended by a meeting held here the 26th ult.) and advising that it be carried into immediate effect:

This meeting seeing the necessity of immediate and active exertion, do enter into the following resolutions:

1, That they will at their own expense, purchase FOUR BRASS SIX-POUNDERS, with their Carriages and proper appendages, to be placed upon the Hill commanding the Harbour of Swansea and adjacent coast, and to be under the care and direction of the Commander of the Sea Fencibles, and exercised by a sufficient number of his best Gunners . . .

——◇——

The Queen's Birth-day. Yesterday, being the anniversary of the festival in honour of the birth of our most gracious Queen, who completed her 59th year on 19th May last, and who, as it was once elegantly and truly said in the House of Commons, "has so lived as to starve the malice of the world." . . . On the entrance of the Queen into the Drawing-Room, the performance of the Ode immediately began; music from the works of Handel, adapted to it by Sir Wm. Parsons.

Her Majesty, who appeared in good health, and received her visitors with her accustomed good spirits and affability, wore a bright orange coloured satin petticoat, with a border of black velvet, white rich silver fringe round the bottom; a drapery of black velvet vandyked, trimmed round with very rich Turkish balvine chains and tassels. An elegant turban and sash of very fine black lace, looped up with silver rolio; beautiful silver cords and tassels . . .

. . . all the ladies (with the exception of a few) wore very large plumes of ostrich feathers – none less than 4, and many 6 or 7. The hair was univerally dressed in Grecian style with, pearl and diamond combs.

. . . The prevalent colours were purple, scarlet, and yellow; with very rich embroidery.

. . . The dresses of the gentlemen in general consisted of velvet coats and breeches of the same colour, with a white satin waistcoat; the whole richly embroidered. The prevailing colours were bottle-green and brown.

——◇——

Swansea Assembly last night, exhibited, as usual, a numerous and elegant display of company.

——◇——

FEMALE DRESSES
FOR FEBRUARY

Morning Dresses – Of plain India muslin are likely to supersede entirely the cambrics, in consequence of the former being patronised by the Duchess of St. Albans, and Lady Charlotte Lennox, &c. These dresses are made quite in the Parisian style, short in the waist, close up to the neck, with a double row of lace, and long sleeves, with a large ruffle. A cord tassel to fasten the waist.

Evening Dresses – Figured short sarsenets are quite new, and extremely genteel: made very long in the train, low behind, and white lace sleeves, very short above the elbow. The back and shoulders finished with silk ornaments.

Dress handkerchiefs are much worn. They are chiefly composed of either muslin and lace, or entirely of lace. The newest form, buttons on each shoulder, with a row of lace around the neck.

The full dress turbans are universally worn *a la Mameluke* . . .

. . . . Large Parisienne shawls of silk, richly figured, have made their appearance at the Opera . . .

——◇——

SWANSEA
TO BE LET
And may be entered
upon immediately

TWO commodious HOUSES situate in WIND-STREET, replete with every convenience which can possibly be desired; each comprising a large under-ground arched kitchen, pantry, cellar, and coal-house occupying a depth of 40 feet; on the ground floor a capital shop, 25 feet by 16, with two handsome bow windows, having a counting house adjoining, and a kitchen pantry; brew-house, scullery, and pumps of soft and hard water behind; on the first floor an elegant drawing-room of the same dimensions as the shop, a lobby, and two bed chambers; on the second story another drawing-room, 18 feet square, a lobby, and three bed-chambers; on the third floor an excellent dining-room, a lobby, and three bed-chambers; with four good attics above.

The front of these Premises is handsomely finished with polished brick, supported by free-stone pillars, plasters, arches, and cornices, with parapet walls coped with free-stone. The shops, counting houses, and all the front rooms, are corniced, and together with the lobbies and stair-cases, beautifully stuccoed. The best rooms are fitted up with Bath-stones and marble chimney-pieces, and all the others with good grates. Behind each house there is a double coach-house and four stall stable, both cieled, with hay-lofts over the same, and an inclosed yard, with handsome gates, and a road into Fisher-street. – Gardens may also be had, if required.

The back rooms command a delightful view of the sea, from which they are not more than 200 yards distant; and the premises are situated in the most desirable part of the town of Swansea, being exactly opposite the principal Inn, where the Mail Coaches to and from London and Ireland arrive daily, and within a few yards of the Post-Office, Theatre, and Market.

These premises are admirably adapted for carrying on an extensive line of business, and the tenants cannot fail of letting any part of the houses they may appropriate for Lodgings during the summer season, when the town is filled with fashionable company to breathe the salubrious air for which Swansea is so justly celebrated, and to enjoy its warm and cold bathing. Each floor forms a complete suite of rooms for a family, with separate kitchens, and other domestic conveniences.

Further particulars may be had by personal application, or letters, post-paid to Thos. Williams, Surgeon, Swansea.

To MONEYED MEN

A GENTLEMAN who has Discovered a New, and improved Method of Manufacturing several articles of trade with more expedition and greater saving than is now done, and whose large profits would in every respect supersede the many opulent Gentlemen engaged in it at present, tho' the said articles are always wanted and prove very lucrative in their actual method of manufacturing: Wishes to meet with two or three Gentlemen of fortune to become concerned, and assist in all pecuniary matters to connect the three Branches of Manufacture into One Concern, and to construct, erect, and place all the necessary Engines, with their Implements, calculated to carry on the Business on a new Plan.

Apply, by letter (post-paid) to P. R. Benson, Esq. at Mr Galloway's, Engineers, No. 56, Holborn, London; or to Wm. David, Esq. at the Printer's Wind Street, Swansea.

DIED,

Thursday last, much lamented, John Vaughan, Esq. of Golden Grove, Lord Lieutenant of the County of Carmarthen. – A Situation which he always filled with universal satisfaction. – But the principal object of his Life was to make those around him happy; and the comforts of his numerous Tenantry occupied a considerable portion of his attention. Residing the greater part of his time in the country, he attended much to the improvement of Agriculture; was always open to the call of Humanity, and indigent and unprotected Merit never went unrewarded. His political principles were strictly constitutional; dissipation was not a feature of his Character, and it may be truly said that he entertained his Friends with ancient Hospitality. The Farmer, the Peasant, and in short the Country will have to deplore his loss, but his Memory will long exist in the hearts of all.

DOCKS, CANALS &c.

Amidst the warfare in which we are now engaged for our preservation and existence as a nation, it is matter of exultation and self-confidence to reflect that the most considerable and most important of our public works suffer, comparatively speaking, but little interruption. A scarcity of hands will naturally rather retard the completion of them, and such materials as are wanted must be purchased at an increased price, particularly the articles of timber and bricks.

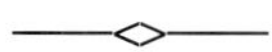

The West India Docks, occupying a surface of thirty acres for unloading *all* vessels coming from the West-India Islands and Colonies, have been completed sometime since, and there is now sufficient accommodation in the substantial and extensive stacks of warehouses for such merchants as wish to bond or house their commodities within the walls, unexposed to fire or plunder, as no lights are suffered at any time, nor any person allowed to remain on board, or within the walls after dark. The excavation of the Dock for loading, which is to occupy twenty-four acres is proceeding with great spirit:– In the mean while, it is highly gratifying to the subscribers, and encouraging to these grand national undertakings, to find that the profits warrant a dividend of ten per cent. on the sums already subscribed, and which the subscribers have already received.

THE GRAND JUNCTION CANAL, a concern of immense importance to the commerce of the country, is now pretty well known to the public. – They have lately experienced some impediment from the drought during the summer; but on the other hand, it has enabled them to repair and cleanse the bottom in some parts where it wanted. The sum subscribed for this concern is about 1,350,000l, and when the tunnel and aqueduct at Blesworth are completed, which is expected will be so at the end of this year, this immense undertaking will be considered as quite complete, and well supplied with water, without interruption; then the subscribers will begin to look forward for a rapid increase of their dividends, which there can be no manner of doubt will very happily remunerate them for their long patience and spirit of perseverance, in assisting a work of this national consequence.

1st. February 1806.

SKETTY HALL, SWANSEA.

TO BE SOLD BY AUCTION

By D. PERROTT,

On Monday, February 3, 1806,

and following days until the

whole is disposed of,

ALL the modern elegant FURNITURE belonging to the Proprietor of Sketty Hall, comprising four-post, tent, and other bedsteads, with hangings complete, down and feather-beds, and rich appropriate suites of furniture for drawing-rooms and other apartments of the highest fashion and stile of workmanship, being the manufactory of Mr. Kaye of Ludgate-Hill, and other London upholsterers of celebrity; also a French Clock, elegant pier-glasses, and various other useful and and ornamental articles by the first manufacturers in their respective lines.

At the same time will be Sold the Kitchen Utensils which constituted the whole culinary department at the Savoir Vivre, late Weltjie's Club; and a variety of Agricultural Implements, Stock &c, including waggons, carts, double-furrow plough by Chieslie and Yowle, chaff-cutting machine on an improved principle, about 40 tons of well-ended hay, seven waggon-horses, a capital saddle-horse, six years old warranted, a remarkably handsome cart and a fine colt rising two years old; a modern curricle with suitable harness, and a set of carriage wheels by Leader, never used; fruiting pines of the most luxuriant growth.

And on Thursday the 6th will be Sold, that excellent well-bred Stallion ROLLA – six months credit will be given.

Rolla was got by Overton, brother to Hambletonian, (who never was beat) out of a Highflyer Mare, her dam Platina, sister to Gnawpost by Snap.

Rolla, at three years old, was esteemed the best horse of his year, having beat Champion and Lignum Vitae.

Most of the Mares covered last year by this excellent horse have proved in foal.

Catalogues are preparing, and may speedily be procured at the Bush and Mackworth Arms; and the principal inns at Neath, Pyle, Cowbridge, Cardiff, Merthyr-Tidvil, Newport, Chepstow, Carmarthen, St. Clears, Haverfordwest, Llandilo, Llandovery, and Brecon.

——<>——

The Dangers and Disagreables of

The PASSAGE over the SEVERN SEA avoided,

By a New and

COMMODIOUS CONVEYANCE

From

LONDON to CARMARTHEN,

By way of

GLOCESTER, CHEPSTOW, CARDIFF, SWANSEA &c.

THE Public are most respectfully informed,

that

A TELEGRAPH COACH,

called

The Prince of Wales

Sets out from *the Bell-in-Tun,* Fleet-Street, London, every Sunday, Tuesday, and Thursday at twelve o'clock at noon, for Carmarthen; arrives at the *Boothall Inn* Glocester, every Monday, Wednesday, and Friday mornings at nine o'clock, and proceeds from thence, at one o'clock in the afternoon of the same days, through Newnham, Lidney, Chepstow, Newport, Cardiff, Cowbridge, Pyle, Neath, Swansea; &c. to the *King's Arms inn,* Carmarthen; returns from thence three times a week; arrives at the *Boothall-inn* Glocester, every Tuesday, Thursday, and Saturday mornings; and proceeds thence from at twelve o'clock at noon to London.

N.B. The Coach meets at Glocester, the Coaches to Bath, Bristol, and the West of England, and to Birmingham, Liverpool, and the North of England; which, with the London, Hereford &c. Coaches meet at the Boothall inn as usual, where Travellers will meet with comfortable accommodation, neat post Chaises, able Horses and civil Drivers.

We, whose names are undersigned considering the present Rates of Carriage by the Mail Coach to be exorbitant agree to support any New Establishment for the conveyance of Passengers and Parcels between LONDON, and SWANSEA, through GLOCESTER, which may be carried upon more reasonable terms than is now done by the Proprietors of the Mail Coach; and that the same be communicated to the Public in some of the London and Provincial papers.

Milford; Thos. Wyndham, J. Capper; J. Morris; J. Morris jun; Edward Powell; Griff. Llewellyn; J. Goodrich; Thomas Davies; J. Wood; E Jenkins; R. T. Dere; John Franklest; Thos. Franklin; R. Bevan, jun; W. Vaughan; R. Mansel Philipps; J. Wood jun; J. Richards; Jeremiah Homfray; Wynd. Lewis jun; Thomas Thomas; Row. Williams; Chas Brown; W. Taitt; W. Meyrick; Powell Edwards; Henry Hollier; Robt. Jenner; Fendall and Co.; H. Hurst; H. Reece; John Miles; Harford and Co; Ll. Treherne; R. L. Blosse; R. Lascelles; Robert Jones; Robert Wrixon; John Richardson; John Williams; Thos. Davies, jun; John Jones; Thos Morgan; John Bassett; Edw. Pearson; Daniel Jones.

——<>——

Caution to Waggoners – The practice of wanton driving teams through brooks or water, when there is a bridge to pass over, having increased amongst waggoners to an alarming degree, it becomes a duty incumbent on masters to forbid their servants so doing in the winter, especially at a time like the present, when the swell of water has increased every rill so much as to render the passage extremely dangerous. Many accidents have lately resulted from this practice; and, amongst others, in the town of Wrexham, last week, it was with difficulty a team of horses was rescued from destruction, and one animal was actually drowned.

——<>——

SWANSEA BATHING HOUSE.

THE Corporation of Swansea are ready to receive PROPOSALS for TAKING the BATHING HOUSE and FIELD, either together or in lots. The premises may be entered into immediately.

Persons desirous of making proposals are requested to transmit the same in writing on or before the 1st. day of March next to Messrs. Thomas Boryen and John Grove, Committee Attornies of whom particulars may be known.

Swansea, Jan. 8 1806.

BALL,
At the NEW TOWN HALL,
LLANDILO
on
FRIDAY, Feb. 14, 1806.
Under the Direction of Mr. HART.
Tickets 5s. 6d. each to be had of Mrs. Jones, Bear Inn, Llandilo.
To commence at seven o'clock.
N.B. To render the Assembly Room well aired, Fires are kept therein daily.

———◇———

The Abu and Theresa, Cullins, from Burry bound for Newham, with copper, struck on the Sker Point on Wednesday last, and sunk. The cargo is expected to be saved.

———◇———

SALE OF TIMBER,
Glamorganshire,
TO BE SOLD BY AUCTION,
By Mr. PERROTT,
Either together or in Lots,
At the Mackworth Arms Inn, Swansea.
Some time in the month of March next, as will hereafter be appointed,

SIX Hundred and Forty three capital OAK-TREES, (Marked and numbered.) growing upon the following Estates:

Lot 1 – TWO HUNDRED TREES on Penderry, in the parish of Llangevelach.

Lot 2 – THREE HUNDRED and TWELVE TREES on Gwenlais fawr, in the parish of Llandilo-Tallybont.

These two lots are marked and numbered in red paint.

Lot 3 – ONE HUNDRED and THIRTY-ONE TREES on Lower Sketty or Sketty Issa, marked and numbered with white paint.

The greatest part of this timber is fit for the navy. The first lot is within two miles of the port of Lloughor. The second within four miles of Swansea and about the same distance from Lloughor; and the last within half a mile of the sea and a good shipping space.

The respective tenants will shew the Timber, and for particulars apply to Mr. James or Mr. Phillips, Attornies Swansea.

———◇———

Wednesday last a meeting of the Society for the Education of the Children of the Poor was held at the Town Hall, which was attended by a number of the most respectable inhabitants in this town and neighbourhood. A President, Vice-President, Treasurer, and a Committee were appointed; a subscription entered into, and subscription lists ordered to be left at different places in the town. The amount already subscribed is upwards of 65l per annum. The objects which this institution professes to embrace are, the instruction of the children of those parents only who are debarred by poverty from affording their offspring any education whatever in reading, writing, and the first rules of arithmetic – the engrafting on their minds the principles of religion and morality and enforcing a proper observance of the Sabbath by causing all the children to attend some place of Divine Worship twice every Sunday. For the carrying out of these laudable and benevolent purposes, the subscription has been instituted, and will, we hope, be filled up with a promptitude equal to that displayed by the first founders of the institution.

———◇———

THE CAMBRIAN

SWANSEA, Friday, Jan. 31.

The arrivals from the continent this week have put us in possession of an official copy of the Treaty of Presburgh, an analysis of which is given in our preceding columns. The terms are sufficiently hard to convince us of the extremity to which the Emperor of Austria was reduced – his resources are dried up, and his territories parcelled out at the will of a victorious foe. Nor is this the darkest side of the situation: by the creation of new Sovereigns, we behold Bonaparte forming to himself new and perpetual allies – bound to him by the strong tie of gratified ambition. The passages from France to Austria, occupied by friends and dependents, will, in future, present no obstacles to his incursions, should he ever again attempt to push his armies into the German Empire. But, alas! what further humiliation can Austria endure; what ills can await her more destructive in their nature than those which have already befallen her! While these lamentable revolutions are taking place on the continent, the eyes of this country are fixed on the projected revolutions in the British Cabinet. From the conference which has taken place between his Majesty and Lord Grenville, it is inferred, with a great degree of probability, that the Administration about to be formed will comprise all the leading characters of the Opposition, thus, undoubtedly, embracing the greatest talents which now exist in the country. From an arrangement of this sort, the public will naturally look for exertions corresponding with the professed principles of the new Ministry. Much will, much ought to be expected from the united constellation of talents, which will illumine the cabinet and we trust the country will not be disappointed.

———◇———

WANTED, an APPRENTICE in the PAINTING and GLAZING BUSINESS. A creditable Youth will have an opportunity of acquiring a knowledge of Painting in all its branches, viz. House Painting, Heraldry, Furniture and Fancy-work, together with Glazing.
Enquire of Mr. Goldstone,
Druggist, Carmarthen.
A premium is expected.

———◇———

Accounts from Montgomeryshire represent the injury occasioned by the late violent storms in that county as very extensive and truly lamentable. Torrents of rain which fell were such as have never been remembered; and the inhabitants are stated to have been compelled to forsake their habitations till the fury of the storm was, in some degree mitigated.

From several parts of England distressing accounts have reached us, houses have been unroofed, and the most stately trees uprooted. Rivers and brooks have overflowed their banks, and the inundation of the Severn, when at its height, is represented as awfully tremendous; its restless torrent sweeping away everything before it, and occasioning the utmost alarm to the neighbouring inhabitants.

To the King's' Most Excellent Majesty

"We, the Gentlemen, Clergy, Freeholders, and others of the County of Caernarvon, beg leave to approach your Majesty's throne, in consequence of the unparalleled successes, and the indelible glory, recently achieved by your Majesty's fleets.

"In our reflections on these momentous events, our minds are filled with the most awful and powerful emotions of grief for the loss of our departed and ever to be lamented Hero; and of pious gratitude to the Divine Providence, that watched over and secured our brilliant and unexampled victories, finally preserving to us those surviving ornaments of the British navy, who are ordained to be the future supporters of that character to which it has been so eminently raised.

"Being thus guarded by our natural shield; relying firmly on the wisdom, and vigour of your Majesty's councils and on the active bravery of your military forcc; entertaining also a fervent hope (through the interposition of Divine Mercy) for the prolongation of your Majesty's life and happy reign, we contemplate with implicit confidence, and with veneration the permanence of our invaluable constitution, and the consequent prosperity of these realms."

———◇———

The following singular charge has been made before the magistrates:–

A young female, pupil of a celebrated Italian singer, charged her mistress with bewitching her. The complainant stated that she had roused the indignation of her mistress by receiving the addresses of an old gentleman, who had long been her suitor, and she being apprehensive that the marriage state would soon deprive her of the complainant's services at balls &c. she was informed that if she continued to listen to her lover, she, the mistress, would dispossess her of all personal charms, and indict vengeance on her body by deforming it. The mistress stated herself to be in possession of her powers by a brown breast. The complainant in a few days after lost her voice, which was before melodious, and her frame became covered with sores, which induced her to prefer this complaint, as the only way of obtaining redress. The mistress in a fit of rage, uncovered her breast, and exposed herself to the magistrates to convince them that the charge was false, and it was discharged, after exciting much laughter.

———◇———

Kidwelly District Turnpike Trust

CARMARTHENSHIRE

NOTICE IS HEREBY GIVEN, that the several TOLL GATES in the said District will be LET by AUCTION, to the best bidder at the Pelican Inn, in Kidwelly, on Monday the 3d day of February next, between the hours of 11 and 12 o'clock in the forenoon, in the manner directed by the Act passed in the thirteenth year of the reign of his Majesty King George the Third "For Regulations of the Turnpike Roads:" They were let the last year as follows, viz.

	£.	s.	d
Pensarn & Croesllwyd	350	0	0
Pontyberem	99	0	0
Murkey & Pontyates	119	10	0
Llanelly	50	10	0
Rhylltymurdy	60	0	0
Spudders Bridge	92	0	0

and will be put up at the same. Whoever happens to be the best bidder, for the whole, or either of them, must, at the same time, give security with sufficient sureties to the satisfaction of the Trustees of the said District Trust, for the payment of the Rent agreed, for and at such times as they direct.

JOHN STACEY, Clerk.

Carmarthen Jan. 14 1806.

———◇———

Mr. Pitt's funeral is, it is said, to be attended with the same ceremony as was observed in regard to his father, with the difference only of the procession taking place from the House of Commons to Westminster Abbey, instead, as was then the case, from the House of Lords.

Mr . Pitt.

Mr. Lascelles, agreeably to his notice, rose yesterday in the House of Commons, which was numerously attended, to make his motion for some signal mark of honour to the memory of the late Right Hon. William Pitt, &c. who had sacrificed so much for the good of his country. After an introductory speech, in which Mr. Lascelles dwelt on the great merits of the deceased, the pride and ornament of the age in which he lived, he submitted to the consideration of the House the following motion: "Resolved, That an humble address be presented to his Majesty, that his Majesty will be graciously pleased to give directions that the remains of the Right Hon. William Pitt be interred at the public expence; and that a monument be erected in the Collegiate Church of St. Peter, Westminster, to the memory of that excellent statesman, with an inscription expressive of the public sense of so great and irreparable a loss; and to assure his Majesty, that this House will make good the expences attending the same."

The Marquis of Tichfield seconded the motion. It was opposed first by Lord Folkestone, and afterwards by Mr.Windham, Mr. W. Smith, Mr. Pytches, Lord Douglas, and Mr. George Ponsonby. The ground of the opposition was this:– They professed to allow Mr. Pitt every credit for brilliant talents, and the most spotless integrity, in as far as concerned pecuniary matters; but having had frequent occasion, in the the course of his administration, strongly to disapprove of the direction of his talents, they could not now consent to a motion which, by implying a general approbation of his measures, would thus involve them in inconsistency . . .

Ayes 258

Noes ...... 89 Majority 169.

———◇———

His Majesty came from Windsor to town yesterday about one o'clock, and, being seated on his throne, received the addresses of both Houses of Parliament. His Majesty looked extremely well, except appearing somewhat lame when he walked; when the passage was read alluding to the loss of the Duke of Glocester and Lord Nelson, the King discovered considerable emotion.

5th. March 1808.

NEW THEATRE, CARMARTHEN,
Notice to Builders, &c.

ALL Persons who wish to CONTRACT for BUILDING the above THEATRE, agreeable to a New Plan, to be seen at the Chamberlain's Office, are desired to send their estimates under seal to the said office, on or before Saturday the 20th. day of March next.

Feb 26, 1808.

TO VIOLIN PLAYERS.

ANY Person who can play well on the VIOLIN, and having likewise some other employment or occupation, may meet with good encouragement, by residing at Cardigan, in South Wales.

TO DEBTORS.

ALL persons indebted to the Estate of DAVID GWYNNE, of Swansea, mercer, are required forthwith to pay the same to Mr. John James, of Swansea, otherwise they will be proceeded against without further notice.

Swansea, Feb. 26 1808.

JOHN KNEATH,
(*Late of the Milford),*

BEGS leave to offer his grateful acknowledgments to his Friends and the Public in general, for the encouragement he received while in business at the above house, and respectfully informs them, he has taken the Talbot Arms-Inn. which he has fitted up with every necessary accommodation, and hopes, by a due attention, to merit a continuance of the favours which he lately experienced.

Good Stabling, and the greatest care taken of Horses.

N.B. *An Ordinary provided every Saturday.*

Swansea, Feb 26 1808.

BEAR-INN, COWBRIDGE.

THE THIRD SUBSCRIPTION BALL, will be on THURSDAY, the 10th. Instant.

N.B. Post-Chaises as usual.

March 1 1808.

To Owners and Masters of Vessels from 70 to 200 Tons Burthen.

WANTED to FREIGHT, from the Port of LLANELLY, a considerable quantity of COALS, CULM, FIRE-BRICKS and CLAY, to the different ports of IRELAND. Such Owners or Masters of Vessels as may be disposed to treat for same, are desired to send their proposals addressed to Mr. Jeremiah Thomas, Llanelly, which will be immediately attended to.

Also, several SMALL CRAFT, from 30 to 70 Tons burthen, for a regular trade from the same Port to Carmarthen, Neath, Swansea, and the coast of Devon. – Enquire as above.

It is a singular circumstance, and strongly expressive of the present restricted state of our commerce that for three days past no vessel, either inwards or outwards, passed Gravesend, and that there has not been a single arrival in the River since Monday. There is not a period within the memory of of any person connected with the port of London, during which so little business was done, either as to shipments or unlading, as at present.

SWANSEA
TO BE SOLD BY
PRIVATE CONTRACT,

THE UNEXPIRED LEASE of 94 years of TWO valuable HOUSES, pleasantly situated in Nelson-Place, SWANSEA, one of them in the occupation of Captain Carder, and the other lately held by Capt. Barber. They consist each of two parlours, a good drawing room, three bed-chambers, back-kitchen, cellar, gardens, fore-courts, and an excellent pump of water, with suitable accommodation for servants; entirely adapted for the reception of genteel families. The situation is one of the pleasantest in Swansea, having a full command of the Bay, the Bristol Channel, and the surrounding Hills. – They are at present let for £45 per annum, but well worth £50.

For further particulars apply, (if by letter, post-paid) to the Printer of this Paper.

Intelligence has been received of great exertions making at Antwerp, to fit out a powerful armament, intended to operate in favour of Russia and Denmark against Sweden, in the Baltic, and it is said to be in such forwardness as to have excited some anxiety lest it should be ready before our Expedition, which is preparing for the same scene of action.

The Entreprenaute cutter, arrived at Plymouth, from off Ferrol, left the British Squadron off that port on the 15th instant. consisting of the Achille, 74; Audacious, 74; Alcmene, and another frigate under the command of Commodore Sir Richard King. The enemy's squadron in Ferrol consists of three sails of the line, one a three decker, apparently without any intention of putting to sea. On the 4th. inst. Sir Richard Strachan's squadron passed by that station. Sir Richard made signal to go under the lee of Cape Finisterre, to divide water and provisions, and then proceed in search of the Rochefort squadron. A boat with an Officer and 12 men belonging to the Theseus, had been captured, and marched up to Corunna. They were taken in an unsuccessful attack to destroy an old Spanish line of battle ship lying off Vigo. A flag of truce was sent in hopes of getting them restored, but without effect.

A reinforcement of troops is about to be sent to Gibraltar, and it is supposed that a portion of the force originally intended for Sicily, will stop at that fortress.

. . . nearly five hundred voyages were made from America to Liverpool alone in the course of a year, in ships, the burthen of which amounted to more than 123,000 tons; that the amount of British manufactures annually exported to America, was more than 10,000,000l.: that government derived from the Liverpool portion of the trade alone, not less than 1,000,000l a year, and that the average debt due from America to this country is not less than 12,000,000l. – the payment of which is now interrupted by the embargo in the American ports.

IMPERIAL PARLIAMENT.

HOUSE OF COMMONS.

Monday, Feb. 29. – . . .

After some conversation between Lord Castlereagh and Mr. Whitbread, as to postponement of their respective motions, the former wishing to bring on the motion for the erection of a monument to the late Lord Lake, Mr. Whitbread hoped the Noble Lord would hold him excused, if he pressed the consideration of the resolutions of which he had given notice several days ago. He rose under circumstances of great personal responsibility. The subject was one of the most important which could be submitted to the deliberation of Parliament; for it related to that state and condition of society which constituted the chief happiness of mankind. The Commissioners appointed by his Majesty to open the present session, had stated that this was the crisis of the fate of the country. Now, before that crisis came on, he was anxious to to ascertain how it might be avoided. This crisis, if properly employed, might produce the salvation of the country; but, on the other hand, if we persevered in the same manner which had been used towards the foreign Powers since the last Parliament, it might terminate in the ruin of every thing that was dear to us . . .

. . . If the petitions presented at the commencement of the war with France had been listened to, we should not have witnessed the enormous aggrandisement of that Power, or have to contend with all the disadvantages resulting from it . . . After reviewing the situation of Russia and Austria he stated that Bonaparte had three times made distinct overtures . . . There could be no humiliation in sending a message to the French Government. There was no degradation in offering peace . . . A direct overture could attach no disgrace, if it failed or succeeded . . .

. . . The French Emperor was described as a man of inordinate ambition. Granted; but he was a man of talents. He never seemed to be led beyond where he saw it to his advantage to stop. He thought that it was Bonaparte's interest to make peace, and to maintain it. If, therefore peace was attempted in the spirit of conciliation, he must think it might be made. Bonaparte had been represented as having sworn the destruction of this country. When, how, where? Was it when he was made First Consul? No: for he offered peace. Was it when he became Emperor? No: for still he would negotiate. Was it at the peace of Tilsil? No: for then he accepted the Russian mediation. Had he now sworn it?. Try a negotiation again and prove it . . .

According to the returns of the Navy, up to this day, there are in commission 774 ships of war, of which 114 are of the line; 21 from fifty to forty-four guns; 175 frigates; 215 sloops of war; and 219 gun-brigs and other armed vessels. There are besides in ordinary, 53 sail of the line; and building 57 sail of the line, and a great number of other ships in a state nearly ready for sea; making a grand total of 1061 ships of war, of which 254 are of the line; 36 from fifty to forty-four guns; 254 frigates; 286 sloops of war; and 251 gun-brigs, and other armed vessels.

TO BE SOLD

To the Best Bidder.

In the presence of Mr. Barrallier, at the Dockyard in the town of Milford Haven on 20th March 1808.

THE WRECK

of

His Majesty's Ship LEDA

Now lying in West Angle Bay near the entrance of Milford Haven.

For conditions of sale, and for further particulars apply to the Commissioners of the Navy-Office, London; or to Mr. Barrallier, Dockyard, Milford Haven.

The inhabitants of North Wales were much alarmed by the meteor on Sunday evening se'n night; it was accompanied by a noise like distant thunder, and fell into the the river Menai, near the Swilles, with a loud and sudden report.

Sale by Public Auction

1808.

TO COVER this SEASON, at the DOBBIN-Pitts Farm, near Cardiff, at TWO GUINEAS a MARE, and HALF-A-CROWN the Groom.

GREEN DRAGON,

By St. George, Dam by Paymaster.– Match'em, Regulus, &c. St. George was got by Highflyer; his dam, own sister to Soldier, by Eclipse.

Green Dragon is six years old, fifteen hands, three inches high; from his great bone strength, beauty, and action as a roadster, he is far superior to any horse that ever appeared in this country, for getting Coach-Horses, Hunters &c. with proper Mares. He is a beautiful bay with black legs.

GRASS for MARES, at 5s a week.

WANTED a WOMAN SERVANT, capable of undertaking the Brewing department at a small Public Inn near Swansea; her constant attendance will be required, and her duty will be to brew once a week in the winter months, and twice in the summer. Liberal wages will be given to a person who is competent to fill the situation. Apply to the Printer of this Paper (if by letter, post paid.)

The anniversary of St. David on Tuesday last, was celebrated with much festivity in various parts of Wales, as well as in London and several provincial towns of England. A short account of the Saint may not be unacceptable to our readers:– St. David was a man of great respect, fame, and dignity in his days, of royal descent, and according to Popish legends, many miracles are said to have been performed by him. His father was a Prince, and Lord of Cardigan, brother to Einion-y-dwr, or the valiant King of Cambria, and was a nephew to King Arthur. He was very learned, and abstemious even to austerity. He lived to the age of 141 years, and died 642 A.D. He was canonised a Saint by Pope Calisus 11 in the year 1119, 477 years after his death. His nativity was foretold thirty years before he was born. He by a miracle made hot the Bath water in Somersetshire, which still retains that quality. It is also asserted that he had an angel always attending him. The above, and many more, are Popish stories. It is true he was a very learned man, prudent and sagacious, very diligent and active in his profession. He received his education in the great College at Monmouth. Then he spent a long time in the Isle of Wight. He returned to Monmouth, and lived in a monastery there, of his own erection. After this he travelled to Rome and to Jerusalem, in company with the Saints Teilaw and Padarn. On their return they attended a synod, summoned by Dubritus, or Dufrig, Archbishop of Caerllean, for the purpose of suppressing the Pelagian heresy, which, at that time, had spread itself alarmingly in the Christian world. David by his consummate erudition, deep knowledge in the Scriptures, and his eloquent reasonings, exposed the fallacy of that pernicious doctrine. After this, Dufrig, being then very old, resigned his episcopal charge to St. David, and retired to the great monastery at Enlli, or Bardsey Island, and there he died and was buried. David, after this removed the archepiscopal chair from Caerllean ar Wysg to Mynwy, now St. David's, about the year 521, and it continued an archiepiscopal see to the 11th. century, when it was, by Henry I. King of England made subject to Canterbury, and continues so to this day.

Vaccination. – By the indefatigable exertions of Mr. Llewellyn, surgeon, of Llanymynech, considerable progress has been made towards exterminating that baleful disease the small pox from Montgomeryshire. He has, we understand, vaccinated upwards of 100 children, within the last three months, *gratis.*

Wednesday, a fine boy fell from the top of the mail-coach between Carmarthen and Abergwilly, and the hind wheel passed over his body: although much injured, he was yesterday expected to recover.

The following is copied from a provincial print:– "Wanted, a Sexton for the parish of Harleigh. He must be sober of *a grave* disposition, and have no connection with *resurrection-men.*

In addition to the the calamities of the dreadful storm on Thursday, the 27th ult. we have to add the following:– The brig, Fortitude, John Skelton, master, was found early on on the Friday morning a complete wreck, in a small creek within three miles of Amlwch, known by the name of Porth y Gwychiaid. She was the property of a Liverpool merchant, bound from Gibraltar, laden with wine, figs, raisins and nuts. What could be saved was protected and sold by Mr. Thomas Jones, an officer of the customs in Amlwch. All the persons on board and one of the pilots, unhappily perished. Two of the bodies were found, and an inquest was held over them on the Monday following. This is the fifth melancholy accident of the kind that has happened in this neighbourhood since November, and from which three lives were saved.

The following singular circumstances took place at Sheffield recently:– A young woman was married on the Thursday, brought to bed on Friday, the child died on Saturday, was interred on Sunday, the husband enlisted for a soldier on Monday, and marched away on Tuesday.

We are sorry to state that the Industry, Capt. Bowen, of Swansea, from Cork to Plymouth, with provisions, was captured, together with three other vessels, by a French privateer From St. Maloes, on the 21st. ult. One of the prizes was given up to the crews, in which they arrived at Cork on the 25th.

In England there is a number of *perpetual Curacies*, and in Wales a greater number of *perpetual Curates.*

. . . a Clergyman, on Sunday last, lamenting the rapid decline of religion and morality, observed that such was the depravity of the day, that even *women* turned highway-*men!*

FOR THE CAMBRIAN

HINTS FOR COUNTRY COFFEE-ROOMS.

1. Gentlemen learning to spell, are requested to use *yesterday's* papers.

2. Those who have already attained that art, are desired not to put it into practice, by reading the paper *aloud,* to the annoyance of the whole room.

3. It is a bore to all present, and does not add one atom to the consequence of any Gentleman, who may take pleasure in disseminating the following *important* fact; viz.– *That he dined yesterday, or that he dined today, or that he is to dine tomorrow, with some Great Man!*

4. The door of a coffee-room is just as easy shut as the door of a drawing-room, and the comfort of its being so, as justly appreciated by the inside passengers.

Monthly Agricultural Report:– The state of the season since our last has still continued unfavourable to the young wheats, especially such as were put into the ground late, and they would without doubt have been very materially injured, particularly those which were in a forward and luxuriant state of growth, had it not been prevented by the snow with which they have been covered and protected during a great part of the month. The sharp dry winds and frosts in the latter part of the month have given a favourable check to the too luxuriant vegetation of some crops of this kind. – The luxuriant forward tare crops have been much protected and preserved by the falls of snow as have the wheats, though in exposed situations they have suffered considerable injury . . .

——<>——

The late combination entered into by certain Postmasters, &c. throughout England, to advance the price of posting, has been in a great degree given up, many of them being willing and desirous to post at the former prices.

——<>——

7th. April 1810.

THE OLD-ESTABLISHED
FLY-WAGGONS
from
London, Oxford, Glocester, Manchester, Shrewsbury, Birmingham, Worcester; &c.&c.&c.

NORTH, REES, & CO. Proprietors of the above Waggons, impressed with the truest sense of gratitude, beg leave most respectfully to inform their Friends, that from a wish to accommodate them to the utmost of their power, they have established ANOTHER WAGGON WEEKLY from LONDON, which regularly loads at the King's-Head Inn, Old Change, every Tuesday evening, and delivers goods at Landovery and Landilo, on that day and at Carmarthen on the Wednesday morning following.

Their other long established and regular Waggons continue to set out from the usual places viz. from

London – The George Inn, Snowhill; The King's Head Inn, Old Change; and the Castle and Falcon Inn, Aldersgate Street; calling in coming out and going in, at the Black Bear Piccadilly, and the Green Man and Still, Oxford Street.
Oxford – Hunt's Warehouse.
Gloucester – Heane and Co's ditto All goods from Bath, Bristol, or the Clothing Country, is desired to be directed to the care of Mr. Kendall, or Mr. Walker, Wharfingers.
Birmingham – Ashmore's Warehouse.
Worcester – Mole and Co's ditto.
Manchester – Mason's ditto; from whence the goods from Leeds, Wakefield, Huddersfield, Dewsbury, and all the North of England are regularly conveyed.
Shrewsbury – Ditto.
Leominster – Price and Co's
Hereford – Ditto.

They are happy in having an opportunity of returning their unfeigned thanks for the unexampled suppport they have so many years received, (*particularly during their late SHORT LIVED OPPOSITION which proved to be FOUNDED IN FOLLY by terminating in its PROJECTOR'S DISGRACE.*) and being convinced that no concern whatever can accomodate the public, in the manner their's can, they much more solicit a continuation of those favours they have so long experienced, pledging themselves, as the best mark of gratitude, to continue to pursue the same unwearied exertions to give satisfaction as they have always hitherto done.

No Money, Plate, Jewels, Watches, Writings, Glass, China, &c.&c.will be accounted for, if lost or damaged, except entered as such and paid for accordingly at the time of delivery.

Brecknock, March 21 1810.

——<>——

South Wales Soap Works, Swansea

THE Public are respectfully informed that SOAP is now ready for delivery at the above works. The great pains taken by the Proprietors to secure an article of the first quality will, they trust, entitle them to the encouragement of the public. The prices will be regulated by the London and Bristol Markets, and as there will be a constant supply kept at the Manufactory for the retailers, it will preclude the necessity of their keeping large and expensive stocks by them. Captains of Vessels trading to different ports in the Channel will find great advantages in this establishment.

Orders addressed to Henrie and Co. Swansea, will be punctually attended to.

N.B. A good price will be given for any quantity of Wood or Fern Ashes, well preserved. The best time for burning fern is about Midsummer; the plant should be cut down green, dried, and burnt to a white ash, after which it should be kept free from damp.

——<>——

The intended match between Capt. L. of The Royal Pembroke Fusiliers, and the rich heiress Miss B. of Hastings, is off by mutual consent, and the parties have retired to their different country seats.

——<>——

BUSH-INN, SWANSEA.
Day Coach

WM. JONES and Co.

Beg leave to state, that they have, for the accommodation of the Public, ALTERED THE TIME of the PRINCE of WALES COACH leaving SWANSEA for London, Bristol, Glocester, Birmingham, Manchester, Liverpool, Oxford &c. In future it will leave Swansea at FIVE O'CLOCK IN THE MORNING, on MONDAYS, WEDNESDAYS and FRIDAYS, arrive at Glocester and Bristol the same nights, and will then meet all the London, Birmingham, Manchester, Liverpool and Exeter Coaches. Passengers will then be conveyed to London without being more than one night on the road; and by this means also a communication is opened with all parts of the North and West of England, Particularly with the principal manufacturing and commercial towns above mentioned and to which places and countries passengers and packages are immediately forwarded by their respectively connecting Coaches.

The Proprietors will not be accountable for the loss of Parcels above Five Pounds value, unless entered and paid for accordingly; nor for damage by improper packing.

——<>——

TO BE SOLD

SOME remarkably fine OLD HAY, six, eight, or ten Tons.

Enquire (if by letter post paid) of Henry Nunn, Esq. Fairy Hill House, Gower.

TO BE SOLD

A Commodious TRAVELLING GIG, upon Springs, having a shifting Head and Trunk behind, with a Driving and Seat Box, Lamps and Harness. The price – *Twenty Guineas* – Apply to Mr. Young, Saddler, Cowbridge, if by letter, post paid.

The Labourers employed by Mr. Yalden, in the limestone quarries at the Mumbles, near Swansea, lately cut through a complete cemetery, in which were found immense quantities of human bones of a very large size; from the position and confused state they were discovered in, it is highly probable that this spot was the burial place of a vast multitude who perished nearly at the same time, either by pestilence or the sword, at some very remote period.

The sloop Invincible, supposed from Aberystwith to Liverpool is lost on Bray beach.

On the 26th ult. the Severn Tunnel Bill passed the House of Commons . . .

CARDIGANSHIRE,
SOUTH WALES.
ELIGIBLE FAMILY RESIDENCE.

TO BE LET
READY FURNISHED.
For a Term of Years and entered upon of May next.

CASTLE HILL, most delightfully situated on a pleasing eminence, above a lawn of 40 Acres of rich Land, bordered with Plantations, Walks and Shrubberies, beautifully laid out, with a most excellent Walled Garden well stocked with fruit tree; distant six miles from the town of Aberystwith, a place of very fashionable resort for sea bathing, where there is a good market and provisions extremely moderate. The house commands a most delightful view of the beautiful vale of the Ystwyth, is in substantial repair, and consists of an entrance hall, dining and breakfast parlours, drawing room, a small study, a suitable number of bed-rooms with all necessary domestic offices, cellaring, coach house, and stables. The roads in the neighbourhood are very good, and rides pleasant and romantic.

For further particulars apply (if by letter, post paid) to Wm. Tilsley, Esq. Severn Side near Newtown Montgomeryshire; or of Hugh Hughes, of Aberystwith.

ESCAPED out of the House of Correction, at Cowbridge, on Monday evening, March 26 1810, DAVID HARRY, by trade a Shoe- maker, about 25 years of age, five feet nine inches high, swarthy complexion, grey eyes, brown hair; had on when he went away, a round hat, short blue coat, striped waistcoat, and velveret small clothes; he is a native of Carmarthenshire, straight and well made, and has the appearance of being a soldier.

Also DAVID REECE, a labourer, 26 years of age, about five feet five inches high; had on when he went away a round hat, a short blue coat, white waistcoat, and canvas trowsers; a native of Gower Glamorganshire.

Whoever will apprehend the said prisoners, and lodge them in any of His Majesty's Gaols, shall receive a reward of TWO GUINEAS each, by applying to Evan Deere, Keeper of the House of Correction at Cowbridge.

Cardiff Assizes concluded on Monday last, the business at which was unusually heavy. The following prisoners were capitally convicted, and received sentence of death, viz, Thomas Grimes, alias Thompson, alias Smith, for breaking open and robbing the house of the late Mr. Perry, at Merthyr; this man was condemned at Glocester some time ago, but was reprieved, and afterwards escaped from the officers while they were conveying him to London for transportation. The 18th instant is appointed for his execution. John Thomas for sheep stealing; Richard Jones for horse stealing and Edward John for felony; the three last mentioned were reprieved and will be transported. Elizabeth Rees, for stealing cotton and handkerchiefs was ordered to be imprisoned for two months, George Williams, indicted for stealing a colt; and William Davies for robbing his master, L. W. Dillwyn, Esq. of Swansea, were acquitted; the latter much to the surprise of the Court and auditory, and Mr. Justice Hardinge commented on the verdict with marked severity.

DIED

At her house in Glocester Place, London, on Wednesday the 28th ult aged 64, Mrs Vaughan, relict of Richard Vaughan, Esq. formerly of Golden-Grove, Carmarthenshire. By the death of this excellent and worthy lady, the Right Hon. Lord Cawdor will be benefitted to the extent of about 800l. per annum.

Odd Will. – Mr. Lewis Evan Morgan, of Gwyllgyth, Glamorganshire, at the age of almost 100, bequeathed the whole of his property to his housekeeper, who had lived with him many years. His will is comprised in these words – "I give to my old, faithful servant, Esther Jones, the whole that I am possessed of, either in personal property, land, or otherwise. She is a tolerably good woman, but would be much better if she had not so clamorous a tongue.

She has, however, one great virtue, which is a veil to all her foibles – *strict* honesty."

MILFORD BANK.

IN consequence of the unprecedented attack on the CREDIT of this BANK, Nathaniel Philipps, *Esq, of Slebech, for the satisfaction of the public, signed the following Declaration, which he made before a number of the Gentlemen and Merchants of Milford:*

"I Nathaniel Phillips of Slebech, in

the county of Pembroke, do hereby assure the inhabitants of South-Wales and elsewhere, that I have undertaken to be accountable to the Public for the Payment of the notes issued by the Milford Bank as far as the sum of Thirty Thousand Pounds will extend to pay.

(Signed)

"NATHANIEL PHILLIPS."

"Milford." March 22 1810."

—◇—

LLANRHIDIAN FAIRS

(TOLL FREE).

WILL be held annually at the village of Llanrhidian 22d of February, Palm-Monday and 3d. of October, for the sale of Cattle, Horses, Sheep &c. The day following each of those days a Fair will be held for the sale of pigs.

N.B. Shoemakers, Hatters, Hawkers &c. will find a ready sale for their goods. Llanrhidian village lies 11 miles E. of Swansea to which place there is a good road.

—◇—

The prisoners in the gaol at Cardiff, for the County of Glamorgan, return their thanks to the gentlemen of the Grand Jury at the last Great Sessions, for 3l 12s, given by the hands of J. Richards, Esq. and laid out in provisions for them.

—◇—

2nd. May 1812.

VERY DESIRABLE PROPERTY

TO BE SOLD

WORCESTER-HOUSE, eligibly situated in the town of SWANSEA, and commanding delightful views of the harbour and bay, and adjacent coasts. The house comprises a dining and drawing-room, each 21 feet by 14 and 11 high; library 13 by 11 and 11 feet high; three best bed rooms of same dimensions; two smaller ditto; kitchen 16 feet by 15, and 13 feet high; commodious cellars, closets, servants' rooms, scullery with pump, four-stall stable, gig house, and yard adjoining the same; together with a coach house, two cottages, and a plantation in front of the house.

Half the Purchase Money may remain on the security of the respective Premises. *Also, TO BE SOLD* A singularly eligible FREEHOLD ESTATE consisting of 25 Acres of excellent Meadow and Pasture Land within a ring-fence, distant only half a mile from the flourishing town of Swansea, situate on a gentle eminence within 200 yards of the sea, and commanding most extensive and fascinating views of the town, bay, and surrounding country; and now let to a responsible tenant at £125 p.a.

The above Estate is one of one of the most eligible for the erection of one or more gentlemen's residences, the country abounding with game, coal and close to cheap and plentiful markets. For further particulars apply (if by letter, post paid) to Dr. J. C. Collins, Swansea.

—◇—

Yesterday a Cabinet Council was held on the contents of the recent communication from the French government, and in the evening a messenger was sent from the Foreign Office with an answer, which was forwarded this morning to Calais, by the Cordelia with a flag of truce. Nothing has transpired with respect to the purpose of the communication, but it is generally conjectured that it contained an insidious repetition of those pacific overtures to this country, which have been the usual prelude to fresh aggressions upon the States of the Continent.

—◇—

PEMBROKESHIRE-SOUTH WALES

Capital Mansion House, Freehold Estate, and Manor,

TO BE SOLD BY

PRIVATE CONTRACT,

With Possession at Michaelmas 1812.

THE Mansion House, Offices, Gardens, Hot-houses, Peach houses, Conservatory, Demesne Lands, and Manor at ROBESTON HALL, containing 338 Acres or thereabouts of rich Meadow and Pastureland, including 12 Acres of Wood and Plantation. The whole lying within a ring fence

The Manor of Robeston is very extensive, comprising the whole of the parish of Robeston West, and parts of the parishes of Stainton, Harbrainston, and Nolton.

The Mansion House is a substantial stone building containing spacious breakfast, dining and drawing rooms, library and lobby, excellent bed-chambers and dressing rooms, servants' apartments, extensive offices, stabling, coach houses, farm-yard, and buildings, the whole forming a complete residence for a Gentleman of fortune. The lands are well fenced, and have a constant supply of water, and are now in full heart and condition, having been for several years occupied by the proprietor, under a judicious course of husbandry. There is also a Corn Mill, worked by water on the premises, together with a convenient set of Cottages for labourers.

Robeston Hall is situated within three miles of the market and post town of Milford, and six of Haverfordwest, with turnpike roads to each, and in an excellent neighbourhood. For particulars, apply by letter (post paid) to William Evans, Solicitor, Haverfordwest.

—◇—

WESLEYAN

THE NEW WESLEYAN METHODIST CHAPEL in NEATH will be OPENED on WHIT-SUNDAY, May 17, 1812. The service (English and Welsh) will begin at ten o'clock in the morning, at half past two in the afternoon, and at six in the evening.

—◇—

It will be recollected that some time since Lieut. Gibbons, of the Alphea schooner, was tried by a Court-Martial for ordering the wife of the Corporal of the Marines to be put on a buoy in the Passage way, and sentenced to be dismissed his vessel. An action was also brought against him, and having suffered judgment to go by default, the damages were on Friday last assessed at Plymouth under a wilt of enquiry 1500l.

—◇—

MARRIED

On Tuesday, the 14th of April, at Weston-on-the-Green Oxfordshire, Richard J. Nevill, Esq. of Llanelly, Carmarthenshire, to Anne, eldest daughter of the late James Yalden, Esq.of Loweington Hall, Hampshire.

A NEW & ELEGANT POST COACH,
called

The Prince Regent,

THE Public are respectfully informed that a new and elegant POST COACH, carrying Insides only, has commenced running from the Bull and Mouth, London, and will continue every Sunday, Tuesday, and Thursday, through Oxford, Cheltenham, Glocester, Ross and Monmouth, to the Angel Inn Abergavenny, where it will arrive the following evenings, and proceed every Tuesday, Thursday, and Saturday mornings, to the Ivy Bush-inn, Carmarthen; return from thence every Monday, Wednesday, and Friday mornings at six; will sleep at at Abergavenny (where it meets the Bristol Coach, and where Passengers are booked) and proceed the following morning through Monmouth, Ross, Glocester, and Cheltenham, for London, where it will arrive early on Wednesday, Friday and Sunday mornings. Passengers may be booked all the way through.

The public are respectfully informed, that arrangements are making to continue the above coach to Milford.

Performed by NOTT Carmarthen
LONGFELLOW Brecon
HEATH and Co. Glos,

The proprietors will not be acountable for any jewels, plate or money, however small the value, nor for any other articles above the value of £5, unless regularly entered and paid for accordingly – nor for Passengers' luggage.

Mr. Lancaster delivered several Lectures in Scotland, during the last month, on the education of poor children. He was every where received with the most cordial welcome, and was present at a public dinner in Glasgow, where a very numerous company, from respect to his religious opinions, instead of drinking his health, testified their sense of his worth, by a general burst of acclamation, for which justly merited compliment he expressed his acknowledgment with greatful feeling and sensibility. On the health of the Duke of Sussex being drunk, Mr. Lancaster stated a fact not generally known of the Marquis of Huntley's Regiment of Royal Highlanders, who had received the benefit of education and when on duty during the rebellion in Ireland, although allowed to live at free quarters would '*not even take a drink of buttermilk without paying for it.*'

The University of Oxford has ordered all *pastry* to be discontinued in the Colleges during the present scarcity;— a measure worthy of imitation in private families.

We have received a letter from Birmingham announcing the restoration of public tranquility in that town, and containing an eulogium on the conduct of Lieut. Thomas of the Hansworth Cavalry (son of Mr. Charles Thomas, of Landough, Glamorganshire.) to whose prompt and zealous exertions the inhabitants are stated to be much indebted.

To the EDITOR of The CAMBRIAN

Sir,

At a time like this, when bread corn is not only at an exceedingly high price, but not enough even to be had in our markets, and when this misfortune is apparently on the increase without a prospect of any help coming to us from the Continent, it behoves every person not only to practice a strict economy, but to endeavour by every means to lessen the consumption of wheat. It is on this principle that I trouble you with this letter, to inform you of a mode of making bread that increases prodigiously its quantity, and adds, as I think to its goodness.

I read in a newspaper, the title of which I am sorry to have forgotten, a method of making bread, that appeared to me so marvellous, I doubted the facts, and determined to try it. I have the pleasure to say, that it has answered in every respect, and is now the bread used by myself and family, and I think the public should also be made acquainted with the process. It is simply this: to every five pounds of flour add one pound of rice, but the rice must be boiled over a slow fire until it becomes like a jelly. You then, when lukewarm, add the barm and mix up your bread; should the sponge be too thick, you add a sufficiency of luke warm water. By this mode thirty pounds of flour and six pounds of rice will make eighteen quartern loaves, of four pounds and one quarter each.

I am, Sir, your obedient servant

Hafod, April 23d 1812 T. Jonnes

SHIP NEWS

Carmarthen, – Arrived, the London Packet, Roberta from London: and Mermaid, Thomas from Liverpool with sundries: Betsy, Jones, from Pembroke, with wheat: Sophia, Rogers from Glocester: with salt: Ceves, Norman, Louisa, Lonsdale, and Providence, Taylor, from Lymm with barley; William & Mary, Roberts from Barnstaple, malt and earthenware; Rebecca, Treharne, from Newport, with pig iron: Mary Ann, Mathias, from Cardigan, with slates: Bedford, Harry, and Batchelor, Lloyd from Kidwelly: Mary Ann, Morgan, Creswell Castle, Lewis, and Two Friends, Morgan, from Llanelly with coals.

Cleared out, the Mary Ann Morgan, for Llanelly: Elizabeth and Mary, Rowe, and Welcome, Davies, for Bristol, with sundries: Betsy Jones, for Llanelly, with ships' anchors: and Theta, Harris, for London, with tin plates.

3rd. September 1814.

NOTICE is hereby given that the TOLL-GATE, on the WICHTREE BRIDGE near Morriston, in the county of Glamorgan, will be LET to the best bidder, at the Guildhall, in Swansea, on Monday, the 5th day of September 1814 between the hours of twelve and two, in the manner directed by the Act passed in the 13th year of the reign of His Majesty King George the Third, "for Regulating the Turnpike roads," which Toll will be set up at such sum as the Trustees then present shall think. Whoever happens to be the best bidder must at the same time give security with sufficient sureities to the satisfaction of the Trustees, of the said Bridge, for payment of the rent agreed for, and at such times as they shall direct. Dated the 1st. day of August 1814.

W. GROVE, *Clerk to the said Trustees.*

The Mary, Murphy from Newfoundland to Ross in Ireland is carried into Ilfracombe, by Wm. Ray, pilot of Bristol, who boarded her on Thursday six leagues to the westward of Lundy, at which she was in possession of Americans, having been captured off Cape Clear, by the Mammoth, American privateer, but the prize master had lost his way supposing Lundy to be an island on the French coast.

On Friday last a schooner was cruising a little below Lundy, supposed to be an enemy, as she was seen to chase several vessels.

Preparations are making for carrying into effect the resolutions of the Magistracy of the counties of Monmouth and Gloucester, for erecting a Cast iron Bridge over the Wye at Chepstow, on a very grand scale. A native poet has said of the present bridge,

> "*The startled traveller gives God his thanks,*
> *When pass'd in safety o'er the rattling planks.*"

SOUTH-WALES,
Most valuable Freehold Mansion & Estate.

TO BE SOLD BY
PRIVATE CONTRACT,

THE ESTATE of TALIARIS, situated in the parish and at an easy distance from Llandilo, in the county of Carmarthen, a most beautiful part of South Wales; together with the right of Presentation to the Perpetual Curacy thereof.

This desirable and truly important Estate, consists of a MANSION HOUSE & DEMESNE, with sundry FARMS, WOODS, and ORNAMENTAL PLANTATIONS containing together 2800 Acres or thereabouts; Land is redeemed.

The Mansion-house posseses every accommodation for a family of the first consequence, and with the Demesne containing upwards of 730 Acres, is now, and has been for many years in the occupation of the Proprietor. The remainder of the Estate, which is let to responsible tenants at will, is in a good state of cultivation and abounds with capital thriving Timber. The neighbourhood is the most respectable, and the country extremely beautiful and picturesque, abounding with game and river fish of every description.

Llandilo is on the great post road to Milford; and is distant from Carmarthen 15 miles, from Swansea 24, Gloucester 98, and London 202 miles.

Mr. Bowen, at the Mansion House will appoint a person to shew the Estate. The printed particulars preparing, and may be had by applying to Mr. James, No. 5 New Boswell court, Lincoln's inn, London.

Part of the purchase-money may remain on security of the Estate.

Last week a handsome woman, of genteel appearance, approaching her accouchement, took her place in the Chester mail from London, to go to Chester, and from thence to Ireland, where her husband, who is an officer in the army, and had recently returned from Bourdeaux, awaited her arrival, having received orders to proceed with his regiment to America. On her arrival at Oxford on Sunday morning, she complained of being unwell, but recovering her spirits soon afterwards, she determined to proceed on her journey. There were three gentlemen in the Mail with her. She had not long passed Wolverhampton, however, when her indisposition returned, and she soon had reason to lament her the precipitrosy of her progress, for she was assailed by the pains of labour; the gentlemen instantly quitted the coach, and sent a young woman, who happened to be on the outside, to their fellow traveller's assistance. She was so much alarmed, and so little experienced in such scenes, however, that she was of little service. Fortunately an elderly female, accidentally passed at the moment, and being called, with her matronly skills, a fine boy was ushered into the world. The mail was detained half an hour, but the lady and her offspring were safely conveyed to the lodge of Sir John Wrottesley between Wolverhampton and Stafford, where she now lies, to use a technical phrase "as well as can be expected." The child is also doing well. It is but due to state to Sir John Wrottesly, that he received his unexpected guest with every possible attention and hospitality.

The Principality of Wales has been more than usually attractive this season; and persons of the first respectability and import have taken up their temporary residence at, or made excursions to, the seaports of Swansea, Tenby, Aberistwyth, Barmouth &c. &c. Hafod, the classic abode of the Member for the County, has, of course, had its share of all those visitors who have any pretensions to taste, any reverence for literature and the arts or any curiosity to witness agricultural and other improvements which have transformed a Desert into an Eden. – Considerable improvements have taken place at the Devil's Bridge, under the direction of Mr. Johnes. The Bridge itself is quite a new object; and Mr. Johnes has laid the foundations of a new and spacious hotel, which will be completed next spring – the present house being found quite inadequate to accomodate the visitors to this interesting spot.

To the EDITOR of THE CAMBRIAN
Haverfordwest 1st. September 1814.

Sir,

The repeated losses which our shipping have experienced so close to our shores, and the ruin which has been the consequence, induced us to petition the Admiralty for protection, and the answer which we have just received, is as concise as most of Mr. Croker's letters – I have known the time when such an application would have been immediately followed by the appointment of a competent naval force; but at the present moment not a ship of war has arrived; on Thursday night two of our devoted merchant vessels were seen on fire within a few miles of Fishguard Head. Although petitions have been sent from every city and town, yet as no effectual remedy has been applied, I feel it a duty, through your Paper, to make a public call on the commercial world to come forward and represent their wrongs to a higher power than the Secretary of the Admiralty Board. I cannot omit alluding to his reply to the Exchange Assurance Company, "that there was at the time a competent naval force in St.George's Channel." From my own knowledge, I deny the assertion. It is true, there is a naval force stationed at Cork, which lies at the *entrance* only of the Channel, and it has for the last four months cruised only to the southward. – The Americans well know this fact; they contrive to pass this station in the night, and then deal out destruction to our defenceless vessels at their leisure. Applications, I am told, arrive at Milford frequently from, Liverpool, Bristol, &c. for the immediate sailing of ships of war from that part; but they are informed in return, that it is no longer a naval station. The valuable Lanzaretie Establishment, The Town, and a Royal Dock-yard, with Timber valued at 300,000l, lie at the mercy of any petty privateer that may attempt their destruction.

NAVALIS

———<>———

Mermaids – Two mermaids it is asserted, have been lately seen by T. Johnson and W. Gordon, fishermen, residing at Port Gordon, a small village in Scotland, who have attested the account of what they witnessed to Mr. George McKenzie, the schoolmaster of that village.

On the afternoon of the 15th instant, about three or four o'clock, and about a quarter of a mile from shore, the sea being perfectly calm, they observed at a small distance from their boat, with its back towards them, and half its body above the water, a creature of a tawny colour, appearing like a man sitting with his body somewhat bent. Surprised at this, they approached towards him till they came within a few yards, when the noise made by the boat occasioned the creature to turn about, which gave the men a better opportunity of observing him. His countenance was swarthy; his hair was short and curled, of a colour between a green and a grey; he had small eyes, a flat nose, his mouth was large, and his arms of an extraordinary length. Above the water he was shaped like a man, but, as the water was clear they could perceive that from the waist downwards, his body tapered considerably; or, as they expressed like a large fish without scales, but they could not see the extremity. The men, however, had not long time to observe him; for, after looking stedfastly at them for about a quarter of a minute, he suddenly dived, but rose again some distance from the boat, accompanied by another, whom the men supposed to be a female, as they could perceive she had breasts, and her hair was not curled, but reached to a little below below the shoulders; the skin of this last one too was fairer than the other's. By this time the men had become considerably alarmed, and made to the shore as fast as possible, and for some time they could perceive the mermaids looking after them.

———<>———

Air Balloon, – Mr. Sadler, jun. ascended with his balloon on Wednesday the 24th. from a field called Kettlewell Orchard adjoining the Cathedral, at York. The ascension was a remarkably fine one; the weather which had been very stormy during the whole of the forenoon, cleared up, and was as calm and favourable as could be wished. The balloon ascended at 21 minutes after one, and was seen with the naked eye from the place of ascension for 45 minutes. From the ascent to the descent 65 miles. His descent was near Craike and Easingwalde, where he was received by Rev. Dr. Guise. He was fortunate in alighting near a populous and hospitable neighbourhood: had he passed the bleak and desolate hills which were before him, he might have spent the night unassisted and in distress. Exactly on the same day, 28 years ago, Lunardi ascended from the same spot. Mr. Sadler returned to York safe, at half past seven o'clock.

———<>———

6th. July 1816.

Mackworth Arms Inn, Swansea

CAMBRIAN & GENERAL PICTON

COACHES

THE Public are respectfully informed that the CAMBRIAN COACH to Bristol, will leave Swansea every Sunday, Tuesday, and Thursday nights, at twelve o'clock, and arrive in Cardiff at seven in the morning, where it will meet the PRINCE of WALES COACH to Gloucester, at which place the latter will arrive at five in the evening. The Cambrian will proceed immediately to Bristol, and arrive there at two o'clock in the afternoon.

The GENERAL PICTON COACH will leave Swansea every Tuesday, Thursday, and Saturday mornings at four o'clock, and reach Bristol at six in the evening.

Both coaches will leave Bristol at six o' clock in the morning on the alternate days, and arrive at Swansea at ten the same evening; from whence the General Picton will start every Monday, Wednesday, and Friday mornings, at seven o'clock, through Llanelly, and Kidwelly, for TENBY, and arrive there at eight the same evenings. This Coach will return from Tenby on Tuesday, Thursday and Saturday mornings at seven o'clock and arrive at Swansea at eight each evening. Passengers and Parcels by the above Coaches, may be booked at either of the towns on the road, for Bristol or Gloucester.

The Public may rely on the exertions of the several Proprietors to ensure regularity and attention throughout the whole line of the road.

No Parcel will be accounted for above the value of Five Pounds unless entered as such and paid for accordingly.

The MILFORD and BRISTOL MAIL COACH every morning at three o'clock from Swansea to Milford; and each evening at eight for Bristol.

WHEAT-SHEAF INN, SWANSEA

Messrs. BENNETT & LONGFELLOW

RESPECTFULLY informs the Public, a New POST COACH called the ACCOMMODATION, to carry four inside, is now running and will continue to run, every Wednesday, Friday and Sunday, from the Wheat-sheaf inn, Swansea, through Neath, Merthyr Tydvil, Brecon, and Hay, to the Hotel, Hereford, where it arrives early the same evening, and meets Coaches from Gloucester, Oxford, London. Worcester, Birmingham, and all parts of the North; also, Ludlow, Shrewsbury, Chester, Holyhead, and Liverpool. Will return from Hereford to Swansea every Monday, Thursday, and Saturday . . .

——◇——

TENBY THEATRE

TO BE SOLD BY AUCTION

On Saturday the 20th day of July 1816 at the Townhall, Tenby.

THE LEASE of the above THEATRE, Ninety-two years of which are unexpired, held under the Corporation of Tenby, at the yearly rent of of One Shilling; with the Scenery, Dresses, Books &c.

——◇——

SHIP NEWS,

Swansea,–

Arrived . . .

Susan Foreshaw from Genoa, ordered to Milford to perform Quarantine .....

——◇——

WESTPHALIAN ESSENCE

FOR preserving and flavoring all kinds of Fish and Flesh, AND RECOVERING MEAT THAT HAS BECOME TAINTED.

Particulars of the excellent qualities of this Essence accompany each Jar.

Originally prepared by Samuel Rogers, Hydrogen Laboratory, near Pontypool; and sold by Mr. Dawe, Swansea; Mr. Dyke, Merthyr; Mr. Abraham Jones, Newport; Mr. Bradford, Chepstow; Mr. Dawe, Monmouth; Mr. J. Price, Abergavenny; and by druggists and perfumers in every principal town, in Jars, with ample directions.

Price 1s.6d.

Dicey and Co's True Daffy's Elixir,

SUPERIOR to every other Medicine for giving immediate relief in the most painful fits of cholic, and in all complaints of the stomach and bowels. It has also been found no less successful in attacks of the same diseases in horses, cows and other cattle; and, as a general family medicine. DICEY'S DAFFY has long become so justly celebrated, from its superior quality to all other preparations sold under the name of *Daffy's Elixir* that no family, particularly in the country, ought to be without it;- but, as effectual relief, is only to be expected by those who use the *Genuine Medicine*, purchasers are cautioned not to rely merely upon the glass bottle bearing the name of *Dicey & Co.* as there are unprincipled people who buy up the empty bottles for the purpose of filling them with their own *Counterfeit Preparations,* and which are therefore foisted upon the public as *True Daffy's Elixir* – the only certain criterion is to examine whether the stamp label in red ink which is pasted over the cork, has the words Dicey & Co. printed thereon; and to observe that the bill of directions is signed

"*W. Sutton & Co. late Dicey & Sutton.*"

Sold, wholesale, at the Original Warehouse, No. 10, Bow Church-yard London, in bottles at 2s. 1d. and 2s. 9d. each; and retail by all respectable Medicine Vendors.

——◇——

The five persons left for execution at Ely, underwent the sentence of the law on Friday. They all evinced great repentance, and voluntarily signed a written confession of their offences. The execution was attended by an immense concourse of spectators who behaved with the greatest order, and upon whom the awful scene seemed to make a deep impression.

——◇——

GLAMORGANSHIRE

A Desirable Residence, near Swansea.

TO BE SOLD OR LET,

And entered upon immediately, for the unexpired term of 99 years, determinable on three good healthy lives.

A LEASEHOLD ESTATE, called LOWER SKETTY, a neat commodious House in good repair, consisting of two parlours, dining room, a drawing room, six bedrooms, one housekeeper's room, a large convenient kitchen, scullery, butler's pantry, larder, dairy, cellar's, with other convenient offices, a good pump in the yard, and excellent Garden, with choice fruit trees, with about 18 Acres of excellent Meadow and Pasture Ground, in high cultivation. More Land may be had, and contiguous to the premises, if required.

The Mansion House is delightfully situated on an eminence, with a lawn in front of about one acre.

It commands a view of the bay and harbour of Swansea, with the opposite coasts of Devon and Somerset, as well as the romantic country around: distant three miles from Swansea, and half a mile from the sea, in a dry healthy situation and genteel neighbourhood. It altogether forms a most compact and desirable retreat for a respectable family. The Furniture, which is modern, may be taken at a valuation, if desirable.

. . . Apply to James Masters Esq. Sketty . . .

——◇——

Chepstow bridge will certainly be opened on the 24th. inst. The engineer (though attended with considerable inconvenience) has extended the former indulgence, by allowing persons to pass the bridge from half past five in the morning until half past nine in the evening, each foot passenger paying one penny, and for each horse sixpence, with double tolls on Sundays. When it is considered that the little fund that may be thus raised will be applied wholly towards discharging expenses unavoidably incurred by those of the poor workmen with families, who have met with serious accidents during the arduous undertaking, the humane will feel a pleasure in making the trifling deposit for so laudable a purpose; especially as they will be immediately by the accommodation afforded them. The boats continue to pass as usual.

The Graniens frigate has sent into Milford a fast sailing lugger-rigged boat, called the Witch, of Fowey, suspected to be a smuggler; and the Bat

Admiralty cutter has carried into the same port a French smuggling vessel called the the St. Joseph, of Rouen with 150 ankers of brandy and geneva, which have been deposited in the Custom-House warehouse.

We are sorry to state, that the hopes which were entertained of a good hit of fruit in the orchards have in great measure vanished, so destructive has been the blight with which the apple and pear trees have been visited.

Swansea fair, on Tuesday last was plentifully supplied with cattle and horses; but few purchases were made, and those at indifferent prices; – fine wool produced 18d. a pound, and coarse 13d.

Llandilo Barnabas fair exhibited a considerable shew of cattle, horses, and pigs; and we regret to say that the prices of neither were at all improved. A young man who had taken a copious libation of *cwrw* fell asleep on the bridge, and had his pocket picked of 26l.

1st. August 1818.

PENTWYN HOUSE, LOUGHOR.

TO BE LET

For a Term of Years, and entered upon immediately.

A Desirable RESIDENCE, called PENTWYN HOUSE, consisting of a breakfast-parlour, dining-room, spacious kitchen, back kitchen, pantry and cellar on the ground floor; drawing-room and five bed chambers on the first floor; palisaded court in front, about half an acre of pleasure ground and garden in the rear; an excellent stable for three horses and a coach house.

The premises are delightfully situated, commanding fine land and sea views, within seven miles distance of Swansea and four of Llanelly.

For particulars apply to Mr. James, Attorney, Swansea.

A Commission has just passed the Great Seal, appointing a Board to inquire into the best means of preventing the forgery of Bank notes, to examine evidence and to receive any plans that shall be offered. The Members are – Sir Joseph Banks, Sir Wm. Congreve, Wm. Courtenay, Esq. M.P., Davies Gilbert, Esq. M.P. Jeremiah Harman, Esq. Governor of the Bank, Wm. Hyde Wollaston, M.D; and Charles Hatchett Esq. The first sitting took place on Tuesday last.

The following occurrence lately happened in the old church-yard of Tulliallen Perthshire. The Sexton, whilst digging a grave, had his attention attracted by an unusual noise under ground, which encreased as he proceeded in the operation, until having reached a coffin, on breaking which, he was assailed with swarms of bees, which had there taken up their residence. The breast of the skeleton was found completely filled with honeycombs; and from its quantity it appeared the inhabitants had remained in undisturbed possession of this singular station for many years previous to the discovery.

The present summer has been the warmest since that of 1779. The previous winter and spring were so mild, that green peas were sold in May at one shilling the peck measure. The thermometer was at 78 on the 15th. of April, and the hawthorns were in blossom three or four days after that period.

The Philadelphia Mercantile Advertiser of the 20th June mentions that mountains of ice have been seen in lat. 29, outside the Gulf Stream.

TO BE LET,

And entered upon immediately,

A Convenient and extensive DWELLING-HOUSE, situate in Castle Bailey street in the town of Swansea, late in the possession of David Jenkins, Printer, Bookseller, and Law-stationer; consisting of a large shop, with counters and other fixtures complete, a parlour in front, a hall, two kitchens adjoining, an underground cellar, a drawing-room, dressing room, pantry, and store room at the back of the shop, communicating with a small garden, a well of excellent water, and a back-entrance into Worcester-place, four bed-chambers on the first floor, and two servants' rooms in the attic.

If the premises shall be thought too extensive, the Proprietor will engage to detach the drawing-room, dressing-room, pantry and store room, last mentioned by annexing them to the adjoining house.

For further particulars, or a view of the premises, apply at the Counting-House of Wm. Grove and Sons, Swansea.

A vessel is now moored off the Tower, for the purpose of enlisting seamen for the navy. It is reported to be the intention of the Admiralty to fit out 12 sail of the line for the naval review so long talked of, and which is again put off until the end of August. This statement is, however, not credited among nautical men; and speculation is busy in finding some better employment for our seamen than a naval review.

FOR THE BENEFIT OF ALL CONCERNED.

TO BE SOLD BY AUCTION,

For home consumption and exportation, at the Custom-house Warehouse in the town of Cardigan, on Wednesday, the 9th day of September next,

TEN Casks of BORDELAISES VIN DE MONTAGNE, Twenty-five ditto MUID DE VIN RONGA, and One ditto DE VIN BLANC, saved from the Cargo of the Brig Eliza, wrecked the 14th December, 1816, within the limits of the port of Cardigan, on her voyage from Cette to Havre de Grace.

Also, Pieces of MASTS, YARDS, CABLES, and other materials belonging to the said wreck.

For further particulars apply to D. P. Lucas, Esq. Custom-House Cardigan.

SWANSEA INFIRMARY.

Abstract of the House Surgeon's Report to the Weekly Board, from the 21st to the 27th July, 1818 inclusive.

In-door Patients

Remain as per last report	4
Admitted since	1
	5

Out-door Patients

Remained by last Report	126
Admitted since	13
	139
Discharged Cured & Relieved	22
Ditto incurable	2
Ditto for Non-attendance and irregularity.............................	3
	27
Remaining	112

[*From the Literary Gazette and Journal of the Belles Lettres.]*

FINE ARTS – ENGRAVED PRINTS.

Six Views in and near Swansea, drawn and etched by T. Baxter.

It has been our invariable practice, in remarking on works of art, to bestow attention upon the rising artist, as well as upon his more successful and established contemporary: and as far as was in our power to seek the unobtrusive, and to distinguish merit, whether it lay too low, or was raised too high for general notice, either in exhibitions or the passing publications of the day. Accordingly we present to the public these apparently faithful delineations of the county in and about Swansea. The views are as follows:–

1. Caswell Bay, fom the Spring.
2. The Willows and Mount Pleasant.
3. Mount Pleasant.
4. Oystermouth, from the Castle.
5. The Church at Briton Ferry.
6. The Castle at Oystermouth.

In these etchings there is great adroitness in the execution and even minuteness of detail, without any visible sacrifice of truth either to style or skill. There is much of that simplicity which characterised the early periods of art, where the aim of the engraver was solely to give a faithful copy of a painting or drawing.

Mr. Baxter's choice is various and judicious. Caswell Bay and Oystermouth are of a bold and picturesque appearance, and would afford an opportunity to exercise the talents of our first landscape painters: as it is, we can form from the etchings a very fair idea of the extent and magnificence of the scenery.

To those interested in the local character of the views we feel assured that nothing has been omitted that could identify the scene; and we sincerely hope the artist will be encouraged to appear in future with advantage to himself and credit to the art.

Before quitting the subject, we shall just offer a passing hint to the artist engravers of our own country; and though many have highly distinguished themselves by their abilities, it is still necessary to recommend to their serious attention that fidelity of representation so essential to good art, without which, what we are called upon to admire is merely the dexterity of the mechanic, and not the efforts of of a liberal profession.

These remarks were suggested by turning over a volume of Divine Emblems from the designs of Otho Veurns published at Antwerp 1680, which, without the advantage of etching, or other means since brought into use, have in them so much of character and expression, with such judicious attention to keeping and the other principles of art, that we lament to say is not often found in the present day; and, it must be further observed, by means in the execution as simple in their quality, as might serve no higher purpose than is now used in engraving coats of arms, crests &c.

Bolswert in his landscapes after Rubens, has attained similar effects by as simple a process. It would be well if our engravers were to cast their eye occasionally on these examples as on first principles . . . which might give their works an equal value in the eyes of *posterity.*

NOTICE.

ANY qualified Gentleman taking out a Game Certificate, who may be desirous of SPORTING upon his Grace the DUKE of BEAUFORT'S HILLS, in Breconshire this season, is hereby permitted to do so from the 12th to the 20th of August, and no longer.

No Gentleman will be allowed to kill more than Two Brace of Grouse each day.

All *Unqualified* Persons found trespassing will be dealt with according to law.

July, 1818.

Arrived in Swansea, – Mr. Smith, Mr. and Mrs. Edward Davies and family, Sir Thomas Warmington, Rev. Mr. Clarke, Mr. and Mrs. Ackland, Mr. and Mrs Lewis, Mr. Blackwell, Dr. and Mrs. Briant, Mr. and Mrs. Price, Sir J. and Lady Nicholl and family, Mr. Ward, Lieut. and Mrs. Harrington R.N. Miss Holbrow, Mr. J. Beard, Rev. Mr. Hancorne, Mr. and Mrs. Griffiths, Miss Wrankim, Mr. and Mrs. Badenton, Mrs. Henry Murcott, Mrs and Miss Turbervil, Mr. and Mrs. Lloyd, Capt. Davies R.N. Mr. J. Hill, Mrs. Crawshay and family, &c. &c

——◇——

2nd. September 1820.

NOW LOADING
At Carpenter Smith's Wharf, Southwark, London,
THE ASSIDUOUS,
Wm. Trick, Master; Round to *Swansea, Neath, and Ports adjacent,*
And will sail in twenty-one days.

For Freight and Passage apply to the Captain on board; or to Geo. Dawkins, High street Swansea.

August 21 1820.

——◇——

FREEHOLD PREMISES:

Lot 1, ALL that MESSUAGE or DWELLING HOUSE situate in Goat-street, in the town of Swansea, together with the Garden behind the same extending to the White-Walls, now in the possession of Thos. Lutus, as tenant at will, at the low rent of £12.

Lot 2, All that other MESSUAGE or DWELLING-HOUSE, adjoining Lot 1, together with the Garden behind the same, extending to the White-Walls, now in the possession of Mr. Lewis, as tenant at will, at the low rent of £13. The above premises are situate in Goat Street, opposite Bank-street and measure in front 33 feet, and in depth 200 feet-a most desirable property to be purchased in order to open a new street to communicate with the White-Walls, and which may be continued from thence in a direct line through the Rope-Walk, and the adjoining Lands (the property of C. R. Jones, Esq.) being also a desirable situation for building. For further particulars apply at the Office of Messrs. James and Collins, Solicitors, Swansea.

——◇——

ESCAPED FROM JUSTICE,

To the Chief Constables, Constables of Hundreds, and to whom it may concern, in the County of Glamorgan,

WHEREAS EVAN THOMAS EVAN, THOMAS EVAN the Younger, THOS. HOWELL, SAMUEL GRIFFITH, WM. EVAN REES, OWEN FRANCIS, HOPKIN WILLIAM, WM. MORGAN, JOHN DAVID, WILLIAM HUGH, WILLIAM JOHN, JAMES HOWELL and WILLIAM REES, Coppermen, in the employ of Messrs. Williams, Grenfell & Co. of the parish of Lansamlet in this county, have been convicted for unlawfully combining to raise the price of wages, and were severely sentenced to various periods of imprisonment, some of whom have been rescued and others have absconded, you are hereby required to make diligent search after them, and to lodge them, or either of them, in either of his Majesty's Gaols, and give notice of your having so done to Mr. Withecombe, Clerk to the Magistrates at Swansea.

——◇——

Searjeant Cummings, a colour searjeant of the Royal Marines Artillery, has been dismissed the service after 17 years faithful discharge of his duty, for having, a few days previously, drunk the health of the Queen in a public house! – *West Briton.*

At Brecon Great Sessions, Wm. James for stealing a lamb; and Morgan Thomas, for robbing the house of David Vaughan at Llanthew, received sentence of death; Thomas Swift, for stealing a pocket book, to be transported for fourteen years; and Samuel Apperley, for stealing in a dwelling house, seven years; Wm. Fox, for circulating base coin, twelve month's imprisonment. Four others were acquitted.

On Monday morning one man was killed, and another had his arm broke and otherwise much bruised, by the falling of stones at the Box Colliery, Llanelly.

——◇——

TO BE LET

THE HOUSE and TAN-YARD at Cardiff. The Tan-Yard is now in full work, with every convenience, and will be let separately from the House if required and entered upon the 25th of September next, with the advantage of the incoming tenant working in his stock in the backward boxes, for the term of two years and a half, which is the unexpired term of the lease to the present tenant, but any further terms will be granted by the landlord if required. The premises are eligible, and the House a good one, and the whole in ample repair.

Being the only Tan-Yard in so populous and rising a town, or within twelve to twenty miles off, being the best market in the county, in a country abounding with oak bark, and every facility of conveyance to any part of the kingdom, its advantages are obvious.

Further particulars known by application (if by letter, post-paid.) to Mr. Williams on the premises.

——◇——

GAME

ALL Persons are requested NOT to SHOOT or COURSE on the several Manors of *Wenvoe, Wrinstown, Cadogstown, Denispowis and Castle Moil.*

——◇——

THE flattering and gratifying testimonials of the public approbation conferred upon Miss DESMOND, by the Ladies and Gentlemen of Swansea, who honoured her BENEFIT with their presence, calls forth her most grateful thanks and warmest acknowledgments, which it will ever be her pride to and ambition to merit.

August 26 1820.

Theatre Swansea

Early as Patronage can be obtained,
MR. LLOYD
ANNUAL LENT ASTRONOMICAL LECTURER,
From the
Theatre Royal, Haymarket, London,

WILL give his COURSE of ASTRONOMICAL LECTURES, Illustrated by the

DIOASTRODOXON,
Or, GRAND TRANSPARENT ORRERY.

The Course will introduce all the splendid Scenery and Decorations annually displayed in London, on a scale of grandeur and magnificence never yet witnessed in this Principality, the whole forming the desideratum of astronomical beauty and intelligence.

The Dulcet Notes of the Celestina will accompany the Changes with Sacred Music.

Subscribers to the Course, Three Lectures, *Half a Guinea;* Tickets transferable.

Subscriptions are received at Mr. Jenkins's, Cambrian Office. – where likewise may be had a Compendium of the Lectures, with Plates, price 1s.6d.

THE CAMBRIAN.

SWANSEA, Friday, Sept. 1.

We are concerned to state, that a difference in respect to wages, has arisen between some of the Copper Companies in this vicinity, and the men employed in the works. Thirteen of the latter were convicted, before our Magistrates, of a combination, and committed, but escaped from the constables. On the following day three of these were again apprehended and lodged in our temporary place of confinement previous to their removal to the house of correction; but they were speedily released by force by a body of their comrades.

Our magistrates used every persuasive method to induce the people to return to their work, and if not satisfied with their situations, then to give the usual notice to their employers; but all to no purpose. We are happy to add that this complaint has not originated, nor is it in any way connected with any political feeling, and we are entirely free from any disorder or turbulence. It has, however, been deemed prudent to swear in an accession of constables, and to embody our Volunteer Cavalry in support of the Civil Power. We hope that the people concerned will shortly resume their wonted labour, and that the business will be happily adjusted.

Breconshire Turnpike Trust.

NOTICE is hereby given, that the TOLLS arising from the several Toll Gates undermentioned, will be LET by AUCTION, to the best bidder, at the Shire-hall in Brecon, on Wednesday, the 15th. day of September, 1820, between the hours of eleven and twelve in the forenoon, for One Year to commence on the 29th. September, 1820, at noon, in manner directed by The Act of Parliament in that behalf.

The sums of money set opposite the lots are the annual rents at which the same are respectively let this year, clear of all deductions; but they will be put up at such sums as the Trustees shall think fit.

The bidders must be then and there prepared with sufficient sureties for payment of the money monthly.

Lot 1. Furnace and Pencerrig Cochion Gates	£350
Lot 2. Llanvaes, St. John's Watton and Court Gates and the Canal Bridge Side Gate	1395
Lot 3. Pontcumbeth and Crickhowell Bridge Gates and Pontybrinhirt Side Gates	480
Lot 4. Llangunider and Llangunider Bridge Gate and Llansaintfread Side Gate	135
Lot 5. Builth Gates	327
Lot 6. Pontneathvaughan Gate	28
Lot 7. Cwmdu Gate	46
Lot 8. The Hay Pound, Dishpool Lane, and Glasbury Gates	287
Lot 9. Cefn Llanddewy Gate in Llangammarch	17
Lot 10. Clydach and Danygraig Gates	45
	£3120

By order of the Trustees,
WALTER CHURCHEY, Clerk.

MACKWORTH-ARMS, SWANSEA.

WM. JONES,
Importer & Dealer in Wines, Spirits, &c.

BEGS leave to thank his Friends and the Public in general for their favours and support bestowed upon him for twenty-four years in the Wine and Spirit Trade, as well as in the Tavern Line.

He now respectfully informs them that, in consequence of a depression in the Spirit Trade, he is enabled to offer them for *ready money* –

	Per Gal
Real cognac Brandy – direct from the grower	26s.
Fine Old Jamaica Rum	18s.
Real London Gin and British Hollands	17s.
Skiddam Hollands	26s.

Fine Old Port, Bucellas, Madeira, Teneriffe, Vidonia, Sherry, and Claret, together with a small lot of Mount Etna Wines in pint and quart bottles.

Bottled Porter, Beer, Perry and Cider in perfection.

Horses and Carriages taken at Livery, with lock up coach houses.

New Post Chaises, a Town Chariot, and Open Carriage, to Let on Hire.

5th. October 1822.

PUBLIC APPROVAL

THE New Lottery Scheme (as I anticipated.) appears to have met with public approval; I cannot, therefore, do better than remind my best friends of its principal features. – It contains

3 **M**oney **P**rizes of £20,000!
2 **M**oney **P**rizes of £10,000!
2 **M**oney **P**rizes of £5,000!
3 **M**oney **P**rizes of £2,000!
110 other **M**oney **C**apitals!
5600 other **M**oney **P**rizes!

Not any Fixed Prizes. – All the tickets in the Wheel before the first day. – All the capitals may be drawn in First

Hour of First Day.- Not any Classes. – In fact, it is only a plain Old fashioned Old English Scheme; as the Contractors are determined to try which the majority of the Public like best, viz. the present sort of Scheme, or those with Classes, Re-Drawing &c. as it of course is immaterial to the Contractors which are adopted. Their only aim being to please the Public.

Tickets and Shares are selling at my Offices 4 Cornhill and 9 Charing-cross, London, & by the following Agents.
W. FAGG, Bookseller, Swansea;
BARRY & SON, Booksellers, Bristol
D. EVANS Journal Office, Carmarthen
W. BIRD Post Office, Cardiff . . .

In the late Lottery I sold the Grand Prize No. 4660. Prize of £30,000, and several minor Capitals, parts of which were sold by some of the above Agents. I have the honour to be, the Public's devoted Servant.

T. BISH, STOCK-BROKER

***SCHEMES GRATIS.*

Drawing Begins 30th. of this month,

OCTOBER.

———◇———

On Saturday night, about twelve o'clock, an armed party of men attacked the farm-house of John Hare, at Kildonnell, in this county. They fired a shot through the door, and demanded it to be opened, which was refused by Hare, who saw some of the party armed with poles, and bayonets on the tops. They fired through the windows. Hare's mother, who lay in a bed opposite, received a ball in her cheek, after passing through the centre of a hand saw, which hung near her. They made several attempts to break into the house; but the shrieks of the inmates, and the firing of the shots, having given alarm to the neighbours, the villains made off.

The neighbourhood of Donegal has been lately a scene of continued outrage. An armed party attacked the house of D. Hickey, and demanded and obtained arms. Another party set fire to a stack of tithe corn, the property of Archdeacon Maunsell, which was totally consumed. The sounding of horns, and loud shouts, accompanied these daring outrages. Another party, still larger, and well armed attacked the house of Mr. Curtis, of Ballinlea, demanded arms, and took from him a gun and pistol. This party then proceeded to Mr. Nash's, Woodbine Lodge, and searched for arms.

———◇———

In consequence of the King not having appeared in public since his return from Scotland, it is reported that his Majesty is not so well as could be wished

———◇———

Theatre. – This place of rational amusement, after a cessation of four weeks, re-opened on Monday evening, with a grand new spectacle called *Joan of Arc*. The tale is well told, the dresses admirable, and the performers seemed quite *at home* in their respective characters, owing, as we suppose, to their having so recently appeared in them on the Bristol stage, where it has been represented three times with *increased applause* on each repitition. Mrs. Inchbald's Play of *Every One has his Fault* was performed on Wednesday: it is generally thought to be amongst the best of our modern Comedies, and never fails affording satisfaction when even *tolerably* performed, but, on this occasion there was not a *fault* to be found. The benefits and a liberal public, we trust, will not overlook or neglect the *meritorious or the industrious.*

– *The Bristol Observer,* in its report of *Joan of Arc,* pronounces it one of the most interesting features of French History. The interest never flags; all the speeches are short, giving no time for bombast or meretricious clap-traps; and the pictures with which several of the scenes terminate are truly imposing. Even the Coronation at Rheims, much as we have seen of a coronation nearer home, is far from being tedious: the ceremony is relieved by an original chorus, containing more of music than noise. Mrs. M'Cready's Joan of Arc, her figure and dresses, brought to view the best picture we have seen of her prototype; and as companion to Mr. Hancock's portrait of her in Queen Elizabeth, we should like to see her painted in Joan, both in her village attire and at the instant of her kissing the mark of a tear that had dropped upon her sword, when she first rescued *Charles* from peril.

———◇———

A GENERAL TURNPIKE ACT

We before referred to this Act, passed in the last Session of Parliament, by which the former Turnpike Acts are repealed from Jan. 1st. 1823.

After Jan. 1 1826, all wheels of waggons and other carriages are to be so constituted as not to deviate more than a quarter of an inch from a flat surface in wheels exceeding six inches in breadth; the nails of the tires of such wheels not to project above a quarter of an inch above the surface. Penalties for non-observance 5l. on the owner, and 40s. on the driver.

No waggon or cart to be used after Jan. 1, 1826, with wheels of less breadth than three inches on any turnpike road. Penalty not exceeding 5l. on the owner, and 40s. on the driver . . .

Nothing contained in the Act relating to breadth of wheels, or the tolls payable thereon, to extend to coaches, &c. . . .

The following weights are to be allowed:

Power is given to Trustees or Commissioners of Turnpike roads, and Collectors or their deputies, and to every person acting under their authority, to measure wheels: penalty on obstructing measurement, not exceeding 5l. Penalty on toll collectors allowing waggons to pass before measurement(the same having been required) not exceeding 5l.

	Summer.		Winter.	
	tons.	*cwt.*	*tons.*	*cwt*
To every waggon with nine inch wheels.	6	10	6	–
To every caravan, or four wheeled carriage, for the conveyance of goods & built with springs.	4	5	3	15

It shall be deemed summer from May 1 to October 31, both inclusive, and Winter from November 1 to April 30.

Trustees are empowered to demand the following additional tolls for overweight:– for the first and second hundred of overweight, 3d. for each hundred . . .

and for every hundred exceeding ten hundred, 5s.

The above regulations as to weight are not to extend to waggons, &c. carrying only manure or lime for the improvement of land, or hay, straw, fodder, or corn, carried for sale; nor to waggons &c. carrying only one tree or one log of timber, or one block of stone, or one cable or rope; nor to any coach, gig &c. . . .

Penalty for unloading goods, &c. to evade toll, or obstructing the weighing, 5l. on the owner of the waggon, &c. and not exceeding 40s. on the driver . . .

Tolls payable on waggons going empty for road materials &c. to be repaid when returning laden . . .

Exemptions from Tolls. – Tolls are not to be demanded on waggons, &c. conveying materials for roads or bridges; or manure (except lime) or implements of husbandry (unless laden also with some other thing not exempted from toll); or agricultural produce not sold or for sale; or for horses employed in husbandry, such horses not going more than two miles on the turnpike road on which the exemption shall be claimed; or from any person going to or returning from their parochial church or chapel, or usual place of religious worship tolerated by law, on *Sundays* or on any day on which divine service is by authority ordered to be celebrated; or from persons attending funerals; or from any rector, vicar or curate, attending his parochial duty within his parish; or for any horse, waggon, or cart, employed only in conveying a vagrant sent by a legal pass, or prisoners sent by a legal warrant; or for any horses or carriages conveying persons to county elections; or for any horses or carriages which shall only cross any turnpike road, or shall not pass above 100 yards thereon . . .

———◇———

Domestic Telegraph. – This is a very superior invention to bells. It is intended to convey orders to servants, which they can instantly execute, without the usual loss of time in going to receive a verbal command. Mr. Pearson (the inventor) a resident at Boston in America, conceived the possibility of surmounting the difficulties that walls and distance opposed to his success, and of preventing the necessity of speech. The master is obeyed as promptly as possible, and the servant, certain of understanding his orders, need not fear the effects of the want of memory. The telegraph consists of two dials, divided in the same manner, each of the needles is subject to the same movement at the same time, and over the same space. – The communication of the movement from one needle to the other was the only difficulty in this mechanical problem; the obstacle has been ingeniously surmounted. One of the dials is placed in the master's room, and can be made an elegant decoration; the other in any situation most convenient to the servant. Every one of the divisions, which can be multiplied with pleasure, represents an order by an understood sign or figure; the master points the needle of his dial to the sign or command he wishes to be obeyed, and that instant the signal is repeated on the dial fixed up for the servant's use. The telegraph is easily made, and of very trifling expence.

———◇———

Sad News for the Fair. – By the late returns it appears that in England there are 294,083 females more than males – in Wales, 16,464 – in Scotland, 126,352, making a total in Great Britain of 434,804 – almost half a million ladies fair, doomed by the unlucky course of nature to single blessedness – which is rendered worse by the waste occasioned by at least 150,000 inflexible bachelors. – How it is in Ireland, we have no means of ascertaining; but we hope affairs are more prosperous.

———◇———

6th. November 1824.

Saturday to Monday's Posts.

———

LONDON, OCT 30.

———

THE French Papers of Wednesday are filled with the details of the ceremony used in the interment of the late King, on the preceding day. The accounts of this pageant furnished by the Journals, though sufficiently particular, make no mention of any expression of popular feeling upon the occasion, beyond the homage which a Frenchman's heart offers to *Spectacle* of every kind. In truth the memory of Louis appears to have perished among the subjects, with a celerity outstripping the proverbially rapid oblivion of deceased Sovereigns; and though there was much in his character, as well as in his history, to keep alive remembrance

These papers contain the copy of a sanguinary Decree of the blessed Ferdinand, affixing the penalty of death to certain seditious cries and expressions, such as "Long live the Constitution"; "Viva la Liberte"; Death to Tyrants &c. &c. Freemasons, Sectarians, and Constitutionalists, being regarded enemies to the throne, are all to be considered as guilty of high treason, and as having incurred the same penalty. The King has further fenced himself round with a considerable addition to his body guard, and another park of artillery; not an unwise step, perhaps, after such a decree. And further, as if the measure of Ferdinand's fanatical violence was not complete, the *Journal des Debats* says, that he is about to re-establish the Inquisition, and to appoint for its Chief a barefooted Capuchin. – It is superfluous to reason against such intense stupidity and wickedness; it is to be punished, not animadverted upon; and we do not distrust the retributive justice of time. – *respice finem* . . .

———◇———

Duke of York, The Prince Leopold. Printed for Whittaker, Ave Maria La.

The steam engine at the paper mills of A. H. Holdsworth Esq. at Dartmouth, exploded last week, by which accident several persons were severely injured.

W. Twiss common carrier between Chester and Rhyddlan, was fined 7l. for taking passengers into his cart for conveyance. It is not, we believe, generally known that a liability to fine exists.

Sudden Death. – On Sunday last, just as Mr. Goss, master of the brig Perseverance, of Ilfracombe, lying at Truro, entered the Independent Chapel at the latter place, and whilst he was in the act of offering up a short prayer, usual on such occasions, he was observed to fall, and before he could be removed from the seat he was quite dead. Captain Goss was the first who held divine worship on board of ship.

Cure of Hydrophobia. – Mr. John Cook of Minchinhampton in a letter to the editors of the Gloucester Journal, gives the following recipes for the cure of Hydrophobia:

"Mix and pound common salt in a quart of water, and then squeeze, bathe and wash the wound with the same for an hour, but not drink any of it, then bind a little more salt to the effected part for twelve hours. The discoverer of this recipe declares that he was bit six times by mad dogs, and always cured himself by it."

"Take native cinnibar, and cinnibar faciti, of each 24 grains; musk 16 grams; mix it into a powder and give it in one dose in a glass of French Brandy, as it was given in the following case:– A poor man was bit by a mad dog, and after using divers medicines, was invaded with a strong hydrophobia; and being confused at Greenwich, was treated with the above medicine as follows: his teeth being forced asunder with a knife, he took one dose; three hours after, the hydrophobia symptoms were abated; when he swallowed a second dose, which, by the next morning almost totally recovered him, he took a third dose in a fortnight, and a fourth in a month after, and never felt more of his complaint."

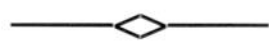

A smuggling vessel was captured last week in the channel, by the Harrier and Pelarous, worth 8000l.

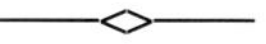

His Majesty's ship Phaeton, Capt. Sturt, arrived in Portsmouth on Friday, brought 22 Spanish refugees from Gibraltar, men of excellent character, whom Captain Sturt took on board through feelings of commiseration.

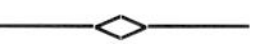

Monthly Agricultural Report. – The late hurricanes which have occasioned so much mischief on the north coasts were attended with heavy rains, extremely injurious to the remnants of harvest remaining abroad in the low and backward districts. Lincolnshire, the fens, and some parts of Yorkshire, have been deluged, and the beans and some oats remaining abroad have been greatly deteriorated in quantity. Clover seed is the worst crop of the season, great part of it is entirely spoiled. It will require full the remainder of the current month, to clear the fields generally. Both Scotland and Ireland, as it appears have to boast of superior crops of all kinds, both in quantity and quality, however abundant we may deem our own. We have now reached the period in which we can avail ourselves of nearly decisive tests, and thence it seems generally acknowledged that the wheat crop is a full average. The crops of rape and cale are super abundant; but in some districts where the grass is equally so, the heavy rains have so bent down and soaked it that it is likely to produce little nourishment to cattle, and may prove fatal to sheep. Latter sown turnips having been forced too much into foliage by the warm rains, in course are at present deficient in bulk; but there will be no dearth of that root. Potatoes likewise will be fully adequate to the demand. Hops prove superior to expectation some time since, but the avidity with which good samples are bought up shows the state of the case.

To the Subscriber's to the Swansea Infirmary,

Swansea, October 20th 1824.

Ladies and Gentlemen.

MR. Osler having resigned the appointment of RESIDENT SURGEON to the SWANSEA INFIRMARY, I beg leave to offer myself as a Candidate to succeed him. Having served my apprenticeship to the Institution, I have had an opportunity of becoming fully acquainted with the general routine of the duties of the appointment, and with the mode of conducting the Establishment; and having since devoted nearly three years to the study of my Profession in the Medical Schools and Hospitals in London, I trust you will think my pretensions entitled to your favourable consideration. Should I be so fortunate as to obtain the appointment, I shall endeavour, by my conduct to justify the confidence reposed in me by the Friends of the Institution.

I am,
Ladies and Gentlemen,
Your most obedient servant,
WILLIAM ROWLAND.

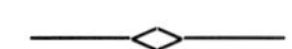

A farmer named Leigh, about 77 years of age, residing at North Curry, near Taunton has, according to his own calculation, drunk on an average fourteen pints of cider daily, for fifty years, excluding all other liquor, which amounts to 501 hogsheads. He is in perfect health . . .

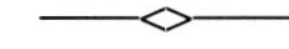

Aberystwyth, Oct 31. – *Dreadful Occurrence.* – On Monday last the weather being favourable and a prospect of a good take of herrings, a number of boats, as well at this place as along the coast, collected for the purpose of fishing. All went out in the night, without suspicion of impending danger, and their hopes in a great measure were realised; but at five o'clock in the morning a storm arose at west, and continued to blow hard until about eight, when it increased to a perfect hurricane. The boats which had previously come to their anchorage, were instantly driven from their moorings and sent in all directions on shore; at this time all was bustle and confusion; the alarm bell ringing, houses unroofed, and windows broken, to an extent seldom known before – but, melancholy to relate, in the midst of this horror, a most appalling scene presented itself, by the appearance of two fishing boats advancing towards the bar, and both soon after in the most distressing state stranded. The one got on shore to the north of the harbour, and with the greatest difficulty her crew were saved; but the other sunk in the harbour's mouth – and seven poor men perished in sight of several hundred spectators, who, although very near, could not possibly render them the least assistance. Thus, with many similar instances at different periods, have we to lament the want of of a place of safety for vessels in distress – the harbour being open to the west, and dangerous to approach in bad weather – when, at a comparatively trifling expense a pier might have been erected, which not only would have saved the lives of these poor fellows, but many others, and property to an immense extent. Six of the bodies have been thrown on shore, but the other, as yet, has not appeared. What a sad tale to tell, and what reflection upon those who, for want of exertion have suffered a situation, perhaps not to be equalled, for the erection of a pier, to be left open to the merciless storm, when a small sum would not only be the means of preventing the loss of lives, but in a material point of view would preserve property to an extent not to be calculated upon. It is a subject not only worthy of the attention of the mercantile part of the community, especially those trading to all parts of the world through St. George's Channel, but to the Government of the country, for by a slight view of a map of England and Ireland, it is obvious that that a communication between the Sister Kingdoms, by this place, would be of the greatest benefit to all parties.

2nd. December 1826.

Wednesday the General Committee of the National Society, for the education of the poor in the principles of the established church, held their meeting at St. Martin's Vestry room; the Lord Bishop of Exeter in the chair. Eighteen fresh schools were united to the National Society, and ten grants of money were made towards the erecting, enlarging and fitting up of school rooms.

The Bank of England have at length determined to open a branch bank in Liverpool, on the same plan as those lately established at Manchester, Gloucester, Swansea &c.

We understand that a reduction is to be made in the naval estimates, from those of last year to be laid before the new Parliament. Five lines of battleships, several frigates and sloops, are to be paid off, which will discharge about 3000 seamen from the service.

Earl Pembroke has generously intimated to his numerous tenantry, his intention of deducting 25 per cent, on their respective rents, in consequence of the depressed state of agriculture.

At the last meeting of the Trustees of the Turn-pike road leading from Warminster and Frome to Bath, a Committee was appointed to prepare a petition to Parliament for a reduction of the present enormous expenses in procuring local Turnpike Acts. Upwards of 450l. were paid to one of the Clerks of the House of Commons upon passing the the last Act for the roads of this Trust, exclusive of the solicitor's bill and other expenses.

—◇—

To PARENTS and GUARDIANS

WANTED, by a *Surgeon and Accoucher,* in good and genteel practice, a Young Gentleman, who has received a decent classical education, as an APPRENTICE. According to the old routine, young men, after their indentures are executed, *are left entirely to themselves* to glean what they can of their profession, without any effort being made to put them in a regular and progressive train of improvement. – Most respectable references will be required and given.

Applications directed (post-paid) for A.B.C. to the care of the Editor of this paper, will be promptly attended to.

—◇—

The tunnel of the Manchester and Liverpool Railway, by which the carriages are to enter Liverpool, is proceeding securely and rapidly. In a few days the cutting of the road for the railway will be commenced at Olive Mount, near Wavertree, and at Whiston, near Prescot.

We are extremely sorry, says the *Edinburgh Observer*, that the condition of trade seems to be getting colder, and clouded with the season. The symptoms of revival, which never, indeed, were very promising or definite, appear to have lost the vigour they at one time possessed; and we have now before us the prospect of a long and inclement season, without any provision, on the part of thousands of the working classes, to combat its rigour, or sustain their existence. Something of this depression, it is true, may be referred to the natural turn of the winter; the home markets of November being usually insignificant and dull. But with so much misery and so little to meet it, the most casual depression must be dreadful. And though something may now be doing for the Mediterranean and the Brazils, and though a little more may be done next month for the northern States of America, it will be all, we fear, much too trifling to support us through anything like a season of severity and starvation.

It is proposed to erect a Mausoleum at Stratford-on-Avon in commemoration of Shakespeare, to which his Majesty has offered a subscription of 100l.

—◇—

Lunatic Asylum – A letter on lunatic asylums, written by Sir Andrew Halliday to the Magistrates of Middlesex, contains the following remarkable statements:–

The crowded and uncomfortable state of the majority of the private asylums in the neighbourhood of London must be known to many of you; they can be considered as nothing better than large prisons, where the insane are are confined; as hospitals for the treatment and cure of insanity, all of them, I maintain, in as far as the parish poor are concerned, are wholly unfit, and perfectly useless. Yet you will allow, that a lunatic asylum ought to be an hospital, and is what the Legislature has ordered that county asylums should be.

Lord Roberts Seymour, a most active and intelligent member of your body – a Nobleman whose exertions in the cause of humanity have never been surpassed – has informed you, in a letter, dated the 12th. of June last year (a copy of which is now before me), "that at Bethnall Green, in one of Mr. Warburton's houses, he saw three hundred and fifty two, one hundred and ninety two private patients and fifty three attendants, making altogether five hundred and forty four patients; and that the physicians who visited the paupers, by order of the parishes, had repeatedly declared that the crowd in Mr. Warburton's house made the recovery of these paupers highly improbable." His Lordship informs you further, "that each of the dormitories contained from sixteen to twenty beds; and, on the female side, that many of the paupers lie two in a bed, the bedsteads being only 18 inches from each other; and that the exercising yards were more crowded than ever yet was a dog kennel." From my own knowledge I affirm, that this description will apply to a very great majority of the private asylums in the counties of Middlesex and Surrey.

It is not in the power of any man, or number of men, to bestow upon the inmates of such establishments either the medical or moral treatment that their cure imperatively calls for. Look at our well regulated public asylums, as they now exist in the metropolis and the counties where they have been established under Mr. Wynn's Act. Look at the numbers discharged, cured from these public hospitals, and compare them with the numbers discharged from even the best regulated and least crowded of our private institutions, and they tell me, if you have done well in allowing the present system of providing for your insane poor to exist so long.

———◇———

Tradesman and Mechanic's Institution.

AT a numerous Meeting held at the Town-hall on Wednesday evening last, it was unanimously determined to establish a TRADESMAN'S and MECHANICS' INSTITUTION for the TOWN and NEIGHBOURHOOD of SWANSEA, on the basis of Rules and Regulations there read and assented to; and the Provisional Committee have further the pleasure to inform the Public that the First GENERAL MEETING of the said INSTITUTION will be held at the Town Hall, on Thursday, the 7th December inst., at seven, for half past, exactly, in the evening, when an Introductory Address, including a concise view of the first principles of natural history, will be delivered.

The Public will, on this evening, be admitted free of expense, and seats will be reserved for Ladies.

———◇———

THE CAMBRIAN

SWANSEA, Friday, Dec. 1.

In consequence of the appeal to the Public through the advertisement inserted in our Paper of last week, and by hand-bills distributed by direction of the Provisional Committee appointed at the Meeting, held last week at the Mackworth Arms, a very numerous and respectable Meeting of the Friends to the dissemination of *useful knowledge* amongst the industrious classes, was held at the Town Hall in this place. Notwithstanding, from the crowded state of the body of the Hall, the usual provision of benches was found to be inadequate to the comfortable accommodation of a great proportion of the auditors, their marked attention and enthusiastic concurrence in the different resolutions proposed, demonstrated the deep interest that was excited by the proceedings of the evening. M. Muggridge having taken the Chair, in compliance with the expression of the general wish of the assembly, opened the business of the Meeting by demonstrating, in concise but clear terms, the advantages to be derived, by the working classes in particular, from the establishment of Mechanics Institutions generally. He then made a verbal report from the Provincial Committee elected at the the previous Meeting which proved that they had not been unmindful of the task they had undertaken – in proof of which Mr. Richard Aubrey read the the Rules and Regulations which they had selected chiefly and indeed, nearly verbatim on all material points from those of the London and Bristol Institutions; – after which the Chairman explained how the interests of the Members of the Institution and the great object of its establishment would be secured by the adoption of the Rules and Regulations that had been read, and insisted at length on the advantages to be derived from such an establishment to Swansea and its Neighbourhood (which including the mineral district with which it is so intimately connected, he said it appeared to him nature had destined to be one of the most important and flourishing of the British Empire.) and to the nation at large. In the course of a speech of considerable length, Mr. M. considered, in succession and separately, all the different known remaining objections of the present day to the general diffusion of useful knowledge; amongst which, if we understand him right, he enumerated, those of servants being taught things that would unfit them for the discharge of the duties of their respective situations; the working classes being taken out of their proper sphere in life; there being none left to perform the menial services in society, or as the Chairman expressed it to be, "hewers of wood and drawers of water;" the fear that the working classes will be made wiser than their superiors; the apprehension that the spirit of insubordination and combination would would be generated; and the notion that the working classes *thus taught* would get a habit of reading novels and writing love letters:-all of which he separately, distinctly, and most triumphantly answered in a manner that we much regret that we have neither time nor room to detail at large. "But," said the Chairman, "though it have entered into the consideration of these objections, because they have been made, and sometimes by very respectable and well meaning persons; these objections are not applicable to Mechanics' Institutes; they apply, if at all, to the *previous* instruction of the working classes,— to the schools in which they are taught to read, write, and to cast accounts; the objections to which have been long refuted both by argument and experience and now, the question is *not* whether the working classes *shall be taught,* but whether they shall be well or ill *taught. Taught* they must be; *learn* they will; let then the youth be taught useful knowledge, and have Mechanics' Institutes to go to, instead of learning, as they otherwise would, frivolity and vice, and having no place of amusement or interest to frequent but the haunts of drunkenness and obscenity." . . .

An idea of the progressive increase of the Tonnage on the Swansea Canal, may be formed by the following Comparative Statement of the Quantities of Stone, Coal and Culm brought down:–

In 1818	.. .. ..	77,215
1823	.. .. ..	96,628
1824	.. .. ..	124,551
1825	.. .. ..	126,439
1826	.. .. ..	145,309

The Swansea Hounds will throw off on Tuesday next at Norton, and on Friday at Waunllestyr, at nine o' clock.

5th. January 1828.

The use of Salt, (observes a Correspondent) in abating the flames of fire is known to most cooks, who damp or lessen them by throwing salt on the ignited coals, and this is generally done when meat is broiled on the grid iron; it is rather strange that a fact known so well should be neglected when most required. In all cases of fire it is desirable the salt should be mixed with the water previous to its being thrown on or pumped on the burning materials, as it would be doubly efficacious in extinguishing the flames and the low price of salt is favourable to its use on such occasions.

. . . Potato Bread. – At the Edinburgh Agricultural Meeting, on Wednesday week, at which above 300 noblemen and gentlemen attended. Sir John Sinclair addressed the party after breakfast, and informed them that a great part of the bread they had been eating was composed chiefly of potato flour; and that if the public would be contented with such bread, Britain would never require a bushel of foreign grain.

. . . Steam Carriages. – A considerable degree of misunderstanding prevails respecting the origin and progress of this branch of practical mechanics. The person who first conceived the idea of propelling land carriages by steam was the late Oliver Evans of Philadelphia, who made various experiments commencing in 1772; and in 1786 he obtained a patent for a high pressure steam waggon; but the public mind, both in England and America, was not at that time adapted for the encouragement of such an undertaking, and Mr. Evans' pecuniary resources were inadequate to overcome the obstacles which he met with his proceedings; although the public trials made in Philadelphia of his steam-waggons afforded demonstrated proofs to scientific men of their economy, and of the practicability of their construction; but no capitalist was found disposed to advance the requisite sum for carrying the proposition into full effect. In 1802, Messrs Trevithick and Vivian took out a patent in this country for a locomotive engine; and in 1804 it was successfully applied to the Merthyr Tydvil Railroad. From that period up to 1825, near 20 patents have taken out for steam carriages; and at the present time there are building or altering in London, only, the following steam carriages of different constructions:– Gordon's, Jame's, Gurney's, Burstall's, Brown's, Hancock's, and Beale's, beside several others. "Mr. Gurney's, which was was to have started some weeks since, and for which it was said that depots of coals and water had been prepared on some of the principal roads, is not, we hear," (says the Morning Herald) "likely to drive the present stage coaches out of the field quite so readily as was imagined; and the agriculturists, who had so feelingly taken the alarm, may, if we are rightly informed, sleep quietly on their beds for some time to come. The utmost rate at which these vehicles have hitherto been propelled, has, we understand, been about five miles an hour, and that only upon the smooth road in the Regent's Park. Instead of increasing this pace, we hear that the present power, taking the rough and smooth, hill and dale, it is not likely to urge them beyond two miles an hour, or about two thirds the rate of the slowest stage waggon. This certainly would be what is called travelling by the "slow coach." Besides this, the present proposed machinery for the conductor, or coachman is, we hear, quite out of the question, and that no human arms could stand for an hour the rough test of guiding the 20 horse power which would be applied to the elbows. This, we understand, may be remedied – but that the smoke never can. The pure carbonic gap which the outside passengers would would have to inhale, when the wind was "in their favour," might be death to moderate lungs; while the smoke, when the gas was not so pure, would carry suffocation with it. In fact, when on a journey to Bath, would consequently spend a whole day sitting on top of a chimney! We are no enemies to scientific inventions and improvements where these are in fact such; and on the subject, if we are misinformed, the result will set us right. But what we have heard we think it right to disclose. In the end the truth will out."

After the battle of Navarin, a wounded Turk swam to the Alcyone. The crew observed him with his arm broken and hanging. He was taken on board, when he made signs for them to cut off his arm. M. Martineax, surgeon-major, complied with his wishes. The sufferer then called for a pipe and tobacco, which being given him, he smoked; after the operation was performed, quite at his ease, looking calmly on those about him. In a short time afterwards, it was discovered that he had thrown himself into the sea, and swam his own ship!

The Shrewsbury Union coach was accidentally upset on Wednesday at Gerrard's Cross: one gentleman had both his legs shockingly crushed, and lies in a dangerous state.

The Bridge erected over the Severn at Holt Fleet, a few miles above Worcester, was opened to the public on New Year's Day, and by a strange coincidence, the tolls of carriages and horses, at Worcester Bridge ceased at twelve o' clock on Monday night.

THE CAMBRIAN

SWANSEA, FRIDAY, JAN. 4.

. . . **The Cambrian** retains its original aim, which was to form a plain useful Provincial Newspaper, devoted emphatically to *the Public* and not to any peculiar portion of it. The suffrages of our numerous and respectable subscribers justify us in concluding that this honourable aim has been accomplished; and whilst we eagerly seize the present occasion for assuring them that we are most anxious still to advance in their good opinion, we wish them *a happy new year* with the greater glee, as we enjoy the consciousness, not only of our own sincerity, but also that of their kindly response to our salutation. May it often and cordially be interchanged between us!

Our readers will observe that we have presented them, at the commencement of the new year, with an enlarged paper, a change which will furnish them with an additional quantity of matter, equal to two columns weekly.

Cardiff Bridge has been repaired, and is now perfectly safe for carriages &c. to pass over.

On the night of of Friday, the 21st. ult. the sloop Cambria, of Carmarthen, was upset in Loughor river, and the master (David Owen) and the mate were unfortuately drowned. It appears that the vessel, without any pilot on board, had arrived at Spitty Quay on the night preceding the the accident, and that the master had moored her, if not improperly, at least incautiously, with her stern to the flood tide, and in such a position that the tide took the vessel on the quarter, so causing her to sheer off from the quay, and as the tide was one of the highest, and consequently the most rapid, which had occurred for several years. The consequence was that when taken by the flood tide, the vessel broke from her moorings and drifted before the stream until she struck on a sand bank above Spitty, where she at once upset, and her crew, consisting only of the captain and the mate, were, as before stated, drowned. – the vessel is now in the sand, but it is expected that on the next high spring tide, the vessel may be raised.

The prevalence of southerly and westerly winds during the last month, has prevented the sailing of vessels from Swansea and other parts of Wales; and in consequence a scarcity of coals is beginning to be felt in different parts of Cornwall.

TYNYRHEOL, near NEATH.

THIS ESTABLISHMENT for the Education of Young Ladies will RE-OPEN on Monday the 28th. inst. Terms may be had on applicationto the Misses Thomas at Tynyrheol.

Tynyrheol, January 1828.

THE PALMERSTON

Steam Packet.

THE Public are respectfully informed that the above PACKET in order to receive a new Boiler, will remain at Bristol for two or three weeks. Due notice will be given when she is ready for sea.

Bristol, Jan. 1 1828.

The Prisoners in Brecon County and Borough Gaol most repectfully express their heartfelt gratitude, and humbly return thanks to Samuel Church, Esq. for an excellent dinner on Christmas day, consisting of roast beef, plum pudding, bread, and a quart of beer.

To be SOLD by
PRIVATE CONTRACT,

A SHARE in the PENCLAWDD CANAL, Glamorganshire. This Canal runs through a coal country, and every probability appears of considerable traffic over it in a short period.

For further particulars apply to T. Rogers Jones Solicitor, Swansea.

To the EDITOR of The CAMBRIAN,

The measures hitherto either proposed or adopted by the British Government, for the amelioration or extinction of Slavery in its colonies, appear to me to be prospective, and in anticipation of beneficial results at some future and indefinite period, dependent on contingencies, which many intervening circumstances may either greatly protract or totally annihilate. Having been for many years familiar with the progress of slave emancipation, knowing that only between seventy and eighty years ago some of my ancestors were slave proprietors, – that, and considering the imperfection of all human systems, and the frailty of human nature operating on mankind from various circumstances, – I have all along considered, that much was due to the present slave proprietors, and therefore I have been desirous of meeting the question *on neutral principles*:– that is emancipation by compensation, which induced my submitting to the public, in April 1824, and repeatedly since, through the newspapers and other channels, my idea of a plan for effecting it; namely, for Government immediately to purchase the freedom of all slave children, both male and female, now of the age, say from eight to ten, or from ten to twelve years, and to continue to purchase the freedom of every other slave child on its attaining such determined age, all at a fair relative value, to be fixed by Commissioners appointed for that special purpose; and when so purchased to be apprenticed out by the Commissioners to suitable masters and mistresses, till they reach the age of twenty-one. – such masters and mistresses to be required to give these apprentices a Christian education, and to send them to some place of worship on Sabbath-days . . .

FOR SWANSEA.

WILL TAKE IN GOODS,

Until the 10th inst. at Hayes Wharf, London.

The New Schooner

THE BROTHERS

Thomas Lewis, Master.

For freight or particulars apply to Captain on board, or to Mr. Joseph Lewis, Agent, 54 Orange street, Swansea.

Jan. 3.1828.

Execution. – Monday morning being appointed for the execution of *Joseph Swan* and *John Thompson* at Horsemonger-lane gaol, for a burglary in the house of Mr. *Biser*, a lace merchant, about a stone's throw from the place of execution, hundreds of people assembled to witness their dreadful fate. They were both well known to the police as finished *cracksmen,* and were convicted on three indictments for burglaries in Newington and Camberwell. In the first case, between three and four hundred pounds worth of lace was carried off, and in the others property to nearly the same amount. A few minutes before their awful exit they were conducted into the chapel where they joined in prayers with the Rev. Mr. Mann, apparently with great fervence. Thompson was the first brought into the open air to be pinioned. He came with a firm step.

He sighed deeply and frequently while being bound and gazed on the blue sky and the prison walls for the last time with an unmoved countenance. Swain maintained the same undaunted firmness. The haggard paleness of his countenance, however, bore witness to his mental suffering. He was a thick and muscular young man, with a rather inoffensive countenance. He had sometime since been convicted of cutting and manhandling a watchman, in attempting to escape after a robbery at Alderman Waithman's in Fleet Street. He was then sentenced to die, but his friends, who are respectable, exerted themselves, and by means of great interest his sentence was commuted, and he suffered a minor punishment. On that occasion no less than eight Members of Parliament signed his petition. He had previously lived with his sister and her husband who keep a respectable hotel, but whose names in delicacy forbear mentioning. – Everything being in preparation the unhappy men moved to their last scene. Swain was first placed on the fatal drop, and, while he was being tied, a person conversed with Thompson, on his unfortunate situation, and was apparently trying to offer him Christian consolation. Thompson turned to him, with a smile on his pallid face, and coolly exclaimed, "I'm a heavy man – I can meet death with a smile – death is nothing to me!" The executioner then reminded him that it was his turn. – He shook hands with the person who had spoken to him and mounted the steps with the same apparent indifference. Each placed himself under the fatal beam with an air of willingness, and left the world without a tear. They died almost instantly – Thompson though the smallest, without a struggle. Two females, with whom the prisoners had cohabited, were convicted of receiving part of the stolen property, and sentenced to fourteen years' transportation. They were in the gaol while the death note was peeling for their fellow prisoners.

A Child with Two Faces – A most extraordinary caprice of Nature occurred in this town on Sunday morning last, in the birth of a female child having two distinct and perfectly formed faces. Elizabeth Verrier, the mother of the child, is the wife of a carpenter residing in Halway lane. She had previously seven healthy children neither of them exhibiting the least deviation from ordinary nature. In the present instance there was no prematurity of birth; the child lived three quarters of an hour, and in the course of that time cried very audibly three times. From which of the two mouths these issued is not ascertained; but there is nothing in the structure of either of the faces to indicate a superior faculty in one over the other; every component part of the face is distinctly in each, and both of them present the pleasing countenance of two fine babes. At that part of one of the faces where the usual formation of the ear takes place, the additional face commences, with a slight undulation towards the cheek of the second face, which then proceeds through all its regular features until it terminates at the left ear – so that the face on the right side has one ear, and the face on the left one also. The space on the back of the head is, from the encroachment of the faces, very limited; but it is, as well as the front of the head covered in hair. In all other respects the child is well formed. – A very accurate drawing has been made of the child, and is now in the hands of the lithographer. The mother is doing well, and has been benefitted by the receipt of a considerable sum, in various donations, from the great number of persons who have been to see the infant, which has been put in spirits, and will present an interesting addition to the *lusus nature* with which the museum of the curious are already furnished.

Taunton Courier. Dec. 26.

Elopement in High Life. – The late elopement has furnished much gossip in the county of Essex, and will, no doubt, be "fine nuts" for the gentlemen of the long robe. The injured husband is son and heir to a wealthy Baronet whose name is remarkable for its connexion in English history with the late William Rufus. The "gay Lothario," for whom this frail but lovely young lady has left a splendid home, and deserted a young family, is the illegitimate son of a Baronet. We have been favoured with the following curious particulars of the elopement:- Not long since, the Essex Baronet and daughter in law took a trip to Chelmsford, to enable the lady to make sundry purchases, at which place they separated, but agreed to meet at the home of a mutual friend in the town. The worthy Baronet, however, might have wasted the end of time for his fair companion, who had gone of with her *cher ami* in a very different direction, as appeared by the sequel. His patience being exhausted, he drove home, thinking to overtake her on the road. But alas! on reaching B______, no one had seen or heard of the lady since she left. The alarm was then given, messengers despatched to make enquiries, when it was ascertained that a lady answering her description was seen stepping into a chaise that drove furiously off.

The guilty pair were speedily followed to London by the husband's brother, who was, however soon acquainted that her determination remained unalterably fixed, and dismissed in rather an unceremonious manner. The parties are now on the Continent.

——◇——

6th. February 1830

Orders have been received to Chatham Dock-yard to discharge fifty-nine men at the end of this week, with pensions according to service, varying from 8l. to 24l. per annum. The allowance for chips is also to be discontinued. It is calculated that the saving in that yard alone will be 6,000l per annum, and the total saving in all the yards 30,000l per annum.

——◇——

The snow on the Mendip hills is represented to be from 10 to 20 feet deep. Upwards of 20 waggons and carts were on Thursday completely blocked up near Oakhill, and so covered with snow, that only the top of one of the waggons was visible.

On Tuesday the body of the late Mr. Tierney was opened, when it was found that a quantity of water had accumulated in his heart, and, as is usual in such complaints he expired suddenly, without the slightest indication of approaching death. In consequence of suddenness of the death of the Right Hon. Gent, it was deemed advisable to hold an inquest on the body, and a most respectable jury was accordingly summoned on Thursday at the White Horse Tavern, Burlington street. – Dr. Johnson and Dr. Pettigrew gave evidence to prove that the deceased died of an organic infection or enlargement of the heart. The countenance exhibited a serene and placid appearance, indicating that he died without a struggle. On their return they delivered a verdict, "That the deceased died a natural death by the Visitation of God, that is to say of an enlargement of the heart." Mr. Tierney was found dead in his chair by his servant, on entering to announce a visitor. He has left two daughters and a son. The latter is Charge D'affaires at Munich.

——◇——

Fashions for February. – *From La Belle Assemblee.*

– *Evening Dress* – A dress of *gaze satinee,* the ground rose-colour, the stripes of that peculiar shade of drab colour, which resembles unbleached cambric. The skirt, somewhat more ample than last month, is slightly goted, and trimmed rather below the knee with a fringe of uncommon breadth and beauty. It has an open worked head, very richly wrought in lozenges. The *corsage* is cut very low, but not quite square round the bust, being rather higher in the shoulders than evening dresses generally are. Sleeves, *a la Sultane;* very wide; fastened at the wrist by gold bracelets, and drawn round the arm just above the elbow, by a row of fringe to correspond with that on the skirt, but narrower. The hair is arranged in loose full curls, which fall low on each side of the face, and parted in the middle to display the forehead and eyebrows. The hind hair is disposed in two very large knots on the crown of the head. A scarf of Circassian gauze, corresponding in colour with the ground of the dress, and fringed at the ends, is tastefully arranged in *conques*, which are intermixed with the bows of hair. One of the ends falls on the left side to the neck; the other forms a tuft on the right side. The necklace, earrings, and bracelets, worn with this dress, are a mixture of pink topazes and filagree gold. A bos tippet, of the finest sable, is thrown carelessly round the neck. White kid gloves. Slippers, white *gros de Naples.*

Walking Dress – A *robe redingote,* composed of French Cachemire, of a light shade of *grenet.* The *corsage*, made right, turns over *en schall,* so as to display very much the Cambric *chemi-ette* worn with it. The facings are of black velvet. Sleeve, *a la Caroline,* fitting close to the arm from the elbow to the wrist, and extremely full, above the elbow; the fulness is divided in the middle of the arm by a broad band of black velvet. The cuff is also of black velvet; is very deep, and, finished at each edge by a rich but narrow black blend face. The trimming of the skirt consists of a bias band of black velvet of moderate breadth. Black velvet *ceinture*. The *chemisette* is fastened in front with small gold buttons, and finished round the throat with a full ruff of the same material. Black velvet bonnet worn over a cap of the *demi cornette* form, which is trimmed with *Valencienne*'s lace. The shape of the bonnet is rather close; it is ornamented on the inside of the brim with three *coques* of satin ribboned, figured with velvet. Two large *nauds* of this ribbon adorn one side of the crown, and three ostrich feathers placed upright fall over it. *Brodequtus* of black figured silk. Pale lavender gloves. The boa tippet is of chinchilla.

——◇——

The Welsh Iron Trade. – We regret, in presenting to our readers the quantity of Iron delivered by the respective Iron Works at Cardiff, during the year ending 30th. December last, to find that the great depression of the trade has already affected the Works in this county, and that many furnaces are at this moment out of blast, and probably, more will follow, as the price of Iron is now so exceedingly low as not to nett, when sold the bare amount of cash paid for actual labour by the manufacturer to his workmen . . .

——◇——

Highway Robbery. – On the night of Wednesday se'night, about nine o'clock, a journeyman cabinet maker, on his way from Hereford to Leominster, was knocked down about two hundred yards on the Hereford side of Broadward bridge, in the Turnpike road, about a mile from Leominster, by two ruffians, about five feet, five inches high, dressed one in a waggoner's frock and the other in a light jacket, after which the villains thrust into his mouth a quantity of coarse grass tightly bound up with packthread, and tied it once round the sufferer's head and then under his chin, and his hands they also tied behind him. The ruffians then stole from his pockets seven sovereigns and some silver, a silver hunting watch, No. 672, maker's name "Verney" and a bundle of shirts and other articles marked, 'J.H.' After plundering they left the poor fellow to his fate. He was discovered on the road in an almost lifeless state, by two persons who were passing that way, and who conveyed him to the house of Mr. Edwards at Broadward, where every kind attention was paid him, and surgical assistance was immediately procured. On the sufferer being taken to Mr. Edwards's, some time passed before it could be discovered what was the matter with him, and till Mr. Edwards happened to hold a light towards his face, when he found the coarse grass tied into his mouth, and that his hands were tied behind his back. It was more than an hour after he was released before he was able to speak, and if he had remained undiscovered ten minutes longer than he did, it is believed that he must have ceased to live.

Chepstow was lit on Tuesday night for the first time with gas, which burned brilliantly, and appeared to give general satisfaction. The bells rang merrily upon the occasion, and a band of music, followed by a large concourse of men, women, and children paraded the streets, which resounded to their cheers.

ASSEMBLY-ROOMS,
SWANSEA.

THE Nobility and Gentry of Swansea and its vicinity are respectfully informed, that in consequence of the severity of the weather,

The Third Subscription Ball
is POSTPONED until Tuesday the 23rd. of February. H. LUCAS. Esq.
J. H. H. SPENCER.Esq.Stewards.
Dancing will commence at nine o'clock.

THE CAMBRIAN

SWANSEA, Friday, Feb. 5.

In addition to the many efforts now making for relieving the sufferings, of the labouring poor of Swansea and its neighbourhood, it is with pleasure we record the liberal gift of a barge of the best coal (23 tons.) by C. H. Smith, Esq. of Gwernlwyniaith. Coal at the present moment is an invaluable article to the comfort of the indigent, and we sincerely hope to record similar acts of benificence.

Scientific Notices.

Substitute for Steam – At a lecture delivered at the Royal Institution on Friday last, Mr. E. P. Fordham developed a plan, for which a patent has been taken out, whereby a preferable substitute for steam could be applied to the purposes of impelling carriages along a turnpikeroad. The principle is the compression of common air, which on being allowed to expand, was shown, by experiments made with a model to possess sufficient power to act, in all cases instead of steam.

Clifton Suspension Bridge. – In ordinary cases, the sublimity of nature can receive no improvement from the efforts of art; but singularly magnificent as is the scenery of the Avon, where the Suspension Bridge is proposed to be erected, it has also the advantage of affording points d'appui as imperishable as the universe itself, and of presenting the means for the achievment of another triumph of science in addition to those which have already exalted the intelletual character of our country, beyond all other nations of the earth.

The structure is intended to cross the Avon in a direct line with Gloucester-row, at an altitude of 210 feet above high water mark. We can scacely imagine a more beautiful object than will be then exhibited amidst the gigantic rocks that skirt the river.

Novel Exhibition of a Steam Omnibus. – On Wednesday afternoon, between three and four o'clock, an immense number of persons assembled in Regent's Park and the New road, to witness the exhibition of a new invented steam Omnibus, which proceeded from Mr. Braithwaite's manufatory in Albany street, Regent's park. The steam apparatus is in the front, in a machine something similar to a light cart guided by two men and an engineer; and the Omnibus is attached to it, with a boy to attend passengers, in the usual manner. The Omnibus was filled with passengers. The velocity with which it proceeded along the roads was surprising, passing every other vehicle that attempted to compete with it From the general appearance, there cannot be any doubt of its answering in every respect; and there is a great advantage by the machine containing a plentiful supply of coals and water. From the speed with which it proceeded, passengers could at any time leave Paddington, and reach the Bank in a quarter of an hour.

On Friday week an eagle was shot in the neighbourhood of Bridgewater by a man who was in the pursuit of wild fowl. Its wing only being broken, the bird escaped, and seated itself on the summit of a tree, from which, it was dis-lodged by a second shot from a stranger who chanced to be near. The monarch of the air, perhaps with the intention of inflicting summary vengeance, alighted on the arm of his assailant and would probably have most amply avenged himself had not the man dextorously seized him by the throat, and, notwithstanding the repeated and violent blows which he received from the powerful pinions of the enraged bird, held it firmly until he was rescued from his perilous situation by the first sportsman. The majestic bird was then secured by banding his pinions. It measures eight feet from tip to tip of the wings.

4th. February 1832.

Execution of the Bristol Rioters – The four convicts, *William Clarke, Christopher Davis, Thos Gregory and Joseph Kayes,* underwent the extreme sentence of the law on Friday noon, in the presence of a very large number of spectators. A respite arrived the previous day for Vines. The convicts were evidently altered for the worse, since their trial, but their demeanour was patient and resigned; and the scene was altogether so affecting that not a dry eye was to be seen during the awful preparations in the yard. Soon after twelve o'clock, the executioner made his appearance. Davis was then conducted up the stairs to the scaffold followed by Gregory; the latter bowed to the populace. Davis took no notice of those beneath, and but once cast his eyes up to the fatal beam. The executioner then put the eye of the rope upon the book. Clarke then ascended followed by Kayes, and the same sad ceremony was gone through. The Rev. Divines having prayed with them a short time, and again taken leave of them, the caps were pulled down over their faces, and the bolt was drawn. Kayes apparently suffered much; the others died almost instantly. Perhaps more becoming conduct, in such a trying moment, was never witnessed. The crowd did not express a word during the time of the execution. A great number of women were present.

Assembly-Rooms, Swansea

THE Nobility and Gentry, are respectfully informed, that **A BALL** will take place at these Rooms on FRIDAY February 24th.

In celebration of the Queen's Birth-Day.

L.W. DILLWYN Esq.
Stewards
Capt. RICHMOND,

Dancing to commence at nine o'clock.

St. David's College.

THE BUSINESS of the ensuing TERM will commence on **Thursday**, the 16th. inst. when all Members of the College are expected to be in residence.

The Principal desires it may be distinctly understood that any Member who does not appear on that day will incur the forfeiture of the Term.

Candidates for Admission will be examined on Saturday the 18th.

By order of the Principal,
STEPHEN STANFORD.
St. David's College, Feb. 1 1832.

WILLIAM PHILLIPS

RETURNS his sincere thanks to the Nobility and Gentry of Swansea and its Vicinity, for their patronage and support, and at the same time begs leave to inform them, that, having declined further Partnership with Mr. Alfred Dean, he has quitted the Wheat Sheaf Stables, and entered upon the LIVERY STABLES, situated in CHAPEL STREET, BURROWS, where he hopes, by unwearied assuidity and constant attention, to merit a continuation of their favours.

LANDAU FLYS, &c. at the shortest notice.

THE FATE OF GENIUS –
By Ann of Swansea.

Fame's thrilling voice each throbbing pulse delights,
On – onwards still – its luring smile invites.
Whither? – "aye, there's the rule." – to want, and woe,
For seldom doth deluded Port know
Aught else, save aching head, and that dire curse,
That worst of all life's ills, an empty purse.
Send not, ye rich – 'tis not wild fancy's dream,
But sad reality supplies my theme.
Ill fated genius with desponding gaze
Beheld Wealth's pampered sons in crowds pass by;
Some freely *gave* – his odes and sonnets praise.
Others bestow'd a glance from scornful eye.
Better the siren blast had never shed
On him her dazzling, her illusive fay,
To climb Fame's laurel'd steeps had never led,
Or lur'd him from life's safer paths astray.
Sick, broken hearted, stifling fruitless moans,
The hapless wretch to his damp garret hied.
There famished, friendless, hopeless and alone –
Shudder, O world! – neglected Genius *died.*
Young mother Peace! – ah! do not rashly pray
That Genius with thy children may be found;
Plain Sense will guide them on that surer way,
Where *common efforts* are by *fortune crown'd.*

SHIP NEWS

SWANSEA – Arrived, the Favourite, Jones; and Jane and Mary, Jones from Gloucester; Hinton, Samuel, from Cork; Eleanor, George, from Bristol; Sarah, Johns, from Liverpool; and Blossom, Hole, from Minehead, with sundries; Bedford, Ashton, from Ross with cattle and pigs; Cardiff, Howells, from Aberthaw; Jane, Davies, from London; Princess Royal, Morgans, and Sarah Ann, Julian, from Dundalk with corn; Commet, Wedger from Poole, with clay; Prince Waterloo, Fox; and Crawford, Keaton from Wicklow; Catherine, Roose from Amlwch; Two Friends, Burke, from Dungarron; Palace, Featherbridge; Eliza, Lelean; Emerald, Climo; New House, Todd; William and Thomas, Scantlebury; Polgooth, Rollings; Olive Branch, Peters; John and Edward, Melhuish; Abeans, Longmaid; and Rashleigh, Vounders from Fowey; Maria, Heathrington; Endeavour, Morgan; Two Brothers, Wheddon; Apollo, Dawson; Rebecca, Chalk; Calstock, Lewis; Four Friends, Hockin; Joseph and Mary, Harry; Youghall, Shean; Truro, Carter; Brothers Towell; and Three Sisters, Barch from Falmouth; Pennelly, Barch from St. Ives; Villers, Dalton; and Phoenix, Taylor, from Plymouth, with copper ore. Severn, Cridland; William, Thomas; Devonshire, Lowther; Harmony, Bedford; Perserverance, Mathias; Betsy, Meredith; Somerset, Barwell; Lady Kenmare, Thomas; Sarah, Thomas; Fortitude, Ware; Jerimiah, Fisher; Bristol Trader, Johns; Peggy, Lloyd; Swan, Galgey; Ann and Betsy, Thomas; Union, Vittery; Mary, Pinnet; Lord Eberington, Day; Ann, Bushing; Ceres, Slocombe; . . . in ballast.

Llanelly Field Sports – The harriers of William Chambers, Esq. of Llanelly, met on Tuesday last, on Pembrey Mountain, where they started a fine hare. Puss took a circuitous route over a heavy and dreary country for upwards of three hours, and was killed at last near Lanon, after running a distance of 30 miles. The friends of the chase in the evening sat down to an excellent dinner, at the Thomas Arms Llanelly.

——◇——

THE PARENTS NEW YEAR'S GIFT.

Dedicated, by special permission, to the Lord High Chancellor.

———

Price 10s.6d. cloth or 11s. handsomely bound in embossed morocco.

THE YOUNG GENTLEMAN'S BOOK; containing a Series of choice Readings in Popular Science and Natural History, together with Retrospective Essays, Conversations Literary Reminiscences &c.

It was held by the ancients, and moreover written by the late Dr. Edward Young, that a "serious mind" is the true and genial soil of every virtue, and the single character that does real honour to mankind. This axiom, then we will select and apply to our present purpose, as one we could hope to see engraven on the foundation stone on which we shall endeavour to raise a superstructure for the completion of The Young Gentleman's Book.

A land of levity is without doubt, a land of guilt, and consequently one of crime and misrule. In the present day of universal talk, and malapplication of speech, and when there are, at home as well as abroad, so many surface persons, assuming a knowledge they cannot be supposed to possess; comporting themselves unworthily, as well as unwisely, toward men of learning character and genius, infinitely their superiors in every respect, it may not be thought unbecoming to offer a work of the class now before the reading public, the primary objects of which shall in no wise be secret; suffice it then to state, that it was considered well worth the trial, however successful or otherwise that trial might eventually prove, to send forth a book calculated in some measure to lessen, if not destroy, that silly and degrading personal pride, which is being manifested by not only the higher but the middle, and even the lower orders of society; and which alone constitutes a foul blot on the character of common humanity – by means of precepts found on truth and justice, as well as by examples of the highest order, and commensurate experience – to subdue that reckless frivolity and thoughtless indolence concerning the works of nature, and the providence of nature's infinite God, so conspicuous among the grown up, but particularly in the rising generation whose education for the most part having been neglected from a variety of causes, have long wandered from the high road both of virtue and religion, scorning and mocking at the truth. To introduce a book which might safely be put into the hands of the youth of Britain, with a view to aid and assist their usual definite course of education, comprising choice readings in Natural Science and Natural History, together with retrospective Essays, Conversations, Literary Reminiscences &c. and as containing no matter calculated to incline the mind to a wrong direction, much more an evil bias, or give an impetus to scepticism and infidelity – was the desire of the compiler.

As the occasion of the YOUNG GENTLEMAN's BOOK was real and not fictitious, so also was the the motive which impelled and actuated the compiler rather of a religious than a merely moral order. To conduct youth to the better and more substantial walks of study – studies which enlighten the mind and render glad the panting heart – to walk with them, as it were arm in arm, through nature's magnificent domain; demonstrating by slow and guardian like efforts the sublimity of animated nature, and, above all, the preponderating and omnipresent Majesty of Truth; always rejoicing in the good work set before him to perform, and not merely to do, but to accomplish with all diligence – were among the highest aims and pardonable ambition of the compiler.

The youth who has learnt to derive enjoyment from observing the operations of the bees and the silk worms; from watching the metamorphoses of the dragon-fly, the cockchafer, the butterfly, and other insects; who knows the history of the ant, the grasshopper, the ephemerides, the aphides, and even the common house fly; who has learnt to mark the contrivance that nature has bestowed on them; their structure, habits and curious economy; will not pass these circumstances unnoticed in animals higher in the scale; and ascending to his own species, will learn also the elevation of his own nature. The mind rationally occupied with studies of nature will no longer seek resource from ennui in bad novels; and the same superior taste for information, and the same admiration of the wisdom of nature, as displayed in her works, will lead to a more select choice of companion.

"Such are the enjoyments and the interest that attach to the study of Natural History. To procure the greatest number of these advantages at the easiest rate of labour, recourse must be had to scientific study, which is to the aquirement of knowledge what machinery is to the production of manufactures." To render this machinery available to every reader, and especially to young persons is, the principal object of The Young Gentleman's Book. At such a period as this, when the great importance of education is duly appreciated, and seems to be publicly recognised by the general diffusion of knowledge, a new publication adapted to these circumstances cannot be deemed unreasonable, and may be found deserving of public support. That the knowledge which will be communicated through the medium of The Young Gentleman's Book, and the activity which will be excited by this early cultivation of the mind, should

A view of Swansea from the Bay – 19th century.

A view of Cameron's Wharf, Swansea, c.1847 (William Butler).

Castle Square – near the Cambrian Office.

Wind-street – near the Cambrian Office.

receive a right direction, and be under the control of correct principles, is universally acknowledged to be an object of the utmost importance.

London: Printed for Hamilton, Adams, and Co; John Cumming, Dublin; Constable & Co. Edinburgh; Galiganni, Paris; and W.Jackson, New York.

The following particulars respecting the increase in population in England and Wales are extracted from the Returns:–

Population of England.
1801 ... 8,331,434
1811 ... 9,551,888
1821 ... 11,261,437
1831 ... 13,089,338

Increase in 30 years, from 1801 to 1831 57 per cent.

Population of Wales
1801 ... 511,546
1811 ... 611,788
1821 ... 717,438
1831 ... 835,236

Increase in 30 years 49 per cent.

In the town of Swansea the increase in Population has been still more rapid.

In 1801 the population was 6,000.
1811 .... 8,190.
1821............................ 10,255.
1831............................. 13,694.

And on the 30 years ending in 1831, the increase was 154 per cent.

SWANSEA FRIDAY, FEB. 3.

Our justly popular Ministry must mind what they are about, or that experienced old fox, Toryism out of Office, will yet be too cunning for them. – The Dutch loan question gave them a smart jog the other night, which ought to keep them wide awake for the remainder of the Session.

If they do not retain office, and carry the Reform Bill triumphantly, everlasting disgrace will be upon their heads – and we are morally certain that those who now lie in wait for their places, would only hurl the country into an abyss of anarchy, by foolish attempts at satisfying the people with some less effective measure; – we therefore consider the peace and prosperity of our beloved country identified with the stability of the present Government, at least till we shall have obtained such an amended representation as the Bill provides for. Mr. Perceval's *general fast* motion, is of a nature too serious for laughter, and yet the mode of it was too burlesque for our gravity. – We certainly think Hunt's quotation from Scripture much more apposite than those of his more worthy opponent, and are glad to find that the Member for Preston is so biblical in his reading – he may stumble upon many passages deeply instructive to him as a politician. – As regards what is termed a "general fast," we must leave everyone to his own individual conviction as to its duty or conviction as to its duty or utility – but as the cholera is almost exclusively destroying the already *fasting* and ill clothed poor, we would suggest, whether a liberal contribution – say from every family in good circumstances, the value of their customary substantial dinner for one day – towards clothing and feeding, and otherwise comforting this suffering portion of our fellow subjects, would not be a more acceptable token of national contribution, than any ostentatious public ceremonies, or the most scrupulous dining upon fish and egg since, from one end of the kingdom to another?

Skinless Oats

PERSONS desirous of cultivating this most valuable Oat, may procure seed by applying personally, or by letter (post paid) to Richard Tucker, Heanton, Punchardon, near Barnstaple.

Price 20s. – the Imperial Bushel, which weighs 50lbs.

5th. April 1834.

A deputation of 17 Members of the Trades' Unions, headed by Dr. Wade, had an interview on Sunday with Lord Melbourne. Upwards of 10,000 had assembled early in the morning at the Institution Hall, Fitzroy Square and sanctioned a Memorial agreed to on the previous evening on the subject of the sentence of transportation passed on the Dorchester agricultural labourers. After a lapse of nearly two hours, the Deputation returned; and it was stated amid tumults of applause, that his Lordship had consented to stay the execution of the sentence until he had ascertained his Majesty's pleasure on the Memorial. The meeting then peaceably adjourned.

TO BE LET, for a Term,

A Very desirable FAMILY RESIDENCE, called LOWER SKETTY, now in the occupation of Henry Bath Esq. situate in the parish of Swansea, about a quarter of a mile from the sea, and midway between Swansea and the Mumbles. The House, which is pleasantly situated, commanding extensive views of the much admired Bay of Swansea, and the surrounding neighbourhood, consists of a drawing room and dining room, each 23 feet by 18 feet, small study, water closet, six bedrooms, and two dressing rooms, man servant's room, and every requisite office; Coach house, Stable, &c. There is a very good well stocked Garden, and about 20 Acres of good Meadow and Pasture Land.

Enquire (if by letter, post-paid.) of John James Esq. Solicitor, or of James Hall, Surveyor, Swansea.

FOR NEW YORK,
WITH PASSENGERS AND GOODS,
THE FINE BRIG
BRITANNIA.

This vessel is intended to sail about the middle of April, and as she will only take a limited number of Passengers, an early application is recommended

Apply to Messrs Francis, Richardson, and Co.

TO BE LET, by Tender.

THE Commissioners acting under and by virtue of of the Swansea Paving and Lighting Act, do hereby give notice, that they are willing to TREAT for the LETTING of all those commodious and lately erected premises, called or known by the name of "The PUBLIC SLAUGHTER HOUSES," situate in the town of SWANSEA. The public department contains accommodation for Slaughtering 40 Head of Cattle, 300 Sheep, and 130 Calves and Pigs. There are seven *Private* Slaughter Houses affording accommodation for Slaughtering 6 Head of Cattle, and about 30 Sheep, Calves, and Pigs each. There is also an excellent DWELLING-HOUSE on the premises, and a PUBLIC YARD for the SALE of CATTLE, together with an abundant supply of Water, and every other possible convenience.

Sealed Tenders, stating the amount of Rent proposed to be given, to be sent to Mr. Thomas Thomas, Solicitor, Swansea, on or before Tuesday, the 6th. day of May next.

Swansea, 3d April, 1834.

NOTICE is hereby given, that a GENERAL MEETING of the COMPANY of PROPRIETORS of the SWANSEA GAS LIGHT ESTABLISHMENT will be held at the Mackworth-Arms Inn, in the town of Swansea on Wednesday, the 10th. of April instant, at eleven o'clock in the forenoon.

JOHN NICSON.

Swansea, April 3 1834.

We last week alluded generally to a project which has attracted much attention in this county, for a Railway from Llanelly in Carmarthenshire, to Cardiff, in Glamorganshire, as one great section of the "Great Western Railway" communication with London; and we stated our intention of again touching on the subject this week. We apprehend in this country, no Railway will be formed by a body of private individuals but such as holds out a fair prospect of remuneration to the subscribers; it is on this principle, we understand the project scheme has been brought forward, and received the sanction of so many leading mineral proprietors, and active men of business in this and other counties. When Mr. Wooddison, in October last, adduced his plan for a Railway from London via Gloucester to Swansea and Milford Haven, a general impression prevailed among our most influential men of business, that such a scheme could only be effected by Government, inasmuch as that on the lower or most western part of the line no sufficient traffic could reasonably be expected to produce the revenue required as a compensation for so large an expenditure; and since it is not the habit of our Government to enter on such works in England, but that their execution is left to the public spirit and enterprise of private individuals, so large a project is not very likely to be soon effected; the want of probable revenue to induce capitalists to embark their money in the undertaking, operating we fear as a bar to it. There is, however, no lack of capital and of enterprise in this country when a fair, legitimate and profitable scheme is adduced; and such, we venture to say, will be found in the project now under our consideration, for a Railway from Llanelly to Cardiff, which may ultimately be carried on to a bridge across the Severn. To those who are unacquainted with the subject, or who have not taken pains to examine it, the idea of a Railway running parallel to the sea for 88 miles, the distance from Llanelly to Sharpness Point, which is the site for the intended bridge over the Severn, may at first appear a startling proposition; and if were only for heavy goods and such matters as are usually borne by sea for the whole distance that the Railway would be applicable, we fear there would be little prospect of dividends for the proprietors of such an undertaking. In this case, however, if the Railway was constructed on the best principle of such modern works, we shall have a road over which the public may travel at the rate of from 25 to 30 miles per hour, with the most perfect safety: from Llanelly to Cardiff will be something short of 50 miles, and thence to Sharpness Point about 36 miles, over a dead flat, near the banks of the Severn, the whole distance. Thus to travel from Swansea to the bridge, above the entrance to the Gloucester and Berkeley Canal, will only require about three hour's time; and who that would travel at this rate would with perfect safety, would go back to eight or nine miles per hour?

There can be no doubt that the public would readily pay even a higher rate of fare, if necessary, for the more rapid conveyance, and thus the Railway, once made will have a decided preference. In a mineral district like that in which it is our good fortune to live, we have, however, a very powerful adjunct to the kind of traffic we have named, in the rich and inexhaustible mines of coal and iron, which lie intermediately between our several sea-ports, over and along which the Railway must pass, and which alone hold out a very sufficient inducement for the formation of a Railway from Llanelly to Cardiff; the ordinary traffic of the public roads will, nevertheless super add a considerable income to the subscribers. Between Llanelly and Swansea there lies a rich district of bituminous coal of the very finest quality, several thousand acres of which belong to his Grace the Duke of Beaufort, besides whom Col. Cameron, J. Dillwyn Llewellyn, Esq. Sir John Morris, Bart. and many other proprietors have very extensive tracts of valuable coal. The country has remained long unopened from the want of Railway communicatios to the ports of Swansea and Llanelly; several collieries are at length in the process of being opened; the Railway from Llanelly to Swansea is thus become indispensable, and must be very shortly made, if not by a public company, by the duke's lessees alone whose single traffic will be sufficient to make it pay a fair return. Bridges at Swansea and Briton Ferry have long been considered desiderata: the ordinary and existing traffic of the county will alone yield a fair return on their cost, and parties can be found who would readily join in such a speculation, even apart from the Railway; this latter being added the speculation becomes more tempting; and since means have now been devised by the engineers of this undertaking for the construction of bridges, through which wide opening for navigation can be given, in an incredibly short space of time, there no longer remains the same objection as formerly (as regards navigation) to the construction of these two bridges. The iron and tinplate manufacturers of Aberavon, and many proprietors of mines and minerals on the eastern side of our Bay, together with the leading proprietors of Porthcawl and Duffryn-Llunvi Railway, are very desirous of having a Railway communicating with the ports of Swansea and Neath, joining that Railway beyond Pyle, and there can be no doubt but the valuable coal of that district, which is said to be fully equal in quality for domestic purposes to that of any coal in this country, would find a ready sale in our market. Between the Porthcawl Railway and the valley of the Taff, which runs down to Cardiff, is a county full of excellent coal and iron, hitherto entirely shut out from an export trade from the want of a Railway to Cardiff: the valleys and glens in this district run generally north and south; when our Western Railway be formed through the beautiful Vale of Glamorgan, giving a sort of base line to the mineral district, there can be no doubt but every valley will have its tributary branch Railway, and will pour down a vast supply of coal and iron, partly to the port of Cardiff and partly to the more Western ports, according to the demand in the respective markets. When we reflect that in a well constructed Railway, the whole expense of transit need not exceed one penny farthing per ton per mile, including tolls and locomotive power, for a descending trade, which would be the case from these intermediate districts to the sea; that much of coal brought upwards of 16 miles down to Newport in Monmouthshire, over an old fashioned tram road, costs full 2½d. per ton per mile, we have no difficulty in arriving at the conclusion, that there is nothing extravagant or chimerical in the scheme before us; but on the contrary, that it will prove equally advantageous to the subscribers and to the public. Of all places affected by the measure, Cardiff will perhaps be most benefitted; it cannot fail to bring to that port a vast accession of trade, and will in this respect admirably chime in with the magnificent project in which the spirited Lord Lieutenant of our County, the Marquis of Bute, is now engaged for improvement in that port.

It is, moreover, now universally admitted that Swansea and Llanelly produce the best steam packet coal in the world; if, therefore, a three hours' railway communication be had from Swansea to the Severn Bridge (within 120 miles of London), is it not obvious that Irish and Foreign Steam Packets, would be established to start from this port with passengers, thus avoiding the long and dangerous navigation of the Bristol Channel, and saving all the the freight and breakage of the coal which now falls on this type of kind of conveyance? We have already extended this article to a greater length than we intended; we conceive, however, it is a duty we owe to the public to treat largely of of a project so legitimate in its objects, and calculated to confer such immeasurable benefits on the country in which we live. We hope next week to advert to the subject again.

SWANSEA and NEATH
Horticultural Society.

THE FIRST SHOW of the above SOCIETY for FLOWERS, FRUIT, AND VEGETABLES, will be held at the Public Rooms, Swansea, on the 24th. of April instant.

ROBT. BYERS, Hon. Sec.

Subscribers are referred to the first and second Rules.

N.B. Mr. Williams and Mr. Dawe, of Swansea, and Mr. Hayward of Neath, are supplied with Cards of Admission to deliver to Members on application for them.

HOUSE OF COMMONS
WEDNESDAY, March 26 – . . .

Great Western Railway – *Mr. Ramsbottom* presented a petition from the Mayor, corporation, and principal inhabitants of New Windsor, against the proposed line of the Great Western Railway, and praying that the line be altered to so as to go through that borough: – *Sir J. B. Pechell* presented a similar betition from the same place. Both the petitions were referred to the committee on the bill.

Carmarthenshire Railway Bill – Mr. Vivian brought in a bill to enable the Carmarthenshire Railway Company to raise a further sum of money, which was read a first time. On the motion of the same Hon. Member, the Monmouth Market Bill was read a second time.

Mr. Ewart moved "for leave to bring in a Bill for abolishing the punishment of death for stealing letters, returning from transportation, and in certain cases of felony. The Hon Member said that, within the last two years, capital punishment for seven crimes was done away. The consequence was, that crime had greatly diminished, and it was found that secondary punishments had increased as compared with the number of commitments." Mr. Ewart and Mr. Lennardwere appointed to bring in the Bill.

Trades Unions. – *Mr. H. Hughes* presented a petition from Oxford, complaining of undue severity of the sentence passed at the late Dorchester Assizes on the men convicted of belonging to an illegal union. – *Mr. H. Bulver* inquired whether it was the intention of Government to advise an mitigation of the sentence. – *Sir J. Graham,* after stating that the matter did not fall within his department, expressed an opinion that the Government did not intend any mitigation. – *Mr. Hardy* complained of the extension of the Trades' Unions. Their conduct was most reprehensible. They not only fought to regulate their own trades, but to compel other trades to strike; and they were spreading throughout the country, from one end to the other. They bound themselves by the most frightful and terrifying oaths, and acted by compulsion on others. He rejoiced that the Judge had found it his duty to pronounce so exemplary a sentence: and he trusted that it would not be without the most salutary effect. – Mr. Rotch also applauded the sentence, and deplored the continuance of the Unions. He gave notice that after the recess he should move for leave to bring in a Bill to put down these Unions, by punishing such combinations and administration of oaths. – Laid on the table.

The Cambridge Petition. – The remainder of the Morning Sitting was occupied by the discussion on this petition, which was again adjourned till the first meeting of the House after thr Recess.

Sir Robert Inglis contended that to interfere with the Universities would be to risk the safety of education and the maintenance of the established religion of the country. If the House thought that the Dissenters would be satisfied with the matters mentioned in the petition, they had a much lower estimate of the claim of the Dissenters than that body itself. The present possession was held by law, and a possession of 300 years, without any abuse being proved, ought not to be disturbed. In conclusion he expressed his earnest hope that this question would receive the deliberate attention which it deserved.

Mr. O'Connell supported the petition at considerable length. There was, he said, no instance in which the temporal interests of the establishment did not influence the conduct of the clergy educated at the Universities of Oxford and Cambridge. They had preached up the doctrine of passive obedience, and non resistance, and continued Tories in every change and phasis of Government, down to the passing of the Reform Bill – and now they oppose the admission of Dissenters to the Universities, as if they had something as powerful as the Inquisition at their backs. Hon. Members might say that they were supporting the Established Church; but had an Established Church continued long in any country where the opinions of the educated and the enlightened middling class has been attempted to be destroyed. No Established Church continued long unless it possessed the sympathy and affections of the people. (*Hear, hear.*) . . .

Mr. Shaw said that the Dissenters in this country were not satisfied with requiring that the Universities should be open to them, but they demanded a separation of Church and State, and the total dissolution of the of the connexion between them. – (Hear, hear.) – Look at the motion which was made a few days ago in that House to expel the Bishops from the House of Lords. Look at the petition from Edinburgh, signed by 14,000 persons, who, not confining themselves to the subject matter of the prayer of petition from Cambridge, declare also that the very existence of a Church Establishment is an evil, and that it should be extirpated . . .

7th. May 1836.

Bristol, Ilfracombe, and South Wales.

The Powerful New
Steam Packet
BENLEDI,
Of 120 Horse Power. – B. Matthews, Commander.

Is intended to perform Voyages at the following times with light GOODS and PASSENGERS, between BRISTOL and ILFRACOMBE:–

From Cumberland. Basin.	*From Ilfracombe*
May.	May.
10 Tues. 2 after.	11 Wed. 5 morn.
17 Tues. 9 morn.	18 Wed. 9 morn.
24 Tues.12 noon.	25 Wed.2 after.

Fares:– Cabin, 15s. Fore Cabin, 8s. – Children under twelve year's, Half price. – Steward's fee, 1s.6d.

SWANSEA

From Cumberland.	*From Swansea. Basin.*
May.	May.
12 Thurs.5 morn.	13 Fri. 6 morn.
19 Thurs.9 morn.	20 Fri. 9 morn.
26 Thurs.2 after.	27 Fri. 3 after.

Fares:– Best Cabin, 12s. Fore-deck 6s.6d. Children under 12 years, half-fare. Horses, 17s.6d.; 4-Wheel Carriages 32s.6d.; 4 ditto, one horse, 21s.6d.; Gigs 16s.; including the Dock dues on Horses and Carriages; Dogs 2s.6d.; Pigs 1s.9d.; Sheep, 1s.3d.; Lambs 1s.

Steward's Fees for Ladies and Gentlemen, 1s. each; Children and Servants, 6d.

TENBY

From Cumberland	*From Tenby. Basin.*
May.	May.
7 Sat. 10 morn.	9 Mon. 6 morn.
14 Sat. 6 morn.	16 Mon. 6 morn.
21 Sat. 9 morn.	23 Mon.11 morn.

Fares:– Cabin, 21s. Fore-Cabin 16s.; Children under 12 years, half price; Servants in Cabin 15s. – Steward's Fee, 1s.6d.; One Horse 4 Wheel Carriage, 32s.; Gigs 25s.; Horses 25s. Dogs 3s.

Refreshments at stated prices. – a Female Attendant.

This splendid and powerful Steamer performs her voyages with great rapidity and punctuality.

SWANSEA, MILFORD, AND LIVERPOOL.

The New and Swift-going
Steam Packet,
MOUNTAINEER
140 Horse Power.
JOHN EDWARDS, Commander.

IS intended to Sail as follows from SWANSEA, calling at MILFORD on her way to LIVERPOOL and LIVERPOOL to SWANSEA:–

From SWANSEA.	*From Liverpool*
May 1836o'clock	May1836 o'clock
4 Wed. 7 morn.	7 Sat. 1 after.
11 Wed. 8 morn.	14 Sat. 11 morn.
18 Wed. 7 morn.	21 Sat. 1 after.
26 Thurs. 2 after.	29 Sun. 11 after.

REDUCED FARES.

Best Cabin, 25s.; Deck, 12s.; Horses, 30s.; four wheel Carriage 40s. four wheel ditto one Horse 25s.; two wheel ditto one horse, 20s.;Dogs 5s.; Pigs, 2s.6d.; Sheep, 2s.; Lambs, 1s.; Horned Cattle 12s 6d. Children under twelve years of age Half Price.

From Swansea to Milford – Best Cabin, 12s.6d.; Fore Cabin, 7s. ——

From Milford to Liverpool – Best Cabin 25s.; Fore Cabin 12s.6d.

Steward's Fees 2s.6d. each Lady or Gentleman, and 1s.6d. each Child above seven years of age, and each Servant.

A Female Steward attends the Ladies' Cabin.

Horses and Carriages shipped with the greatest care. They must be brought alongside one hour before the time of sailing. The Neath Goods are conveyed from Swansea without delay. The BRECON FOREST SWANSEA CANAL PACKET meets the Steamer at Swansea every Friday, to convey Goods to Brecon, Trecastle, Devynock, Llandovery and the interior of the country; and arrangements are made for the conveyance Goods direct from Liverpool via Swansea to Bristol, Gloucester, Birmingham, Carmarthen, Llandilo, Llandovery and the adjacent towns.

The Mail and other Coaches from Swansea to Bristol, Gloucester, Carmarthen, Milford, Merthyr, Brecon &c. &c. REES' WAGGON meets the Packet every Thursday for Carmarthen and the interior of the country.

——◇——

Dutch Mechanical Surgery. – *The Hague Journal* states that a Dutch artilleryman, named Van der Boll, having lost both his arms below the elbow, by an explosion, the Sculptor V. F. Freil of Flushing, has contrived and executed for him two artificial fore arms and hands with which he can feed himself, put on his clothes, perform all other ordinary offices, and even write. The poor man was also deprived of one of his eyes, but for this we suppose no substitute can be found.

Borough of Swansea. – A meeting of the Council of this Borough was held at the Town-Hall, on Thursday last (yesterday). Colonel Cameron, Mayor in the chair; present Messrs Aubrey, Grove Glover, Johns, Michael, Owen, Richardson, Smith, and Sanders. After the minutes of the last Meeting were read over, the tender of Mr. Thos. Bowen was accepted for building the quay wall, according to the plans and specification of Mr. James Hall, at ten shillings per perch, and tenpence per foot for the coping; and two sureties were proposed and accepted in the sum of fifty pounds each, for the due performance of the contract. The Surveyor was directed to commence the projected quay wall with all due dispatch. Licence was granted to Mr. Tardrew, to assign the lease of the house, now held by him under the Corporation of Swansea, situate near the Ferry, to Mr. John Rosser. Mr. Hall was directed to pay John Lace ten pounds, on account of his demand against the Corporation for meetings. On the motion of Mr. Michael, which was seconded by Mr. Grove, it was resolved that as the funds of the Corporation were at present in such a condition as to retard several projected and necessary improvements and more especially the contemplated improvements of the public quay, that Capt. Richardson's handsome offer of a loan of a sum of money, at four per cent per annum, without security, to enable the Corporation to carry into effect the above named last improvement, be accepted, with the full understanding that he be paid off as early as the Corporation funds will permit . . .

It was resolved unanimously that the handsome offer of John Grove Esq. to relinquish his privilege to exemption from Corporation Tolls, be inserted in the minutes of the present Meeting; and the Council trust that so good an example will act beneficially, and induce others similarly circumstanced to relinquish their rights to exemption from tolls.

——◇——

Swansea Philosophical and Literary Institution. – The following are the donations to the above Institution during the month of April:– A piece of terra cotta, several ancient seals, red oxide of zinc, and galena on carbonate of lime, from D. Nicol, Esq., surgeon, Swansea; several centipedes and scorpions from R. Prichard, Esq. Swansea; a groat of the new currency 1836, from R. Aubrey, Esq. jun., Swansea; three volumes for the Library, a white owl, and a rabbit for stuffing, from Mr. J. Williams, Cambrian Office; a piece of ancient quern, found at Loughor, from Mr. J. Morgan, surveyor, Swansea; a specimen of peacock ore from Valparaiso, from Mr. Todd of the Customs, Swansea; a number of fine engravings of animals from the Secretary; a green lizard, a snake, a blind worm, several scorpions from Mr. Geo. Hexham, Swansea; a Mexican silver coin from Mr. William Sibbering, Swansea; two silver English coins from Mr. Rayner, Swansea; an old wood engraving 13(5?)02, and two copper coins from Mr. Sullivan, Swansea; a silver model of a tea kettle made from 1-18th. part of a dollar found in Gower, made and presented by Mr. R. E. Mosely, Swansea; a piastre of Turkey, rare even in that country, from its being out of circulation very many years, it is now a nominal money only, from Mr. J. Grove, Wind street, Swansea; a cyriona kitten, with two perfect bodies and one head, from Dr. Gibbon, Swansea; a model of a canoe from Master W. H. Michael, Swansea; a specimen of purple quartz from Mr. W. Sibbering; a snake from Master E. Turner, Swansea; a stuffed mole from Mr. Crutchley, Swansea; fan coral, from G. G. Bird, Esq., Swansea; a very fine and delicate specimen of carbonate of lime from Devonshire, from Miss Jeffereys, Swansea; quartz and crystals found at Hill, in the Isle of Nevin, from G. G. Bird Esq., Swansea; 113 copper coins, chiefs tokens, from Mrs. Staniforth, Veranda; hippocampus from Mr. Geo. Cemmins, Swansea; copper coin of Louis 14th., from Mr. J. Rivers, Swansea; a green woodpecker, from J. H. H. Spencer, Carmarthenshire; skull of an ox, from S. Benson, Esq., Swansea; polished specimen of topaz, quartz, chrysophrase, agates, Mocha-stones, neat spar, and smoky quartz, a crystal of Amethyst, containing a drop of water, ferruginous coarix and a variety of other minerals and cut specimens from Mr. G. G. Francis, Swansea; several specimens of copper ores from H. Bath, Esq. jun., Swansea; a gold fish from R.Higgs, Esq. Swansea; Kennett's Roman Antiquities, from S. Padley, Esq., Swansea . . .

——◇——

A man named Warren Hathaway, and a lad, were going down the Severn, near Beachley, on Thursday week, in a small sloop laden with salt from Lydney. The wind was very high and boisterous at the time, and as they were attempting to enter the mouth of the Wye, the vessel took in a considerable quantity of water and went down. Hathaway jumped into the small boat, but unfortunately not having a knife or any means of separating the painter, the small boat was dragged down with the vessel, and Hathaway drowned; the lad climbed up the mast, which providentially remained above water, and was afterwards taken off by a boat.

——◇——

To the EDITOR of The CAMBRIAN.

Sir, – After the two letters that appeared in your paper last week, complaining of the laziness of the Swansea Police with regard to the number of dogs allowed to run at large in the public streets, and calling on the Mayor to use a little more vigour in getting rid of the nuisance. I think, in common justice, thanks are owing to that gentleman for his praiseworthy assuidity during the past week. Let him not, however. relax in his exertions so auspiciously commenced; there is still a wide field before him – there are some hundreds of curs yet to be destroyed, were it only on the score of humanity, to save them from starving; and although some few private individuals might have felt aggrieved from their darling imp-dog . having met with so ungracious a death as the Policeman's pistol, yet let them be philanthropic enough to consider it is for the public weal. Laws are not made for the few, but for the better guidance and safety of the many.

I remain, Mr. Editor.

Swansea, May 5 1836. A Cur Hater.

——◇——

"WINE IS A MOCKER."

(From " The Patriot'.)

1. Drink! for the tide of mirth flows high;–
Though soon it ebbs again;
And on the sand will leave thee dry,
In bitterness and pain.

2. Drink! and forget-although, tomorrow,
Remembrance come again,
And find thee well awake to sorrow,
To bitterness and pain.

3. Drink! 'tis a health; and though your own
In every cup you drain,
Be sacrificed, let this alone for bitterness and pain.

4. Drink! be a man; – though who computes
His manhood thus, in vain;
And to a sense below the brutes,
Adds bitterness and pain;

5. Drink! be a Deity! and know
The drunkard shall attain
To immortality; – although
Of bitterness and pain.

In Vino Veritas.

INTERESTING NOTICES.

———

Railroad – In a lecture Dr. Gardner of Southwark detailed the processes by which the improvement in locomotive engines had been attained and remarked that he had lately travelled at the rate of 60 mph and that 70 or even 80 mph may be accomplished . . . the Doctor exhibited a model of the engine which overturned causing all the steam to escape to the great alarm of the females sitting near the Lecturer.

——◇——

WHAT WILL THE LORDS DO?

(From the Dumfries Times.)

What will the Lords do? is in the mouth of everyone – so as to be tiresome. The reply is plain and simple – "They will play the fool." How can anyone be so weak or so absurd as to suppose that the House of the Lords, composed as it now is, should act with discretion, and much more so with wisdom. Unfortunately the great body of their Lordships are of that age and of that school as to be buried in ignorance. To many, and to the most violent, Nature has been unkind. What can be expected from men of such mental capacity as the Duke of Newcastle, the Earls of Winchlesea and Falmouth, and Baron Kenyon; then the infirmity of the Earl of Vase, known commonly as the Marquis of Londonderry; and the affliction which has fallen on the Earl of Roden – his bigotry, his religious prejudice. What can be hoped for, while there is yet so much honest darkness which hangs over the Earl of Mansfield – poor man! One cannot but respect him, for one feels he is sincere in his opinions, but yet one pities him, for he is not deficient in intellect, – that he in these days should be at least two centuries behind the great body of his fellow countrymen; – what makes his blindness the more lamentable is, that as a boy at Westminster, he showed capacity; and distinguished himself at Oxford – that he is a good scholar, and not wanting in information, and in private life is not only a respectable, but an estimable gentleman. There are several Noblemen in his unfortunate condition; they live to and by themselves – they mix not with the world – they move in limited circles – they are governed by antiquated opinions, and can neither believe nor understand the intellectual changes which have taken place, not only at home but abroad; nor the progress in knowledge which has spread over the mass of the population of the empire and of Europe. My Lord Mansfield adheres to all the habits of his boyhood. You may read the man is remarking his dress. The tight web pantaloons, the Hessian boots, and a particular cut coat, and old fashioned hat. His Lordship may be supposed to have a horror of the power of steam, or is ignorant of its application and the changes which it has produced. He is a good classic, but has made little or no advance in the knowledge of the sciences; and as his Lordship is, so *are many of his compiers. Three* are of a certain age, and will work out by degrees, and be succeeded by a race more suitable to the general enlightenment of the present and the forthcoming period. What can be expected but folly from the House of Lords, or even worse than folly, when the representative Peers of Scotland and Ireland are returned by such Constituencies as now exist! In Scotland in particular, where an unprincipled Renegade directs, and in Ireland, where the majority of the Peers are bigoted, corrupt, intolerant or unprincipled. What can be looked for from a body where there are so many lawyers, who have been advanced to the honours of nobility for their apostacy and political profligacy? What can be expected of a body who shall select for their leader such a person as my Lord Lyndhurst, talented enough indeed, and a powerful speaker; but can anything more be said of his Lordship, who was known at College and for many years after being called to the bar, to be so extreme in his political and religious opinions, as would even now cause an ultra-Radical to be driven from all decorous society . . .

——◇——

2nd. June 1838.

Great Western Railway

THE Public are informed that this Railway will be OPENED for the conveyance of Passengers between London, West Drayton, Slough, and Maidenhead station on MONDAY 4th. JUNE.

The following will be the times for the departure of trains each way, from London and from Maidenhead, until further notice:

TRAINS EACH WAY

8 o'clock morn.	4 o'clock after.
9	5 .. ..
10	6 .. ..
12	7 .. ..

Each Train will take up or set down Passengers at West Drayton and Slough.

FARES OF PASSENGERS

From Paddington

	First Class		Second Class	
to:	Posting Carriage	Passenger Coach	Coach	Open Carriages
WD	4s.6d.	3s.6d.		
S	5s.6d.	4s.6d.		
M	6s.6d.	5s.6d.		

NOTICE is also given, that on and after Monday June 4th., Carriages and Horses will be conveyed on the Railway and Passengers and Parcels booked for conveyance by Coaches in connexion with the Railway Company, to the West of England, and also to Stroud, Cheltenham, Gloucester, as well as to, Oxford, Newbury, Reading, Henley, Marlow, Windsor, Weybridge, and other adjacent places.

By order of the Directors,
CHAS. A. SAUNDERS
THOMAS OSLER.
Secretaries.

YOLAND'S SPECIFIC SOLUTION.

FOR the cure of Gonnorhoea, Gleets Strictures, Irritation of the Kidnies, Bladder, Uretha, prostrate Gland and all diseases of the Urinary Organs, &c., is offered to the public upon the authority and recommendation of several Medical Men of the highest standing in the profession, and is WARRANTED to cure the above diseases in a much shorter space of time than any medicine that has ever been prepared or sold in this country.

In addition to which it is agreeable to the palate, and invariably improves the constitution, however much it may have been impaired by the disease, or by those injurious remedies, mercury, Copaiba, turpentine, balsams &c.

Yoland's Specific Solution is now universally kept and prescribed at several of our principal Hospitals, a fact which speaks volumes in his favour, – *one bottle having more effect than* four of *any other remedy* for the care of any of the above diseases. Captains and Seamen should make a point of taking a few bottles with them, as it is *utterly impossible to procure any medicine that will effect half as quick and certain a cure.* The following testimonials selected from numerous others will satisfy every one of the value of this remedy.

I hereby certify that I have prescribed Yoland's Specific Solution in very many cases of Gonorrhoea, Gleets, Strictures and Whites that have come under my care; it certainly has a most astonishing effect in resisting diseases. I have repeatedly seen a perfect cure performed by it in three days after many boxes of pills, and many bottles of Copbaia in various forms have been taken without the disease diminishing. One trial will convince the most incredulous the superiority of Yoland's Specific Solution, and how quickly it eradicates disease from the constitution. London, July 1837.

ASHLEY B. COOPER.

....

A Physician, who has testimonials of the highest character, attends daily from nine till four, at Messrs. Graham's 138, Holborn, who may be consulted for the above or any other form of disease.

Prepared and sold at Graham Co's 138, Holborn, adjoining Furnival's Inn, London; wholesale and retail by by . . . J. Williams, Cambrian Office Swansea . . .

Price 2s.9d., 4s. 6d., and 11s.

Mr. John Cook, eldest son of Mr. Philip Cook, surgeon of Tygwin, near Clydach, was, on Monday last admitted a member of the Royal College of Surgeons, London.

Thomas Williams, from Bridgend, aged 16, underwent the operation of amputation of the leg, on Monday last, at the Infirmary, under the care of Mr. Bird. We are happy to learn that the patient is going on as well as possible.

It may not be generally known that by an Act lately passed two magistrates may order any person brought before them, whose insanity can be satisfactorily established, to an asylum instead of a gaol for trial, and that two magistrates may order any person in similar circumstances now in prison to be removed to a lunatic asylum.

The fact of 36,000 mackerel having been sold in the 24 hours, on Friday and Saturday week, in Swansea, by one fish salesman, proves the great consumption of the town.

One of the Cardiff and London Shipping Company's crack schooners, the *Celerity*: John Williams, master, completed her last voyage, from London in 80 hours, – Having left Gravesend on Friday the 25th. and arrived at Cardiff on Tuesday last, at day break.

Swansea Teetotal Procession and Tea Party.

THE MEMBERS of the above SOCIETY intend MEETING. ON Wednesday Morning, next, June the 6th., at ten o'clock on the Burrows, from whence they will walk in Procession to St. John's Church, where Divine Service will be performed by the Rev. H. Crowther

At half-past two they will again meet at the Infant School Room, and proceed in the same order to Bethesda Chapel, where Service will be conducted principally in the Welsh language.

A PUBLIC TEA PARTY will be held at the Infant School Room, after which the Company will be addressed by a number of Reformed Characters.

The attendance of our Friends from the neighbourhood will be esteemed a favour.

Concentrated
ESSENCE OF JAMAICA GINGER,
A certain cure and preventive of all Nervous Complaints, Spasms, Gout, Rheumatism, &c.

THE utility and benefit of Ginger as a family or domestic medicine has been long known and deservedly appreciated; and as a stimulant or tonic is acknowledged by many eminent Medical Practitioners to be one of the most valuable Medicines in the Materia Medica; but useful as it is acknowledged to be, its application has been hitherto very limited, in consequence of the unpleasant sensations often experienced in administering a sufficient dose of the powder, such as excessive heat and irritation of the fauces in the act of swallowing, and a subsequent uneasy sensation in the stomach and bowels &c. All these objections are now completely overcome by the introduction of this elegant preparation, which is made from the pith of the finest Jamaican Ginger that is imported, the exterior coat or bark being rejected. This pith (one ounce of which is equal in strength to four ounces of powdered Jamaican Ginger) undergoes a tedious chemical process, by which almost the whole of its active principles can be separated, and is now offered to the public in the very desirable form of a Concentrated Fluid Essence, in one tea spoonful of which the whole active principles of half an ounce of the best White Jamaica Ginger is concentrated, and from its extreme pleasantness can be taken in any vehicle.

In all nervous complaints and hypochondriacal affections, it is wonderfully successful, acting as a genetic stimulus on the stomach, diffusing a mild and cordial warmth over the whole system, it assists digestion, removes flatulency, pain in the stomach, giddiness, head ache &c. and exhilarates the spirits thereby avoiding the necessity, which too often compels nervous persons to have recource to ardent spirits in the hope of obtaining a temporary relief, to which practice they soon become habituated, and the fatal results are too well known to require repitition. In this preparation they will experience all the relief afforded by some baneful practices, unattended by their subsequent injurious effects. In the above complaint, one tea spoonful should be taken in a glass of wine, or any other vehicle, three times a day.

The Essence proved in numerous cases, during the prevailing epidemic of 1831 to be decidedly successful in cases of cholera or spasms of the stomach and bowels . . .

Newspaper Stamps

The following is the number of Stamps issued to the specified Papers, from the 1st. of January 1837 (the period when the distinctive die came into operation), to the 31st. of March 1838, according to the Returns:–

CAMBRIAN	107,000
CARMARTHEN JOURNAL	47,118
CARNARVON HERALD	54,595
MERTHYR GUARDIAN	71,475
N'TH WALES CHRONICLE	21,833
SILURIAN	49,950
WELSHMAN	66,276

We refer our readers with satisfaction to the above Returns, as they indisputably shew that the CAMBRIAN still maintains its distinguished position as an advertising medium.

To Builders and Contractors.

NOTICE is hereby given that the COMMITTEE appointed to conduct the NEW BUILDING for the SWANSEA PHILOSOPHICAL INSTITUTION are ready to receive Proposals for executing the same.

Specifications of the several Works to be done and the necessary Working Plans &c. may be seen at the Town Hall on and after Monday next, where printed copies of specifications can be obtained on application or of the Secretary.

Wind Street. J. W. G. GUTCH. Esq.
Swansea, June 1 1838.

The Coronation. – Though the Government has resolved that the Coronation of her Majesty shall not be attended with wasteful and unnecessary expenditure, yet it appears that everything really conducive to the greatness and solemnity of the ceremony will be on a liberal and magnificent scale. The performance of the sacred music, in particular, which forms a part of the religious service within Westminster Abbey, will be in a style of unprecedented grandeur. At the Coronation of his late Majesty the temporary orchestra in the Abbey contained 187 performers; too small a number to give full effect to choral music in that setting. It has been found practicable, we understand, to erect an orchestra capable of containing 400 performers; the number to be assembled on this occasion, which object will be effected by taking down the Abbey organ and erecting a temporary organ, placed much further back, and connected by a long movement with the keys in front of the orchestra, where the director will be stationed. A number of the most eminent English vocalists will be engaged, and, in addition to them members of the choirs of the Chapels-Royal, Westminster Abbey, St. Pauls and Windsor, a body of female choristers will be introduced. This being unprecedented in our Cathedral music, gave rise to some deliberation; but the proposition was adopted, as being liable to no rational objection and calculated to increase immeasurably the beauty and effect of the choral harmony. The most splendid steps have been taken for the reception of the Foreign Ambassadors and their numerous suites, and it is reported, no doubt, with great truth that, *fetes* on the most extensive scale will be given by these representatives, that suitable honour may be done to this court, and that the Sovereign whom they respectively represent may be reflected with with becoming magnificence.– The arrangements for due solemnity are rapidly advancing in the Earl Marshall's Department. The Peers and Peeresses have all received their letters of summons, and the 11th. day of June is the last day upon which they can signify their intention of being present. The requisite accommodation in the Abbey will then be appropriated to them, and the lower classes. The 2nd. of June is the last day that any application for admission will be received for persons who on account of their offices would have had the privilige of walking had there been a procession. Lords of Privy Council have decided against their own competency to invite Baronets to attend.

Negro Apprenticeships. – Among the Members who voted in the House of Commons, on Monday last, for the immediate abolition of the Negro Apprenticeship, were – J. J. Guest, Merthyr Tydfil; B. Hall, Marylebone; J. Jones, Carmarthenshire; D. Morris, Carmarthen; J. H. Vivian, Swansea. Among those who voted in the Majority against the measure, were – Lord Adare, Glamorganshire; Sir J. Graham, Pembroke; G. M. R. Morgan, Brecon; P. Pryse, Cardigan; Lord Somerset, Monmouthshire; C. R. M. Talbot, Glamorganshire; Hon. G. R. Trevor, Carmarthenshire; W. A. Williams, Monmouthshire; Col. Wood, Breconshire. – Sir R. B. Philipps, Member for Haverfordwest paired with Major Vivian in favour of the immediate abolition of the Negro Apprenticeship system.

Awful Shipwreck. – The *Sunderland Beacon* gives the following account of one of the most calamitous shipwrecks that has ever come under our notice; by which, of 41 human beings on board, only two were miraculously preserved, one of whom the second mate, furnished that paper with the following particulars:

The *Margaret,* of Newry, transport of the burthen of 826 tons, commanded by Wm. Mowbray, after taking in a quantity of stores in the Thames for the use of her Majesty's troops in Canada, proceeded to Cork, at which place they completed lading, sailing from thence to her place of destination on the morning of the 26th. ult., having on board, in addition to the crew (which consisted of the captain, the chief and second mates, and 25 able seamen), two officers' ladies, with their children, (seven in number), the captain's wife and child, two ostlers and 12 horses. The weather, at the time of her departure was fine; but shortly after noon a fresh breeze sprung up from the SSE., which, as the day advanced, increased to a gale, accompanied with thick showers of snow. At about half-past 11 p.m., the ship being still on the same tack, in the darkness of the night, and during a heavy fall of snow, she struck on the rocks lying off Cape Clear, at about the distance of about a mile from the main, the sea making a complete breach over her; and shortly after the captain, his wife, and child were successively ingulfed in the raging abyss. The chief mate, with a view to steady the ship, which was beating violently on the reef, ordered the carpenter to cut away the main shrouds and main mast, which was promptly done, the mast being left about two-thirds cut through. The whole of the crew and passengers then sought refuge in the fore part of the ship, with the exception of the survivors, Mr. Willis and a seaman of the name of James Johnson, a native of North Shields, who lashed themselves to the main-mast, on the windward side. Shortly afterwards the main-mast went over the lee carrying with it the two hapless seamen, who, on their again rising to the surface, floated freely. A few minutes afterwards the foremast went by the board, hanging over the lee side of the vessel, only attached to her by the shrouding, with the unfortunate ladies and children lashed thereto for safety, the remainder of the crew clinging to various parts of the ship. At this moment the universal shriek of despair which burst from the devoted group was of the most heart-rending description. Mr. Willis and his companion in misfortune at length drifted clear of the wreck, surrounded by the accumulation of horrors. Exposed to the fury of the sea, pelting of the snow-storm and enveloped by the deepest shades of night, the mast to which they were lashed continued to drive in the direction of Cape Clear until six o'clock a.m., when they perceived a large dog of the Newfoundland breed, which had belonged to the unfortunate chief mate, swimming towards them, and which they contrived to place on the mast beside them. In this helpless condition they remained until half-past 10 a.m., when they reached the shore, well nigh exhausted. The sagacious brute which accompanied them immediately on landing set off to a preventive station, where by the singularity of its actions, it attracted the attention of four of the coast-guard, who were eventually induced to follow it, which circumstance led to the discovery of the suffering mariners.

The great Montgolfier Balloon. – An immense multitude of persons assembled on Thursday in the Royal Surrey Zoological Gardens, to witness the ascent of the great Montgolfier, or fire balloon, which has for sometime past excited public attention. They were, however, disappointed – the aerial giant, like Pope's tall belly "lifted his head and lied." At seven o'clock the balloon appeared to be completely deflated, and though it did not exhibit violent struggles to get free from the ropes which restrained its ascent, it seemed sufficiently full of rarified air, or air of some kind ("all smoke," as it afterwards appeared), to render its rise into a loftier element a matter of certainty, and the spectators were on tiptoe for the wished-for event. In vain, however, they waited all their patience gradually away. At length placards were exhibited in front of the platform, on which was the following announcement:– "The balloon cannot ascend but to compensate for the unavoidable disappointment, an eruption will take place at dusk." The Company, at least a certain portion of them became exasperated; yells of the most discordant nature commenced; these were followed by throwing stones at the balloon. The shower, at first a slight one, gradually increased in force and energy until the sides of the "giant" gave way beneath the attacks of his assailants, and presented a thousand wounds, from every one of which the vapour of his life-escaped with fearful rapidity. The harmless monster swayed backwards and forwards in the agonies of approaching dissolution, and at length fell over the edge of the scaffold, and bent its head into the water. The disturbance gradually subsided. The company admitted could not be estimated at far short of 15,000 persons.

4th. July 1840.

THEATRE, SWANSEA.

– By Authority.

THE Public are most respectfully informed, that this Theatre having been RE-DECORATED and EMBELLISHED in a most superior and elegant style (by Mr. CONNOR and Assistants). will open for the Season.

On MONDAY, JULY 6th, 1840.

Under the Management of
Messrs. NEWCOMBE
and J. BEDFORD.

The Evening's Entertainment will commence with the
National Anthem.
GOD SAVE THE QUEEN, with an additional verse by L.N.
To be sung by the whole Company.
After which an OVERTURE, composed expressly for the occasion
by D. HERVEY, Esq.
(Of the Bath Concerts) will be performed by the Band.
To be followed by the
Musical Comedy of,
SWEETHEARTS and WIVES.
Admiral Franklin ... Mr. TILBURY,
(From the Theatre Royal, Covent Garden-his first appearance here).
Charles Franklin ... Mr. JOHNSTONE.
(From the Theatre Royal, Newcastle)
Mr. Sandford ... Mr. T. BISHOP.
(From the Theatre Royal, Bath.)
Who will introduce the Songs.
"The Sun, its Bright Rays."
and "The Mountain Maid."
Billy Lackonow ... Mr. WOULDS.
Who will sing, "*Surely Mortal Man was born for Sorrow."*
Curtis ... Mr. ROYER.
(From the Theatre Royal Bath).
Eugenis ... Mrs. ASHTON.
(From the Theatre Royal Bath).
Laura ... Mrs.G. NORMAN.
(From the Theatre Royal, English Opera and Bristol). who will sing.
"*Pretty Star of the Night.*" and "*Why are you wandering here, fair Maid.*"
Mrs Bell ... MRS.DARLEY.
(Her first appearance these two years)
Susan ... Mrs. ROYER.
(From the Theatre Royal Bath.
Her first appearance here).
After the first Act of the Comedy,
A NEW DROP SCENE, taken from the LAKE OF COMO, and Painted by
Mr. Connor, will be Exhibited.
In course of the Evening, a Dance by
Miss EARNSHAW.
(From the Theatre Royal, Sheffield – her first appearance).
Between the Acts of the Comedy the Band will perform several of Strauss's most Favourite Waltzes.
The whole to conclude with a Drama of intense interest, entitled.
THE SERGEANT'S WIFE.
Old Cartouch (a Wounded Veteran).
Mr. TILBURY
Frederick Cartouch (his Son),
Mr. T. BISHOP,
who will introduce
"The Toast be Dear Woman."
Robin (Attendant at the Old Chateau)
MR.WOULDS.
Lissette (the Sergeant's Wife),
Mrs. COLEMAN POPE,
(From the Theatre Royal Sheffield. – her first appearance).
Margot, MRS. ROYER.
Cecile, Mrs. JOHNSTONE.
Maria, Miss EARNSHAW.
Leader of the Band – Mr. R. GUY.
Stage Manager – T. H. WEBB,
(from the Theatre Royal,
English Opera House)

Nights of Performance – Monday, Tuesdays, Thursdays, and Fridays.

Tickets to be had at the Misses Jenkins's Library Wind-street, where Places for the Boxes may be secured.

Boxes, 3s.; Second Price, 2s. – Pit, 2s; Second Price 1s. – Gallery, 1s; Second Price 6d.

Box Transferable Ticket for the Season, (Benefits excepted). Three Guineas; Box Single Ticket, Two Guineas; Pit Transferable Ticket for the Season, Two Guineas; Pit Single Ticket, £1 8s.

Doors open at Half-past Six and begin at Seven precisely. – Second Price at a Quarter before Nine.

TO BE SOLD, or LET for a Term,

EARLSWOOD COTTAGE, situated near Briton-Ferry, consisting of two parlours, a sitting room, five bedrooms, kitchen, dairy, cellar. &c. with a Gig house, three stall Stable and every other requisite convenience with a small detached Cottage and Garden; also a good walled-in Garden, and about nine acres of Land. Rent and Taxes very moderate.

The Cottage is delightfully situated, commanding extensive views of the surrounding country, and within three miles of the market town of Neath, and five of Swansea, and well adapted for the residence of a genteel family.

For terms apply to Mr. W. Lewis, the tenant.

Preparatory School
for Young Gentlemen.

From four to nine years of age.
Conducted by
Mrs. LE COURTEUR,

WHO will conscientiously attend to the health and comfort of any Young Gentleman placed under her care. The situation is healthy, and near the sea. Swansea enjoys the advantage of warm and cold sea bathing, and the climate is particularly mild. School opens on Monday 28th. July. Terms for Boarders and Day Pupils may be had from 4 Nelson Place, Swansea.

Swansea Academy.

AT this ESTABLISHMENT, conducted by Mr. KNEATH and ASSISTANTS.

A few Vacancies now occur.
Particulars may be obtained on application.
Oxford-street, Swansea, July 2d 1840

THE CAMBRIAN.

There is no question about which the country is likely to take more interest than that which was last week brought before Parliament by Mr. Fitzroy Kelly – that is to say whether the punishment of death ought to be abolished in the case of all crimes, murder and treason excepted. If the feelings of humanity alone were to be consulted, there can be no doubt that most, if not all, would say, "Abolish capital punishment at once – give your criminal code a merciful character – recommend yourselves to the people, and obtain a lasting reputation in history, by keeping pace with, or perhaps going before, the spirit of the age, and the demands of public opinion." But unfortunately in matters of this kind, it is not enough to consult the sentiments of the heart we must have resource to the stern dictates of reason, and if possible, ascertain not what will be most pleasing to the country, but what will make most for the country's permanent good. We are aware that the opinion prevails, and perhaps somewhat widely, that society possesses no right to take away human life under any circumstances. But if this view of the matter be correct, it proves, not merely that the majority of men have hitherto been in error on the subject of the penal code, but that civilised society is altogether based on false principles. In the self same arguments by which the right to inflict capital punishment is denied, the state deprives it of the principle of taking up arms in self defence, and exposes even the individual to be cut off by an assassin in the street or on the highway, without permitting him to have recourse to such means as Providence may have placed at his disposal for effectually resisting violence; since if a man or a state be justified in repelling force by force, and in putting in the open field, the enemy or the highwayman to death, if no other means be left of counteracting their intended villany, then by purity of reason society has a right to take the only step by which it can effectually secure itself against the designs of the murderer, who by cutting off one of the members of the state, proclaims war against the whole, and must be dealt with exactly in the same manner as a lion, a tiger or any other wild beast. The opponents, however, of capital punishment are in the habit of maintaining that, to say nothing of justice or humanity, it is impolitic, because unnecessary, to put murderers to death, seeing that solitary confinement during life would be a far severer and more effectual punishment. But if in reality it be a severer punishment, that is to say, if it inflicts a greater amount of suffering on the criminal then it is the advocates of solitary confinement who in reality trample humanity underfoot, by seeking to visit offenders with aspects of retribution from which they would gladly be delivered by death. To comprehend the subject thoroughly however a little beyond the malefactor, he must consider the effect of solitary confinement upon the community at large, and ascertain whether, by preserving the life of one guilty of blood, very great injustice and very great cruelty be not perpetrated against the innocent members of society. For example – it is admitted on all hands that extreme poverty of the lower orders must consequently multiply the number of individuals disposed to transgress the law. Now, to erect a prison for the confining and securing of criminals, who, according to all laws human and divine, have forfeited their lives, to maintain such criminals during twenty, thirty, or even forty years in silence, and not only so, but to support and pay a whole army of gaolers, turnkeys, and other officers of prisons, as the liveried attendants of transcendent guilt – all this, we say, must inevitably press hard upon the honest and industrious poor cut short the lives of many of them through starvation and precipitate others of them perhaps into the commission of offences which may reduce them to be the companions of those caitiffs whose villany, caused their impoverishment. Thus the adoption of the system of solitary confinement might, to preserve the existence of the murderer, ruin half-a - dozen innocent and humble families, and thus perpetuate enormous injustice through a reprehensible affectation of humanity and the desire to appear excessively merciful. This view of the question it appears to us is altogether decisive. Connected however with the subject is another inquiry, namely, admitting it to be just and salutory to execute murderes, the same arguments will justify the execution of political offenders, and the perpetrators of other acts, deemed criminal or illegal by society. Our own decision is in the negative, and the reasons on which this decision is founded are among others the following:– first the execution of political offenders is rarely or never justified on any other ground than that of state necessity – that is to say the injustice and moral enormity of its execution are confessed, but excused upon the plea that society must protect itself. In a Christian country this necessity ought to be carefully sifted – that is, it ought to be established beyond the possibility of contradiction that unless political misdemeanours of a certain class be visited with capital punishment, greater evils would accrue to the community than are supposed likely to spring from the perpetration of certain acts of injustice. Now this, in our opinion, can never be shown, for by committing injustice, the state itself becomes a criminal, and exposes itself to that direct vengeance which, whether in great matters or small, tracks the footsteps of iniquity. Besides a wise legislature would without difficulty discover far better preventives of treason than sanguinary executions. Here mercy is of great potency: it invariably ranges public opinion on the side of authority and gives transgressors the appearance of at least acting as much in opposition to the wishes of the country as to the interest of its rulers, another reason why political misdemeanours should be visited leniently by the laws in the consideration that, although we are now blessed with a liberal and benificent government, it is altogether uncertain how long we may enjoy it – how soon the reins of power may pass into the hands of the Tories, who would convert the provisions of the penal code into an instrument of revenge, and prosecute men for treason, those whose only object might be to save the empire from their oppressive grasp.

"Notre lieu, notre reine, notre pays."

– Druid's Cre

Widening Loughor Bridge.

To Conractors and Others.

Persons desirous of Contracting for Widening the Wooden Bridge at Loughor, and for Laying a Railway over the same, are requested to forward Sealed Tenders to Mr. J. J. Stacey, Clerk of the Kidwelly Turnpike Trust, Carmarthen, on or before the first day of August next.

The Bridge is constructed of Timber 670 feet in length, and 20 feet in width, and is to be widened to a breadth of 25 feet, and to have a railway laid down thereon.

A Plan and Specification of the Work required to be done may be inspected after the 24th instant, at the Office of Mr. R. W. Jones, Civil Engineer, Loughor.

The Trustees will not pledge themselves to accept the lowest Tender.

– R. W. JONES Mem Inst. C.E.

Swansea Infirmary.

THE Committee beg to announce that a Vacancy in the OFFICE of RESIDENT SURGEON to this INSTITUTION, will occur in September next, by the resignation of Mr. Ll. P. Mortimer, and that a GENERAL MEETING of the SUBSCRIBERS, for the purpose of ELECTING a SUCCESSOR, will take place on Tuesday, the 18th. August next, at the Town-Hall at twelve o'clock precisely.

Salary £100 per Annum, with Residence, Coals, and Candles.

For further particulars apply (if by letter, post-paid.) to the Secretary.

2d. June 1840. GEO. T. STROUD. Secretary

A.O.D.

THE EISTEDDFOD and PROCESSION of the BARDS and BROTHERS of the SWANSEA DISTRICT of the ANCIENT ORDER OF DRUIDS will take place on the 11th. day of August. 1840, when PRIZES will be awarded for the best compositions on the following Subjects:–

1. For the best Poem on the Providential escape of our Beloved Queen from Assassination. Prize – £3. 3s. and a copy of Davies's "Celtic Researcher."

2. Am y Bryddestawd buddigawl ar Waredigaeth Rhagluniaethol ein Anwyl Frenhines rhag Llofruddiad, – gwobr o £3.3s. a chopi o "Hanes Cymru" gan y Parch T. Price.

3. For the best English Address on Druidism, delivered in the ensuing Eisteddfod – prize £2. 2s.

4. Am y Cyfarchiad Cymraeg buddigawl ar Dderwydddaeth, a draddodir yn yr Eisteddfod dyfodol – Gwobr a £2.2s.

5. For the best original Druidic Song in English. Prize £1. 10s.

6. Am y Can Dderwyddawl buddugawl yn y Cymraeg. – Gwobr £1.10s

7. For the best Essay in English or Welsh on the A...O and the Oak, Mistletoe &c. as Druidic symbols. – Prize £3. 3s.

8. For the best Translation into Welsh of the *"Mynstrel's Song and Ode."* by Chatterton.

N.B. Druids only are allowed to compete for Prizes 3 and 4.

Prizes will also be awarded for Penillion singing, for the best player on the Single and Pedal Harp, for the best singers (male and female) with the Harp, to the Airs *"Ar Hyd y Nos" "Codiad yr Ehedydd" "Merch Megan"* &c.

Particulars will be given at an early period, stating the amount of of the different Prizes for the successful Harpists, and Singers, with or without the accompaniment.

All compositions on the above subjects to be directed to the Secretary on or before the 4th day of August. 1840.

Every candidate to sign his production under assumed name and the real name of each to be written in a corner of his paper, and sealed up.

All the successful compositions to be the property of that section of the Order which originated and supported the Eisteddfod.

Ladies and Gentlemen wishful to encourage the literature of their country, and to patronise the melodies which Handel admired, are respectfully requested to send their names as contributors, and a subject for a Prize, as early as possible, to the Editor of the Cambrian, or the Secretary; and as the time of the Proclamation and the Eisteddfod, are unavoidably so near each other, the Committee will esteem it a favour if Ladies and Gentlemen, in selecting their Prizes will bear this fact in mind.

Signed on behalf of the Committee.

REES PRICE, Secretary.
Mor Alarch Lodge, No. 304 A.O.D.
Rutland Arms Inn, Swansea, July 3 1840.

6th. August 1842.

The Thames Tunnel is rapidly approaching completion; on Monday next the entrance on the Wapping side will be open to visitors, the shaft at Rotherhithe being closed in order to finish the new staircase.

When this is completed the tunnel will be thrown open, not merely as an object of curiosity, but as a thoroughfare for foot passengers, and its practical utility as a medium of communication from one shore to the other will then be tested.

Her Majesty, attired in a splendid purple riding habit, with the ribbon of the Order of the Garter, and a military cap reviewed the 15th. Regiment of Foot commanded by Lord Charles Wellesley. In the Home Park, Windsor on Thursday morning, in company with Prince Albert, Her Majesty reviewed the 2d. regiment of Life Guards which are now garrisoned at Windsor. In the Great Park Windsor, yesterday, habited in her splendid riding dress which she wore the preceding day, and mounted on her favourite chestnut African barb rightly caprisoned.

A horse from Java, of the diminutive size of only 27½ inches in height, scarcely as tall as a Newfoundland dog, was yesterday received as a present by her Majesty at Windsor.

The Lords of the Treasury have ordered that Carnarvon shall be a boarding port. The priviliges of a boarding port will not only contribute to the prosperity of Carnarvon town, but must prove highly beneficial to the county as well as to the county of Anglesea.

Railway Accident – On Wednesday morning last, when the train which leaves Birmingham for Derby at seven o'clock, had passed the Barton station, Mr. Gruggari, who was one of the passengers, observed an unusual smoke from a luggage waggon near the engine; after several attempts to make himself understood, he succeeded in getting the train stopped; the guard lifted the cloth, which covered the luggage, and after desiring the passengers, who in alarm had left their seats, to "jump in" called to the engineer to "run into Derby as fast as ye can"! The train was no sooner put in motion than the flames burst out with great fierceness; the fire soon reached the second luggage waggon, and threatened the destruction of the passengers, among whom were many females, who were riding in a third class carriage attached to the luggage waggons; the shrieks of the women were frightful and the blaze most awful; but so rapid was the speed at which the train had been urged, that the engineer could not stop until it reached the approach to the Derby station, where several persons were much injured by jumping out of the carriages as soon as they came to a halt; every exertion was of course then made to extinguish the fire; one of the luggage waggons was completely consumed, and the other much burnt. Surely the engineer and guard ought to have detached the luggage carriages when the fire was first discovered, instead of risking the lives of the passengers by taking the dangerous course they did. The fire is supposed to have originated from the spontaneous combustion of some article among the goods conveyed, as the luggage was well protected from the effects of sparks from the engine. – *Nottingham Journal.*

Miraculous Escape – An inquest was on Friday week held before J. Barnett, Esq., on the body of T. Sollis, farmer, of Bishop's Cleeve, near Cheltenham. A jury of fourteen farmers, after having been sworn, repaired with the coroner, the surgeon and the police, to view the body, which lay on six chairs in a small room, on the ground floor, adjoining a kitchen, in the house, the property of the deceased, and in this room there was scarcely room for all to stand. The two last two jury men were just entering it, followed by a reporter from one of the Cheltenham Papers, and Superintendent Russell (a nurse and two female neighbours had just retired by desire of the coroner), when an extraordinary noise like cracking was heard, and in an instant every board in the floor was cracked to pieces, and the whole floor gave way in the centre, with the joists and beams under precipitating twelve of the jury, with the coroner, surgeon and police, into the cellar below, and over them rolling, with the chairs on which it rested, the body of the deceased. The clouds of dust enveloped all in momentary obscurity. At length one of the two jurymen managed to escape from being near the door, and, being a rather tall man, he recovered himself by placing his foot on the bare head of the coroner, who was in the cellar below, being landed on his feet there. Not a voice or outcry was heard up to this time, but all were as silent in this painful situation as he about whose death the living were assembled to inquire; but immediately on his being assisted up, the coroner gave orders for a ladder to be sent for to enable the others to get out, and himself cleared the way down the steps, directing the jury and others the safest and quickest means of escape; he then superintended, with the aid of one of the jury and a policeman, still in the cellar, the elevating the body out of this premature and unceremonious grave, into which it had, carrying the living before it, been thus cast; the end wall and the rest of the floor outside the doorway all the time appearing ready to fall. We are happy to say no limbs were broken, although sundry sprains, scars and bruises were complained of by all. – The inquest then proceeded.

The Prince of Wales's Nurse. – It will be remembered, that her Majesty selected the Nurse of the Prince of Wales from among the servants of King Leopold of Claremont, under the approval of Dr. Lacock, from her very healthy appearance. Her husband was in his Majesty's establishment, and her father a most industrious trader at Esher. The prospect of the whole family were of course in the ascendant under the Royal patronage, and the nurse, on the day of the Christening received at least *150l.* in presents, and subsequently sums to the amount of *500l.* Her perquisites, on weaning the Royal Infant, the Heir Apparent to the Throne, were estimated at *2000l.* From her own imprudence, however, she has lost her all these prospective advantages, as, three weeks ago, on her Majesty entering the the nursery, she found her in a state of drunkeness, and a bottle which had contained gin by her side, in which there was a small remnant of the intoxicating beverage. Her Majesty, as every other mother would have done, instantly discharged her, and sent her home to her father. Although her Majesty inflicted this just punishment on the delinquent, with that kind consideration for the feeling of an old servant in the family of her uncle, she immediately despatched a letter in her own hand writing to the unhappy husband, acquainting him with the cause of his wife's sudden dismissal; and we understand he Majesty has expressed her intention of providing for him and his unoffending children. —*London Paper.*

Longevity. – The following most extraordinary instance of longevity appears in the *Cork Reporter,* and its accuracy is is vouched by a gentleman of fortune in the county of Cork, Mr. Nagle of Ballinamous Castle, who in a letter dated July 26, thus writes to the Editor:– "I think you will have not have any objection to insert in your next publication the death of a very old man, my pound keeper, on part of the land of Clogher near Doneraile, named Louis Wholeham. He died yesterday at the age of 118 years and seven months; he was married to his first wife more than 50 years, and had no offspring. He married a second wife at the age of 109 years, by whom he had a son, a fine boy, and very like the father. From his great age I have given him his house and the parish pound many years rent free, which made him comfortable and prolonged his life. He never lost a tooth, nor had a grey hair on his head.

In our advertising columns of this day will be found a notice that an examination of the Children will take place on Tuesday next, at the Swansea Infants' School. We have pleasure in recommending to the attention of the public this interesting and useful institution, remarking at the same time, that a little additional pecuniary support would be very acceptable.

Swansea and Liverpool

The First Class Powerful
Steam Vessel
TROUBADOUR,
James Beckett, Commander.

IS intended to Sail between SWANSEA and LIVERPOOL, with Goods and Passengers, calling at BRISTOL on her way from Liverpool to Swansea, in the month of August, on or about the following days, Wind and Weather permitting:–

Frm S'sea to L'p'l Aug1842 o'clock.	Frm L'p'l to S'sea Aug 1842 o'clock
3 Wed ... 2 after.	6 Sat ... 9 morn.
10 Wed ... 6 morn.	13 Sat ... 2 after.
17 Wed ... 2 after.	20 Sat ... 10 morn.
24 Wed ... 6 morn.	27 Sat ... 1 after.
31 Wed ... 11 morn.	

From Milford to Liverpool, about five hours after leaving Swansea.

From Milford to Bristol, about eighteen hours after leaving Liverpool.

Fares:– *Swansea to Milford:–* Best Cabin, 10s; Deck, 5s.

Swansea to Liverpool:– Best Cabin, 20s; Deck, 7s.6d; Horses, 30s; Four - wheel Carriages, 40s; Ditto one Horse 25s; Two-wheel Ditto, 20s; Dogs 5s; Pigs, 2s.6d; Sheep 2s; Lambs 1s; Horned Cattle 12s.6d. . . . The Llanelly Mail Coach leaves the Mackworth Arms, Swansea at half-past four every evening, returning the following morning at seven. North Rees' Waggon meets the packets every Wednesday, for Carmarthen, Cardigan, Llandilo, Llandovery and the interior of the country.

On the evening of Friday the 24th ult. the plate glass in the shop window of Mr. Joseph Ward, tailor, Wind Street Swansea, was mischievously or maliciously cut with a diamond, or some other hard substance. We cannot sufficiently deprecate such gross and wanton mischief, and a reward of five guineas having been offered by Mr. Ward for the discovery of the party who committed the act, we trust the miscreant will be discovered, and meet the due reward of his folly or wickedness.

The Corn Trade. – We have now arrived at a very critical period, one at which a week's rough and unfavourable weather may occasion an almost incalculable difference in the prospect of the future; the nearer the crops approach maturity, and the more weighty the ear, the greater are the chances of injury being sustained by unpropitious atmospherical vicissitudes; every change of temperature, and every shower of rain which may take place during the present month will therefore be anxiously considered, and the spirits of all engaged in the cultivation of the soil, as well as those embarked in the grain trade, will for some weeks rise and fall with the barometer. Harvest operations have been more or less interrupted by showers, still a tolerable amount of work has been done, much corn having been cut round about London, and some quantity carried; hitherto, however, very little new grain has made its appearance at any of the country markets, farmers having been too busy in the field to afford much time for threshing. The accounts we receive from those districts where the reaping of Wheat has been pretty generally commenced, bear out our previous opinion as regards the probable result of the harvest that viz. not withstanding the extraordinary fine weather experience for many weeks past, and the immense benefit accruing therefrom, the original cause – a deficiency of plant universally complained of early in the year – will prevent the yield being large, and we have no hesitation in repeating a remark made a fortnight ago "that we still doubted whether under the most auspicious circumstances the produce of Wheat, taking the entire kingdom, would amount to an usual average."

7th. August 1844.

The Union Iron Foundry,

SITUATE upon the Strand, Swansea, and running back to the tramroad near the river, together with the WORKMEN's COTTAGES belonging thereto.

TO BE LET

Apply to Mr. Wm. Walters, Castle-square, Swansea.

TO BE LET

And entered upon at Michaelmas next

SEVERAL FIELDS, comprising the White Stile Fields, and several others part of Ffynone Lands.

Apply to Mr. Thomas Walters, Wind Street, Swansea.

Glamorganshire

TO BE SOLD BY AUCTION
Mr. J. G. HANCORNE,

For the benefit of whom it may concern on Wednesday, the 11th of September,1844, on Whitford Burrows, near Lanmadock, Gower,

SEVERAL Cases of GERMAN WINE, a Lot of HEMPSEED, and a large quantity of OILCAKE, &c. now lying on the said Burrows, being part of the Cargo saved from the MARGARET, of Bristol, lately wrecked in Brufton Bay.

Sale to commence at eleven o'clock in the forenoon.

Felony – Between the hours of nine and ten o'clock on the evening of the 25th. ult. the harness room of Nash Edwards Vaughan Esq. of Rheola, in the county of Glamorgan, was burglariously broken and entered, and the following articles, the property of the servants, stolen there from:– an old fashioned silver watch, a blue frock coat with white buttons and crest, a black hat with crepe, which has been on some months. We understand that a handsome reward has been offered, for the production of such evidence as will lead to the conviction of the offenders.

It is with much pleasure that we notice the liberality of our fellow townsmen, Messrs Rogers and Son, towards the New Church of this town, in presenting to it a beautiful chaste and well executed font which harmonizes with the general architecture of the Church. The eight panels of the bowl bear the inscription, *'Jesus est numen quod est super omne numen'* which is peculiarly appropriate seeing that the baptized person is baptized into the name of Jesus, to be his follower.

Distressing Deprivation – A daughter of Mr. Stephen Stephens, smith, of Llandilo-fawr town, named Anne, aged 10 years, died after a few hour's illness on Sunday the 1st. inst., at ten o'clock, also Thomas a son aged 3 years, at 3 o'clock of the same day; and on Tuesday the 3rd. inst., David another son aged 6 years On Wednesday the three were buried in the same grave in Llandilo churchyard. Thus suddenly Mr. Stephens was deprived of all his children, who, a few hours previous were pictures of innocence and health.

Mad Dog, – A dog in a rabid state, has been seen in this neighbourhood during the last few days. The Mayor has, consequently, thought necessary, for the public safety, to have notices to the effect, tbat all dogs found at large, will be destroyed by the police.

Swansea and Merthyr Cricket Clubs. – A match came off between eleven gentlemen of the Swansea and Merthyr Clubs, in the neighbourhood of the Lamb and Flag, in the Vale of Neath. Mr. Penrose kindly giving them the use of his field, which had been prepared by him for this occasion. The following is the score:–

Swansea	1st inn.		2nd. inn.	
W. Cameron	n.o.	47	b. Davies	17
E. Gregory				
b. J. Russell		0	not out	1
P. Benson				
b. J. Russell		0	b. Davies	0
S. Benson				
b. J. Russell		2	b. Russell	3
– Fredricks				
b. J. Russell		7	b. Russell	8
R. Price				
c. Meyrick		0	c. Russell	0
Capt. Napier				
b. Davies		18	b. Russell	27
J. W. Willioams				
b. J. Russell		6	b. Russell	1
I. Thomas				
run out		3	b. Davies	1
L. L. Dillwyn				
c. Davies		2	b. Davies	1
Byes &c.		7		7
		—		—
		92		66

Merthyr	1st. inn.	2nd. inn.	
E. Thomas			
b. Fredricks	0	b. Fredricks	0
J. Russell, jr.			
b. Fredricks	2	not out	1
J. Russell			
b. W.Cameron	10	b. Fredricks	14
W. Meyrick			
b. Fredricks	0	b. Fredricks	1
Bathhurst			
b. Fredricks	1	c. W. Cameron	6
Davies			
c. Gregory	0	b. Fredricks	35
Homfray			
b. Cameron	3	b. Fredricks	0
Sims ?			
c. Napier	0	b. W. Cameron	0
Jas. Russell			
run out	1	b. W. Cameron	0
Pate			
not out	2	b. Fredricks	5
Hopkins			
b. W.Cameron	1	c. Cameron	0
Byes &c.	7		5
	—		—
	27		67

Swansea winning by 64

After the match had been played, the whole company adjourned to the Lamb and Flag, where Mr. Price had provided an excellent dinner. The return match comes off at the same place on Saturday next.

The Rebecca Riots. – (*From the Bristol Mercury*) A piece of plate purchased by subscription, which it is intended to present to Mr. J. G. Powell, jun. of this city, one of the reporters of London *Times,* in acknowledgment of his services in exposing and promoting the redress of Welsh grievances during the period of the late Rebecca riots, has just been manufactured by Messrs Chilcott of this city. It consists of a handsome silver vase weighing upwards of 60 ounces. On one side is represented a dragon passant, with wings elevated: the badge of Wales, originally adopted by Henry the Seventh, and settled by royal warrant of George the Third. On the other side the following inscription:–

"To John George Powell, one of the faithful and indefatigable reporters of the *Times* newspaper, of facts connected with the 'Rebecca' disturbances of the Principality of Wales 1843, who, in the discharge of their professional duties became the patriotic expositors of grievances in which those disturbances originated. This Vase is respectfully presented as a small token of the feelings of grateful Welshmen, and other friends, for an impartial writer, who calmly traced, amidst popular tumult, the existence and source of legitimatised abuses, and, through the powerful medium of our glorious free press, fearlessly disclosed to public view insufferable wrongs, so as to ensure from a British legislation the speedy restoration of just rights."

Steam Boat Collision, – a collision, of a somewhat serious nature, took place on the morning of Thursday s'en -night, in the river Avon near Sea-Mills Reach, between the old company's Newport packet, *Usk*, Captain Dando, and the new company's screw propelled packet, *Severn*, Captain Brown, which runs on the same station. The accounts given by the two parties of the occurrence differ widely. The captain of the *Usk* states that he left Cumberland basin at 20 minutes past seven o'clock, a.m. It was a little hazy, but he could see both sides of the river, and vessels to a considerable distance. The *Lord Beresford,* Swansea packet, was ahead and the *Usk* in her wake. On getting to Sea Mills Reach he saw the flag of the *Severn,* which was coming up the river, over Sand Bed Point, and he imediately ported his helm, slowed his engines, stopped them, running the *Usk* close alongside of the rocky bank on the Gloucestershire side of the river. So close was she to the land that that a passenger was enabled to jump on shore. Seeing the *Severn* crossing the *Beresford's* bow at speed, and coming direct for his vessel, he called to the captain by name. " Slow your engines, or you'll be right into our vessel". The captain of the *Severn* seemed to take no notice, and the vessel came against the *Usk,* and carried her stanchions, netting, boat, and everything on the Larboard quarter clear to the bands. The *Severn* sustained injury, but not to so great an extent, and she sailed away without her commander appearing to take any notice of the occurrence.

The passengers were greatly alarmed, but no one was injured. In confirmation of this statement the captain has a written paper, exonerating him from blame, signed by twenty-three of the passengers. The account given on the other side is that the *Lord Beresford* and the *Usk* were racing abreast of each other, and that, there not being room for the *Severn* to pass, the collision was, as far as he was concerned, unavoidable. Until an investigation takes place, it is impossible to say which of the preceding statements is the more accurate.

South Wales Railway – A gentleman influentially connected with the Great Western company, has been to Newport this week, and made important communications in reference to the line proposed as a South Wales Railway in the published prospectus. He states that the Government have, through a leading personage, signified their approval of the line; that three thousand shares have already been applied for; and that, encouraged by these and other circumstances, the Company will lose no time in preparing for Parliament. The high professional character of the gentleman to whom we refer, is to guarantee for the truth of these representations.

———◇———

South Wales Railway

A numerous meeting of landed proprietors connected with Gloucestershire, Herefordshire, Monmouthshire and Shropshire, including deputations from the Gloucester and Berkeley Canal and the Gloucester Chamber of Commerce was held on Tuesday week, at Barratt's Hotel, Ross, to consider the question of a railway through South Wales. Mr. Blakemore M.P. for Wells, Sir Hungerford Hoskins, the Right Hon. Frankland Lewis, Mr. Sergeant Taddy, the Dean of Hereford, Mr. Vaughan, Sir Herbert Price, Mr. Clive M.P. and Mr. Bailey Jnr. M.P. were amongst those present. The deputations from Gloucester included Mr. Baker, Mr. Shipton, and Mr. Kimberley. To make the proceedings understood, it may be as well to mention, that a prospectus has been issued for some months, soliciting capitalists to take shares in a railway to run from a point of the Great Western Railway at Stonehouse (eight miles below Gloucester), crossing the Severn at Parton, and proceeding by the sea coast to Chepstow, Cardiff, Swansea &c. It is not disguised that this scheme is under the auspices of the Great Western Railway Company. The circumstances, however, of the scheme placing Gloucester, Ross, Hereford, Monmouth, the Forest of Dean and other populous towns, in an isolated position, has raised resistance to it. Monmouth last week rose up in arms against it, but Newport espoused it. Resolutions were passed pledging the meeting to oppose the Stonehouse scheme, and to support a line which should have Gloucester for its terminus, passing through, Ross, Monmouth, Newport, &c. with branch lines to Hereford and the Forest of Dean. One principal feature of interest at the meeting was the introduction by the Dean of Hereford, of the model of Kollman's patented railway improvements, for which he is desirous of contracting an independent line from Hereford *via* Ross – the model worked well, and was greatly admired. The Dean did not like to give up his independent scheme, and place it in jeopardy by sanctioning the principal of a great trunk line, running many miles from Hereford; he, therefore stipulated for a branch line, and so did the Gloucester people, as regarded the Forest of Dean. Mr. Blakemore who took the lead in the proceedings, seemed to regard their stipulations as a dead weight on the carrying out of the great trunk line. The resolution, however, was carried and a committee was appointed to correspond with the Great Western Railway Company, on the subject of of changing the Stonehouse line, so as to meet the views of the meeting – Another meeting was held at Tolsey, Gloucestershire, at which similar resolutions to those of the meeting at Ross were passed, a report of which was given in our last.

———◇———

2nd. October 1846.

South Dock – opened in 1859.

The Market – built in 1897.

Mumbles Village.

Mumbles Lighthouse.

Reduced Fares
FROM SWANSEA AND BRISTOL

The Fast Going
Steam Packets
LORD BERESFORD,
ROBERT DAVIS, Commander,
And
COUNTY OF PEMBROKE,
WILLIAM ROSE, Commander,

ARE intended to Sail as follows during the month of OCTOBER:–

Lord Beresford Tues and Fridays – County of Pem broke, Thurs and Saturdays.	*Lord Beresford Thurs and Sats – County of Pem broke Tues and Fridays.*
From Swansea	From Bristol
Oct. 1846 o'clock	o'clock
1 Thursday 3 morn.	3 morn.
31 Saturday 4 morn.	3 morn.

Fares: Best Cabin, 10s. Fore Cabin 5s. Children under twelve years of age, half fare; Horses, 17s.6d. Fat Cattle, 10s. Store ditto, 8s. Cow with Calf, 10s. Dogs, 2s.6d. Sheep, 1s. Lambs, 9d. Pigs, 1s. 6d. Fat Pigs, 1s. 9d. Gigs, 16s. Phaeton, 21s.6d. Carriages, 32s.6d.

Steward's Fees for Ladies and Gentlemen, 1s. each, Children and Servants, 6d.

Female Stewards attend the Ladies' Cabins.

Refreshments may be had on board at moderate charges.

Carriages and Horses shipped with the greatest care, – Horses and Carriages to be shipped two hours before sailing.

A COACH leaves the Mackworth Arms at eight o'clock every Morning, through Llanelly and Kidwelly for Carmarthen and returns the same day.

The LLANELLY MAIL COACH leaves the Mackworth Arms, Swansea, at half past one every afternoon, returning the following morning at a quarter past eleven.

PRICE's SPRING VAN leaves The Beaufort Arms, Swansea, every Wednesday and Saturday morning at eight o'clock, for Llandilo, Llangadock, Llandovery, Carmarthen

THOMAS's SPRING WAGGON meets the Packets for Goods to Neath, Aberavon &c.

From SWANSEA to ILFRACOMBE, and ILFRACOMBE to *SWANSEA.*

The LORD BERESFORD – Mondays
COUNTY OF PEMBROKE – Wednes.

Fashionable Dancing, Deportment and Calisthenic Exercises.

MR. SECOND, of His Majesty's Theatre, and many years patronised by the Nobility, respectfully informs the Gentry, Schools and Inhabitants of Swansea, Neath, Llanelly, and Carmarthen that he has arrived in Swansea, and intends giving Instruction in all the fashionable DANCES of the present time, and hopes, by strict attention to merit a share of public patronage, to maintain that flattering high position which he has hitherto held in the profession.

Mr. Second has taken the Assembly Rooms, Swansea, in which Mr. S. intends opening an ACADEMY, the ensuing Quarter.

Terms and particulars may be known at the Assembly Rooms.

Parties forming their own circle attended at either their own residence or at the Rooms Schools and Families attended any distance round Swansea.

Dr. Williams of this town has just published in the annual volume of Guy's Hospital Reports, an *Essay "on the Structure and Functions of the Liver".* The author states that he has traced this organ from the lowest animal up to man, with a view to obtain a complete history of its varieties and development. The Work is enriched by beautiful wood-cut illustrations, taken from original dissections, laboriously executed under the microscope by the author. Dr. Williams alludes to the facilities and advantages afforded by the neighbourhood of Swansea for the study of natural history and comparative anatomy. We understand that the work will be immediately translated into the German language.

The Theatre. – It will be seen from an advertisement in the *Cambrian* of this day, that a grand and extensive scientific entertainment takes place in Swansea on Monday and Tuesday nights. The immense Planetarium, which covers 200 feet, showing at one view the primary and secondary planets in actual motion round the sun, with an extensive panorama of the heavens, must have a splendid effect on ages from all parts of the house. Many years have elapsed since such a display of the Stellar universe was given in Swansea. The Ciomatrope and Chinese Fireworks are also to be exhibited, with upwards of fifty dissolving illustrations of many remarkable places in the world, amongst which will be found a view of Neath Abbey, situate in our immediate locality. We can assure our readers that this exhibition will be worthy of their attention. We have no doubt the house will be crowded. We understand the Planetarium is not equalled in Europe or America.

Accident. – On Saturday last, while a young seaman named John Griffin was in the act of passing through the entrance to our pig market, the heavy gate gave way, and fell on him, causing a serious fracture of the leg in two places. The poor fellow was promptly attended by Mr. W. H. Michael and is now progressing favourably. Blame is certainly attached to the party whose duty it was to inspect the state of the gate.

A Dangerous Nuisance. – Some weeks since we directed attention to the dangerous state of the road leading from Greenhill gate to the New Bridge, on the Landore road. We then blamed the Roads Board, but were subsequently informed that this portion of road came within the management of the Swansea Paving Commissioners. Be that as it may, the evil still remains unremedied, the road being covered with large holes, rendering it absolutely unsafe for vehicles to travel, while the thick mud accumulated renders the bridge almost impassable for pedestrians. In addition to this a portion of the parapet of the bridge has fallen, being quite on a level with the road, so that on a dark night, any man, child or horse is liable to walk over, and be precipitated to a depth of thirty or forty feet. It certainly reflects no credit on the authorities that so dangerous a nuisance should be suffered to exist for a single day, at the very entrance to a town of the magnitude of Swansea, and on a road traversed by thousands of people, many of whom, we are sorry to say, are frequently in a state of inebriety. We hope some member will bring the subject under the notice of the Paving Commissioners, at their next meeting, to be held on Wednesday next.

Coach Accident. – On Saturday se'nnight, while the Collegian was on its way from Aberystwith to Brecon, the fore axle broke on the road, about five miles from Lampeter, on the Llandovery side, and, we regret to state that Mrs. Williams, late of Gweryllan, near Brecon, was thrown off, and some of the luggage falling on her leg, fractured it very severely in two places. Her little girl was also slightly hurt on the arm; and the coach man was very much bruised. The other passengers, 14 in number wonderfully escaped without injury. Mrs. Williams was removed to the Black Lion Inn, Lampeter, where surgical aid was immediately obtained, and every possible attention was rendered. We are glad to state, that up to the latest account on Thursday, she was doing as well as could be expected.

——◇——

Vast shoals of pilchards, extending miles in length, were seen lately off the Pembrokeshire coast, by one of the pilot boats, and it seems they make their appearance every summer, but, as no one goes out to catch them, they pass on to our neighbours on the opposite side of the channel, where they have recently been taken in countless numbers.

——◇——

To the EDITOR of the CAMBRIAN.

Sir, – It may, perhaps, not be known to you, that on Monday night last, our native Brass Band called "Foresters," was prohibited playing in the streets by one of the Policemen, in accordance with the Inspector's order, but such is the fact. I know, Mr. Editor, you will feel it your duty to inform the public of this act of supererogation (as I believe it) of the Inspector, for there is a difficulty in coming to the conclusion that any man or body of men, possessing any taste, education, or influence in the town, would have been so careless of their reputation as to offend three-fourths of its inhabitants, by depriving them of music, so freely and gratuitously afforded them.

I should be proud to be able to say that this is the doing of an individual, and not of those in authority, for otherwise our neighbours, and the world indeed, will think us Savages. I can venture to assert that the above Band is a credit to the town of Swansea, and cannot be surpassed by *any of the kind* in the principality. It consists of young men of the town, was assisted at its formation (not two years ago) by Mr. Williams, and can now boast of some skilled in music above mediocrity: capable of great execution. It was engaged to play at the Bazaar at Clydach, where the principal ladies and gentlemen of this end of the county were congregated, and gave great satisfaction; so did it also at the Concert for the benefit of our Mechanics' Institution, where it played gratuitously.

Is it not strange that Foreigners and strangers find it worth their while to come to Swansea as street players while our own band is not allowed to contribute to the amusement of the inhabitants without any reward.

By inserting this in you next *Cambrian* you will oblige yours &c.
Swansea, October 1st, 1846.

(????)

——◇——

3rd. November 1848.

HARBOUR MASTER WANTED,

WANTED a Person competent to perform the duties of HARBOUR MASTER and GENERAL MANAGER of the HARBOUR of PORTHCAWL, in the county of Glamorgan – the salary is £100 per annum and security will be required. Applications, with testimonials enclosed must be addressed postage free to the Board of Directors of the Llynfi Valley Railway 440 West Strand. London.

——◇——

TO BE SOLD BY AUCTION,
At the Custom-House, Swansea, on
Monday, the 5th. of November 1848,
at twelve o'clock at noon.

THE FOLLOWING SEIZED GOODS:-
25Lbs SEGARS
2 Gallons of FRENCH WINE
W. Barker, Collector, T. S. Todd, Comptroller – Custom House Swansea

——◇——

South Wales Railway

Important Sale of Draught Horses, Harness &c.

Pembrokeshire.

Mr. W. Morse Allen

Begs respectfully to announce that he has been favoured with instructions from the Proprietor, Mr Samuel Garrat, contractor on the above line.

To Offer by Public Auction

At Robeston Watham, on Wednesday 8th. of November next.

Forty splendid Draught HORSES, and, BROOD MARES, of the English, Belgian and Prussian breeds, purchased regardless of expense. Also, two Galloways, steady in harness, one Entire Horse "Hercules" of immense power; Waggon and Cart Harness in prime condition, together with various other Articles.

Credit will be given subject
to conditions.
Sale to commence at 12 o'clock.
Narberth, October 23rd.1848.

——◇——

SWANSEA HARBOUR TRUST.

Notice is hereby given that a SPECIAL MEETING of the **Trustees of Swansea Harbour** will be held at the Council Chamber at the Guildhall of the Borough of Swansea, on Friday the 17th. day of November next at twelve o'clock at noon, when it will be proposed, and if considered advisable, resolved that the said Trustees shall make and convert into a WET DOCK the Bed of the river Tawe from the Point where the river Tawe is by the said Act of the 6th. and 7th. William 4th. – 126 – authorised to be diverted at or near the Pottery, and for that purpose to erect, contract and maintain a Lock or Gate across the Bed of the said River, at or near the Corporation Public

Quay in the Town of Swansea aforesaid; and to erect and maintain a Bridge over the said Wet Dock, also near the Corporation Public Quay aforesaid; and also to erect, make, and construct a Gate or Gates across the Bed of the said River Tawe, at a place opposite or near the Cambrian Hotel, on the Burrows in the Franchise of the Town of Swansea, so as to form a Half-tide Basin, to communicate with the said Wet Dock, together with such Docks, Wharfs, Warehouses, Quays, Buildings and other Works, as may be deemed necessary for the accommodation of Vessels resorting to and using the said Dock and Tide Basin.

Dated at Swansea, the 24th day of October 1848

S. PADLEY, Clerk.

LEWIS THOMAS, Solicitor to the Trustees.

——◇——

SWANSEA DOCKS

To the EDITOR of the CAMBRIAN.

Sir, – I wish to make a few observations on the attempt now making to prevent the formation of these Docks, for which the Act was obtained in June 1847 after a protracted struggle and considerable expense.

If the Dock Company find it difficult to raise the necessary funds owing to the present depreciation of such schemes in the eyes of the monied men of the day, how can it be expected that funds will be forthcoming for floating the Old River?

Mr. L. L. Dillwyn, in his evidence before the Committee of the House of Commons, in May 1847, stated "that the Act by which the Trustees were empowered to make a Flood in the River, was obtained in 1836, and in 1844, was renewed, and again expired in January, 1847. He did not think the Harbour Trustees were in a position to contract a Flood – indeed they had no means of carrying out such a project, as they frequently tried to borrow money without success. He had always been of the opinion that flooding the river would operate most injuriously on the interests of the port, and after describing, and of course objecting to Mr. Starling Benson's rival scheme of Eastern Docks, he was candid enough to allow that not withstanding the disadvantages, that scheme laboured under, Eastern Docks were less objectionable than a Flood in the river.

Mr. T. B. Essery, in his evidence corroborated Mr. Dillwyn as to the inability of the Harbour Trustees to raise money, "they had advertised for money, but did not succeed in raising any."

Mr. Starling Benson on the same occasion, gave evidence that "the estimate in 1836 for the gates &c. for the purpose of floating the Town Reach was 30,000*l*." and further "that the credit of the Trustees was in a bad state, because a portion of the Trustees were very fond of running down their own credit; and in fact after repeated advertisements in the *Cambrian*, they had the offer of 100L. only."

If the Dock Company are only anxious to save the 4850*l*. 13s. 6d. (which it appears from their balance sheet, exhibited at their meeting, is all they have expended), surely they will be disappointed; for how is it possible the Trustees of the Harbour could give a *valid* bond for that amount without special powers conferred by a new Act. Is there a reasonable prospect of the legislation sanctioning such a scheme? Would the present bond holders tamely submit? Surely the Court of Chancery, by injunction or the Queen's Bench by mandamus, would interfere to prevent. But supposing the Western Dock Company simply forego their scheme in favour of the Harbour Trustees, without asking for their 4850*l*., and suppose the the old bondholders do not interpose, does any reasonable man believe that the necessary funds for floating the Town Reach will be raised?

Perhaps, after all, the present agitation is only got up as a prelude to the Company winding up its concerns by a sort of friendly Fiat in Bankruptcy.

As "Looker On," a correspondent in last week's *Cambrian*, puts it, between the two stools. Floating accommodation will fall to the ground, and the wants of the merchants and traders of Swansea will be as little likely to be provided for as they ever were.

Yours &c. Observer.

31st. October, 1848.

Diet and Cholera, or the Board of Health *versus* Vegetables. – The gentlemen costituting the Board of Health have, by some very unaccountable process, arrived at a conclusion, opposed both to the teaching of science and to the authority of testimony: they have in the otherwise masterly document published lately in the *London Gazette* put a veto on vegetables as articles of food leaving it to inference that the obedience to the injunction "thou shalt eat the herb of the field" cannot be complied with, saving on the condition of the contingency of an attack of cholera. We are quite at a loss to understand the principle of this prohibition. Those who have sent this dogma abroad ought to back such mandate with *reason*. The laxative tendency of vegetables is no reason against the usual mode of using such food; for independent of that mode being found by constant experience to be beneficial, an acknowledged therapeutic principle is conformed to in the adaptation of the principle; namely, *"similia similibus curantur"* – the like cures the like; and more strongly, the like prevents (by forestalling) the like. We repeat, experience and science negative the soundness of prohibition. Our remarks last week on this subject gave a clue to the scientific bearing of the question; we shall now append the opinions of some of the most eminent medical men of our country, on the use of vegetables. These opinions were delivered at the time of the former visitation of cholera, and Dr. Paris, President of the College of Physicians, now fully coincides with the views of these gentlemen:–

"The first great object," says Dr. Paris "appears to me to sustain by every practicable means, the highest possible standard of health; and to accomplish this object it has been recommended by authority that the quantity of vegetable food should be diminished or withdrawn. *The probable consequence would be to substitute a less healthy diet* than persons have been accustomed to, and *to prepare the way for* the incursion of *disease*. I think a hint of this kind would be highly salutary. The fallacy is so mischievous that the public mind should be disabused without delay."

"I consider good ripe fruit, and sound cooked vegetables, eaten at the proper season, and in moderate quantity not only not likely to originate cholera, but jointly with animal food, absolutely necessary to maintain individual, and consequently, public health." David Barry, M.D. . . .

Assembly-Rooms, Swansea.

For a Short Time Only

WILL OPEN on Monday next Nov. 6th. 1848, the original Models of Ancient and Modern

JERUSALEM,

patronised by the Clergy of every denomination, and already visited by a Million of persons, and 1000 Clergy.
Doors open at one o'clock;
Descriptive Lectures at two and four.
Doors open in the Evening at seven.
Lectures at eight o'clock.
Prices of Admission –
Morning, 1s.6d.
in the Evening, 1s.
Children, Half – price.

N.B. Boarding Schools on moderate terms, and Sunday-Schools on a more nominal charge, on application being made by the Head of the Establishment.

These models have been attended in Clifton by more than 50,000 Persons, and upwards of 20,000 Children of the different Schools, accompanied by their Ministers, have visited this instructive and interesting Exhibition.

"Where Ignorance is Bliss." &c. – A couple very well known in Paris are at present arranging terms of separation, to avoid the scandal of a judicial divorce. A friend had been employed by the husband to negotiate the matter. The latest mission was in reference to a valuable ring, given to the husband by one of the Sovereigns of Europe, and which he wished to retain. For this he would make a much desired concession. The friend made the demand. "What!" said the indignant wife, "do you venture to charge yourself with such a mission to me! Can you believe that I can tear myself from a gift which alone recalls to me the days when my husband loved me! No, this ring is my souvenir of happiness departed." "Tis all – (and here she wept) – that I now possess of a once fond husband." The friend insisted – the lady supplicated – grew obstinate – grew desperate – threatened to submit to a public divorce as a lesser evil than parting with this cherished ring, and at last confessed that – she had sold it six months before!

Wreck at the Mumbles. – On Thursday se'nnight the *Eagle* of and for Aberystwith from Porthcawl, after running out of the Mumbles struck a rock near the Mumbles Head and immediately went down. The crew fortunately were saved. It is expected she will become a complete wreck.

. . . "that the main (Swansea) sewers and street drains are greatly out of repair, insufficient in number and use; have been constructed without regard to a general system of sewerage, and are wholly inadequate for sanitary purposes."

6th. December 1850.

Loss of another Emigrant Ship. – On the same night that the *Edmond* so fatally suffered wreck in Kilkee-bay, another ship laden with migrants, bound for New Orleans, was totally lost on the Black water bank, along with three other vessesls laden with cargoes of the value of 35,000*l.* The emigrant ship was an American, named the *Adeline*, last from Liverpool, with it is said 500 passengers. She struck on the south end of the shoal. Her signals of distress were perceived by the coastguard, who with the inhabitants immediately put off in their boats to the wreck, and, by extraordinary exertions, they succeeded in saving every soul. The ship, however, went to pieces.

NEW DECIMAL PALM CANDLES.
2d. *per lb.* 10 *to the lb.*

THESE CANDLES, though ugly, burn well, and without guttering. They are admirably adapted for all who require a great light. For Artisans, Turners in metal, Sempstresses, Tailors, Shoemakers, for the windows of small shops, and for persons of weak sight, where the light is of primary and appearance of secondary importance, these candles are incomparable; in short one Decimal Palm Candle gives the light of three ordinary Candles, and does not require snuffing.

Sold by Grocers, Candle Dealers, and Oilmen, and Wholesale by PALMER and Co. (the Patentees), Sutton-street, Clerkenwell, London.

TWO HUNDRED POUNDS REWARD,
as below

MY Fellow-Sufferers – I sympathise with you, under your Nervous or Mental Affliction. But having discovered the means of cure myself of a deep-rooted Nervous Complaint of fourteen years' duration, I take this method of informing you that I am (D.V.) both able and willing to cure your Nervous Suffering; – especially

Depression of Spirits, – This is one of the most distressing symptoms. It prevents riches, learning, society, &c. making man or woman cheerful. It is the chief cause of suicides.

Involuntary Blushing, – This keeps the Nervous out of Society, or renders them uncomfortable in it.

Sleeplessness. – This treatment never fails to restore sound sleep.

Restlessness. – This prevents the sufferer from settling to anything, or finding contentment or satisfaction anywhere.

A dislike of Society; Unfitness for Business or Study; Failure of the Memory; Confusion of Thought; Giddiness; Delusions; Blood to the Head; Groundless Fears; Indecision; Hysterics; Wretchedness; Blasphemous Thoughts; Thoughts of Self Destruction; Fear of Insanity, &c. &c.

For these and other Nervous or Mental Sufferings and Insanity, no other CURE is known. I challenge the Nation to produce any other. And I offer a REWARD of ONE HUNDRED POUNDS to remove these Mental or Nervous Afflictions, by any other means. And another HUNDRED POUNDS, to cure as many (50) of Insanity in the same time as I have. These Cures have not been effected by Pills, Powders, Draughts, Bleeding, &c., nor can any such means cure diseases of the mind. No, my great Discoveries consist in means that act on the nerves, and enable me to restore the brain to perfect health, which is the organ on which the correct working of the thoughts and feelings depend. Having for thirty years been successful in the cure of these Complaints, it is no matter of surprise that thousands have applied to me from all parts of England, Ireland, Scotland, France, America, the Indies, &c. And no wonder, as of nearly 20,000 applicants, 50 are not known uncured who have strictly used these rules. Indeed, the the time has arrived when the feeling is general that no other means of care are known; and that all who cannot avail themselves of the EXTRA MEANS at my house, or the ordinary means at their own, may give up all hope of a cure. I therefore advise Nervous Sufferers and Friends of the insane, to come or write. Thirty years' successful practice, leaves no doubt but they can but be cured, unless malformation prevents, and this is a rare case. Let none, therefore, be discouraged by the idea of expense, as benevolence rather than gain is my motto.

WM. WILLIS MOSELEY,
A.M.L.L.D., &c.
18, Bloomsbury-street, Bedford Square, London

P.S. If you will send me the particulars of your case, I will tell you if I can cure you. And if you enclose a Stamp, I will send you Free my PAMPHLET (26,000th.), which will give you all the information you require on your Case, Means of Cure, Terms, &c. EXTRA MEANS and Accommodation here, when required.

For SAN FRANCISCO, California,
Direct.
THE FINE SHIP "ALCESTE,"
Capt. J. D. Cann,
550 Tons Register, A 1 at Lloyds, and Coppered, has room for Two or Three Cabin Passengers, on moderate terms.

For particulars apply to THOMAS WALTERS, Jun.
Ship and Commission Agent.
27 Wind-street, Swansea.
December 5th. 1850.

THE CAMBRIAN.

Swansea, Friday, Dec. 6, 1850.

South Wales Railway.

An account of Business for the week ending December 1st, 1850.

	£	s.	d.
Passengers	534	5	5
Parcels	23	19	7
Goods	114	10	2
Total, exclusive of Mails	572	15	2

Taff Vale Railway

Traffic Account for the Week ending Nov. 30th. 1850:–

Total	£2101	13	10

Gipsey George Again. – This notorious vagrant was again brought up, although his Worship only discharged him on Wednesday morning, and gave him a shilling in his pocket. It appeared he went as far as Loughor, and there entered the Bush Inn, and demanded ale and food. Out of charity this was supplied him liberally. He was however, not satisfied with what he received. After enjoying a good meal, he commenced a furious attack on Mr. Thomas's windows, and broke several panes, and afterwards threatened to demolish every window in the ancient borough of Loughor. The landlord, at last, succeeded in arresting him, and anxious to have him secured, paid 14s. to bring him to Swansea. Remanded to Saturday.

NEWPORT.

The Western Valley Line of Railway was inspected on Tuesday last and will be opened for passenger traffic on Monday next.

John Williams, landlord of the Green Meadow beerhouse, Newbridge, was charged by Superintendent Thomas with keeping his house open during divine service in the afternoon of Sunday the 17th. instant. Defendant admitted the charge and was fined one shilling and costs.

MERTHYR

The Early Closing Movement. – We are happy in being enabled to state that the drapers here, without exception, agreed to a petition of their assistants respecting early closing and have consented to close their shops at seven o'clock Tuesday, Wednesday, Thursday, and Friday; nine o'clock Monday, and eleven o'clock Saturday evening. We were not prepared for the exhibition of such good feeling existing between the drapers; in fact we must confess to our being pleasantly disappointed. Of course, no objection can be raised by the other tradesmen to adopting the same course immediately for such a good plan is deserving of being carried out generally.

Sanatory. – The Committee appointed by the Board of Health met at the Vestry on Monday, when it was finally decided that 100 public gas lamps should be erected in and around Merthyr.

Dowlais. – The Exhibition of 1851. – Sir John Guest has shown an example well worthy of imitation. He has seen that amongst his workmen there are many eager to go to the Exhibition of 1851, but, in consequence of the lowness of their wages, compelled to refrain from ever hoping to feast their eye on the wonder which the genius of the world will next year spread before a million admirers; he has therefore formed a club (to which he has very handsomely presented 50*l*) and all his workmen who are desirous of visiting the Exhibition will have to pay into it 6d. or a shilling a week until May next to enable them to defray the expenses of their visit. The deficiency will be made up, we believe, by subscriptions amongst the generous-minded of Dowlais. After this, no one can accuse Sir John Guest of "self interest being at the bottom of every deed". This of itself evinces his desire for the mind's improvement of his men, and is an act of charity and goodness which we hope to see repayed by the better attention of the men to the interests of their employer. The evil of strikes, so well demonstrated in many a lecture, will never be repeated if such worthy examples be followed. Let the men but know by deeds of the like nature, that the master considers them as something higher than mere serfs and tools to construct their own greatness, and we prophecy an almost utter extinction of strikes, for the men will rely with confidence upon the justice of their employers.

Preaching in the Streets. – *William Carlett* a poor emaciated looking personage with huge moustache whose face was "sicklied o'er with the pale cast of thought". and whose worn out scanty clothing indicated too clearly that he had borne fortune's buffets, but had received few of her rewards – was brought up by P.C. Thomas Jones, for preaching in Fisher street thereby obstructing the thoroughfare by collecting a crowd of people. The Inspector stated that he had warned him on the subject once before.– Mr. T. Edward Thomas, to the defendant: What have you to say to this charge? This is an offence that cannot be alloyed. Defendant, with all the solemnity of a puritan: I must say I was preaching according to the word of the Lord, for – Mr. Thomas My good man we don't want any preaching here. You must not collect a crowd of persons in the public street, and annoy the inhabitants. Defendant interrupting – I have not annoyed any of the inhabitants of this town possessed of Christian feeling. – Mr. Attwood: What are you by trade? Defendant – I am a baker by trade. – What are you doing here? Defendant: I must say I am here on a little business, and it will take me about three days to complete it. – I preach the gospel, for I am not happy in my mind, only when I am preaching. – Mr. Thomas: Will you promise not to repeat this offence, if you are now discharged? Defendant with much gravity – With God's blessing, I will endeavour to preach the Gospel in all towns and cities – Defendant being inexorable on this point, he was sent back to his cell to meditate on his position until next morning.

On Sunday last the town of Llandovery was inundated by the rivers Bowddwr and Brane, which had risen to such a height that had not been witnessed for the past sixty years. With but few exceptions in the highest parts of the town, the water covered the ground floors of the houses, and in some places several feet deep. Strong and powerful currents poured down along the streets, on which the coracles were passing to and fro. Divine Worship was only attempted in the parish Church and in one chapel, where the congregation amounted to 9 and 15 individuals, they had either to be conveyed home by carriages or on horseback.

To the EDITOR of The CAMBRIAN.
Maesteg House, 5th. December 1850
Sir, – Having been appointed to preside at the meeting held at the Assembly Rooms, on Monday, and the Committee on Tuesday, from which the Address to the Queen, now in course of signature, emanated, I must be allowed to intrude on your columns with a few remarks.

I was voted to the Chair, though the Mayor and the Vicar were both present, either of whom were better qualified to fill it, in order to take from the meeting any appearance of party spirit and to remove any cause of cavil. It had first been intended that the Meeting on Monday should have been preliminary to a General Meeting; but, as the community of Swansea had pronounced, in a public meeting, legally convened, and presided over by the Chief Magistrate, against any approach to the Throne on the present occasion, we deemed it our duty to bow to the decision of the majority, however unfortunate and mistaken we might deem such decision to be. We might still have held an open meeting of persons favourable to an address to the Queen, in reprobation of the Papal aggression; and though we had no fear that sufficient arguments would not have been adduced in support of our views, we were unwilling to take a step which while it would have only permitted a one-sided expression of opinion might have disturbed the public peace, and aroused feelings calculated to widen rather than heal any breach lately created. It was therefore deemed more advisible to empower a committee consisting of five Clergymen, five Dissenting Ministers and five Laymen to prepare an address to the Queen, to be signed by all who approved of it, and which will be regarded as the individual act only of such inhabitants of Swansea and its neighbourhood who have affixed their signatures to it. I believe, in taking this course, we have acted costitutionally, and for the best interests of the community.

When I look at the character of the meeting on Monday, and especially to the names and station of the Dissenting Ministers who have united with us on this occasion, I am confident that, though in a minority, we are fully entitled from the influence and character of those it, to give this public expression of our feelings on the question which has roused England, almost as one man, in defence of our common Protestantism. As a statement has been made of "great diversity of opinion" having existed amongst us, I beg to state, that in my experience, I have seldom presided over any meeting, and especially one comprising such various shades of creed and profession, at which there was less.

I am, Sir, your faithful servant,
P. St. L. Grenfell.

Swansea Bay.

TO BE LET

And may be entered upon immediately

A Very desirable FAMILY RESIDENCE, called "THE RHYDDINGS," consisting of breakfast, dining and drawing-rooms, six good bed-rooms and dressing room, manservant's room, kitchen, scullery, dairy, water-closet, Pantries and an excellent Walled Garden, commanding a fine view of the Bay, and distant about a mile from the town of Swansea.

Also about Thirty Acres of MEADOW LAND, adjoining the above, which may be had together with it or separately.

For further particulars and to treat, apply to Messrs. Jeffreys and Gaskoln, Solicitors, Swansea.

——◇——

SOUTH WALES RAILWAY

Reduction of Charges on Merchandise and Cattle Rates.

ON and after the 2d. December, a REDUCTION will be made in the TONNAGE and CATTLE RATES between all Stations on the South Wales Railway, – particulars of which can be obtained at the various Stations on the Line.

FREDERICK CLARKE,
Superintendent.

——◇——

2nd. April 1852.

WELSH INTELLIGENCE

CARMARTHENSHIRE

The other day a Woodcock flew into a cottage, called "Goose Hill." and perched upon the shelf; but upon the landlady, Mrs. Davies, getting up to secure the prize, by shutting the door, the strange visitor took his flight. The occurrence has caused no small degree of excitement among the old women of Pendine, as it is looked upon as ominous of something "wonderful" which will shortly occur at Pendine, more especially as Mr. Longbeak should "take it into his head" to visit a cottage which is known by a name appertaining to the feathered tribe "Goose" Hill.

PEMBROKESHIRE

Pembroke Yard.—The works on the *Windsor Castle,* first rate, are progressing with considerable speed. It may be remembered that this is the line of battleship that was lengthened thirty feet amidships That space is now so filled up with its *joins* can scacely be detected, and the stern alterations are fast completing. It is intended to launch her this summer, so that the experiment of adapting her for the auxiliary screw may at once be tested for which purpose almost all the shipwrights of the establishment are engaged upon her. A drawing of the boat, which has made such a stir, has been called for, and furnished to, the Admirality. The establishment altogether is in a state of great activity. The contemplated removals and superannuations have been suspended; and under the effective superintendence of Captain Sir Thomas Pasley, Bart., everything goes on in the most efficient manner.

CARDIGANSHIRE.

The harbour dues were let by auction on the 18th. inst., to Mr. William Lewis, of Swansea for 1,600*l.*, he having produced the required surities.

Caution to illicit Malt Makers. – On the 19th. ult., Messrs Monk and Stephens, two of the officers of the Inland Revenue, stationed in Cardigan obtained intelligence which induced them to keep a sharp watch upon the movements of a woman named Ann Llewellyn, residing at Llynvelin, Cardigan, and in the course of the day Mr. Monk, finding her house, in a stealthily manner followed her in, and surprised her in the act of turning over some grain then in preparation for malt; Mr. Monk at once took her into custody and sieved the malt. On Saturday, Ann Llewellyn was brought before the Mayor, Thomas Edwards, Esq., and proof of the facts being given, the defendant was fined the mitigated penalty of 30*l.*. The money not being paid, the prisoner was committed for three months.

——◇——

Screw Steamers at Liverpool. – The rapidity with which screw steamers trading with foreign parts increase at Liverpool is truly astonishing. On Saturday no less than three large and powerful screws sailed from the Mersey, namely the *Pelican,* for Rotterdam, the *Arabian,* for Constantinople, and the ——- for Messina. Two also arrived, viz., the *Orenitce* from Alexandria and the *Astrologer,* from Constantinople. Mostly all the screw steamers sailing from Liverpool for foreign parts are well freighted, and must be bringing a fair return for the capital which the owners have embarked therein.

——◇——

John Pemberton, the driver of the train on the South Coast Railway which met with a collision near the bridge over the Arun, some time since by which Martin the Stoker was killed, has been tried at Lewes Assize for the manslaughter. The accused did not obey the signals to stop at the bridge over the Arun, where there is only a single line of rails: after the collision he cut his throat, and jumped into the river, endeavouring to kill himself. On behalf of the prisoner, it was argued that, having through unforeseen necessity, a fresh fireman on the night in question, he was compelled to look after him to see that the steam was properly kept up, and having looked at the fire just before he arrived at the spot in question, the glare of it dazzled his eyes, and prevented him from seeing the signal. The jury returned a verdict of "Not Guilty."

Conviction for Murder – At Kingston Assize, John Keene, aged 20, and Jane Keene, aged 25, man and wife were indicted for the murder of the latter's illegitimate child, aged 3 years, by casting it into a well. It was proved that the man threw the child down the well, when nearly all the bones of the unhappy infant were fractured. Its remains were not removed for twelve months after the murder. The verdict was "guilty" against the man; the woman was acquitted. He was sentenced to death without hope of mercy; and the miserable wretch heard the sentence passed upon him without betraying the least emotion, and walked carelessly away from the dock.

Execution of Anthony Turner – *Derby, Friday,* This morning Anthony Turner underwent the extreme penalty of the law in front of the county gaol, for the murder of Mrs. Barnes of Belper. Turner never denied having committed the deed, consequently the usual "confession" was not necessary. He expressed his deep regret to the chaplain at having perpetrated the awful crime which doomed him to the gallows, and said he was astonished that he should have been betrayed into the comission of such an act. On being questioned as to what had become of the knife, he replied that he had put it into the fire at the house of a friend. On Sunday last the condemned sermon was preached by the chaplain from 1st. Timothy, chap 5. Turner paid great attention to the discourse. On Monday, his wife, his brother's wife, and her child, for whom the unhappy man formed so strong an affection took a last farewell of him. The scene was a most painful one. The chaplain read the burial service and Turner seemed for a few moments engaged in prayer. After taking a farewell of those on the scaffold, Colcraft, the executioner, drew the rap over his head, adjusted the rope, the fatal bolt was drawn, and the unhappy wretch was launched into eternity. There was no manifestaion of feeling on the part of the spectators, who quietly dispersed after the body had been cut down.

Coals Superseded. – *Polytechnic Institution.* – On Saturday the 20th. inst. some very curious experiments were made at this establishment in the presence of several scientific gentlemen to test the results of a recent invention of Dr. Bachhoffner, for which patents have been obtained by the inventor and Mr. N. Defries. The invention consists in the substitution of thin pieces of metal in the place of coals in fire grates, which being acted upon by a small jet of gas immediately become red hot, and emit a prodigious degree of heat. The flame which is produced by the proper but very simple management of the gas, cooperating with the metal laminae, give the appearance of a brisk and cheerful coal fire, and can scarcely be distinguished from it.

The heat can be regulated by turning the cock of the gas-tube. There is no deposit of soot, no smoke, nor any of the annoyances which attend coal fires, and the gas can be extinguished *instantly* or the fire kept as low as may be convenient. It will be seen that this useful invention is of general interest, and not only as affects private houses, but as affects breweries, manufacturies, and all places where large fires are required, and by its adoption the use of enormous chimnies might be dispensed with, as no smoke is generated. The expense with the gas now used for lighting, would render a fire on this new principle about the same expense as if coals were employed, but were what is termed non-carbonized gas employed, a great diminution of expense would be obtained. This invention is of public importance, and is well worth the attention of the public.

Use of Photography – One of the most useful applications of photography is that recently brought into operation for copying or taking photographs of machinery. By means of a camera-obscura and a few sheets of prepared paper, copies of the most elaborate mechanisms, from a watch to a weaving-room, can be obtained in a few minutes; possessing the advantage of being perfectly correct in regard to the relative size of the parts, and from which it is easy to calculate their proper dimensions. Civil engineers and mechanics will find it of infinite service.

Correspondence

The Free Trade Meeting.

To the *EDITOR of the CAMBRIAN.*

Sir, – Having no little interest in the welfare of my native town and county, I cannot forbear making a few remarks on the proceedings at the meeting which was held on Monday evening, to consider the propriety of petitioning Parliament in favour of free trade. I did not consider it right to do so at the meeting (where I was present), because it might have interfered with the general amusement, as well as because I do not pretend to any knowledge of a subject which has so long occupied and continued to engage the best, although divided attention of our greatest statesmen. What "Free Trade" may be did not appear to be very satisfactorily explained by any of the speakers at the meeting. One of them indeed, whose statistical array, was not the least entertaining part of the proceedings, stated that though he was a Free Trader "to the back bone", he did not quite approve of the part of it which induced the gentry of the town and neighbourhood to buy all their shop goods in London and elsewhere instead of at Swansea. But whether it is "Free Trade," or whether the recent and present prosperity of the country at large is to be attributed to "Free Trade," or to other causes such as the disturbed state of the rest of Europe during the last five years, Californian and Australian gold, or the continual and rapid improvement in the arts and sciences – it is beyond my province to say or conjecture. It seems to me that the enigma has yet to be solved. One thing, however, is certain, that truth, although deep hidden and long concealed, *must,* sooner or later, be brought to light, and

"Quinquid sub terra est, in apricum
proferet artos
Defodiet condet qur notentia."

However, another matter, which more intimately affects the welfare of this town and county, was brought forward at the meeting. My particular object in troubling you with this letter is to advert briefly to it. It is the representation of the county in Parliament. Now, it cannot be forgotten that, in the severe contest which took place between the manufacturing and landed interests in 1837, the latter was successful. Although on that occasion our respected Lord Lieutenant and many other landowners aided the weaker party. It is now understood (and I believe with good reason) that those landowners would not renew their former alliance with the manufacturers, and to these may be added the numerous and influential body of shipowners and others interested in commercial navigation. Under these circumstances, then, a renewal of the contest is, I cannot help strongly feeling, much to be deprecated, for many reasons. This feeling is, of course, most disinterested on my part; but I have had some experience of such matters during my professional career, and I know their injurious consequences in a social point of view. Such a contest in this county would also, if I am rightly informed of the name of an expected candidate, and of the declared intentions of several supporters of the present Government, in all probability cause a disturbance of our reformed representative's seat in tis borough – a state of things which no one of his numerous friends and supporters would regret more than myself.

Apologising for thus occupying so much of your valuable paper.

I am, sir, your obedient servant,
J. GWYN JEFFERYS.
Swansea 30th. March 1852.

Scenery of the Neath Valley.

To Excursionists and Tourists.

Directors of the Vale of Neath Railway have provided COVERED FIRST-CLASS and OPEN EXCURSION CARRIAGES, specially adapted for viewing the justly renowned scenery of the Valley and its tributaries. Parties-taking not less than 12 tickets may have an excursion carriage attached to either of the Ordinary Trains, or a Special Engine can be obtained upon giving due notice to the undersigned, or to Mr. Clarke, South Wales Railway, Swansea; from either of whom the terms of hire may be known.

Principal waterfalls in the valley are –

"MELINCOURT,"

"SGWD EINION GAM,"

"SGWD GWLADYS,"

"UPPER" and "LOWER" "CILNEPUTE,"

"UPPER" "MIDDLE" and "LOWER" "GLYN GWYN,"

The first of these may be reached by the Ordinary Trains from Neath Station, the remainder together with the far famed "Porth-yr-Ogof Cave," the "Dinas Rock," and the "Bws Maen," from the Glyn-Neath Station; but special trains may be stopped at the option of passengers.

By Order,
JOSHUA WILLIAMS

31st. March 1852.

A book to the Scenery of the Valley is now in active preparation.

A Flat Between Two Sharps. – On Saturday, information was received that Mr. Collagon of Weymouth, while proceeding to take the train at the South Western Railway, was accosted by two men, who pretended they could not read, and having just picked up a parcel that contained a paper, they would be obliged if he would read it for them. Mr. Collagon consented and read an invoice receipted and made out for articles of jewellery to the amount of 150l. The fellows appeared pleased at what they called their good fortune, and invited him into Gould's coffee house, Waterloo-road, and displayed what appeared to be a quantity of chains, ear-rings &c, which they had just found. No doubt a large reward would be offered; they were going to emigrate; and, if Mr. Collagon liked they would sell him their chance. After some huckstering, he consented and gave them 20*l.* in notes of the Blanford and Weymouth bank. On proceeding to a jeweller's he found, to his dismay that the articles were only metalic gold.

English and Yankee Yacht-builders. – We understand that Mr. Mars of Blackwall, has invited the commodore of the New York Yankee Club, or any gentleman in America, to compete with a vessel which he will construct, in a contest similar to that in which the *America* was successful last year, to come off, at Cowes in next August or September; the conditions to be referred to umpires chosen by the respective parties. Mr. Mars stakes 1000*l* on the result. The American yachtsmen must be aware that the *America*, built almost entirely for speed, came to England to contend with yachts already constructed to combine as much speed as would be consistent with comfort – hitherto a *sine que non* in British yachts; and Mr. Mars in the same spirit of courtesy and generous rivalry as characterised the proceedings at Cowes on the late occasion, invited the Americans to the trial; and although Mr. Mars by no means presumes that the British yacht will be successful, yet he ventures to think a better test of the respective vessels will be obtained when they are both built for the same purpose.– *United Service Gazette.*

SWANSEA.

TO BE LET,

with Immediate Possession.

FYNONE HOUSE and GROUNDS, a very desirable Residence, delightfully situated on a rising ground, within a quarter of a mile west of Swansea, commanding extensive views of the Bay and Bristol Channel. It consists of a breakfast-room, library, dining-room, drawing-room, opening to a Vinery and Conservatory, china pantry, butler's pantry, kitchen, scullery, wash-house, and dairy; five bed-rooms, two dressing-rooms, and two servants' bedrooms, four-stall Stable, Coach-house, and Cow-house; very spacious and productive Fruit and Kitchen Gardens, with Forcing Pits for melons, cucumbers &c. A good supply of Spring Water on all the premises. Pasture Land may be had, if required.

Apply to Mr. James Walters, Merchant, at his Office, Wind-street, Swansea.

Melancholy Accident. – A dreadful accident took place at Ravenstonedale corn mill, on Thursday morning, by which Mr. Anthony Dawson, the celebrated wrestler, met with an untimely death. He was at the mill early in the morning, and was placing the belt upon one of the wheels, when he was caught by the axle of one of the wheels and wound up by his clothes, and crushed in most terribly. His body thus entangled stopped all the power and machinery of the mill, and he was held in that painful position upwards of four hours before he was released. He was quite alone at the time. His watch which was in his pocket at the time, was stopped by the crush at 55 minutes past three. He was not taken out until after eight o'clock, at which time the accident was discovered. Two surgeons were immediately in attendance, but could render him no assistance, and he only lingered until one o'clock, when death put an end to his sufferings. Deceased was in the 25th. year of his age, and has left a widow and daughter to lament his loss.

TO BE LET,

at MICHAELMAS Next,

A Desirable FARM, of about 55 Acres, pleasantly situated overlooking Swansea Bay, three miles west of the town. The land is in good cultivation – the house and outbuildings nearly new. The unexpired lease of the above may be had for 3,10 or 17 years.

Address (post-paid) to A.B. Post Office, Sketty, near Swansea.

BUSTIN'S CONCERT-ROOM,
OXFORD-STREET, SWANSEA.

MR. BUSTIN most respectfully begs leave to inform the Gentry and Inhabitants of Swansea and its Vicinity generally, that he has, at great expence made several important additions to his Company, viz:–
MR. AND MRS. HENRY PRESCOTT.
(*Of the Principal London and Provincial Theatres*). For
SHAKESPERIAN and DRAMATIC READINGS, assisted by
MR. AND MRS. C. R. DAY,
(Late of the Theatre Royal, Manchester).
Mr. Bustin begs further to state, that he intends introducing to public notice, a SERIES of ENTERTAINMENTS far superior to anything previously attempted in this town, which, he trusts, will not only prove alike amusing and instructive to all, but be found worthy that patronage and support it is his anxious study to deserve.

Stage Director .... Mr. H. Prescott.
Ballet Master .... Mr. C.R. Gay.
Pianist .... Mr. Palmer.
Musical Conductor .... Mr. Leggett.

N.B. In addition to the above artistes, a CONCERT COMPANY is Engaged, selected from the Principal Theatres and Concert-Rooms in the Kingdom.

A CHANGE OF PERFORMANCE EVERY EVENING.

For Sale by Private Contract.

THE A 1 British-built Barque CUBA, of Swansea, 381 Tons Register, coppered and copper-fastened fitted up with Trunk and Platform, &c. expressly for the Copper Ore Trade, now lying at Swansea. She was built for the present owners, under inspection, at Sunderland, in the year 1844, and is classed at Lloyd's for 10 years; fully provided with Stores of every description, and ready for immediate employment. For inventories and further particulars, apply to Mr. T. A. Marten, or Mr. Wm. Jenkins, Ship Agent, Swansea 23rd. March 1852.

TO ENGINEERS AND IRON SHIPBUILDERS.

THE TRUSTEES for SWANSEA HARBOUR are prepared to receive

Tenders for an Iron Dredging-Machine,

agreeable to Drawings and Specifications, which may be seen by applying to the Engineer's Ofice, Quay Parade. The Engine Boiler and part of the Bevel Gearing of a former Machine, will be used in the construction, and the Contractor will have to take the remainder of the old Machinery at a valuation to be given in with his Tender.

Specification and further particulars may be had by applying to George Abernethy, Resident Engineer for the Float.

Sealed Tenders to be given in, addressed to the Trustees, on or before the 8th. of April.

The lowest Tender may not be accepted.

Quay Parade, Swansea,
March 18, 1852.

5th. May 1854.

NEW YORK Direct,

THE A.1. American Clipper BARQUE "JENETT" has spacious accommodation for Second-cabin and Steerage Passengers, and will leave Port Talbot on or about 12th. May, for New York direct.

Apply, for particulars, to David Jenkins, Ship-broker, Port Talbot.

ELECTRIC POWER LIGHT and COLOUR COMPANY, – The Electric Colour Company are ready to supply any of their DRY ELECTRIC COLOURS, which for brilliancy, durability, body, purity, and price have no equals in the market. For particulars &c., application must be made to the Commercial Manager, William Prosser, Esq. at the Works Frogmore-lane, Wandsworth, London.

Agent, Mr. H. A. FORD, Swansea.

PHOTOGRAPHY,

B. R. HENNESSY,
Optician, &c.,
No. 5, Wind-street, SWANSEA,

HAS the honour of informing the Nobility and Gentry of Swansea, and Town adjacent, that he has just concluded an advantageous engagement with a Paris Manufacturer for the supply of Cameras, Lenses, and every article required in PHOTOGRAPHY, detailed catalogues of which will shortly be ready.

Tripod Stands, of superior construction.
An extensive assortment of Frames, of the newest designs.
Cameras Repaired and Altered to order.
Lenses, by Lerebours & Secretan.
Orders (per post) shall meet with immediate attention.

South Wales & Vale of Neath Railways.

FIRST, Second, and Third Class Sunday Excursion Tickets will be issued at all Stations between Gloucester and Haverfordwest, and on the Vale of Neath Railway, at a reduction on the ordinary Return Fares, on and after Sunday, the 7th. of May.

These tickets will not be transferrable and will only be available on the day of issue. – Third Class Excursion Tickets will not be issued by the Mail Trains, nor can they be used for the Return Journey by these Trains.

For Sydney (New South Wales) Direct.

THE Splendid New SHIP "LOUIS NAPOLEON," Captain Gaidet, burthen about 2000 tons; now at Swansea, and will sail on or about 24th May. Her accommodation is of the best description, and has room for some Seven or Eight Cabin Passengers.

For further particulars apply to the Captain on board, or write to,

G. A. BEVAN, Swansea.

CAUTION NOT TO TRUST.

J MORGAN GRIFFITHS, of No. 8, Gam-street, Swansea do hereby give notice to the Public NOT TO TRUST my wife, MARY GRIFFITHS, as I will not be answerable for any Debts that may be contracted by her after this notice. MORGAN GRIFFITHS,
Dated May 1st. 1854.

THE CHOLERA!!!

Prevented by the destruction
of all noxious effluvis.
Crew's Disinfecting Fluid,
Recommended by the
College of Physicians.

THE CHEAPEST and STRONGEST CHLORIDE of ZINC. – Quarts 2s., Pints 1s., Half-pints, 6d.

Sold at the CAMBRIAN OFFICE SWANSEA, and by all Chemists, Druggists, and Shipping Agents, and at Commercial Wharf, Mile End, London.

The Late Fire at Port Tennant.

LYON'S PATENT FUEL COMPANY tender their sincere thanks to the Mayor, Gentlemen, Mr. Tate, and the Police, and to all those friends who so kindly and strenuously gave their aid in subduing the Fire that occurred on their premises at Port Tennant, on Monday night.

Swansea, May 4th. 1854.

TOWN-HALL, SWANSEA.

ADJOURNED MEETING of the RATEPAYERS, This (Friday) Evening. Men who value their Rights, and who will insist upon them, who understand the Doctrine of *No Supplies,* and *No Surrender,* will be present.

By order of the Committee,
G. P. EVANS.

A PUBLIC MEETING will also be held at LANDORE, on Monday Evening Next, Rev. E. Jacob will Address the Meeting, in Welsh, and Mr. Willett and Others, in English.

***Since the above was in type, the MAYOR, has taken upon himself to REFUSE the use of the HALL, assigning in effect, as a reason, that "Great digressions and irregularities were allowed at the Meetings over which Mr. G. B. Morris, Esq., presided, &c. Under these circum-stances, the RATEPAYERS are, notwithstanding, requested to ASSEMBLE NEAR the HALL, at Half-past Seven o'clock, and avoid the issue of his Worship's determination.*

May 5th. 1854.

Desirable Villa Residence at Sketty.

Two miles and a Half from Swansea,

TO BE LET
with immediate possession,

ALL those TWO COMMODIOUS DWELLING HOUSES and PREMISES, with Shrubberies and Gardens known as *"Montpelier Villas,"* Sketty, and within ten minutes walk of the Sea.

The situation is delightful, commanding extensive views of the beautiful Bay of Swansea and Surrounding country, as well as the opposite coast of Somerset and Devon. Each house contains five bed-rooms, dressing ditto, drawing and dining-rooms (which may be thrown into one.), entrance hall, water closet, kitchen, scullery, wine and other cellars &c. with the advantage of an abundant supply of water.

Also, Two convenient DWELLING HOUSES with gardens attached; each containing two parlours, four bedrooms, two attics, kitchen and scullery.

More ground can be had if required.

For further particulars, apply to Mr. J. M. Ellery, Auctioneer, 90 Oxford-street, or to Mr. Jacob Lewis, Draper, Castle-street.

SOUTH WALES RAILWAY.
Traffic Return

Week ending 30th April 1854
– £4144 6 10
Corresponding week, 1853
– £2950 9 0
Miles Open
1853 131
1854 162

VALE OF NEATH RAILWAY

Week ending 30th. April 1854
– £657 9 4
Corresponding week 1853
– £426 3 7

TAFF VALE RAILWAY

Traffic Account for the week ending April 29, 1854 – £3004 12 0

THEATRE, SWANSEA

MR. & MRS. BATHURST

RESPECTFULLY solicit the favour of your patonage for their BENEFIT, which is fixed
For THIS (FRIDAY) EVENING,
MAY 5th 1854.

The BAND will be considerably Augmented on this occasion.

The Performance will commence with Sheridan Knowle's beautiful Play of
The
WIFE: *a Tale of Mantua*

After which, by desire of several families, the most successful Drama ever produced in London entitled
The
CORSICAN BROTHERS.
Song ... **By a Gentleman of Swansea.**
The whole to conclude with a New Farce, called

THE CAMP AT CHOBHAM;
OR, *THE PETTICOAT CAPTAINS.*

The Box Plan may be seen at the Miss Jenkins's Library, where Tickets and Places may be secured.

Tickets to be had of Mr. & Mrs. Bathurst, No. 17, Singleton-street.

RATEPAYERS OF SWANSEA.

THE EVIL-DOINGS of the TOWN-COUNCIL will be Shown Up This Evening, at Seven o'clock. Fresh Discoveries!!! The most recent Tricks of Change upon the Rate Books!!! The MAYOR'S CONDUCT at the COUNCIL CHAMBER, on Tuesday last, and the ORDER for the POLICE to SEIZE upon the RATEPAYERS, and DRIVE them OUT of their OWN COUNCIL CHAMBER, will be expatiated upon. Will you go? Will I Go? Won't I! That's all! Who is the coward that will keep away? Be there ALL RATEPAYERS and Support the Men who are Struggling for your vital interests.

>>The Letter of the Mayor to Mr. Rogers enclosing a Requisition to call a Public Meeting at the Townhall, can only be inserted but as an advertisement . . .

MELANCHOLY SHIPWRECK
IN THE MEDITERRANEAN

Narrow Escape of Sir R. Peel.

By a telegraphic despatch dated Turin, Wednesday, we learn that the Italian Steamer "Erosland" by Herculameum, has been lost off Villa France. It appears that the vessel was on her way from Civita Verchia to Marseilles, and that out of twenty persons on board, only four were saved. Among the latter, was Sir Robert Peel who miraculously escaped by swimming. Among the passengers lost were were 11 English:– Mr. Thomas Halsey, M.P. for Hertfordshire and family (5), Mr. Knight and family (5), Mr. Joseph Hayes and family (3), Mr. Charles Samson, and Sir Robert Peel's servant. The names of the passengers saved were Mr. Edw. Downing, Sir Robert Peel. Mr. George Wilkinson, Mr. Edward Knight and Mr. Charles Boaten. A subsequent despatch adds that Charles Samson was saved from the wreck in the ship's boat with three sailors. Mr. Halsey M.P. one of the unfortunate gentlemen who were lost was nearly related to the Archbishop of Dublin, and other families of distinction. With these the melancholy occurrence will cause the most profound sorrow.

THE HARBOUR TRUST.

We sincerely congratulate the port on the spirit of unanimity which pervaded the Harbour Meeting on Monday, in dealing with the Report of the Committee appointed to carry the New Harbour Bill through Parliament. Thus far, it has triumphed gloriously; but there are, we regret to find, obstacles still in the way. It is said that that it will be strenuously opposed in the Lords by Mr. Hooper, on behalf of the Duke of Beaufort, although it is a measure calculated to enhance the value of his Grace's property on the river alone several hundreds per annum. We confess we can hardly credit that such a suicidal course will be pursued. Of this, however, we fell assured, that, should the bill fail by dint of a morbid attempt to perpetuate antiquated rights, which are opposed alike to the spirit of the age and the best interests of the port, a serious responsibility will be incurred, and a spirit of antagonism, we are afraid, will rear its head once more amongst us, to the manifest detriment of the Beaufort property, as well as to the town and trade of Swansea.

To the EDITOR of The Cambrian.

Sir, – My attention has been drawn to a letter in your last number, signed "Henry Vincent."

Judging from the whole tenor of which, I am led to suspect that its author is one of the numerous puffers which are employed, in various parts of the country, by the different public brewers, when any of the houses they supply are considered to be in danger.

The hypocritical attempt to make it appear to the public that the writer is influenced by the strictest impartiality and the strongest and most rigid love of morality, while his inferences and insinuations are so diametrically opposed to reason and right, fully warrant me in entertaining those suspicions.

I would, however, warn the writer that this attempt of his to damage the fame of Henry Vincent, who I am happy to say, is engaged by the Committee of the People's Institute to lecture at Swansea in the course of this month, will, necessarily, prove a miserable failure, there being no fear of a discriminating public confounding that popular lecturer with the imbecile writer who in this instance has had the presumption to assume his name.

A LYNXED-EYED OBSERVER.

Exraordinary Quick Voyage. – The barque *Countess of Bective*, owned by Messrs. Nicholson and Son and commanded by Captain Paul Smith, has just completed the shortest voyage on record from this port to St. Jago de Cuba and back, she having sailed from Swansea on the 15th of February – arrived at the port of destination – discharged – took in upwards of 600 tons of copper ore, and arrived safe in the Mumbles, thus having accomplished the voyage in the remarkable short space of two months and seventeen days.

CIRCULATION OF NEWSPAPERS

We have een kindly favoured by Howel Gwyn, Esq., M.P. with a copy of the Parliamentary Return of the number of Stamps issued to the different Newspapers and Journals throughout the United Kingdom. From the subjoined extract it will be found, that the number of Stamps issued to "Welsh Papers" was as follows:–

	1832	1853
CAMBRIAN	66,000	69,000
Swansea Herald	55,000	50,000
Merthyr Guardian	66,000	63,000
Welshman	47,000	44,000
Carmarthen Jral	44,000	32,000
Pembrokeshire Hld	42,000	38,100
Silurian	32,500	26,000

By the above return it will be seen that "The Cambrian" has still the largest circulation of all the Newspapers in South Wales, and as this circulation embraces all classes – the Nobility, Clergy. Gentry and Tradesmen, as well as the Agricultural and Commercial Community – we trust we can state, without having any access to any blatant system of puffing, that it affords incomparably the best medium for every description of Advertisements in the Principality.

The Trades Union. – The walls of our town were last week placarded with bills announcing that a public meeting of the operatives of Swansea, would be held on Monday evening last, at the Bird-in-Hand, High-street. It was also stated that two delegates from the Preston operatives would addresss the meeting. The object of the meeting was for the purpose of amalgamating the various and different trades unions throughout the kingdom, so that all classes would have the opportunity of assisting any portion of this body in any "strike" or difference which should exist between them and the employers. Our reporter attended at the hour named, in order to present a full report of this meeting; but after waiting three-quarters of an hour left, imagining from the paucity of operatives who attended, that no meeting would be held. We have been informed that at a later period of the evening a meeting took place, when resolutions in conformity with the objects of the meeting were unanimously adopted.

"Louis Napoleon" at Swansea. – Like the neighbouring port of Cardiff, Swansea has been visited by some splendid French ships. One of the handsomest crafts in the French merchants' service, named the *Louis Napoleon,* by the Emperor himself, is now in our Float, and has been visited by a large number of the inhabitants. She is a full-rigged ship, and carries upwards of 2000 tons, being the largest that ever entered the dock. Her cargo from this port will be Warlich's patent fuel. Every facility is given for inspecting her, and nothing can be more polite than the conduct of the master and chief officers. One day last week a number of ladies and gentlemen went on board to inspect this vessel, when the captain most handsomely invited them (although entire strangers to him) to dine with him; the only favour which the captain and the chief officer asking in return was, that the company should sing the national anthem, in which the captain and officers joined most enthusiastically.

6th. June 1856

Latest Foreign Arrivals. – From St. Melo, the "Felix," with 45 tons silver ore, for H. Bath. From San Sebastian, the "Aurrera," with 55 tons of copper ore, 640 cwt. of wheat flour, for Henry Bath and Son. From Garrucha, the "Request." with 20 tons copper ore (in bags), 80 tons copper ore, in bulk for Wm. Foster and Co. From Almeria, the "Charles Henry," with 247 quintals of copper ore, 1010 quintals of Manganese minerals, for —— Williams. From Torrevienga, the "Elizabeth," with 96 tons of copper ore, for M. Williams. From Boue, the "Betsy," with 100 tons of copper ore to order. From Coquimbo, the "Bella Donna," with 300 tons copper ore, and 200 tons regulus, for Charles Lambert. From Garruchia, the "Union," with 470 tons copper ore, for M. Williams.

Goods Warehoused during the Past Week. – One box maufactured tobacco, weighing 169 lbs., 17 chests tea containing 1360 lbs., and one hhd. brandy, 57 gallons., for Charles Williams. Six chests tea containing 503 lbs., and one cask white wine, 56 gallons for John Davies. One hhd of brandy, 57 gallons for Edward Hammett. Four pipes red wine, 460 gallons to order. Six chests tea, 522lbs. for Miles and Thomas. Twelve chests tea, 482lbs., for David Walters. Ten bags coffee, 122lbs., for Messrs Matthews, Brothers, and Co. Three casks of brandy, 74 gallons, ten cases of Geneva, and 177lbs. tobacco, for Wm. Whiteway. One puncheon rum, 125 gallons, and one hhd brandy, 58 gallons, for C. Williams and Co. One cask red wine, 47 gallons, for J. D. Wheeler.

LLANDILO PETTY SESSIONS

May 31, before J. W. Philips & W. Du Buisson Esqrs.

Rees Morgan, Llangybi was charged by P.C. David Williams with furious driving. The defendant pleaded guilty to the offence, and was fined 5s. and costs.

Mr. John Edwards, Inspector of the Llanelly and Llandilo Railway, charged John Brewer, a fitter – up at the Llandilo Railway Bridge with being drunk and disorderly, and refusing to quit the platform at Cross Inn Station on the 23rd. ult. It appeared that the defendant was on his way home to London, and being intoxicated began to sing indecent songs, and would not leave the platform when requested by the inspector, who, eventually gave him into the custody of P.C. Berry. John Peter, railway porter, corroborated the inspector's evidence and defendant was fined in the sum of 5s. and costs.

NEATH.

THE GREAT CRICKET MATCH AT NEATH.

This match came off at Neath this week, at a field under the Gnoll. The ground was admirable, and was well protected.

The number of visitors during the week was not so large as might have been expected, considering the fineness of the weather, and the attractive nature of the sport. Indeed, the attendance was extremely thin, not more than between

200 and 300 persons entering the ground during the day; on Tuesday the number of visitors increased to between 600 and 700, thus bringing the total for both days up to nearly a thousand – the precise number, however, will not be ascertained until the close of the game. A large and commodious grand stand was erected on the ground, but it presented a very deserted appearance, most of the visitors seeming to prefer a ramble on the green sward of the meadow to availing themselves of the accommodation afforded. A large proportion of the visitors was contributed by Swansea, whilst almost every family of respectability in Neath and the surrounding neighbourhood visited the ground.

The ground was inclosed with a quantity of canvass supplied by Edgington and Co. of London, so as to prevent the outsiders from witnessing the performance without paying the piper. A number of stalls for the sale of refreshments were on the ground, together with a grand stand for the ladies, a *roulette* table and a target for rifle shooting supplied the means of gratifying those who enjoy such sports. A printing press from the establishment of Mr. Thomas Thomas, attracted great attention, as the scores made by each player were successively printed as the game proceeded. As we are not "up" to the game, nor acquainted with the technical terms to describe the play as it should be done, we will be satisfied by merely stating that at the close the twenty-two found themselves thoroughly beaten as will be perceived by perusing the score.

A ball was announced to wind-up the sports on Wednesday evening at the Castle Hotel, and the only reason we could learn why it did not come off, was that there had been some misunderstanding or mismanagement amongst those to whom the arrangements had been left. We much regret this untoward event, as we know how many of our fair friends who were much disappointed of an opportunity of enjoying a harmless and exhilarating amusement

We cannot conclude this short notice without alluding to *a soiree dansante* which took place at the King's Arms, Old Market-street. We have heard that a great number of tickets were issued. An excellent quadrille band was in attendance, and the room throughout the evening was numerously attended by many of the "eleven" and their opponents, together with some of leading tradesmen of the town and their friends. It was to be regretted that so few ladies attended, and should the worthy host attempt another affair of the sort, we trust the moderate charges and the excellent refreshments provided on this occasion, will induce his friends to rally round him whenever the opportunity may present itself. The band played a selection of polkas, quadrilles and waltzes, and the company did not separate till a late hour, after having spent a most agreeable evening.

ALL ENGLAND ELEVEN.

First Innings

R. C. Tinty c W. J. Kempson b.Grace	7
A. Clarke c Pecock b. Grace	17
Anderson c Worthington b. Grace	3
Jackson not out	...
Stephenson b. Hiskly	14
S. Parr leg b.w. b. Grace	4
Wilsher b. Grace	0
Worthington b. Hinkly	0
Bickley b. Hinkly	0
Clarke b. Hinkly	0
Parr b. Grace	2
Byes 6, lb 1, w 3.	12
	——
Total	59

Second Innings

R. C. Tinty b. Stephenson	18
A. Clarke b. Pocock	19
Anderson b. Stephenson	12
Jackson c. Davies b. Stephenson	2
Stephenson c. Spence b. ditto	3
S. Parr b. Stephenson	3
Wilsher b. Hinkly	2
Worthington b. Stephenson	0
Bickley c. Lark b. Stephenson	0
Clarke b. Hinkly	3
Parr not out	39
B7,w b 9, 1b1	17
	——
	118

TWENTY-TWO OF NEATH AND SOUTH WALES

First Innings

H. Grace b. Willsher	1
C. R. Mais b. Bickley	2
B. Stephenson b Bickley	3
T. Hodge b. Bickley	4
A. C. Bell b. Willsher	0
G. Worthington c. and b. Willsher	3
Pocock c. Worthington b. Bickley	1
Kempson lbw b. Bickley	0
H. Cuthbertson b. Bickley	1
– Selby b. Bickley	0
H. Huxham lbw b. Bickley	0
L. Davies b. Willsher	0
J. Jones b. Willsher	0
B. Rees lbw b. Bickley	0
G. Young c. Willsher b. Bickley	0
H. Eustance b. Willsher	1
Spencer b. Willsher	0
Thomas run out	0
– Hinkly b. Hickley	0
D. James b. Willsher	0
R. Sixsmith b. Willsher	0
R. P. Larke not out	–
Byes	11
	——
	27

Second Innings

H. Grace b. Bickley	0
C. R.Mais b. Bickley	6
B. Stephenson run out	1
T. Hodge bWillsher	5
A. Bell c.G. Parr b. Bickley	0
G. Worthington b. Willsher	7
Pocock lbw. Bickley	2
Kempson b. Willsher	0
H. Cuthbertson c. G. Parr b. Bickley	0
– Selby c. Tinly b. Bickley	4
H. Huxham cWorthington bWillsher	0
L. Davies b. Blackley	9
J. Jones b. Willsher	0
B. Rees b. Willsher	0
G. Young b. Bickley	0
H. Eustance b. Bickley	0
Spencer b. Willsher	0
Thomas b. Bickley	0
– Hinkly b. Bickley	0
D. James b. Willsher	0
R. Sixsmith b. Beckley	0
R. P. Larke not out	2
Byes	6
	——
	42

LLANELLY PETTY SESSIONS.

[Held on Wednesday before J. H. Rees and C.W. Nevill, Esqrs.]

Ann Davies, an interesting looking little girl, about 12 years of age, was charged by Richard Williams, the master of the Llanelly Union Workhouse, with having deserted from the workhouse on

21st. July last, taking with her various articles of wearing apparel belonging to the Guardians, and having stamped on them the words "Llanelly Union." It appeared that she and her brother were found begging about the town, and they were admitted as casual paupers. Three days afterwards she made her escape through a drain under the door, and nothing was heard of her until recently a communication was received from the chaplain of Shrewsbury gaol, stating that she was there undergoing imprisoment for vagrancy, and having ascertained from her that she had been an inmate of this workhouse, it was deemed advisable to send her down to Llanelly to be tried for the offence of running away and taking with her the clothes, in order that she may be sentenced to fourteen days imprisonment, and at the expiry of her sentence sent to Lady Leigh's Reformatory School, called the Allesley Reformatory Farm near Coventry in Warwickshire, whose consent to receive her had been obtained, and there detained for five years. After leaving the workhouse it appears she was picked up by some tramps, and at Shrewsbury she was found in company with a blind beggar (whom she led about,) an old woman with whom he cohabited, and a young woman who was a prostitute. Her mother is dead and her father is said to be living in the neighbourhood of Merthyr, and is a man of low and abandoned character. Much credit is due to both the gaoler and the chaplain of the gaol at Shrewsbury, for the interest they have evinced on her behalf, as were it not for their humane exertions, a career of vice and crime would inevitably have been her lot. – The offence for which she was brought up was clearly established, and she was adjudged to be imprisoned for 14 days, and the order for her detention at the reformatory was made.

———◇———

PEMBROKESHIRE.

Pembroke Dockyard. – Steps are now taking for the accommodation of a large number of troops at Pembroke Dock, as both the fortified barracks and the huts are quite full. A garrison chaplain has been appointed. Once or twice a week as the weather permits, the regiments are brigaded together, and in consequence of these field days (which are held on the heights adjacent to the fortified barracks) the troops are rapidly becoming a well trained and valuable group.

———◇———

———◇———

———◇———

British and Foreign School for Boys,

GOAT STREET, SWANSEA.

NOTICE is hereby given that the ANNUAL GENERAL MEETING of SUBSCRIBERS will take place at the Schoolroom, on Friday, the 20th. instant, at twelve o'clock at noon.

A Public Examination of the Children will take place on the same day, at seven o'clock p.m.

Tickets for free admission may be obtained on application to the Master at the school; or to Mr. C. T. Wilson, Chemist, Castle-Square.

———◇———

Correspondence.

N.B. *We do not hold ourselves responsible for the Opinions and Sentiments of our Correspondents.*

Sir, – I have just read your description of Swansea on the 26th. May, 1856, and my mind is filled with unmitigated disgust. It was a national holiday – at least as much a national holiday as could be made without Act of Parliament. Her gracious Majesty's birth-day was chosen on which to celebrate the return of peace, and how did Swansea join in the demonstration? The discharge of a few wretched popguns was all the amusement provided for the many who allowed themselves a holiday to rejoice in the auspicious event, and who also, you say in the absence of other divertisement, found their way to the public-houses, and spent their hard earned pence in beer and gin. Now, Mr. Editor, there is but one consideration that can bring relief to the reputation of my fellow townsmen, not generally, one must confess, so chary of their money – an ineffectual attempt has been made to gain a share in the fireworks, for the Welsh Metropolis, granted ungrudgingly by Government to the English, Scotch, and Irish, and no wonder feelings of indignation should for the moment overpower even the honest delight which the occasion was set apart to manifest.

Welshmen shared the Fight! How much gallant Welsh blood was shed too many a sorrowing family will evidence. Who rivalled in bitterly proved bravery the Welsh fusiliers? I say it is disgraceful we had not a share in the national rejoicings.

It has pained me, Sir, that such an account of the 29th. should go forth without a word of explanation or a symptom of discontent at such injustice; therefore in the sacred name of Justice, and for the honour of our Principality and Town, I ask you to insert this letter in the *Cambrian.* – the mouthpiece of Wales.

And remain, Sir,

Your obedient Servant,

May 31st. 1856 M.L.

SWANSEA UNION.

ALL Persons desirous to CONTRACT with the GUARDIANS of the UNION for the following ARTICLES, for the next Three Months, are requested to send in Sealed Tenders (addressed to the Guardians) to the Clerk to the Union, on or before Wednesday, the 18th. day of June instant:–

PROVISIONS

Flour and Oatmeal, at per sack; Beef – Hind Quarters (whole), separate tenders for each, at per lb., Sticking Pieces, at per lb., and Shin Bones at per lb., Mutton, Suet, Cheese, Butter (salt), Tea, Sugar, Rice, Mustard, Pepper, Soap, Starch, Blue, Tobacco, Candles (dips and others), and Soda at per lb., Salt and Potatoes, at per cwt; Milk, at per quart; best Boiling Peas, at per bushel; Coals, at per ton; Wine (port), at per Dozen; Beer, at per quart.

SHOES

Men's, Boys, Women's, Girls' and Children's, of different sizes; the men's shoes to be made of the best wax kip; Women's of the best grain kip shoulders; the soles of the Shoes of the best buffalo leather; plates and nails included; and all Materials and Work to be of the best quality.

FUNERALS

Of Paupers, at each, including Coffin, Shroud, Grave, Bearers, Burial Fees, and all the other Expenses, and separate Tenders for same, at the following ages:–

Above Twelve Years,

Twelve Years and above Three Months.

Three months and under.

The Tenders may be for any of the Articles separately; and for all Funerals in all or either of the Districts of the Union.

Samples to be sent in with the Tenders of each Article as will admit of it.

Security will be required for the due performance of each Contract.

CHARLES COLLINS,

Clerk to the Guardians.

Swansea, June 5th. 1856.

OXWICH BAY, GOWER,
NEAR THE MUMBLES.

Here on this yellow glittering sand
This ever golden sea-bound floor,
Who would not bend the knee adown,
The great Almighty to adore.

See how their crowned heads in awe
The surging waves bend low around,
Whilst Echo bears from shore to shore
Their solemn anthem's swelling sound

All nature is a church or book,
Where all mankind may kneel and
pray;
The grandest words God spoke to man
Beam forth in glory night or day.

O Earth; that man should be so vain.
To dream his heart or puny hand,
Could form a floor whereon to kneel,
Fit as this yellow glorious strand.

The Train for June. J. Deffett Francis.

The Concert by the Swansea Orpheus Society, – Tuesday Evening passed off with great success. The audience was most respectable. Mr. Evan Davies, A.M., gave an account of the dramatic musical representations of the ancient Greeks, and explained the circumstances under which, "Anigone" which formed a part of the programme of the evening, was written and performed. The Lyrics were read by Mr. Geo. Melville, in the absence of Mr. W. H. Michael through illness. Mr. Denning presided at the pianoforte, and gave much satisfaction. Mr. Bower's solo was loudly encored and Mr. Hore's flute solo was generally applauded.

. . . Length of railway line open at the end of June 1854, 7803 miles 21 chains; June 1855, 8116 miles 11 chains. Length of line in course of construction at the end of June 1854, 889 miles 17 chains; June 1855, 879 miles 75 chains.

Loss of Life by the War. – Since the commencement of the war England has lost 19,584 gallant men by death in action, wounds and disease: 2873 besides have been discharged from the service on account of the two latter causes. England has sealed her declaration of unflinching devotion to the cause of national independence by the sacrifice of 22,457 gallant soldiers. Of these,1993 fell bravely in action; about 1621 sank under their wounds, 4279 died of cholera, and 11,541 of other diseases. The losses of the French, as far as they can be ascertained, amount to 60,000. Count Orleff has admitted in Paris, that the Russian loss was not less than 500,000. The loss sustained by the Sardinians has not been, and the loss sustained by the Turks never will be, ascertained.

A report from Mr. Newton was also read relative to the improved water supply now brought into the town more especially to the laying of a series of pipes along the Oystermouth-road to Langland-place for still further improving the supply . . . In answer to questions put by Mr. J. T. Jenkins and one or two other members, Mr. Newton replied that the works at the Uplands reservoir were now held on an average about three feet of water. He was not aware that there was a single leakage there. Mr. Thomas, relative to the water supply at Sketty, remarked that a very large proportion of the houses on the top of the hill had no water at all. The stream to which Mr. Newton had alluded in his report was not far off, and if it could be diverted would give a great additional supply, and be done at small cost . . .

Singular Accident. – Danger of Hugging in a Hurry. – An extra-

Singleton Abbey.

Penrice Castle.

Gelli Aur, Golden Grove.

Fairyhill.

ordinary operation, necessitated by a most singular accident, has just been performed in our Infirmary. It seems that a young Irishman, residing in Bristol, while larking with some of his country women and neighbours, ran after a buxom girl, who was engaged in sempstress work, and gave her a hug in sport; but, poor fellow, it proved anything but sport to him, for as he pressed her to his bosom, it turned out all but a fatal embrace, as a needle, which she had in the breast of her gown, literally entered his heart, and broke off short leaving three parts of an inob of the steel in the muscles. He instantly fell sick and faint and was taken to the Infirmary, when it was determined to make an effort to extract the broken needle, as, should it remains where it was, death must quickly ensue from inflammation of the heart. Dr. Green, accordingly, cut through the outer flesh, and having laid bare the surface of the heart, discovered a small portion of the needle fragment protruding; and with a forceps he drew it out. The delicate operation was most successful, but as much inflammation had set in before the needle could be extracted, it is still very doubtful whether his life will be saved. It is, however, a most uncommon operation and singular accident, showing that even the heart itself may sustain a sharp wound with death immediately following. It has also a moral, and ought to teach young men, before they hug their sweethearts, to see that the latter have no needles in their bosoms, for though we hear it said, " true as the needle to the pole," in "affairs of the heart," the needle itself may sometimes be too true; and the lethal character of Cupid's darts is a mere figure compared with the puncture of such a tiny weapon.

——◇——

2nd. July 1858.

The Brig Ocean. – Holland master, of Shoreham, bound to Swansea with a cargo of copper ore, and the collier brig Lustre, Williams, of and from South Shields, laden with 350 tons of coal, got jammed at the East India Dock Gates, Blackwall, on Saturday. The collier with her heavy cargo of coals, careened over the starboard side of the Ocean, crushing her bulwarks, and beams, and, resting as it were upon her, rendering her condition, if possible, more hopeless. A large number of the bags of ore forming the Ocean's cargo were got out, and as it was apparent that she would fill on the return of the tide if the position of the collier was not altered, some 30 or 40 empty puncheons were put down into her hold in order to assist in floating her. The work of discharge and dismantling the vessels went on during the night; but on the flowing of the tide, it was discovered that both vessels had sustained such damage that they filled. Both vessels became wrecks.

——◇——

The Theatre. – This place of amusement will be opened on Monday evening next, by the lessee, Mr. John C. Chute. The *corps dramatique* consists of several old favourites with a Swansea audience, and one or two aspirants for public favours. Amongst the new members, we may mention Miss Annie Ness, who is a clever, pretty actress, and well known to the lovers of drama. On the 11th. and 12th. insts. Captain Horton Rhys and Miss Catherine Lucette will make their *debut*, and on the latter night, and original comedy called "Tit for Tat," by Capt. Rhys will be played. We understand that several novel and popular pieces will be put on the stage in the course of the ensuing season; if so they will, doubtless be appreciated and well supported.

——◇——

SWANSEA NATIONAL SCHOOLS.

The following is the report of the Committee for the year just ended:–

There are few subjects of lasting importance to the welfare of a nation than the instruction of the rising generation in sound religious principles, and especially the children of the labouring classes, which must always form the majority, and it is now universally acknowledged that this can never be carried out satisfactorily without the aid of those whom God has placed in the middle and higher ranks of life.

It is the duty of the Committee of the above Schools to report for the information of the Subscribers their general progress during the past year. They have now arrived at a period when they can look back upon the past and point to present results. They look around and see many of both sexes grown up young men and women, occupying respectable positions, who are indebted to that position for the instruction they have received in the Swansea National Schools. They can appeal to Professional Men, Merchants, Tradesmen, and Tradeswomen, Mechanics, Masters of Vessels, Railway Officials and others, to testify to the utility of such an Establishment, from the numbers from our schools who fill situations under their supervision. Ten years' labour of a large Educational Establishment ought not to be without its fruits and its influence upon a parish with a teeming population, and the Committee confidently appeal to the community whether that influence has not largely been produced. For themselves they claim no merit, but they acknowledge with gratitude the blessing from on high which has attended their efforts, and they are encouraged to persevere under the hope and expectation that still further benefits will accrue to each successive generation, grounded upon the promise, "Train up a child in the way he should go, and when he is old he will not depart from it."

The Committee proceed to give some details of each School and its present state from the independent and impartial testimony of those whose official duty it is to inspect and report.

The Boys' School is still conducted by a Master who holds a first Class Certificate, and has passed examinations for Chemistry and Electricity. He is aided by an assistant and four Pupil Teachers and paid Monitors. The number of boys educated since the opening in the Day School is 1757, and additional in the Sunday School 296. Instruction according to the age and capacity of the boys is given in Book Keeping, Mensuration, Composition, Geography, Arithmetic &c. &c. At the late examinations of the Schools H.M. Inspector reports:– "I am much pleased with the state of which I find Swansea Boys' School. The discipline and instruction are well attended to, and confer credit on Mr. Cole for his skill and energy." The number under education during the present quarter is 359, and a weekly average attendance of 256.

Girls' School is conducted by a Mistress, who holds a Certificate of Merit, with three pupil teachers and paid monitors. The instruction is suited to the capacity of the child and has reference to its future condition in life; and in addition to reading, writing, and arithmetic, the higher classes are taught in other useful branches. Each child is instructed in needlework. The number educated since the opening is 1211, besides 346 additional in the Sunday School. The present quarter shews 203 on the books with an average weekly attendance of 130. The Report written upon the Mistress's Certificates by H.M. Inspector is as follows:– "I am much pleased with the state of the Swansea Girls' School: it is improved in more respects than one, and confers credit upon Miss King for her exertions.

——<>——

Infant School – Boys and Girls. – Conducted by a certified Mistress, assisted by two pupil teachers. Since the opening, 2001 little ones, under 7 years of age, have been trained in the first rudiments. In this nursery they are disciplined and prepared for the higher School; and great is the advantage they derive from such a process, by which they acquire habits of diligence, obedience and application. During the present quarter 230 have entered the school, and the average weekly attendance is 142. The last tabulated Report of H.M. Inspectors has this gratifying remark:– "Schools all in good condition, greatly to the credit of the Managers and Teachers."

——<>——

Summary. — By the foregoing statements it is shewn that since the opening of the Schools, they have afforded instruction to 5,705 children, or at the rate of 570 per annum. Nor is it the least pleasing feature, and shews the estimation in which they are held by the labouring classes, that no less a sum than £1814 5s.1d. has been received in pence from the children, averaging upwards of £180 per annum. About half this annual amount is contributed in Annual Subscription.

. . . Religious instruction is given by the Vicar and his curate, one of whom usually opens the Morning School with singing and prayer. The Bible is a daily class book.

Latest Foreign Arrivals, – From Jersey, the Take Care, with potatoes for W. Hoskin. From Jersey, the Rubins, with potatoes, for ditto. From Jersey, the William and Frank, with potatoes, for ditto. From Calders, the Conrad, with 200tons of copper ore, and 200 tons of copper regulas, for H. Bath and Son. From Coquimbo, the Duke of Beaufort, with 650 tons of copper ore, for Charles Lambert. From Jersey, the Hearty, with 500 cwt. of potatoes, for J. Andrews; a quantity of yellow metal for Vivian and Sons. From Cuba, the Duke of Northumberland, with 650 tons of copper ore, for the Cobra Mining Company. From Aveiro, the Ripper, with 141 tons of copper ore, for H. Bath and Son. From Coquimbo, the A. F. Moore, with 303 tons of copper for W. H. Bath and Son.

Blasting Quarries. – We have received one or two letters complaining of the very dangerous practice of blasting quarries in the immediate neighbourhood of inhabited houses, and the same subject has been brought under the consideration of the Magistrates during the week. The quarry more particularly referred to is that at the back of Clifton Row, and very large pieces of stone have fallen through the roofs of houses, thereby causing considerable damage to the furniture and alarm to the inmates. The danger is easily obviated, and we trust that, after this public caution, proper steps will be taken to put a stop to it.

——<>——

NEATH

Britonferry Docks. – Another slip of a serious nature has taken place at these docks, which, although it may not long delay their completion, will add very materially to their cost.

JAMES WILLIAMS

ROYAL MAIL OMNIBUSES,
FROM SWANSEA
TO THE MUMBLES.

RUN daily from the South Wales Railway Station, on the arrival of every Train. Leaving the Post-Office, Swansea, and calling at the principal Inns in the Town at the following hours:–

Morning. – Half-past Seven. *(Mail)*
.. – Ten.
Noon – 20 minutes past 12 *(Mail)*
Evening – Three, *(Mail).*
.. – Eight

An Omnibus to meet the 11.20 a.m. and 3.20 Express Train.

Starting from the Ship and Castle, Mermaid and Elms Hotels.

MUMBLES,

Morning – Nine *(Mail).*
Ditto – Eleven.
Evening – Half past One, *(Mail).*
.. – Five, *(Mail).*
.. – Half past Six.
.. – Eight.
.. – Quarter past Nine.

An Omnibus to meet the down Evening Express and the Eight o'clock Train.

N.B. Not accountable for passengers' luggage or parcels unless they are properly booked at the Hope and Anchor, Fisher-street, or at the Heathfield Inn, Oxford-street.

James Williams begs to inform his friends and the public that he constantly keeps on hand Saddle Horses, Phaetons, Gigs, Flys, Clarence; and also three superior vehicles suitable for Pic Nic Parties; built to carry 9, 13, and 27 persons. Also a spacious Marquee for the accommodation of Pic Nic Parties.

Horses Broken to Saddle and Harness,

J.W. having had 15 years' experience in this department.

Livery Stables, Fisher-street, Swansea.

Vehicles may also be had at the Ship and Castle Mumbles.

——<>——

Increased Steam Communication between Bristol and Swansea.

THE Liverpool and Bristol Channel Steam Navigation Company beg to give NOTICE that as there is but one Steamer plying between the above Ports, they intend running their powerful new screw Steamer,

"SOVEREIGN"

On that station.

The "Sovereign" will take in Goods at Cannons Marsh, Bristol, every Saturday and Monday for Swansea, Neath, Llanelly, Llandilo, Kidwelly, Merthyr, Dowlais and all the neighbourhood.

For further particulars, apply to Mr. J. Edwards, Ferry Side, Swansea, or to Mr. G. H. Evans, Steam Packet Agent, Bristol.

Crinoline at the Cardiff Cattle Show. – The managers of the late meeting of the Bath and West of England Society at Cardiff, made a sad mistake, owing clearly to their neglect to consult their wives and daughters. Adequate provision was made for the admission of men and children, birds and beasts of every kind, but the hoops and crinoline, the pride and glory of ladies, were forgotten. The fashionable attire found it difficult, indeed to force an entrance, and did so at the risk of bruising and disarranging the circular line of beauty. In one instance three ladies were completely loited. They were surrounded by so extensive an enclosure that they were fairly unable to squeeze themselves through the limits of the turnstile. It was in vain they endeavoured to arrange their robes in an oblique position. After they had ineffectually attempted to effect an entrance, an obliging official suggested his readiness to accept their money and furnish them with a ticket, which would enable them to enter the show yard through the spacious door allowed for the ingress of machinery and steam ploughs. The offer was gladly accepted. The attendant opened wide the large folding doors, and the charming trio sailed through in triumph, but in single file, amidst the admiration of the assembled multitude.

Additional Accommodation,

DAILY COMMUNICATION

Between

Llandovery, Llanwrtyd, Llangammarch, and Builth, and alternate days to Llandrindod.

THE Public are respectfully informed that on and after June 21st. a superior Four Horse OMNIBUS will leave the Lion Hotel, Builth, every Monday, Wednesday and Friday mornings, at eight o'clock, going by way of Llanwrtyd, and arriving at Llandovery Station in time to proceed by the 12.45 p.m. Train, returning the came evenings from Llandovery Station and Castle Hotel after the arrival of 1.45 p.m. Train, through Llanwrtyd, to Builth &c.

The Proprietors of the above old established Omnibus, beg respectfully to return their thanks to the Public for the very liberal support, they have hitherto received, and to state that in consequence of the increased traffic over the above route since the opening of the Vale of Towy Railway, they have rendered this additional accommodation.

RICHARD OWEN
& Co Proprietors
REES JONES

All orders for Post Horses and Vehicles, from Llandovery and Lampeter Road Stations, to be addressed to Richard Owen, Castle Hotel, Llandovery.

A Coach will leave the Lion Hotel, Builth every Tuesday, Thursday and Saturday, at 8.30 a.m. arriving at Kington Station in time to proceed by the 11.35 a.m. Train to Shrewsbury, Manchester, Liverpool, &c.

Castle Hotel, Llandovery, June 16th. 1858.

NEATH.

Alderman Davies's Schools. – It will be remembered by our readers that the foundation stone of these splendid buildings was laid some time since, and the occasion was celebrated here with a procession, headed by our worthy chief magistrates, the members of the Town Council, and a numerous and respectable body of the principal inhabitants, and that in the evening some 150 gentlemen sat down to a dinner, which, for the variety of courses, the qualities of the viands, and the smallness of the charges, only excited the surprise of all present as to how the host of the Castle "could manage it". We now find that the inauguration of these schools will be celebrated by a public tea party to the scholars, in the delightful grounds attached to the Gnoll, and that the public are invited to join the children and witness their pleasures on Monday evening next, at one shilling each. An active canvass for the sale of tickets has been commenced in which the young ladies of the town are taking a prominent part, and, should they beseige all the bachelors in the town with as much success as in the case of your correspondent, a numerous party at the Gnoll, and no insignificant revenue to the funds of the schools will be the result. We trust the weather will be propitious, as we have been informed a variety of amusements for the children and visitors will be provided, including the performance of two brass bands, the ascent of of several variegated balloons and a display of fire-works, which will include some rockets of a novel description.

THE SLANG OF THE PRIZE RING. Slang is rapidly encroaching on the purity of the English language. New words, new phrases, new expressions arise with us each day, or are wafted across the Atlantic, and find a place in our conversational language – some good and expressive, some simply absurd and ridiculous, and others perfectly low and vulgar. "Bush" was a good addition; it was short, and expressed the idea very well. "Bogus", meaning a sham and "high falutin" or "Stuck up" are new recent American importations. But of all slang, whether slang of the schoolroom or college, slang of the racecourse, slang of the casino, or thieves slang, the worst is the slang of the prize ring. In the *Bed's Life* account of the recent fight for the championship, between Tom Sayers and Tom Paddock, in which the former was victorious, are to be found some most remarkable instances of perverted ingenuity in this art. The whole account occupies nearly four columns of small type, and is at once historical, picturesque and poetical in its way. Seriously, as a curiosity of literature, it is worth examination. We have not space or time to enter into elaborate analysis of it, but the following list of slang synonymous for the simple word "Blood" would astonish Dr. Johnson:– 1. Juice; 2. Carmine; 3. Red Port; 4. Home-brewed; 5. Cochineal; 6. Badminton; 7. the Ruby; 8. the Vermillion; 9. Gravy; 10. Claret – the real word never being used, but these phrases being repeated fifty times with singular variations. The eye, the nose, and the mouth, seem unknown; instead we have the Peeper and the Goggle, the Snout, the Smeller, the Nob and the Snuff Box, the Mug and the Potato Trap.

HARBOUR OF REFUGE AT THE MUMBLES.

To the EDITOR of the CAMBRIAN.

Sir, – Having by the courtesy of the hon. member for Swansea received a copy of the Report of the Select Committee on Harbours of Refuge, I trust the great interest on the subject to a large number of your readers will induce you to give me space for such extracts as relate to the proposal for so improving the Mumbles Roadstead as to make for a valuable refuge for the shipping frequenting the numerous ports in the Bristol Channel.

This report gives weight to the opinions expressed on former occasions, and I would earnestly suggest that every effort should at once be made by the various Boards of the several ports *to be prepared with statistics and evidence* to lay before the Royal Commission which will (almost to a certainty) be immediately appointed to make enquiries on the spot . . .

The Coast from Land's End to Hartland Point and the Bristol Channel. – "In considering this part of the coast, your Committee draws a distinction between the part extending from Land's End to Hartland Point, and that further up, embracing the whole of the Bristol Channel on both sides. The evidence goes to show, that the part of the coast up to Hartland Point is frequented chiefly by small coasting vessels; it is shown that out of 3,221 casualties, 2,648 happened to vessels under 200 tons, 367 to vessels between 200 and 350 tons, 93 to vessels from 350 to 500 tons, and 113 to vessels above 500 tons. On the other hand, the Bristol Channel is frequented by foreign going ships, rapidly increasing in number, and of large tonnage. With respect to the first of those two divisions, the two points most strongly recommended to your Committee for the construction of a harbour of refuge within the district are St. Ives and Padstow. The points in the Bristol Channel to which the attention of the Committee has been chiefly drawn, as offering the best security for the shipping frequenting it, are the Mumbles Head, Lundy Island, and Clovelly. Mr. Abernethy, who thinks that the Mumbles is the most important point for a harbour of refuge for the Welsh coast and the Bristol Channel, produced a plan by which he proposed to construct two breakwaters, together of the length of 1760 yards, at a cost of £370,000, and which would afford a harbour of an area of 200 acres, with a depth of four fathoms at low-water spring tides, sheltered from all winds; on the other hand it has been strongly contended by other witnesses that Lundy island is the best point. Much difference of opinion has been expressed before your Committee as to the respective merit of these places, and they will require a much more minute investigation than could possibly be given by your Committee before any point is is actually decided upon. Your Committee would only further state upon this part of the subject, that judging by the state of things which has arisen in the crowded coal ports of the North of England, any place which is finally determined upon for affording refuge to ships frequenting the Bristol Channel should have special reference to the rapid development of the coal and iron fields in South Wales, and to the increasing sea traffic which is arising there-from." . . .

. . . In conclusion, I would congratulate those who took an active part in bringing the claims of the Mumbles Roadstead before Parliament on the success so far achieved, feeling certain that the more its merits are examined, the greater will be the certainty of its being selected as the site most fitting for a Harbour of Refuge for the Bristol Channel; but it must be recollected that no supineness must now be allowed to step in, for there still exist prejudices and jealousies as well as (possibly) convictions in favour of *out-of-the way places.*

I remain, Sir,
Yours respectfully,
Geo. Grant Francis.

Cae Bailey, July 1, 1858.

PEMBROKE DOCK REGATTA.

This Regatta came off under favourable auspices on Monday last. Our nautical friends thought in the early morning that it would be no Regatta day, specially for those who love a "wet sheet and flowing sea," as the atmosphere was unusually sluggish. As noon approached, however, the wind increased until before 12 o'clock it was blowing a fine stiff breeze, promising good races and fine sport to all lovers of aquatic sport.

Race 1. Prince of Wales Cup, 50 guineas, for cutter and schooner yachts of 25 tons and upwards, belonging to any Royal Yacht Club. Time race; half a minute per ton up to 50 tons, and a quarter of a minute above that. Unusual allowances to schooners. Entrance £2 10s.

There were only two entries up to Saturday, viz: the Wildfire and the Rara Avis, but in cosequence of some misunderstanding respecting the Wildfire, the entries were declared void. On Monday morning there was a made up race when three cutters were entered, in competition for the cup.

1. Extravaganza. 48 tons, Sir Percy Shelly.

2. The Glance, 35 tons, Major Longfield.

3. Vigilent, 33 tons, J. C. Atkins, Esq.

The yachts started a little after 11 o'clock, in excellent order, and nearly together, the Extravaganza slightly leading, but pushed hard by the Vigilent. On rounding the point, where we lost sight of the race from the starting vessel, they were still in the same order. On returning the first time the Extravaganza and Vigilent were still in the same position closely waited on by the Glance.

They rounded the starting vessel on

both occasions in the following order and time:

	1st. time.	2nd. time.
Extravaganza	1h. 19m.	4h.49m.25s.
Vigilent	2h. 20m.	4h. 49m.33s.
Glance	2h. 21m.	

The Vigilent according to tonnage, was allowed 6 minutes, and consequently won the race. A dispute, however arose as to her measurements, and she was measured again after the race.

This was the great race of the day, and considerable excitement was manifested by backers of the different yachts.

Race 2. The Pembroke-Dock Cup, 25 guineas for yachts of 25 tons and under, belonging to any Royal Yacht Club. Time race; three quarters of a minute per ton. Entrance £1 5s.

1. The Flirt, cutter, 19 tons, H. H. Bryan Esq.

2. The Vesper, cutter, 15 tons, G. A. Bevan, Esq.

These were two beautiful yachts, and according to the opinions of the knowing ones, were well matched. A good and exciting race was therefore expected. They started to time, and well, and for an hour the contest was gallantly maintained. Unfortunately, however, in rounding Llanstadwell point the Flirt struck the ground, and as it was dead low water at the time, she was forced to lie for some time in the soft ooze off the point. When released from her uncongenial harbourage by the flux of the tide, it was of course too late to do anything in the race. The Vesper consequently had it all her own way.

Race 3. A Cup. £10, for sailing boats – open, half-decked or decked, – of 15 tons and under to 8 tons. Time race of one minute and a half per ton. Entrance fee 6*l*.

Distance from the starting vessel twice round the Stack Rock.

1. The Arrow, 10 tons, Mr. Richard Lewis.

2. The Fairy, 9 tons, Mr. G. Thomas.

3. The Imp, 10 tons, Mr. Morris.

This was a most exciting, and a most gallantly contested race. The Arrow and the Fairy are old opponents, and the best judges were unable to hazard a guess as to the chances of either, so well matched were the boats. On former occasions success had alternated between the two, now the Fairy and now the Arrow beating. The boats started in admirable order and considerable dexterity and skill were evinced by the crews of each yacht in raising sail in the sharp breeze, which rattled through the cordage. They started at exactly 11 minutes after 12 o'clock, and came round the first time in the following order:

The Arrow .... 2h. 38m.30s.
The Fairy .... 2h. 39m.30s.
The Imp .... 2h. 58m.15s.

The second course the Fairy rapidly shot ahead of her two opponents, and gallantly won the best contested race of the day, beating her most formidable competitor, the Arrow by 7 minutes.

The remainder of the day was devoted to rowing matches, which were very spirited.

Considerable merit is due to the promotion of this truly national amusement for the perseverance which, in defiance of many difficulties, they were enabled to give such an excellent bill of fare to the public.

10th. August 1860.

Correspondence.

THE HARBOUR MASTER'S SALARY

To the EDITOR of the CAMBRIAN.

Sir, – I perceive that Captain Herbert, the Harbour Master, has made another application for an increase of salary, and the Harbour Trustees will, with their usual liberality, grant the application, but as the salaries of the officials of the Trust come indirectly, out of the pockets of the public, the public should have some voice in the matter. This is the second application for an increase since his appointment, scarcely two years since, and the present salary being £350 per annum, I am sure the majority of the public will consider this sufficient compensation for the duties which Capt. Herbert himself performs. The trade of the port at the present time is exceedingly flat, and this, therefore, is the most inopportune moment to give any increase of salaries. Would the Trustees, as individual employers, make an increase to a servant under the circumstances of the case – if not (and I feel assured they would not) then why should they do so with the public money? Better husband any resources they have than pay exorbitantly high salaries, and if they have any spare cash, let them further reduce the tolls, which will greatly benefit the whole town and port. Trusting you will insert these few observations,

I am sir, yours, very respectfully,
A COAL SHIPPER.
Prospect Place, Aug. 6, 1860

N.B. Would it not be better to wait until the Half-tide Basin of the Float is completed and then judge of the increase of trade, for most assuredly another application will be made for an increase of salary by the Harbour Master.

The Cambrian

SWANSEA, FRIDAY, AUG. 10, 1860

INCREASE OF SALARIES – WHERE IS IT TO END?

Our public bodies have certainly been afflicted of late with an extraordinary mania for increasing the salaries of our various officials. Not many months ago our very hard worked Town Clerk to the surprise of all was favoured with a most substantial addition to his income. At the Council Meeting in July Mr. Brenton, the Collector had an increase bestowed on him of nearly £100 per annum; and at the Board of Health Meeting held yesterday, an assistant was voted to the Surveyor, incurring an increase of expence of 30s. per week. In addition to this it was intended to apply for another increase to the Surveyor to keep a horse at the public expense. Observing that the current of feeling was evidently against the proposition, Mr. W. Michael very wisely abstained from urging the latter application. On Monday next, the Harbour Trustees will again have "to consider the Report of the Executive Committee upon the application of the Harbour Master for increase of salary in certain departments of the staff of the Trustees". Now we should like to know where all this munificence is to end? We should like also to know are the circumstances such as to warrant all this increase on the part of the Public Boards of this town? We say decidedly not. The present Harbour Master on his appointment, not very long ago received the liberal salary of £300 per annum. He had not long been in office before he applied for an increase of £50 a year for the rent of his house, and this was readily granted. Nor was this all. Since the opening of the South Docks, the Trustees, in a spirit of liberality which is most extraordinary, granted, on the application of the Harbour Master, two additional Assistant Harbour Masters. Thus then we have at present a Harbour Master, at a salary of £350 per annum, a Deputy Harbour Master, at a salary of £130; and two Assistant Harbour Masters, at a salary of £100 a year each; again, there is a Clerk employed exclusively by the Harbour Master at a weekly stipend of 13s., which is paid by the Trust. There is also a Superintendent of Works, who receives £100 per annum; the Solicitor's salary is £300 a year exclusive, we believe, of Parliamentary expenses; there is a Collector at about £100 a year, to say nothing of a number of subordinates at various salaries. Now looking at the depressed state of trade of late, one would have thought that the sums paid to this large staff would be sufficient in all conscience for this port for years to come. But no, the Harbour Master has caught the spirit of kindred officials, finding that he had but to make his application "pro forma," lo and behold! our Trustees become at once his humble servants. Happy man to have such easy-going, pliant masters. In Liverpool we find that the Chief Harbour Master receives only £500 a year, whilst the aggregate tonnage of that great port is no less than 4,697,238. In Glasgow, the salary given is £450 per annum, the tonnage inwards and outwards being above 3,000,000. In Belfast, the salary is £250 per annum whilst the tonnage is 785,338. In the Tyne the salary is £200 a year, the tonnage amounting to above 4,000,000. At Swansea, whose aggregate tonnage is only 600,000, we give the Harbour Master the liberal sum of £350 per annum, together with a number of assistants; yet in the face of these facts, the Executive Committee have again resolved to recommend an increase in Captain Herbert's salary equal to another £50 a year, and likewise to increase the pay of his subordinates in the same ratio. Really to say the least of it, such conduct is little less than downright wanton extravagance. Our space will not allow us to pursue this subject at any length. We cannot, however forbear warning the personal friends of the Harbour Master against the ultra liberality they are about to pursue in this matter. When Captain Herbert was appointed there were plenty of able candidates ready to fill the office at £300 a year. There are still plenty ready to do the same now, and with the same attention and ability – able and attentive as Capt. Herbert confessedly is. If this be so, we respectfully tell the Trustees that they are not justified in taxing the funds of the harbour with additional exorbitant salaries. We tell them, further, that the time is most inopportune. In consequence of the stoppage of the float, the trade has suffered enormously. Since last winter, the staple commodity of the port, by the interference of railway and harbour officials, has suffered to an extent that it will take a long time ere it will recover itself. In the opinion of practical men, the staff is at present paid enough to work both the Half-tide Basin, Float, and Docks. Why not wait then to see the effect of the opening of the Half-tide Basin before more expense is lavished on favoured officials? If the trade will then justify such increase, well and good. Looking at the aspect of matters at present in the port, we repeat that we see nothing to justify the contemplated increase in the salaries referred to. On the contrary, we think the Trustees will incur a grave responsibility by doing so, for the salaries of the port of Swansea are just now notoriously liberal, as compared with larger ports, whilst the expenses are growing at a more rapid rate considerably than the trade. We trust this fact will not be overlooked on Monday next.

——◇——

YSTALYFERA.

One of the richest and most picturesque valley in South Wales is, unquestionably, the valley of Neath, and especially beautiful is it on a bright day, in this delightful time of the year, despite the ravages of a lingering winter, and the smoke of many furnaces, where thousands of human beings daily toil for the bare necessities of a confined existence. The cornfields were full of promise, and nature smiled around in triumphant beauty. In the course of the past week it was our privilige to pass down the valley towards the comparatively unknown village of Ystalyfera. In journeying from Pontardawe, the first object which arrested our attention was its pretty church and singular spire. We next ascended a gentle declivity between two hedgerows, dark with matured verdure of waning summer, and were soon on the the high-road sheltered by the rock-strewn mountain dotted here and there with waving patches of woody scenery, along whose borders scores of rabbits dared the open daylight, apparently fearless of the intrusive foot of man. Passing onwards we occasionally felt the bracing freshness of the perfumed mountain air – perfumed by the mingling odours of garden, orchard, and the late hay harvest; while remoter scenes of kindred beauty stretched away and away in the ethereal distance, seemingly slumbering upon the luxuriant bosom of the earth, beneath the boundless blue of heaven. The shining canal or river, like a stream of silver, glided between the sister mountains in silent splendour, refreshing and purifying in its purling course.

We at length reached the village, with its thousand cottage-houses scattered along the mountain side.

This village is chiefly composed of working people, who are employed in the extensive iron and tin works which form the centre of attraction to the wayfarer. It would have given us much pleasure to have inspected these large works but we were advised not to make the attempt as the more illiterate of the inside workers look with feelings of grim suspicion at the approach of well-dressed strangers; we contented ourselves, therefore, with an outside view from the banks of the Swansea canal. We were particularly struck by one feature of peculiar interest, and which indicated the general character of the inhabitants of this valley – the face of their gardens – which evidenced much taste and industry, and led us to form a favourable opinion of the habits of the owners; we should say that they are a sober, if not reflective people. We met the "Patriarch of the village," who is verging on "three score years and ten," the alloted age of man, who had passed his long and peaceful life in the vale, and who had a decided aversion to intemperate and slothful habits, but we could glean nothing of historical or traditionary interest. In fact this mountain village has sprung up within a few years consequent upon the great influx of labourers who are engaged at the above named iron and tin-works. On looking about for the church, we espied the simple spireless edifice among the trees on the slanting hill-side, and two chapels, after the order of Wesley and Calvin. We were surprised to find that almost every person we had occasion to speak with in this Welsh district spoke the English language with fluency and ease, and even more distinctly than within thiry miles of the metropolis of these realms. Although we have no cause to complain of the sylvan scenery of our own home and its external attractiveness, we are sometimes pleased to change our native scenes for those of other districts when the balmy breeze and the golden sunshine seem to invite us into the serener bye-ways and more sequestered nooks of nature's green domain; and on leaving the flowery glades of Ystalyfera we felt our hearts lighter and more in harmony with the peaceful influence of rural scenes, and as we gave a parting glance at the variegated landscape, we could not help exclaiming in the philosophic language of Wordsworth –

"Nature never did betray
The heart that loved her. 'Tis her privilege,
Through all the years of this our life, to lead.
From joy to joy; for who can so inform
The mind that is waking us, and to feed
With lofty thoughts, that neither evil tongues,
Rash judgments, nor the sneers of selfish men,
Nor greetings where no kindness is, nor all
The dreary intercourse of common life,
Shall o'er prevail against us or distrust
Our cheerful faith, that all that we behold
Is full of blessing." – *Wayfarer.*

WANTED, a Situation as Groom or Coachman in a Gentleman's family of the Church of England. He can also Valet and Brew, if required. Address B.C., Post Office, Neath. A twelve years character can be given.

Bristol to New Zealand.

UNDER ENGAGEMENT WITH THE PROVINCIAL GOVERNMENT OF NEW ZEALAND.

To sail for Canterbury direct, end of August.

THE celebrated A1, full Poop, Regular Liner, "MATOAKA," 1,823 Tons Register, 3,000 tons Berthen; A. Stevens, Commander. This noble Ship made her last passage to Wellington in 89 days, being the fastest passage of the season: she has been brought into competition with some of the most modern Clippers, and always beaten them. She has a magnificent Poop, entirely redecorated, and fitted with every possible comfort and convenience; her 'tween decks are unusually lofty, and will be fitted as on her last voyage, when she earned the reputation of being a *Model Passenger Ship.*

For particulars of Freight and Passage apply to MILES BROS & Co, 81, Queen square, Bristol; or to Mr. Hartwell Morice, Swansea.

Why do we buy eighty million of eggs annually from the continent? and why are chickens and ducks reckoned a luxury in England and Ireland, when there might be poultry reared on every common and in every lane, and housed at the end of every cottage? Working men's wives and children manage to keep fowls in the alleys and yards of our great towns, finding them so profitable that they never eat eggs or chickens at home. If our rural labourers would take to this gainful enterprise at once, we might have a large addition made to our stock of animal food, by this time next year. – *Miss H. Martineau.*

GOWER INN ROSARY, PARK MILL,
Near Swansea, Glamorganshire.
EDWARD WEBB.

BEGS respectfully to inform his friends and the public generally that his superb collection of PERPETUAL ROSES are now to be seen to the fullest advantage, and will continue so in succession till the end of October, and respectfully solicits an early inspection.

House of Correction. – The gaol of Swansea is built to contain 161 men and 45 women, or 196 prisoners. The cost has been £40,439, or about £200 per head. There has been no building constructed in connection with it to receive debtors or persons confined for civil causes, though such provision was contemplated, and it is because there is no such provision, and on account of the obvious impropriety of placing, in criminal cells, persons confined on account of civil causes, that commitals under orders of the County Courts at Neath and Swansea are made to Cardiff. That any gaol should be deliberately left as completed without such provision may well excite astonishment in a county where the immense sum of £87,087 has just been expended on its gaols.

THE MUMBLES REGATTA.

THE above REGATTA is open to all Mumbles Dredging Skiffs, and will take place on TUESDAY, August 28th, 1860.

There will be several PRIZES for ROWING BOATS. All Boats to belong to the Mumbles.

Further particulars in the future advertisement.

J. JOSS, Commodore

CARDIFF

A True Picture of Cardiff, – The Traders in prostitution and vice may well attempt to stop the onward progress of the flowing tide in the Bristol Channel, as to screen the infamy of Cardiff from the public gaze. Every passing stranger notes down the scenes of public debauchery, which are being enacted in the open thoroughfares of the town, – from the sea lock back to Bute-street dancing saloons. The sad story of the fearful vice of Cardiff, is wafted upon the wings of the wind, and carried by the sailors of every nation to their several countries, until the name of this borough has become a bye-word and reproach all over the world. The government authorities having tested the truth of these wide-spread reports, made a peremptory order to increase the Cardiff police force. although it was previously in excess of any other similar town in Wales. Captain Willis, the Government Inspector of Police, assigns that fact as the only reason why the force was thus ordered to be increased. The committee feel that every attempt to screen the the crime of Cardiff, is a suicidal act to the town. To expose vice, is to check it, if not ultimately to bring it to an end. Let the brand of infamy be stamped upon every trader in prostitution, including the owners of the brothels, and the resorts of thieves and prostitutes, and many a man in Cardiff who now makes a fair show of morality, will have his hidden deeds brought to light, and so reproved as to lead to their utter abandonment.

– *The First Report of the Cardiff Associate Institution for Improving and Enforcing the Law for the Protection of Women.*

——◇——

The Regatta. – Cardiff annual regatta will take place on Monday and Tuesday next, wind and weather permitting. The prizes offered are large, and the arrangements to increase the interest in this aquatic gathering are on a most extensive scale. This year, two days sport are provided instead of one as formerly. On the first day there will be two sailing matches; for the winner of the first of which a silver cup, value £25 is offered, and for the winner of the second a silver cup, value £10 and a purse containing ten sovereigns. For the first several fine yachts are expected to run, whilst for the second some very smart crafts will compete.

The day's proceedings will close with that prolific source of amusement, a duck hunt. We are sorry to find that in consequence of the committee having made a second sailing match open to all boats in the Bristol channel, the Cardiff pilots refuse to run their boats. They say it is unfair, in consequence the Bristol, Newport and other ports excepting Weston, acting upon the exclusive system. They are not afraid of being beaten by other ports, but they contend that the regatta in other ports should also be open to the whole channel. In speaking of the qualities of the Cardiff pilots, we might observe that Mr. Moss is willing to run his saucy craft against all comers of the same size, with a stiff breeze, and will back her at from three and two to one. The committee have not yielded to the remonstrance of the pilots, but have issued their programme. The position the committee have taken in making the race an open one, is one in the right direction, and we hope that Bristol and the other ports will follow their example. Although at first sight it might be distasteful to Cardiff pilots, they will find that eventually it will be for their good. We hope that on the eventful day it will be bright up aloft, and that with a capful of wind, many will enjoy a toss on "the heaving wave". The second day will be devoted to rowing matches for which nearly sixty pounds is offered, and most exciting contests are expected.

——◇——

JIM MYER'S MAMMOTH

EQUESTRIAN
ESTABLISHMENT
WILL VISIT SWANSEA

On Tuesday and Wednesday, August 14th and 15th, in a Field in Mumbles Road, for TWO DAYS only.

The Company will also visit:

Llanelly on	Monday,	August	13th.
Neath	Thursday	"	16th.
Aberavon	Friday	"	17th.
Bridgend	Saturday	"	18th.

WITH the largest Stud of HORSES & PONIES. Travelling also the the celebrated PERFORMING BULL, Don Juan, and the

GREAT MUSICAL CALLIOPE,

Which is played by Steam – acknowledged to be the Greatest Novelty of the Day Charity Schools admitted Free by applying to J. W. Myers.

N.B. – All Persons dissatisfied with the Performance can have their money returned by applying to Mr. G. Webb.

W. B.WARD, Agent.

——◇——

GELLIONEN SPA.

SPA HOTEL.

THERE is now a commodious Hotel at Gellyonen Spa, at a short distance from the Pontardawe Station on the Swansea Vale Railway, where every accommodation can be obtained.

Mr. W. M. HUZZEY, Proprietor, –
Conducted by Mr. and Mrs. MILLER.

ANALYSIS OF GELLIONEN WATER,
By Mr. Herapath, Bristol.

"In an Imperial Gallon there is contained in Grains and Decimal parts –

Organic Matters	.16
Chloride of Magnesium	.48
Chloride of Sodium	2.24
Sulphate of Magnesia	1.60
Carbonate of Lime	a trace
Bi-Carbonate of Iron	.80
Sulphate of Lime	.36
Total contents	5.64

From Lime Salts; and that its principal medicinal quality comes from Chalybeate, as it possesses 8-tenths of a grain of Bicarbonate of Iron in a gallon. If the locality is salubrious and picturesque, it might be well to establish a Spa there. The trains leave Swansea three times a day for Pontardawe, and from 1st. of August a Train will leave Swansea on Sundays at 2.15 p.m., returning from Pontardawe at 7.40, thus giving an opportunity to spend four hours at the Spa.

——◇——

Important Improvement
in CARRIAGES.
V.R.
BY LETTERS PATENT.

S&A. FULLER beg to invite attention to their improvemnet in Carriages and more especially to their plan of making Doors of Landaus to open with the glass up or in any position. This invention has been highly appreciated, as the result of injury, in addition to the necessity of lowering the glass before the door could be opened, has long been a source of annoyance.

The Fashionable LANDAU SOCIABLE is rendered much more complete with the Improvement, and it can added to Carriages already built. S. & A. FULLER being the Original Inventor of the patent SELF-ACTING DRAG and BREAK, can from long experience apply them to any description of Carriage with economy and despatch.

S&A FULLER have on SALE the Largest Assortment of NEW and SECOND-HAND CARRIAGES to be found out of London, consisting of

BAROUCHES, BROUGHAMS, SOCIABLES, WAGGONETTES,

PARK and PONY PHAETONS, DOG CARTS, and every variety of Modern Carriages, with the Latest Improvements, containing elegance, lightness, and strength; any of which supplied on Hire, with choice of purchase upon liberal terms.

REPAIRS done with that economy and despatch for which their Establishment has always been celebrated, and carriages Lent during the time free of charge.

S&A FULLER are the Patentees of the Fulcrum Shafts, the action of which contributes so much to the safety and lightness of two-wheel Carriages.

S&A FULLER keep a large Stock of well seasoned materials, and having great experience in Carriage Building they continue to receive the highest testimonials of the durability of their Carriages in all climates.

CARRIAGE AND HARNESS MANUFACTORY, AND SHOW ROOMS,

Kingshead & Monmouth Streets.

Near Queen Square, Bath.

Carriages and Harness

Sold upon Commission.

——◇——

On Thursday next will be Published,

Price Two-Pence.

THE LLANELLY TELEGRAPH and GENERAL ADVERTISER. – Llanelly now numbers Fourteen Thousand inhabitants; at the present time it gives every promise of still increasing prosperity; in number, spirit and general importance, its position is no longer doubtful as the first place in the County of Carmarthen.

It is presumed, that in these circumstances, the people of Llanelly are generally prepared to support a Newspaper of their own, which will be identified with their special interests, serve as a medium of Advertisement, furnish a more complete Local Intelligence than can be otherwise supplied, and discuss their local affairs, besides being replete with the usual matter of general interest and importance.

To meet this want, generally felt and admitted, The Llanelly Telegraph will appear on Thursday August the 9th. and on every succeeding Thursday.

The Telegraph will aim at becoming a welcome visitor into every family in Llanelly and the immediate neighbourhood. Nothing will be admitted into its columns that is not consistent with its mission to instruct, to interest, and to elevate. The great cause of Human Freedom and Progress in all its phases, will command its unwavering sympathies. It will have opinions of its own, and will know how to utter them; but it will be its sedulous care not to inflame either religious or political animosity. It will always appear under the profound conviction that no party under heaven has a monopoly of either wisdom or goodness, and breathing goodwill and charity to all.

In steady reliance upon the rising public spirit of Llanelly and the surrounding country, no effort will be spared to render the Telegraph, in respect of general literary powers, variety of intelligence, and genial catholicity of spirit, inferior to no similar issues of the Provincial Newspaper Press.

It is scarcely necessary to add, that the Telegraph will depend for its success upon a generous appreciation of the difficulties connected with such an enterprise, and upon the hearty support of the Public, whom it aspires to represent. It is therefore confidently hoped that the Tradesmen of the Town and District will largely avail themselves of its Advertising Columns, and that the Inhabitants generally will exercise their influence in every possible way to promote its circulation.

Printed and Published by John Thomas, Water-street, Llanelly.

August 3rd, 1860.

5th. September 1862.

IDYLLS OF GOWER.
(How we lived there.)

I think we shall remember well
The days we passed in Gower:
The pleasant cottage on the hill,
And the bathes of morning hour.

And all the lazy afternoon
We lounged on Cefn Bryn,
And used to hurl Homeric stones
At cannisters of tin.

Then how we crawled to Arthur stone
And at its base sat down,
And wondered why it was set on high
So far from any town.

And how they got it there at all,
And what 'twas meant to show;
And tried to scramble up the sides,
But found it all no go.

I think we shall remember well
the Plant on Pennard Tower:
And how we used to go to see
The Mistries of the Gower.

And how we battled with the dog,
And in the *Cambrian* wrote:
And vainly tried to row and ride
(For want of horse and boat).

A gun we dare not use – for he,
Lord of the Manor round,
Who owned the land and ruled the folk,
Would ne'er permit the sound.

And so thro' him who owned the land,
The 'unco' tree before,
Of Church and State we ceased to prate,
And voted peers a bore.

But soon I found how low degree
And low estate are one;
Churls ape their betters' sins, but leave
Their better acts undone.

Thus now thro' him who owns the dog,
That creed I change once more,
Less grievous pride of gentle birth
Than that of profits-proud boor.

Oh! pleasant, pleasant were those days,
And merry was that time,
When we dwelt in wave-washed Gower Land,
In the summer's golden clime.

Then when the proper hour came
round,
We unto church would go,
To hear the Vicar thunder forth
Anathemas of woe.

There might you may see a clerk of
star,
Who made the one bell clang,
The longest when they drawled anon,
The loudest when they sang.

There might you see the villagers,
And there the village school;
All in a line the children sat,
Each on his proper stool.

And when by chance I looked at you,
And you looked back at me,
Sometimes we had to struggle hard,
With risibility.

And yet we meant not then to scoff,
Nor do I mean to here;
But sights so quaint might move a
saint;
And sounds so very queer

But now adieu fair land of Gower,
A long adieu to thee.
To the pleasant walks on the breezy
moor,
And bathes in the briny sea.

Adieu to the studious man who walks
For the full round moon to shine:
How oft we shall laugh at the things
that are past,
When those days are "Auld Lang
Syne."

Ex Pennard.

GLAMORGANSHIRE.

Cooper's Fields. – Rumour states that this fine piece of land will soon be converted into a deer park for the young Marquis of Bute, and it is intended the park, when made, should be enclosed with a high wall. Repairs are also, we perceive, being carried on in the Castle, under the superintendence of Mr. Roose, architect to the Bute Estate.

Town Hall, Swansea.

GRAND CONCERT,

For the BENEFIT of MONSIEUR ALLARD,

UNDER THE PATRONAGE OF

The Mayor of Swansea,
H. H. Vivian, Esq. M.P.
L. L. Dillwyn, Esq. M.P.
Pascoe St. Leger Grenfell Esq.
J. Palmer Budd, Esq.
John C. Richardson, Esq.
Evan Matthew Richards, Esq.
Horace A. Ford, Esq.
George Byng Morris, Esq.
Charles Bath, Esq.
George Brown Brock, Esq.
James C. Richardson, Esq.
And Others,

Will take place at the Town Hall, Swansea.
On Tuesday Evening, the 9th September, 1862
Commencing at Eight o'Clock

In which MISS FREETH, the eminent London Pianist (formerly of Swansea), MONSIEUR ALLARD, and several distinguished Vocal and Instrumental Amateurs and others will take part.

Programmes and Tickets may be obtained at Monsieur Allard's 10 Cradock-street; at Mr. Brader's, 9, Wind-street; at the Cambrian Office; and of Mr. Herbert Jones, Oxford-street, Swansea.

THE SHIPPING TRADE,

Much has been said and written recently about the depression to which the Shipping Trade of Swansea has been subject to of late. That a very considerable amount of stagnation has existed, particularly in the steam coal trade, cannot be disputed, however much opinions may differ as to the real cause of such an untoward circumstance. This is much to be deplored, no doubt, but let us hope that the crisis is now past, and that better times are at hand. The returns of the harbour for the month just ended have been issued, and it is gratifying to find that the cloud which, for a brief period, overshadowed our commerce and frightened some of our Brokers from their propriety, is gradually dispersing, and that a more propitious horoscope is again gradually, but we trust, surely, unfolding itself. The number of vessels that entered the port in August amounted to 549, having a registered tonnage equal to 55,656 tons. Of this number there were engaged in the Coasting Trade 342, or 27,313 tons; in the European 186 or 20,6586 tons; and beyond Europe 21, or 7685 tons. This presents an increase as compared with the corresponding month last year, of vessels 102; and in the number of tons 8028. As compared with the months of June and July this year, also, August shews a very considerable preponderance of trade. The income of the general harbour estate received in August from various sources amounted to £2818, the expenditure to £2463, leaving a balance in favour of the port between £300 and £400 on the month. Nor has the increase referred to above been of a fitful character. We hear that the arrivals this week have very considerable, thus indicating that the shipping trade is reviving, and bids fair to resume its wontedstate of activity and healthy progression.

Prison Life. – Mary Ann Williams, a well known character, and who spends half her life in gaol, was charged by P.C. Milton with drunkenness, and making use of obscene language, on the Strand, last evening. The defendant was quarrelling with another woman, making use of the most disgusting language, and as she refused to desist when spoken to by the officer, she was taken into custody. She was brought before the Bench last week for similar conduct, but was discharged upon giving a promise to leave the town instantly. She has been frequently committed to prison for disorderly and riotous conduct, and she was now sent to her old quarters for three months. She left the Court swearing vengeance upon the head of P.C. Milton, who had been the means of getting her incarcerated.

The Poor Box Robbed. – A poor fellow, who stated he belonged to the parish of Llangadock, Carmarthenshire, was charged by P.C. Lewis with wandering about the streets, being insane, and consequently incapable of taking care of himself. The man was simply brought to the station for safety. The magistrates sympathised with the man, and expressed their intention to pay his fare back to his parish; for this purpose the poor box deposited in the Police Court was opened, but it was found that some dastardly fellow had submitted spurious coins for the whole of the money which had been placed there by the authorities of the Court, and intended for poor but worthy applicants. This robbery of the poor box was most probably censured by the Bench, and the insane and neglected wanderer, who stood so much in need of a little timely assistance, was thus deprived of help, but he was ordered to be taken to the relieving officer, who will take the necessary steps to send him back to his native parish.

——<>——

Wrecks on the British Coast. – The Board of Trade return of the wrecks and casualties which occured on and near the coasts of the United Kingdom in 1861 have just been published. From this report it appears that the number of casualties is greater than that reported in any of the proceeding nine years, and 261 in excess of the annual average of the last six years. The number (exclusive of collisions) were in 1857, 866; in 1858, 869; in 1859, 1,067; in 1860, 1,081; and in 1861, 1,171; and the increase is ascribed to a great extent to the gales of January, February, and November, in which alone there were 465 casualties (exclusive of collisions). The number of collisions, though slightly in excess of 1860, is under the number of 1859, the three years 1859, 1860 and 1861, having the respective numbers 349, 228, and 323: and on the whole the increase in the number of collisions is not proportionately so great as the increase in of other casualties. In the number of lives lost there is a large increase as compared with last year, caused by the gales of January, February, and November which increased the number of casualties. In 1860 there were 636, while in 1861 there were 854, but this number is less than the numbers in 1858 and 1859. The comparatively small number of lives lost in 1860 and 1861 is owing chiefly to the absence of the loss of any large passenger ships on the coast.

——<>——

TENBY RACES.

These races came off on the 29th ult., and from the favorable state of the weather, was attended by a large concourse of persons, two excursion packets from Llanelly bringing about 900 to swell the lists. The course was in an excellent state, and but for the serious accident that happened to George Leach Esq. son of the Rev. Mr. Leach of Petrux, who rode Marmion, in the Hurdle Race, everything would have passed off very pleasantly; that coming in though threw a gloom over the other part of the day's proceedings, and the last race was hardly noticed.

The first Race was "The Pembrokeshire Trial Stakes" of thirty sovereigns, added to a sweepstakes of three sovereigns each, for horses bred in, and the *bona fide* property of residents of and farmers in the county of Pembroke, or of officers of the army and navy quartered at Pembroke Dock. Second horse to save his stake, 3 years old, to carry 9st. 7lbs, 4 years old, 10st. 7lbs, 5 years and upwards, 11 st, gentleman riders. Professionals 7lbs. extra. Thorough bred horses 5lbs extra. The winner to be sold for 80 sovereigns, if entered to be sold for 60 sovereigns allowed 5 lbs, if for 40 sovereigns, 10 lbs., if for 20 sovereigns 15lbs. Winner to be sold by auction after the race, and the surplus, if any, to go to the fund. The winner to pay 5 sovereigns towards the expenses About two miles on the flat.

There were nine entries for this race, and on passing the post they were placed as follows –

Capt. Glynn's b.g. Marmion, 5 yrs
h.b. 11st 1
Mr. Johnstone's c.m. Mabel, 6 yrs
h.b. 9st. 13lb 2
Mr. Fletcher's b.g. Deerfoot, 5 yrs,
h.b. 9st. 13lb 3
Capt. Macqueen's b.m. Lady Superior,
6 yrs. 9st. 13lb 4

In the first heat Marmion got the better of his rider and took the wall instead of the hurdle, consequently he had to retrace his ground and jump within the flags, which threw him out of the heat, leaving Pegasus to win it. The others pulled up about half way round. In the second heat only Marmion and Pegasus started, and upon arriving at the same wall Marmion again took to it this time, throwing himself and his rider, who lay on the ground one hour and a half, unable to be moved, and then was taken away insensible, continuing in nearly the same state up to Sunday, when he began to rally. Hopes are now entertained of his recovery. He came down upon his head among some stones that were thrown out from the wall, and it was the opinion of the medical men who attended him that he had received a contusion of the brain.

The Ordinary was held at the Coburg Hotel, and the steward's ball at the Gate House in the evening.

——<>——

Cricket – Third Glamorgan *v.* Fourth Glamorgan. – On Tuesday a match came off on the ground of the Swansea Cricket Club, between an eleven of the 3rd. Glamorganshire Rifle Volunteer's and an eleven of the 4th., the former Major Dillwyn's Corps, and the latter Lieut. Colonel Vivian's. A good deal of interest was felt in the proceedings of the day, and by one o'clock a considerable number of spectators thronged the ground, and before the afternoon was over they were increased tenfold. Three tents had been provided, partly with a view to accomodate any ladies who might come to look at the game, and there was besides the wooden erection wherein Miss Bradford dispensed creature comforts to the multitude. Soon after the beginning of the game the 3rd. marched on to the ground and they played at the fall of every wicket, as well as at the dinner which followed. On the whole the game was a spirited one. The Browns won on the first innings, having scored 141, but only 64 in the second. The 4th. then made 82 in the first innings, and 23 in their second. The latter were pulling up well when the stumps were ordered to be drawn at half-past six, with one wicket only down.

The Volunteers at Caswell. – This bay, which is one of the most beautiful in Gower, was the scene of a most interesting Volunteer picnic on Saturday last – a treat given by Captain William Thomas, of Lan, and his officers, to his gallant company. There were about ninety present, exclusive of several officers belonging to the other companies, amongst whom were Adjutant Knight, Captain Strick, Captain Herrman, Captain Bath, Captain Dahne, Hon. Surgeon Essery, Lieut. Daniel, Ensign Price, Sergt.-Major Mc. Conachie, Sergt. J. Lewis, Sergt. Evans, Sergt. Fox, &c. There were also present a great sprinkling of the fair sex. The company headed by the band of the regiment, arrived at the Oystermouth station at 11.30. whence they were kindly conveyed to the Mumbles at the expence of Mr. G. B. Morris, who is an honorary member of the corps. The weather in the forenoon was most unfavourable, but having cleared up about two o'clock, the viands were uncarted, and the whole dined together *al fresco* under the shadow of the rocky eminences which so romantically enclose this bay. Having partaken of the substantial fare provided, together with some potations of *cwrw da,* the order to "fall in" was given, when the company under the command of Captain Thomas, went through a series of evolutions, during which they fired several capital volleys and skirmished in good order, their relative distances being very creditably maintained. Drill being over the men, after being again regaled were arranged in sections and sub-divisions, and a series of manly and invigorating games were then indulged in, such as foot-ball, single stick, quoits, Aunt Sally, &c. These were kept up with great spirit until the "shades of evening" approached, and warned everyone present of the flight of time. The company returned to Swansea between eight and nine, all having enjoyed a most pleasant trip.

——◇——

7th. October 1864.

A Lucky Preacher – The hat was passed round in a certain congregation for the purpose of taking a collection. After it made the circuit of the church, it was handed to the minister, who, by the way, had "exchanged pulpits" with the regular preacher, and he found not a penny in it. He inverted the hat over the pulpit cushion, and shook it, that its emptiness might be known, then raising his eyes toward the ceiling, he exclaimed with great fervor, "I thank God that I got back my hat from this congregation."

——◇——

OPENING OF THE MID-WALES RAILWAY.

Connecting North and South Wales, and forming a new and direct route from Lancashire, Cheshire, & North Shropshire to Brecon, Hay, Merthyr Tydfil, &c., via Llanidloes, Rhyader, and Builth, (The Vale of the Wye)

The Public are informed that the above Railway was OPENED for traffic on Wednesday, September 21st. 1864.

TRAINS will run in connection with the Cambrian, Hereford, Hay, and Brecon and Merthyr Railways.

For further particulars see the Company's Time Bills.

Particulars and Rates for conveyance of Goods and Mineral Traffic may be obtained on application to any of the Stations, or to the undersigned.

Brecon, Sept. 1864 J. A. JEBB,
General Manager.

Local Intelligence.

British School. – The Mayor of Swansea, with his accustomed liberality, has presented the sum of £10 10s. to the funds of the flourishing school.

Local Marine Board. – Passed as master ordinary, William John Briffett; only mate, John Vincent and George Rawlings; 2nd. mate Henry Batchelor.

Heavy Gales on the Welsh Coast. – Porthcawl, Tuesday, – A terrific easterly gale, says Captain Buchan, R.N. has been blowing since ten p.m. on Sunday, with but slight intermission. We are making a floating dock, &c., but last night our navvies could not work, all their fires, lamps &c., being blown out.

Panorama. – On Monday evening next Mr. Henry will exhibit, at the Music Hall, his magnificent panorama of the heavens, together with his colossal planetarium, upon which the press generally passes high encomiums. The whole will be interspersed with selections of music from the Creation, and will conclude with panoramic scenes of the most remarkable places in the world. – *See advertisement.*

——◇——

MUSIC HALL, SWANSEA.

POSITIVELY FOR ONE NIGHT ONLY

Monday, October 10th.

MR. HENRY (of London) will exhibit his magnificent

Panorama of the Heavens & Celestial Scenery

&c., accompanied by MUSIC selected from Haydn's Grand Oratorio of the Creation. – See Programme.

Admission – Body of the Hall 1s.6d. First Galleries 1s., Second ditto 6d. Children and Schools half-price to the First and Second Class places only. Seats reserved 2s.

Doors opened at half-past Seven, ommences at Eight precisely; terminates at half-past Nine.

——◇——

Archbishop Cullen on Prize Fighting. – The following letter has been addressed by Archbishop Cullen to the clergy of the diocese:– "Dublin, Feast of the Angel Guardians, 1864. – Very Rev. Brethren, My attention has been called by some respectable gentlemen to a report widely circulated that this city or its vicinity, is to be made the theatre of a single combat between two foreign pugilists, who are about to expose their lives to imminent danger for a certain sum of money. This report must be the source of great regret to every one who is imbued with the spirit of Christian charity and who recognises in his fellow-man the image of the great Creator of the universe. It is not neccessary to call on you to use all your influence to preserve this Christian country from an exhibition so disgraceful and so well calculated to degrade human nature. I shall merely request of you to publish as soon as possible from your altars that such combats in which human life is exposed to danger are prohibited under the severest penalties by the Holy Catholic Church. Passing over the decrees of the Council of Trent, it will be sufficient to state that the learned Pontiff Benedict XIV, excommunicated the principal actors in such fights, their seconds, all who encourage them, and all who designedly become spectators of such unworthy scenes. If you announce these penalties from the altar, I am confident that the faithful of this diocese, who are so devotedly attached to the Holy Catholic Church, and so obedient to its law, will listen with contempt to the invitation of those who would implicate them in the misdeeds of foreign gladiators, and will abstain from countenancing or encouraging anything condemned by our holy religion, and contrary to the dictates of the Gospel. – Paul Cullen."

——◇——

MUSIC HALL, SWANSEA.

GRAND CONCERT

ON MONDAY EVENING,

OCTOBER 17 1864.

Doors open at 7p.m. to commence at Eight o'clock.

J. BRADER has the honour to announce that he has been favoured by J. H. Mapleson Esq. to arrange for a Grand Recital from Gounod's celebrated and successful new Opera.

"MIRELLA."

The Second Part of the Concert will be devoted to a MISCELLANEOUS SELECTION, comprising the most Popular Music of the day, in which the following Eminent Artistes, all of Her Majesty's Theatre, will take part:–

MADLLE.TITTENS,

Madlle.GROSSI,

Madlle. SINICO,

Signor GARDONI,

Signor BOSSI,

Conductor .... Signor ARDITI

PRICES OF ADMISSION:– Balcony and Area Stalls, Reserved and Numbered, 5s.; Family Tickets, to admit Five, 21s.; Balcony, Unreserved, 3s.; Area Side Seats, 2s. 6d.; Gallery 1s.

Choir Tickets will be issued at Reduced Rates to the Gallery. Form of Application and Tickets must be previously obtained. Bills of particulars of the Railway accommodation may be had at the various Stations

In order to avoid confusion, Seats can only be secured at Mr. Brader's Musical Repository, where a Plan of the Hall can be seen. For Railway Arrangements see Small Bills and Programmes.

The Engagement of the above Artistes having been made in July last for their appearance in Swansea on the date now Advertised, Mr. Mapleton has no alternative but to fulfill his part of the Contract, in order to avoid any serious loss which might be sustained by the gentleman who now wishes to decline the engagement.

——◇——

NEW MUSIC HALL,

Swansea.

GRAND CONCERT.

MADAME GRISI,

MADAME SAINTON DOLBY,

SIGNOR MARIO,

MR. PATEY,

MR. SAINTON,

And,

HERR MEYER LUTZ,

will give a concert at the above Hall, at Eight o'clock, on

FRIDAY, OCTOBER 14.

Admission:

Balcony Stalls (reserved and numbered). 5s.; Area Stalls, ditto 5s.; Balcony, 3s.; Area Sides, 2s. 6d.; Area Back and Orchestra, 1s. 6d.; Gallery, 1s.

Tickets to be obtained at the Misses Jenkin's Library, Wind-street, where a Plan of the seats may be seen.

Special Trains will leave Swansea for the Mumbles, and by the Vale of Neath Railway for Neath, Aberdare, and Merthyr, after the concert is over.

To the EDITOR of The CAMBRIAN.

Sir, – By the merest accident in the world, your excellent paper of 30th. ult. fell into my hands; and having once heard of Talhaiarn as being one of your local poets, it was not without a certain interest that I turned to the letter bearing his name inserted in the paper of the above date. To confirm the Truth, I was much disappointed. That gentleman may be or may not be a great Welsh poet, but one thing he is, judging from the above mentioned production, a most insufferable egotist.

For instance:– "Many of my brother-bards said to me, 'Tal, *if you had been our conductor,* we should have had more life.' I said, no, no, I won't have that." This sentence where it stands in the letter has, in my opinion, no relation with what goes before or after. But taking it in connection with the general tenor of his letter, the plain inference is that if I – Talhaiarn – had been elected to conduct this affair, the whole would have been a decided success.

And this sentence is equally offensive:–

"I recollect reading of an Eisteddfod held, in South Wales, when about a hundred competitors had to sing one song, and, if I rightly recollect, *the song was mine.* What a terrible affliction." Very likely!

The closing part of the letter, however, is certainly the most offensive to good taste.

"I am in the position of Solomon when he exclaimed, 'Wisdom crieth out in the street, and no man regardeth her'". We are not unfrequently in this country in want of a little wisdom, and when Talhaiarn has a holiday perhaps he would come over and cry in our streets, it might have a beneficial effect; of course, taking granted all that he says of himself.

Now, sir, excuse this letter. I have no personal or national prejudice in the matter. But I have written in hopes that Talhaiarn will exercise a little more modesty when speaking of himself in public again; especially when he assumes to dictate to others how and what they should do.

I am, Sir, your most obedient servant,

A Scotchman.

Edinburgh, 5th. Oct., 1864.

Heavy Gale on the Welsh Coast. – Porthcawl, Tuesday. – A terrific easterly gale, says Captain Buchan R.N. has been blowing since 10 p.m. on Sunday, with but slight intermission. We are making a floating dock &c. but last night our navvies could not work, all their fires, lamps, &c. being blown out.

Reynoldston. – On the 28th. ult. the children belonging to the Reynoldston School, mustering about 70 in number, were regaled in a very handsome and liberal manner by Mrs. Wood of Stouthall. The schoolroom was tastefully decorated for the occasion by the young ladies and their governess (Mrs. Rains). with festoons of evergreens and bouquets of the choicest flowers. Among some of the precepts and texts beautifully wrought were the following:– "God is love," Suffer little children to come unto me," "Search the Scriptures," "Wisdom is better than rubies," "Be diligent," &c. The weather being so genial, the pleasures of the day were consisderably enhanced. It is customary on such interesting occasions to put the whole of the children through a course of searching examination, which was done on the present occasion by the venerable and respected Rector of Reynoldston, and the Rev. J. Davies, M.A. Rector of Llanmadock, who has lately been appointed Inspector of Schools by the Diocesan Board of Education, and the master of the school, Mr. E. G. Harris. There were present at the examination Col. and Mrs. Wood and the young ladies,; Mr. Falconer of Bath; Mr. Benson and the young ladies of Fairy Hill. Mrs. Wood expressed her approval of the qualifications of the pupils examined by presenting the most successful with several beautifully bound and valuable books as an encouragement of their assiduity in the prosecution of their studies. The awarding of prizes is productive of much good and produces a very salutary effect on the characters of children generally. Their good conduct and merit acknowledged by their superiors and rewarded, thereby stengthening the endeavours of the diligent to further diligence, and indirectly instilling a spirit of emulation among those who through thoughtlessness, carelessness, irregular attendance, and want of application are not so successful as their coadjutors in the work of learning. This interesting feature in the day's proceeding having terminated, ample justice was done to the good things provided. Tea being over and the national anthem having been sung, the children, to express their deep felt gratitude for so rich a treat, made the place reverberate with three times three hearty cheers for their kind benefactress, which was followed by a long loud shout for the young ladies who had so graciously and unremittingly waited upon them with tea and cake. The remaining part of the evening was spent in athletic sports &c. Colonel Wood kindly provided a balloon and superintended the letting it off, and a capital ascent was witnessed. Altogether the day was quite a fete, and will be remembered with pleasure by one and all. The assistance rendered to the school by the family at Stouthall is very material, and through their instrumentality in a great measure, the successful condition is mainly attributable. – *Cor.*

Rescue of Two Men from a Sinking Barge in the Bristol Channel. – As the Sovereign steamer from Liverpool to Bristol, was proceeding up Channel about nine o'clock on Sunday evening, she was hailed, when off the Nash, by two men in an open barge, who begged to be taken off, as their vessel was in a sinking state. It being very dark at the time, and blowing a gale from the south-east, this was accomplished with some difficulty, and the poor fellows, who were very much exhausted by long exposure to wet and cold, brought under the notice of the Ship-wrecked Mariners Society. Acts of this kind deserve the fullest reward.

New Passage. – On Tuesday evening last, T. J. Ward Esq., of Elberton, gave a capital supper to the servants of the Bristol and South Wales Union Railway engaged at the New Passage end of the line, and to Mr. Bland's superintendents on the piers, and others. On Wednesday the same gentleman gave the men employed in the locomotive department of the line a substantial dinner, and in the evening the men on the New Passage piers were liberally entertained by Mr. Ward. Mr. Robertson, the manager of the New Passage Hotel, supplied these repasts, and they reflected great credit on his catering abilities.

Miss Edmonds' Concert. – This concert came off last evening, at the new Music Hall, and we are glad to report that it proved a bumper, the hall being filled with a most respectable audience, including the Mayor of Swansea, H. Hussey Vivian, Esq,. M.P., P. St. I. Grenfell, Esq., H. A. Ford, Esq., &c. Miss Edmunds was aided by Signor Paggi, flautist; Mr. W. B. Kingston, pianist; Mr. Frost, harpist; Mr. Fricker, Mr. Jones-Hewson, and the members of the York Unity Class, all of whom acquitted themselves with considerable ability, and to the entire satisfaction of the audience. This was Miss Edmonds' first appearance in Swansea since her return from London, where she has been studying for three months under first class artistes. The improvement she has undergone in that short time was most marked. Her style was chaste, her voice flexible, her execution facile, whilst her enunciation was most distinct and clear proving that she has been not only a diligent pupil, but possessed of a musical genius of a high order. She was vociferously encored, and highly deserved the plaudits bestowed on her, especially in her execution of the "Mocking Bird," in which she was most ably sustained by the dulcet notes of Signor Paggi's flute. Mr. Frost's solos on the harp were much admired, and Mr. W. B. Kingston's fantasias were admirably rendered. The Unity Class, too, sang the Welsh Airs with great taste and judgment, whilst Mr. Jones-Hewson contributed his share to diversify the proceedings. On the whole the concert was a great success, and we heartily congratulate the fair cantatrice on the progress which she has made in her profession.

THE SHIPPING TRADE

We observe by the harbour returns, just published, that the Shipping Trade of Swansea last month, although not so brisk as that for August, has been much more satisfactory than we were led to expect, considering the adverse winds experienced of late. During September 417 vessels entered Swansea, having a registered tonnage of 55,410. Of this number 225 ships registering 21,074 tons were in the coasting trade; 157, or 21,699 tons in the European trade; and 35, or 12,637 tons, in the trade beyond Europe. As compared with the corresponding month last year, September, 1864 presents an increase in tonnage of 3,757 tons; and £148. 4s.7½d. in money. The receipts from all sources during the month amounted to £3,747.9s.1d., leaving a balance of about £500 in favour of the General Harbour Estate. This is highly satisfactory, and proves the trade of the port to be in a sound, healthy state. On Wednesday last, the new Narrow Gauge Route between Swansea, Hereford, Birmingham, Shrewsbury, Birkenhead Liverpool, Manchester and the North, was opened. This additional feeder to the harbour will give an immediate impulse to our trade. Swansea can now boast of a direct communication with the great narrow guage network of the kingdom. It is a new era in its history, and there is no doubt that the increased facilities which the new route will afford the public, will tend to foster among us new trades, which cannot fail to be productive of great advantages not only to the town and port, but to the whole district.

Monmouth and South Wales. – Sept. 29. – The Ironmasters of Monmouth and South Wales are well supplied with orders, and in many instances the books are full for the next two or three months. The works are in regular employ, and a large amount of activity is to be witnessed on all sides. The advance in bars is fully sustained, and rails are also in active enquiry, more especially on foreign account. As stated last week, some orders are sent to South Wales which would have been executed in Staffordshire had it not been for the turn-out there. The collieries are unusually busy, and the daily output is at present larger than it has been for a considerable time. Contracts have been entered into to supply several Staffordshire makers with fuel for two and three months to come, and the energies of the railway authorities are taxed to the utmost in conducting what may be termed this immense traffic . . . There is no lack of demand in the house coal trade but the dearth of coasters continues and, in consequence buyers are unable to get their supplies at the required time. Red Ash is quoted 10s., free on board at Newport. Attempts are being made to induce the colliers of this district to follow the example of the Staffordshire men, but it is satisfactory to add that up to the present times these attempts have failed in their object, except in so far as to obtain expressions of sympathy from the Welsh colliers. Expressions of sympathy can, however, be indulged in to any extent without trade being injured, and no one will interfere with such indications of feeling. It is and admitted fact that a good collier can now earn in this district 35s. per week on average; and as there is no lack of employment, would it not be exceedingly unwise on the part of the men to send the trade away by resorting to a strike, and lose the present golden opportunity of making money? No doubt they see this, and they have adopted the sensible course of looking after their own interests, and leaving every other district to do the same.

Skilful Surgery. – The surgery of this army is reaching an extraordinarily high scale as weapons reach perfection. Men wounded in the head or neck are fed for weeks through india-rubber tubes. The following is an instance of the wonderful cures made by our surgeons. A man with throat cut from ear to ear was thought to be mortally wounded by a council of surgeons; but the one under whose care the man was thought, as he was to die, he was justified in making an experiment for the good of others, at the same time having great hopes of saving the man. He first commenced his task by cutting through where the two upper ribs meet the sternum, and through this orifice for forty days this man had been fed with five gallons of milk per week, and sometimes his appetite required five pints per day. He is fat and hearty, and the surgeon thinks in two weeks he shall have him able, and the inside of his throat as nearly healed as to allow him to swallow by the natural passage. He at first introduced a stomach pump, and then fed his patient, and after a few hours would clear his stomach by the same means, thus producing artificial digestion until it was no longer necessary. A silver tube is now need to feed him, and such is the progress made by the medical department in these parts that half of a man's face demolished by a ball or piece of shell is replaced by a cork face. – *Springfield Republican.*

Llanelly Special and Petty Sessions, Oct 5, – [Before Col. Stepney and J. H. Rees, Esq.] – John Francis, of Felinfoel, collier, was charged by Mr. W. Isaac, assistant overseer, with having unlawfully neglected to support his wife, whereby she became and now was chargeable to the parish of Llanelly.

The charge was not pressed, and the defendant promised to maintain his wife in future and pay all expenses . . .

Margaret Thomas, Pottery Row, widow, was charged by Mr. William Isaac, Llanelly, collector, with having on the 27th ult. taken a quantity of water from one of the taps belonging to the Llanelly Local Board, not having agreed for a supply of the same. The complaint was withdrawn on defendant paying the water rates and costs . . .

Mr. John Brodie, Tirdail, Llandybie, was fined 1s. and costs for allowing his cart to be used on the highway in the parish of Llanedy, without having the name painted thereon.

2nd. November 1866.

SHIPPING INTELLIGENCE.

The Saginaw, from Cardiff for Panama, has been burnt at sea.

The Star, hence Jersey, put into Ilfracombe on Friday, with damage.

St. Thomas, Oct. 13. – The barque Cornwall (Watkins) for Cuba (coals and machinery), put in here Oct. 4, dismasted and otherwise damaged and is discharging for repairs.

Swansea, Oct. 26. – The Emma. C. Beal reports that on the 21st of October, in lat 48 N., long. 16W., she spoke a Norwegian bark which had taken off the crew of the Robert Staple, of Nova Scotia, from Newcastle for Halifax N.S.

Milford, Oct. 26. – The Friends, of this port, from Cardigan to Swansea, in ballast struck something supposed to be a wreck, about five S.W. of Caldy, last night, and sunk about 1a.m.; crew saved.

Madeira, Oct. 20. – The Belle of Devon, from Cardiff for Montivideo, put in here on the 18th. October to land the crew of the Saginaw, from Cardiff which was burnt about 170 miles N.E. of this Island.

Swansea. Oct. 30. – The Montonden of Llanelly hence to Cork, was dismasted off Caldy, on the 28th of September, in a squall and brought in here by the Scottish Lass from Runcorn.

———◇———

The Cholera. – This epedemic, which at its onset carried so many of the inhabitants away, has now happily cleared away from our midst – but by close attention to the sanitary condition of the town and other measures being carried into effect, the disease has been got the better of. There has been a great number of cases under treatment. and death at one time came rapidly upon them, but through God's merciful providence, who has stretched out His arm to save, we are now, I am happy to say, free. A correspondent writing to us upon the visitation and treatment of cholera, adds:– "All the recoveries from this direful disease are not owing to the medical skill of the neighbourhood, for they appeared to be baffled in their repeated efforts to save; but there is a gentleman, a tradesman living among us, Mr. Williams, who procured a prescription which proved an infallible and invaluable medicine in nearly every case where administered. This Mr. Williams generously gave upwards of 500 who had been seized by the complaint, besides other comforts to those afflicted, entirely at his own expence; and in many instances where medical skill was found unavailing Mr. William's treatment proved successful, and I am not aware of a single case of death occurring where that medicine was made use of." We understand from undoubted authority that our correspondent is correct in his remarks, and that any person who may still have cause to apply may obtain the like assistance; and we may add that the medicine is not only effectual but harmless, being perfectly safe in the hands of any party. This prescription has also been freely given by Mr. Williams to several persons at Neath, Aberavon, Cadoxton, Glyn Neath and other places where it has been attended with like success. The Rev. David Lewis, Incumbent of Britonferry, was also very indefatigable during the prevalence of this epedemic in rendering all the aid he possibly could to the sufferers.

———◇———

The Health of the Town – We are glad to be enabled to state that the town was on Tuesday last formally declared to be entirely free of cholera, no case having occurred for several days past. Clean bills of health can now be given, and thus the trade of the port is again placed upon a satisfactory footing. The cholera hospital will be broken up in a few days.

Cardiff. – The Mayorality. – No definite arrangement has yet been come to as to the Mayorality, and the office this year will regularly go a begging. To assist the Council out of their dilemma we would suggest that the senior member, who has not yet passed the chair should be uniformly elected, which would be following the example of the first municipality in the kingdom. If it be objected that such a practice would necessitate the election of men who were disqualified in point of position and aptitude for the discharge of such onerous duties, the reply is, the ratepayers should not send such men into the Council. It is highly objectionable to force the office upon those who have already passed the chair, and the course we have suggested, although for a time it would place certain gentlemen in an akward position, would ultimately work its own cure.

SWANSEA POLICE COURT

[Before R. Eates, Esq., N.P. Cameron, Esq., and H.R. Bagabawe, Esq., Q.C.]

Travelling without a Ticket. – Edward Patrick was charged with travelling in a carriage on the Great Western Railway without a ticket. David Richards, the ticket-collector at the Swansea station, said that between eight and nine o'clock on the previous day, on the arrival of the train from Paddington, he collected the tickets from the passengers in the usual way. While so doing, the prisoner came up and gave him a ticket from Liverpool to Cardiff, which he now produced. Witness told him that he had to pay 3s.9½d., the fare from Cardiff to Swansea, and to give a reason why he came without a ticket, and, failing to do this, he was given into custody. Defendant was convicted, and ordered to pay the fare, and a fine of 2s. 8½d., or to go to prison for seven days.

Unlawful Possession of Game. – John Grove, carrier, Porteynon, was charged with being in the unlawful possession of game. Mr. H. Morris appeared for the defendant. P.C. Dunlop said that he was stationed at Sketty, and that about half-past nine o'clock on Saturday morning, the 20th. last, he was on duty in the village of Sketty when he saw the defendant driving an omnibus or covered conveyance, down through the village, on the turnpike road. When he came up to witness, the omnibus, by witness's direction, was pulled up to the side of the road. Witness got up on the omnibus, and defendant asked him what he wanted. Witness told him he was in search of game. Defendant replied, "You need not look here; I've not got any." The defendant's bus that day came from Porteynon, in Gower, and necessarily had to pass through and over land frequented by game. Witness opened the boot, and removed several packages, and found a paper parcel containing four partridges. The parcel was merely folded up, and not directed to any one. He removed several other packages and parcels, and in the bottom of the boot found a bag tied with a string and not addressed to any one. The bag at the bottom was stained with fresh blood. He took the bag out of the boot and put it on the ground, and the defendant was about to

'Druslwyn' – Dr. T. D. Griffiths' home.

Parc le Breos.

The Assembly Rooms, Swansea.

Swansea Union Workhouse (Tawe Lodge).

drive off, when he told him to stop, as he wanted to see what was in the bag. He then opened the bag and took out of it six partridges and three hares. When the partridges were taken out of the paper parcel, defendant said they belonged to Mr. Curtis, and that he had received them of one of the servants at Paviland, and that Mr. Penrice had been down the day before shooting. He said he did not know where they were going, he did not even know they were there. Cross-examined: Defendant's conveyance was a public conveyance. The bus was full that morning. The rabbits and hares were ginned. For the defence Mr. R. Curtis was called,who said that he lived at Paviland with his brother, who was a tenant of Mr. Penrice. Saw Mr. Penrice on Paviland farm, and he gave him (Mr. Curtis) two braces of partridges. Sent the partridges to his sister, Mrs Bevan, on Friday evening by the carrier. The partridges were packed up in a newspaper. Edward Roberts, grocer, Swansea, said that he came from Porteynon, on Saturday last, by the defendant's conveyance. Had a carpet bag, a box, two umbrellas, and a rabbit, which was all his luggage. The Bench, after a short deliberation, said they were satisfied as to the partridges and the rabbit that there was no offence committed; but as to the bag of game, there was no explanation offered, although there had been abundance of time to have obtained it. Defendant was convicted and fined 20s. including costs.

John Taylor, carrier, was convicted of a similar offence on the evidence of P.C.Dunlop, and was fined 20s.including costs.

Our Sanitary Condition.

Llanelly is not favourably situated for draining. The buildings are not compact and well together, but scattered, and in batches at some distances from each other, so that considerable lengths of main drains have to be made to connect the distant batches of buildings with the system of drainage; we therefore drain at a great increase of cost over a more compact built place. Much remains to be done in the way of drainage. A sum of about £4,500 must be expended, to complete the main drains; and as but few of the houses in town are properly connected with the main drains, a sum varying from £3 to £6 per house, will have to be expended by the owners of the houses, to place their premises in a proper state as to drainage. The number of properly constructed water closets in the the district now are only 59, so that much remains to be done by the owners and occupiers of houses, in the shape of providing water closets, but before the Board can call upon them to make this alteration, there must be an improved supply of water to work them with, and further drains constructed. Our district has not for some time been in a satisfactory state of health. You will remember that last year we had a good deal of fever about, and we had Dr. Hunter down. This fever was not confined to any particular corner of the district, but was general all over it. There was a suggestion that the drains we had constructed were nor efficient; this, however, I do not believe to be the case. I believe that at two or three points our main drain has sunk with the ground consequent on old colliery workings underneath. At these points there is, at all times, a certain amount of deposit in the drain, but this deposit always being covered with water, I do not think that much harm can arise therefrom. When the ground has quite settled, these portions will have to be reconstructed to the proper fall; this being done, and the main sewer extended from the Iron Works to the outfall, I believe we shall find our drains work efficiently. In the month of July, in this year, the cholera broke out amongst us, and has carried away, in the district of the Board, about 160 persons. We are now free of this epedemic, and our death rate at present is not excessive. In looking at the localities affected by cholera, we came to the same conclusion as we did to the previous fever, that it was not confined to one or two parts of the district, but was very general over its entire area; the part least touched was the more thickly inhabited part of the town proper, where there are more drains and fewer pig styes. At present, I find we have in our district 1,155 pig styes, and 815 pigs are kept therein. With the view to improve our sanitory condition, our efforts must be directed to improved drainage, more water, suppression of pig-keeping, removal of manure, which must not be allowed to accumulate in heaps for garden uses. These are matters that, I trust this Board will deal with at once with firmness, and a determination to place our district in a state of health that will compare favourably with neighbouring towns . . .

I am not prepared to say what the cholera fee has cost the district, but no doubt a very large sum in hard cash, with loss in trade, disarrangement of most matters, to say nothing of the loss of so many valuable lives, and the many orphans and helpless to be maintained . . .

The matters mostly requiring the attention of the Board now are:–

1. The carrying out cost of the improved Water Supply including the building of the New Water Works.
2. Extending the drainage and improving the Sanitary condition.
3. The establishment of a Public Slaughter-house.
4. The laying out of our Park, or recreation ground, and the providing of a Market.

Longevity at the Copper Works – On Wednesday sen'night death put an end to the active services of an old and respected employee at the Morfa Copper Works, in the person of Mr. John Thomas, foreman of the masons, at the advanced age of 83 years, 70 of which he served as man and boy in the above works, and from his honest and upright conduct won the confidence of his employers and the esteem of all who knew him. The late Mr. Thomas is another of the many instances of longevity in the copper works' district; and it may be said of this old veteran, as of those who have gone before him, that he lived his patriarchal life in the midst of the copper smoke.

The training will embrace, at the option of the pupil, preparation for the Universities' Courses and Public Schools, or Public Examining Boards; or, directly, for the Professions or a Practical Introduction to Commercial and Scientific Paramits.

Terms Fifty Guineas for the Academical year; and separate instructions may be had in Elocution and English Composition on special terms.

Situation, salubrious and picturesque; premises commodious and extensive.

For further details, see prospectus.

THEATRE ROYAL,
SWANSEA.

Sole Lessee .... Mrs. Charles Pitt.
Director .... Mr. W.R.Clifton.
Licensed to play the Pieces of the Dramatic Author's Society.

Fourth Grand Fashionable Night of the Winter Season.

This Evening (Friday), Nov. 2, 1866,
Charles Selby's Romantic Drama of
THE MARBLE HEART! or
The Sculptor's Dream.
To conclude with
SARAH'S YOUNG MAN.

Saturday, Nov 3rd. –
The Grand Nautical Drama of
BEN THE BOATSWAIN!
and the Romantic Melo-drama of
THE CHARCOAL BURNER
or, the Dropping Well of Knaresboro'.

On Monday and Tuesday Evenings,
Nov. 5th. and 6th.
The Grand Historical Play of
CATHERINE HOWARD
Or, the Tomb, the Throne &
the Seaflood.

Gorgeous New Dresses and Splendid Appointments

Girl's Evening School. – We are requested to announce that this school, which is held at Trinity Chapel School-room, Swansea, will be opened on Monday next for the instruction, in reading and writing, of girls over 16 years of age and of adults, and will be continued during the winter months on Monday and Wednesday evenings – hours 7 to 9. There is a Penny Bank held at the above school-room on Saturday evenings from 7 to 8 o'clock – also a Bible Club.

Opening of the New Catholic
Church, Greenhill.

THE NEW CATHOLIC CHURCH, Greenhill, Swansea will be solemnly dedicated on Sunday, November 4, 1866.

High Mass, Curam Episcopa, at Eleven o'clock. Sermon by the LORD BISHOP of the United Diocese of Newport and Minevia.

Music. – Massinghi's Mass in B flat, with "Credo." Passion in G; "Agnus Dei." Wall, E flat; Offertoruam, "Laudate." Zengaretti. Organist, Mr. Wall.

Vespers and Benediction at Four o'clock.
Sermons by the Very Rev.
ROGER BEDE VAUGHAN. O.S.B.,
Prior of St. Michael's Priory Hereford.

Admission to High Mass:
Front Seats, 3s; Second Seats, 2s.;
Third Seats, 6d.
Admission to Vespers:
First Seats, 1s.6d.; Second Seats, 1s.
Third Seats, 6d.
Collection at Each Service.

No Services at Eleven and half-past 3 in St. David's Church, Rutland -street, on that Sunday.

Tickets to be had at the Catholic Presbytery, St. David's Place or at the Convent, Green hill.

Entertainment at the Music Hall. – On Tuesday evening an entertainment was given in the above hall, on behalf of the Swansea Juvenile Dorcas Society. The chair was taken by S. B. Power, Esq., who said that the society was established for the purpose of providing clothing for the destitute poor, and for impressing upon the minds of the young mothers the lessons of self denial. It had, like many other good things, grown from small beginnings; the number of young workers at the commencement being 11, but they were now 36. This was mainly due to the energy of the enterprising Secretary; and the profits of the entertainment named would be devoted to the purchase of material for winter clothing for the poor. The programme was opened by a piano forte solo by Miss Sayer (Mr. Fricker not being able to be present) Glees and songs were sung during the evening, by Messrs Cole, Jones, Robinson and Hennings. The readings were by the Rev. J. C. Gollan and Mr. W. E. Brown. A piano forte solo by Mrs. Moulding received considerable applause. The dissolving views, exhibited by Dr. Evan Davies, included several local scenes, and the portraits of several of the public men of Swansea. The entertainment, which was of a very superior character, closed about ten o'clock, with a vote of thanks to those who had taken part in the entertainment, and who had rendered valuable voluntary service. The Chairman also announced that subscriptions, or articles of clothing, could be sent to Miss Matilda Smith, Melbourne House, the secretary of the society.

Foreign Arrivals. – From Pomeron the Hannah, with 130 tons of copper ore to order, from Hondeklip, the Ottawa, with 350 tons of copper ore for Richardson and Co.; from Pont L'Abbe the Voilier, with 50 tons of potatoes to order; from France the Euphrasto with 70 tons of potatoes for Hoskins; from Pan de Zugar, Beatrice with 595 tons of copper regulus, 68 tons of copper ore, and 11 tons of nickel ore for the Cobre Mining Company; from Havre, the Havre with 50 cases of wine for H. Bath and Co., 100 cases ditto for T. Ford and Co. and 17 cases ditto for Wm. Jones; from San Francisco the Emma C. Best with 535 tons of copper ore, 45 tons of silver ore, 102 bales of whale fins, and 50 pieces of beef for Townshend Wood and Co.; from Cuba the Conqueror, with 600 tons of copper ore for Richardson and Co.; the Maida from Paposa, with 336 tons of copper regulus and 27 ox hides for H. Bath and Son. Rose of England from Tocapilla, with 517 tons of copper ore in bulk, and 86 tons of copper regulus for Elford, Williams and Co. Madeleine from Caldera, with 535 tons of copper ore for H. Bath and Son; Jeane Colome from St. Malo, with 160 tons of zinc ore for Mr. Rowland; Eirene from Rotterdam, with 77 tons of old yellow metal for Vivian and Sons; Florence Danvers from Caldera, with 380 tons of silver ore, 101 tons of copper regulus, and 149 tons of silver ore for Anthony, Gibbs and Co.; Gatanilla from Cuba with 545 tons of copper ore, and 94 tons of copper regulus for Cobre Mining Co.

ORANGE-STREET
AND THE MARKET.

To the Editor of "The Cambrian."
Sir, – As you are always ready to insert in your columns what may improve the interests of the unprotected, I feel you will do so on this occasion.

I observed in your last impression that the widow of the late Mr. John Potter, Orange-street, was brought forward for arrears of *rates* amounting to £26, and *ordered to pay the same.* On enquiry I find that her late husband, in the laudable endeavour to improve his property, made four large shops on the faith of the long promised new gate in Orange-street. "Hope deferred maketh the heart sick," and the long delayed alterations did not improve his health. The shops are not let in consequence of having no entrance to the market. The widow preferred keeping them open herself to seeing them shut up, and the above rates are the consequence.

Is it fair that those who are today professing to represent the interests of the borough should be so partial as to be constantly improving Oxford-street and Union-street and neglecting Orange-street and Nelson-street, equally central and convenient to the public for an entrance to the market?

I also observe that the disorderly house belonging to a Guardian of the Poor is permitted to remain on the very spot where the new gate should be. As our worthy Alderman has acknowledged the money is ready, let them throw the house down, and rid the neighbourhood of a nuisance. The new gate there would cause uniformity, being directly opposite the one in Oxford-street.

I am, Sir, yours faithfully,
A Lover of Justice.
Swansea. October 31st, 1866.

4th. December 1868.

Proposed Great Passenger Ship – We have seen a model of what is probably "the coming" ship of this age. It is to be the same size as the Great Eastern, except that instead of 28ft. it will only draw 18ft.; and it will carry proportionately less tonnage. It is designed to carry four times as many passengers as any present style of ship, and to substitute for bunks Christian beds; it will also give four times the space to a state room. The present mode of bunking passengers is unworthy of the age. Sea-sickness if preventible by construction, should be rendered obsolete. This desideratum is attained in Thomas Silver's coming ship; it is secured by the proportion of the ship and there being 30 ft. less of the hull out of the water than in the Great Eastern: but the motion is rendered almost imperceptible by a new device. The staterooms, instead of being at the outside limits of the vessel are amidships; that is, along the centre line of the ship, where the roll is scarcely perceptible. The saloon is to be 500ft. long and clear of obstructions. It is not for dining. Instead of a public table, there are to be two competing restaurants at the extremities adjoining the saloon. The ship will sell passage only, the board being paid as meals are ordered.

It is contemplated to carry second-class passengers and third class in the same way. The present first class bunks will be for third class berths.

The Fortunate Painter, – A short time ago a paragraph appeared in several papers stating that a painter named Ashton, residing in Cardiff, had been left a legacy of £80,000. The paragraph appeared in some of the London papers first of all, and was then copied into the Swansea papers. Ashton had been for some time a member of the Free Methodist connexion and was apparently a very religious young man. When therefore he left his work, and assumed the garb of a gentleman, many who before doubted believed in the truth of the statement. As usual friends poured in upon him, and offers of temporary assistance were made until the legal formulas had been completed. In the meantime he was very lavish in his promises, and offered to give £1000 towards the purchase of a building as a new chapel. Various sums of money have been advanced to him and his bills at the drapers, clothiers, jewellers and others are said to be very heavy: while one of his brother workmen, it is said, borrowed £80 of a friend to lend him. Numerous tradesmen had become securities for him to the amount of several hundred pounds, and it is said also that the committee of management and the minister of the Free Methodist chapel are all sufferers. Ashton left Cardiff eight days ago to take possession of his property, taking with him a large sum of money, and since then the whole affair has exploded. The police are in pursuit of the fugitive.

The Flirting Farmer. – A certain season of the year when the crops are gathered in, and there is a lull in the business of the farm, a curious style of young man may be noticed pervading the music halls and the livlier theatres of London. He wears clothes of a provincial cut, and adopts an air of supreme knowingness and, with an evident anxiety to appear at home in Fleet-street, succeds in displaying aspects and graces which altogether belong o the country. He has but few friends in town, and after a short time even comic songs begin to weary him, and the charms of the ballet fascinate him no longer. Still, however he remains sufficiently long in the metropolis to catch up scraps for the decoration of his talk and of his manners in his native place. He is not in the county set although he goes regularly to the county ball. His family are of middle class; his father was a yeoman, and is now even reconciled to the position assumed by his son, on account of an uneasy feeling that his son has no right to it. Our friend is the flirting farmer. He is, of course, a dandy, after his own notion of the part. His views on the point tend towards very tight and horsey garments and low crown debits. His healthy, handsome and vacuous countenance is invariably fringed with a borde of whiskers, and of late years he no more hesitates about a moustache than would an officer in the Blues. Although he knows his business often thoroughly, it is his way at times to seem as ignorant of it as any club swell is in reality of most things. With his sisters he is grandiose and stupid; with the sisters of his friends it is at once his pleasure, and his duty, so to speak, to flirt. He is as prossie as a pig, without the chance of being etherianised, as Lamb would, say, into bacon. And yet he tries to play at love, at love of all things in the world. We could wish that he were permitted an hour of sense to be able to disclose his views on this subject; as it is we can only indicate him and his existence to those of our fair readers who may come across him in his beats. He will be found worth studying, if not worth marrying; though whether the game would be worth the chase in the latter alternative is a question which women can always best judge for themselves. A Nemesis attends the flirting farmer. He is married at last, and not always happily. He has put it off so long, and disgusted so many by his flippant demeanour, that, in the end, he is obliged to get wedded almost as a necessity of business. – *The London Review.*

Wholesale Rustication at Oxford. – Considerable excitement was caused at Oxford, on Monday, by the whole of the undergraduate members of New College being ordered "down" in consequence of damage done by them to fellow Collegian's windows. As they positively refused to deliver up the actual offender, the authorities of the College deemed it expedient to resort to this extreme measure, and in the course of the day the undergraduates had left College with the exception of those at present engaged in the schools, but who will have to quit the moment they have finished their examinations. It will doubtless be remembered that last Summer Term, the authorities of University College adopted the same course under similar circumstances; but in this case the undergraduates were permitted to return the next day, the Dons having changed their minds. Whether the New College authorities will follow their course is not known, but at the present time the College is empty.

Improvement of the Severn Navigation. – On Monday last, the plans and actions for the proposed further improvement of the navigation of the river Severn were duly deposited with the clerks of the peace for the counties of Worcester and Gloucester. The additional works proposed to be erected are very important. At present there is a series of five sets of locks and were constructed on the river between Gloucester and Stourport, extending over a length of some 50 miles of river, the object being to raise the natural level of the river and maintain permanently six feet of water for navigation purposes. Practically, it is found that this depth cannot be maintained permanently on account of the deposits of mud, which require frequent dredging. This is especially the case in the tidal portion of the river between Gloucester and Tewkesbury. The present locks and weirs are placed at Tewkesbury, Worcester, Bevere, Holt, and Lincomb, and the tide runs constantly up to Tewkesbury, and frequently over the weir. It is now proposed to place a sixth weir at Gloucester, or rather two, in as much as the river divides into two channels at that place. The eastern channel passes by Gloucester and is very circuitous. The western channel, being almost straight, the great rush of tide passes up it, and, consequently the eastern channel is constantly filling up with mud, of which the Severn tides move an immense quantity every day. By the plans to be submitted to Parliament it is proposed to straighten the eastern channels and so lead more water down it past Gloucester and the mouth of the Gloucester Berkeley ship canal. The two weirs are to be placed, the one below Gloucester, on the eastern channel, near to the point where the two channels unite, and the other, at the upper portion of the western channel lock, will be constructed in artificial cuttings, to be made parallel with the weirs. By means of these weirs, or dams, the water will be penned up to a sufficient height on the site of the Gloucester and Berkeley Canal to allow free ingress and egress of vessels between the canal and the river (which was not attainable during last summer), and it will also pen the water above to a sufficient depth for navigation to the Tewkesbury weir, 12 miles higher up the river. The tide in the Severn runs up very rapidly and ebbs very slowly, which encourages a very large deposit of mud, held in suspension in the river. Constant dredging will, therefore, still be required in the 12 miles between Gloucester and Tewkesbury to maintain the required depth of water for navigation.

Correspondence.

We do not hold ourselves responsible for the opinions and sentients expressed by our Correspondents.

OXFORD AND CAMBRIDGE LOCAL EXAMINATIONS.

To the Editor of "The Cambrian."

Sir, – Will you allow me to call the attention of your readers to the speech of the Chancellor of the Exchequer at Northampton., when the prizes gained by the students at these examinations were publicly distributed. It will be seen that Mr. Ward Hunt goes over the same ground as I have done in my letters to you, and he says almost the same things.

I will take the oppotunity of bearing testimony to the readiness and eagerness with which the gentlemen of Swansea have taken the matter up. It speaks much for the welfare of the town that there are influential gentlemen in it willing to make sacrifices for its benefit.

Schoolmasters and Parents may congratulate themselves that in Mr. Wilson they have a Mayor strongly attached to the cause of Education.

My efforts having now been brought to a successful termination, I have no further occasion for addressing your readers. All information respecting these examinations can be obtained of J. Williams, Esq., M.D., Hon. Secretary of the Local Committee, Union-street, Swansea.

I am, sir, very faithfully yours.

W. L. Vaughan Bristow,

25, Mansel Terrace, Swansea,

NEVER SATISFIED.

A man in his carriage was riding along,
A gaily dressed wife by his side;
In satin and laces she looked like a
queen,
And he like a king in his pride.

A wood sawyer stood in the street as
they passed,
The carriage and couple he eyed,
And he said, as he worked with a saw
on a log,
I wish I was rich and could ride.

The man in the carriage remarked to his
wife,
One thing I would give if I could,
I'd give all my wealth for the strength
and the health,
Of the man who is sawing the wood.

A pretty young maid with a bundle of
work,
Whose face as the morning was fair,
Went tripping along with a smile of
delight,
While humming a love-breathing air.

She looked in the carriage – the lady
she saw,
Arrayed in apparel so fine,
And said in a whisper, I wish in my
heart
Those satins and laces were mine.

The lady looked out on the maid with
her work,
So fair in her calico dress,
And said, I'd relinquish position and
wealth,
Her beauty and youth to possess.

Thus it is with the world; whatever our
lot,
Our mind and our time we employ
In longing and sighing for what we
have not,
Ungrateful for what we enjoy.

Miss Francis's Concert The concert on behalf of this young lady came off at the Music Hall on Monday night, and was in every respect most successful. The hall was filled in every part, the dress circles and balconies being occupied by the leading families of the town and district. It will be remembered that this young lady gained the £50 scholarship at the Chester Eisteddfod, which entitles her to a three years' education at the Royal Academy of Music, London, and the present concert was with the view of providing funds to pay for a year of musical study prior to her entering the academy. The artistes were, Mr. Brinley Richards (solo pianist), M. Paque (violoncello), Miss Francis, and the Morvudd Choir, under the very able direction of Mr. Francis, of Morriston. Mr. Brinley Richards came down especially to Swansea from London in fulfilment of a promise which he gave soon after the Eisteddfod at Chester, and again proved his disinterestedness in promoting the success of the natives of the Principality. It need hardly be said that Mr. Richards, upon his entrance on the platform, was received with loud cheers and that each of his performances was vociferously applauded. We cannot, of course pretend to criticise the extraordinary playing of this wonderful instrumentalist and composer, we therefore simply observe that the enthusiasm by which he was received and applauded shewed the appreciation in which he is held. Mr. Paque is also a wonderful performer on the violoncello, and received, as he justly merited, the loudest cheers. Miss Francis, who is at present a pupil of Mr. Barger Wall, and was accompanied on the pianoforte by that gentleman, has a soprano voice of much sweetness, and is doubtless destined to achieve a high position in her profession. To execution of the chorus and part singing by the Morvudd Glan Tawe choir, led by Mr. Francis, was everything that could be desired and was most warmly received. At the conclusion of the concert a most cordial vote of thanks was proposed to Mr. Brinley Richards, by the Mayor (Mr. C. T. Wilson), and seconded by Mr. Evan Richards, the newly elected member for Cardiganshire, and the resolution was carried with acclamation and was acknowledged in a few appropriate words by Mr. Richards. We should not forget to mention that Messrs Broadwood kindly lent one of their grand pianos for the occasion and the Great Western Railway Company kindly conveyed it free of cost. We should also state that much of the success of the concert, in a pecuniary point of view, is due to Mr. Richard Hughes, of Morriston, who undertook all the duties connected with the necessary details, and was also successful in disposing of a very large number of tickets.

Swansea School of Science.

In connection with the Science and Arts Department, South Kensington.

Chairman:

THE MAYOR OF SWANSEA.

Secretary:

DR. PLATT WILKS.

DR. SCHEFTER proposes to OPEN a CLASS in CHEMISTRY under the sanction of the Local Committee of the Scool of Arts.

For further particulars apply to Dr. Schefter, 8, Mansel street.

THE MERTHYR ELECTION.

To The Editor of "The Cambrian."

Sir, – I was glad to see in your paper of last week a most excellent suggestion with the view of wiping out, as far as possible, the stigma which attaches to the rejection of Right Hon. H. A. Bruce from Merthyr. That suggestion was the raising of a public subscription to defray the election expenses of that gentleman. I sincerely hope that some of our leading men in Swansea will at once form a committee to carry out the scheme. The Right Hon. gentleman has many attached friends in Swansea, whilst all classes feel deeply the verdict of the people of Merthyr. There is no need to enlarge upon the merits of Mr. Bruce, or the benefits which have accrued to the public from his seventeen years' faithful servitude. These are known to all. I feel satisfied that the initiative need only be taken when ample funds will be received in a few days or weeks at the utmost. The public are really anxious to show in some tangible way their respect for Mr. Bruce – their appreciation of his high sterling abilities, and at the same time their utter dissent from the opinion pronounced by the ungrateful electors of Merthyr (at least those who voted against him), for whom he has unquestionably done more good than almost any other man living.

Trusting soon to see a good list of committee men, and that Swansea, as boasting itself the metropolis of the Principality, will set the example.

I am &c.

Swansea, Dec. 1st, 1868 An Elector.

THE SWANSEA BOARD OF GUARDIANS.

To The Editor of "The Cambrian."

Sir, – I should be one of the last to curtail the liberty of the Press, inasmuch as I am fully alive to the very great benefits which have arisen and still arise from the fullest publicity being given on all matters of public interest; but, Sir, whilst admitting this, I think all will agree with me when I say Reporters and those who have the management of such a mighty engine as the public press, should exercise proper discretion in what they write. My object in now addressing you is to protest as strongly as I possibly can against the publicity given in your midweek contemporary to a discussion which ensued at the last Board of Guardians upon a most sickening subject. The discussion in itself was doubtless a very proper one as the expenditure of the public money was involved therein; but why the Reporter should have reported it in such full detail I am certainly at a loss to know. One would have thought he would have passed it over altogether. I can only say as the father of several daughters, I forbade the paper being brought into my house, and I am sure no parent who has any regard for common decency would permit his wife or children to read it. I hope, Sir, when any similar subject is brought on for discussion at the Board of Guardians, that the Guardians will see the propriety of doing so with closed doors, and thus prevent the publicity of a discussion, which certainly possessed no possible amount of interest, and would be productive of no good whatever by being made public.

I am, Sir, yours respectfully,

Oxford-st. A Parent

TREATMENT OF BRITISH SEAMEN.

To The Editor of "The Cambrian."

Sir, – I would feel thankful for a short space in the columns of your widely circulated newspaper, in order to give an account of the disgraceful treatment practised upon the body of an English sailor after death. The case to which I allude and of which I was an eye-witness, is as follows:– While lying in company with other vessels, in this port, a British sailor fell overboard his ship, and was drowned. The following morning, having been missed from among his crew, a search was made, and after some time he was picked up and conveyed on board his ship. The circumstances were reported to H.R.M's Consul, who came on board, accompanied by a coroner and a jury. An inquest was held, and after some formalities were gone through, a verdict of "Accidental Death" was returned. The body was then placed in a singularly shaped box, which answered the purpose of a coffin, and conveyed in a boat to shore, followed by seventeen or eighteen ships' boats, manned by four or five men each, on reaching which a procession was formed, and wound its way to a little piece of unfenced ground on the seabeach, about a mile away from the town, which I afterwards learned was kept especially for the burial of heretics, as the inhabitants call Englishmen. On arriving there we were met by a large concourse of people-men, women and children numbering upwards of three hundred, who had collected together for the purpose of witnessing the ceremony. The box coffin was then laid on the ground, when a surgeon approached it, took out the body and commenced brutally cutting it up, for the purpose, I suppose of dissecting. Unable to remain quietly looking on to see one of my fellow countrymen so shamefully cut and mangled, I enquired of the Consul, who was present, the reason for such inhuman conduct, and remonstrated with him, but he only replied by saying, "It was the custom of the country." After this proceeding (which occupied some time) was finished, the pieces were gathered and again placed in the box, and then lowered, with little ceremony, into its last resting place. The spectators afterwards dispersed, and we returned to our ships, much sickened and appalled by the awful scene just witnessed. In conclusion, I think, Sir, you will not differ with me when I say that the trials and hardships a sailor has to undergo during life are, indeed, great and numerous and it is too bad that after death, his body should be subjected to such botchering and much brutal treatment. I do therefore sincerely trust that this may meet the eyes of some of your readers, who have the power and goodwill to prevent such inhuman practices.

I remain, Sir, yours very truly,

D. B. Shipmaster.

Carloforte, Nov 11th. 1868.

Glamorganshire County Roads Board. – The annual letting of the tolls of several turnpike gates within the district of the County Roads Board took place on Monday at the Town-hall, Cardiff, before J. Cole Nichol, Esq., the chairman of the County Roads Board, and several other magistrates. The court in which the letting took place was crowded with persons who had come from all parts of the country. The gates were divided into eight lots. The first lot, which comprised the Cardiff west and north gates, Pengam, Red-house and Llandaff gates was let to Mr. James Percy for £2550. Lot 2, the Bridgend and Cowbridge gates and the district around, was let to Mr. Gardner for £1375. Lots 3 and 4, comprising the districts around Aberdare, Dowlais, &c. were let to Mr. Percy for £1350. Lot 5 Llantrissant and Newbridge gates, was also let to Mr. Percy for £405. For the 6th. lot, the Bedwas, Llanfabon, and Pwllypant gates, no sufficient offer was made, and those gates were retained by the County Roads Board. The Aberavon, Margam, Neath, and Ystalyfera gates were let to Mr. Percy for the sum of £1500; and the Hafod, Pentre,

Pontardulais, St. Helen's and Gorse lane gates were also let to him for the sum of £2550. The letting of the whole was not quite as successful as last year's letting.

FOR SALE.

BROUGHAM, second-hand, Round Fronted, London-built, in excellent condition, the property of a Gentleman having no further use for it.

STANHOPE FRONTED WAGONETTE, with reversible seats to form a Stanhope Phaeton, with Break, Drag, Shafts &c., complete.

A COBURG, in excellent condition; also an IRISH OUTSIDE CAR.

For Particulars apply to K. and H. Veley, Coach Builders to Her Majesty Long Acre, Bath.

Stamped Newspapers in the County of Glamorgan.

According to the last Parliamentary Return of impressed Postage Stamps issued to Newspapers, we find that the figures of the undermentioned Newspapers stand as follows:–

	1865	1866	1867
The Cambrian Est. 1804.	25500	26200	29000
Cardiff/Merthyr Guardian. Est. 1832.	19500	21000	16000
Cardiff Times Est.1857	3500	7500	9000

These are the only papers in Glamorgan which have guaranteed postal circulation, the Cambrian being the only paper in Swansea to which the Postal Stamp is issued.

14th. January 1870.

The Gale in the Bristol Channel

During Friday night and the fore part of Saturday, Bristol and the Bristol Channel were visited by the heaviest gales that had been experienced there for a long time past. Housetops and gardens in elevated and exposed situations suffered severely, and some large trees which had stood the test of generations were thrown down or snapped off. Had it not been that the absence of the leafy covering of summer cause them to offer less resistance to the wind, there would beyond question have been an immense amount of damage done in that way. Notwithsanding the sheltered character and peculiarly good holding ground at the entrance to the river and in the harbour, considerable damage resulted to shipping. The ship Olivia bound from Cardiff to Cape de Verd, was driven before the gale, losing her chain cable and anchors; and a barque, just arrived in King-road, was driven on to the Swash. A schooner moored high in the river Avon, called the Heroine was torn from her moorings. A large ship called the Star of the West, from Callao, which was in the harbour and moored to no less than three mooring posts, was so acted upon by the force of the gale that her hawsers, refusing to part, actually dragged the posts out of the ground, and she went adrift, and coming into collision with the Prince of Wales steamer, cut away her funnel and otherwise damaged her. She also overrun and sunk some river boats. Fears were entertained that she should proceed up the harbour and carry away a costly iron bridge, but happily she ran ashore and checked her progress. It is feared that further cases of damage will be reported. One fatal occurrence has been reported. A young man named Gunning, a son of the captain, was at the helm of a steam tug-boat named the Start, when a sea struck her and he was carried overboard. Efforts were made to save him, the boat put about, and spars thrown out, but in vain. He sank to rise no more.

SWANSEA HARBOUR TRUST.

The monthly meeting of the Swansea Harbour Trust was held at the Guildhall on Monday. There were present Mr. Starling Benson in the chair, Messrs H. H. Vivian, M.P., L. L. Dillwyn, M.P., P. St L. Grenfell, J. T. Jenkins, J. Glasbrook, F. Price, J. Crow Richardson, J. P. Rudd, S. R. Power, W. H. Francis, S. Hall, J. W. James (superintendent of the harbour), and Leslie Thomas (clerk).

The Clerk read the usual financial statement, of which the following is a summary.

General Harbour Estate.

Income	£ s d	£ s d
Balance B/F		24277 17 5
Ship Rates	1275 19 5	
Rates on goods	708 19 9	
Bridge tolls	210 1111	
Ballast rates	111 7 2	
Rent Harb.Rlwy	250 0 0	
Low level Rlwy.	69 0 7	
Canal Lock Tolls	71 19 2	
Wharfage/ Cranes	83 8 1	
Sundries	247 310	
		3028 9 11
		27306 7 4
Expenditure		
Interest	1838 10 2	
Wages	503 12 5	
Ballast	121 19 8	
Salaries	119 12 1	
Stores	117 12 10	
Sundries	211 2 6	
Rents, Rates, &c.	99 4 5	
		3011 14 1
		24294 13 3

SWANSEA HOSPITAL BALL

The Second Annual Ball on behalf of the General Hospital, came off in the Music Hall on Wednesday evening. To say that it was successful in every respect scarcely conveys sufficient significance – every one present was delighted, and never did the hall present a more brilliant and animated appearance. Even the most ardent and devoted admirer of architecture will admit that there is some little room for improvement in the interior of our Music-Hall in its rude and pristine state! But on Wednesday evening it had been completely metamorphised, thanks to the skill, artistic taste and judgment of the working members of the Executive Committee. We have no hesitation in saying that a stranger would not recognise the hall as one and the same place viewed under the two aspects – that is, in its "unadorned beauty" and "dressed" with its crimson drapery, white muslin, floral wreaths and elegant bouquets, as on Wednesday evening. The committee having the management of the details, consisted of a number of gentlemen, but the real work devolved upon some three or four, to whom all render willing thanks, viz., Mr. F. Clouston Scott, hon. sec. Mr. Goodall, Mr. Thornton Andrews, and Mr. Stone of the Mackworth. These gentlemen worked with a zeal worthy of the good cause. The broad expanse of dingy wall at the back of the Orchestra had been completely hidden on this occasion. Mr. Thornton Andrews, the very efficient manager of the gas works, kindly lent his aid to enlighten the scene. A brilliant illuminated star, kindly lent by him, was suspended in the middle, at the sides, and under which there was a richly illumined scroll, bearing the words "1870 – May it be happy and prosperous to you." The other parts of the room bore tangible proofs of the pains and skill of those who undertook the duties of decoration. On the platform, tastily arranged, were a number of large evergreens, shrubs, plants and flowers, which had a very pleasing effect, and which Mr. Shaw, of the St. Helen's nursery kindly supplied. Mr. Goodall, in the most handsome manner, lent the whole of the crimson drapery, muslin &c., with which the balconies and pillars were so profusely decorated. The drapery was tastily arranged, being looped up with floral wreaths and bouquets of artificial flowers. Mr. Ward, of Castle square, kindly lent the furniture required, whilst Mr. Dobbs of High street, and Mr. Nunns of Penllegare, and others rendered willing assistance in the loan of other articles necessary for the successful carrying out of the event.

The company began to assembly shortly after nine o'clock – dancing commencing about ten. At about half-past 12 o'clock the hall presented the most animating scene, the varied hues of the rich dresses of the ladies being in unison with the artistic floral decorations of the room. Mr. Charles Cook's Quadrille band, consisting of some 25 performers, were stationed on the platform, and it is not too much to say the following programme was executed in most excellent style. The success of a ball depends in a great measure upon the music, and Mr. Cook was quite equal to the occasion – nothing like flagging being allowed throughout.

The following is the programme:–

Programme.

1. Quadrille	The Christmas Echo
2. Valse	Golden Beauty
3. Lancere	Carnival
4. Valse	Court Beauties
5. Galop	Snow Drift
6. Quadrille	La Perichole
7. Valse	Christine
8. Lancere	The Claribel
9. Valse	Cecile
10. Galop	No Thoroughfare
11. Quadrille	Les Calabras
12. Valse	The Harry Clifton
13. Galop	Flick or Flock
14. Lancers	Knight of S. Patrick
15. Schottische	Jenny Bell
16. Valse	Les Roses
17. Quadrille	London by Night
18. Galop	Fizz
19. Valse	Lotus
20. Lancers	National
21 Valse	Belgavia
22. Galop	Night Bells
23. Quadrille	L' Ecocssais
24. Galop	Farewell

The supper and the refreshments during the evening were supplied by Mr. Stone of the Mackworth, the mere mention of which fact is sufficient to prove that the most entire satisfaction was given. It is only right to state also that Mr. Stone undertook the catering at such a price as barely pays expenses, being desirous that the Hospital, in which he takes such a warm interest, should realise the full proceeds of the ball.

We are glad to hear that about 220 tickets were sold. Mr. H. H. Vivian, M.P., and Mr. L. L. Dillwyn, M.P., both with a large party of friends, were present. Not only was Swansea well represented, but many of the principal families from the adjacent towns and districts were present.

We append a complete list of those present:– Mr Graham Vivian, Major Heneage V.C. and Mrs Heneage, Miss Vivian, Mrs Booker, Miss Lindsay, Miss Hankey, Mr Ernest Vivian, Mr Aubrey Vivian, Mr Lindsay and Mr Barton; Mr. Dillwyn M.P., and the Misses Dillwyn, Mr and Mrs Clarke, Dowlais and Miss Clarke, Mrs Wood, Stouthall and the Misses Wood, Miss Bull, Mr Henry Nicholl, Lieut Spencer Nicholl, Captain Franklen R.A., Mr H. C. Bruce, Mr Williams, Aberpergwm, Mr. and Mrs. J. T. D. Llewellyn Ynisgerwn, Mr, Mrs and the Misses Wilmot, Mr Penrice Starling Benson, The Mayor of Swansea, J. Jones Jenkins, Esq. and Mrs Jenkins, and Mr and Mrs Evan F. Daniel, Mr and Mrs John Richardson Pantygwydr, and Miss Layton, Mr and Miss Clarke Richardson, Mr. Peri Richardson and Miss Nelson, Mr and Mrs J. H. Rowland and Miss Aubrey . . .Mrs. and Miss Crawshay, Langland . . . Dr. Williams . . .

Dancing was kept up until about four o'clock, the general remark being made that on no previous occasion had the whole arrangements been more perfect, or a more agreeable evening spent.

——◇——

SHIPPING INTELLIGENCE.

Icebergs.

Swansea. Jan. 7. – The Anne Dymes arrived here from Carrizal, passed through a large number of icebergs on Nov. 5, lat. 44S. long. 43W., also on Nov.10 and 11, between lats.43 and 41 S. longs. 42 and 41W.

Milford Haven, Jan. 8 – The Lass o' Gowrie tug lies sunk under the pier in this harbour. A stern board marked "Joseph Haydn" has been picked up, also a vessel's port, white inside black outside.

Scilly, St. Moryn, Jan. 7. – The Ann Banfield from Swansea to the Cape of Good Hope, put in here on the 5th. inst., after a heavy gale on the night of Dec. 30, carrying away rail, bulwarks, companion wheel broken into small pieces, a great part of the house in front of quarter deck, washing away some of the apprentices clothes, and other damage.

Rio Janeiro, Dec 15. – The Serena from Swansea to Valparaiso, put in here Dec. 6. with cargo on fire.

Vigo, Jan. 7. – The Castor (Norwegian barque), from Newport has been towed in dismasted.

The Etoile du Nord, from Cardiff, has been lost on the Coast of France.

——◇——

Local Intelligence.

Early Lambing – As an instance of early lambing we may mention that some fine young lambs, the first, we believe, this year in that neighbourhood, were to be seen in the earlier part of this week on land belonging to the Rev. Thomas Walters, Ystradgynlais, Swansea Valley.

The New Congregational Chapel. – In our last week's issue we stated that the Rev. Thomas Jones of London, would commence his ministry at Walter Road Congregational Church on the third sabbath of January. Considering how much he was beloved by the members and congregation of his late charge, who so highly appreciated his services that they were prepared to guarantee him a stipend if he would continue to be their pastor; in consequence of this fact being known there has been considerable doubt in the public mind as to the certainty of Mr. Jones coming to Swansea. Now, however, that doubt is wholly dispelled. Last Sunday morning the Rev. J. Waite of Cardiff, announced at the Congregational Church that Mr. Jones would commence his ministry on the following Lord's day. We think all classes of the community will welcome his arrival with unfeigned pleasure for an eloquent preacher, a profound thinker as a teacher and expositor of the sublime truths of our common faith. Mr. Jones has but few equals in the kingdom.

Apology

IN our issue of the 9th October, 1869, an Article was inserted, entitled "The London System in the Provinces," which reflects seriously upon the position of a Firm of Wine Merchants at Swansea, and which refers to the quality of the Goods offered by them for Sale by Public Auction in terms which we feel nothing can justify.

We regret exceedingly that we should have been mislead by our Correspondent, and we express our sorrow that such expressions should have been used in our Circular against the Firm referred to, viz. that of Messieurs REES & SON, Wine Merchants and Importers, Broad Quay, Swansea.

This apology we insert in settlement of an action brought by Messieurs Rees & Son against us They having consented to such settlement on our giving up the name of the parties supplying us with the information on which our Article was founded and inserting this apology.

RIDLEY & CO.,
"Monthly Wine and Spirit Trade Circular," – London.

WELSH VIEWS ON EDUCATION.

At a preliminary meeting of the committee, it has been decided to submit the following resolution to the Welsh Educational Conference to be held on the 25th. inst.

1. That it is the conviction of this conference that any system of education fully meeting the requirements of Wales, must be free, secular, unsectarian and compulsory.

2. This conference deems the direct religious teaching now imparted in day schools of but little value, and is confident that the spiritual training of the young may be fully and safely entrusted to the parents and the Christian Church.

3. Religious liberty being the birthright of every individual, this conference protests against any national scheme of education which shall enforce attendance at any denominational schools, or levy rates for sectarian or even religious instruction.

4. That a system of national free education, in order to be equitable, should, in addition to the elementary forms, provide advanced and higher schools open by graduation to all classes of the community.

5. That in connexion with the establishment of a national system of education for the United Kingdom, equitable arrangements be made with the managers of State-aided existing schools for their union with the national system, and that provision be made for the speedy cessation of State aid where such union shall be declined.

6. That an education association be constituted for Wales, to consist of such persons as concur in the principles embraced in the resolutionsof this conference, and that an executive be appointed to bring the views of this conference fairly before the country, and to watch the introduction and progress of any educational measure which may be brought before Parliament, and that the same gentlemen be appointed a deputation to represent the views embodied in the foregoing resolutions before Mr. Forster and the Home Secretary.

St. John's Church.

To The Edditur of The Cambrian Newspappar.

Sir, – You be allways so good to let peepl tel what they want in your valebl pappar, and i want to tel sum thing about our spiritual state in the upper part of this town. i be glad to hear that sumthing is to be dun att last for poor ould St. John's Church – the news be so good that i be affrade it is nott true. Badd news is allways tru, but good news very offen turn out to be lies, but i hop this is not lies. i sined a pettishun last week to Mr. Vivian who they sae is goin to Bildd a church att the hafod, and to sell the ould church to Mr. Squire who they sae is goin to make a district in this upper part of the town and goin to give it to the chaplin of the jail. if he will doe that the peepl will be very appy for it did their sowls good toheer him prech Welsh, and he used to be so good to call to see us and pray with us wen we be sick, sins he left us to take the jail we have only a skriptur reader to call to see us. We dos like Mr. Morgan very wel, but he do liv at lansamlett and cum to St. John's church only once on Sunday after dinner. We don't have much Dinner but bred and cheese in the weak, and we doo lik too get a Bit of met and tattors on Sunday and a drop of Beer with it, and then we woad rather go too sleep than go too church, but if we had a parson to ourselves and prech too us in the mornin and evenin like other people we would like to go to church and that wood do us good. i was think that thare must be sum awfu sponsebillity sumwhare to leve our sowls without a bit of vittles from one end of the year to the other xcept we go too a dissentin chapel for a mel, that be very good sumtimes, but we want to hav it in our own plas.We heerd that ould Mr. Vivian was think too Bild a church at the hafod before he died, but he did die to soon and we Be very sorry for it. We hop that the present Mr. Vivian wil make haste to doo what his father wished to doo, we will bless him for it and pray for him, and God will bless him for dooin good.Our state now is allmost as Badd as the pagans in affrica for thare is no one too care for our sowls. We finf faut with the parsons, but they sae the faut is on Mr. Vivian – it is sumwhere, and it is a great shame to leve us like this. i was a poor Welshman and cact write much Inglish, an i hop you will pass by tis Badd writin.

Cymro.

To the Guardians of the Poor — Swansea Union.

Gentlemen. – As some of you are already aware, I have offered to the Union the the Townhill farm, consisting of about 67 acres, on what I consider would be to it most advantageous terms – namely at 42s. per acre for the land and the buildings, consisting of cottages at valuation, and to give up my entire term of between 50 and 60 years, or to let you the land, together with the buildings, at 60s. per acre. The cottages, when all let, should bring a rental of over £100 a year.

Although personally interested in this matter, but having been for many years a public man, and as one who must ever continue interested in the prosperity of the town and Union, you will grant me to say that it cannot fail to be advantageous to you to have this land in your possession. All able-bodied poor could have employment; your supplies of milk, meat and all kinds green crops, hay &c., could be secured at a nominal cost. You may have any extent of accommodation for your poor; fever hospitals and a burial place:– or you may, with all your able poor, make roads at a small cost (a capital quarry being on the land, with a right to the stones for any purposes on the said land), and apportion any part of the land for building conjointly with the Corporation, at a great profit to both.

It has been my intention to offer the whole, in the Spring, by auction, in building plots; and if once sold, the chance of securing it to the Union would be lost.

If you will kindly at your next meeting, consider the matter, I shall be most happy to meet your committee anywhere you may appoint.

I am, Gentlemen,
Your most obedient Servant,
Thomas Rees,
Sketty Hall, Glamorganshire,
5th. January, 1870.

Mr. O. G. Williams characterised the offer of Mr. Rees as a Quixotic and the most absurd sort of thing that he had heard in his life. He could not for a moment believe that the Guardians would entertain the offer.

Mr. Phillips: When the offer was first made by Mr. Rees he thought they were to have the buildings that were upon the land. He then favourably entertained it and would have taken the farm on his own responsibility, but now it appears that we must pay for the buildings by valuation.

The Chairman said that the letter was now before the Board, and he wished to have the opinions of the guardians.

Mr. David Jones: If we had the land of the Townhill Farm for nothing we would be out of pocket by it. There was enough work in the garden for the able-bodied paupers to do.

After some further discussion, the Clerk was ordered to communicate with Mr. Rees, declining the offer.

Correspondence.

OUR REPRESENTATIVES.

To The Editor of "The Cambrian,"

Sir, – Already a large number of the County and Borough Members of England and Wales have appeared before their constituents to give an account of their stewardship. I respectfully ask our representatives when they intend to afford us the pleasure of listening to their opinion respecting the proceedings of the last Session, and their views on the great questions likely to be discussed in the ensuing Session, such as Education, the Ballot, the Game Laws, the Sysem of Licensing, Army reform &c. I would suggest that the meeting be held in the Music Hall, instead of the Court House, the latter place being wholly unadapted for for a public meeting. Besides, it will not seat a tithe of the electors

I am, Sir,
Your obedient Servant.
An Elector, Swansea, Jan. 12 1870.

THE WRECK OF THE CHARLES AMELIE.

To The Editor of "The Cambrian."

Sir, – Seeing the account of the wreck of the "Charles Amelia" in today's issue of the "Cambria Daily Leader," I beg to state that the names published in it of those that were first to the rescue is not correct; therefore I send you the following "correct account":– A man by the name of G. Jones, living in Bathhurst-street, was the first person to propose to Capt. R. Rosser to get a boat and lines to save the poor crew, and also to bring a boat and a line; John Wilkins, pilot was the second, and they took with them Captains Mitchell and Rosser, and a man of the name of Turpin, who is in the employ of the Swansea Harbour Trustees – they were the first to go to the vessel – and although G. Jones's name is not published in that paper, he was the *Leader* of the party. Hoping that you will publish this.

Truth. Swansea. Jan 10, 1870

P.S. I am told to-day that the Pilots are grumbling because G. Jones took their boat to try and save some of the poor sailors from a watery grave.

WRECKS INSIDE THE WEST PIER EXTENSION.

To The Editor of "The Cambrian."

Sir, – The recurrence of such a scene as that of the wreck of the French brigantine on the East Pier of Swansea Harbour on the morning of Saturday last, January 8th., may, it appears to me, be prevented, were means provided for a casting a rope aboard any drifting vessel from the end of the West Pier Extension. A ship driving before the gale, and circumstanced as the "Charles Amelia" was, would naturally hug the end of the West Pier closely, for the sake of getting into shelter as soon as possible, and to save lee way. A comparatively small rope would have checked her way and rounded her into safety. Even if the first rope parted, it would have so governed her course as that another might have been hove aboard, and so secured her from drifting on to the flats outside the East Pier.

The timber extension of the West Pier is not capable of safely sustaining the shock which would be occasioned by the check of a large ship suddenly brought up against a strong gale – when only such a check would be necessary or useful – and I would, therefore, suggest that mooring posts should be placed at the extremity, and at proper distances along the eastern side of the Extension of the West Pier – not attached to it, so as to injure it under heavy strain, but anchored to the shore by chains passing back through the under portion of the wooden pier to proper moorings, so that each post should be independent of the Pier. A platform should surround the top of each, touching, but not attached to, the Pier itself, so that a rope might more easily be cast, and a hauser made fast.

If this plan were carried out, and a small hauser or two, and some lines and ropes were kept ready at the end of the Pier, and this known to the channel pilots, a driving ship would be brought so close to the Pier, that, by using the means suggested, her course to probable destruction might first of all be stayed, and then, by getting a couple of hausers aboard, she could be warped up the Pier into the harbour even in the most violent storm.

The Extension of the West Pier appears really to render such wrecks as that of Saturday less avoidable than when a ship could run for the old entrances, and merely get stranded inside the harbour, in calm weather! If this is the case, and it looks like it, and that the Extension has rendered it more difficult for a dismasted ship to make the port in safety, some such measure as I have suggested ought, I submit, to be adopted to enable the Extension to remedy the evils it has itself increased, and thus effect great saving of life and property.

I am, Sir, yours truly,

C. S. Waring.

The Darraz, Jan. 12 1870.

2nd. February 1872.

Public Park for Swansea. – It is with pleasure we inform our readers that a scheme is on the *tapis* for giving Swansea a public park. We are not at present sufficiently acquainted with the details to give even an outline of the scheme, but we may state that it is contemplated to lay out the surplus lands of the Cwmdonkin reservoir, and it is hoped by the exchange of a small piece of ground and with our respected fellow townsman John Crow Richardson, Esq., to secure a park of several acres in extent. When most of our green spots are ruthlessly destroyed by the inexorable march of bricks and mortar, and when our sands are injuriously affected by the railways, and that unsightly and offensive building erected for the outlet of the Oxford-street sewers, a public park is a *desideratum* which all can appreciate and the benefits of which can hardly be over-estimated.

CARMARTHENSHIRE
The Late Shipping Disaster
in Carmarthen Bay.

– The *Welshmen* says – The unfortunate loss of the brigantine Mary B., of Llanelly, with all hands on board, has called forth some animadversions on the conduct of the crew of the lifeboat at Ferryside. They were charged on two counts, firstly, that although the bell, announcing the danger in which the ill-fated vessel was placed, was rung at five o'clock on Thursday morning, the crew did not muster until eight; and secondly, that when they did muster, they were so slow in their movements as to raise suspicion that they had no inclination to proceed to the distressed vessel. Both these charges were the subject of an enquiry before the Lifeboat Committee, at Ferryside, on Wednesday. Mr. Jennings of Gellydeg, in the chair. The accusations were fully gone into, and evidence was taken, some witnesses from Laugharne being examined amonst others. The conclusion arrived at by the committee is embodied in the following resolution which was passed:– "The committee, having fully considered the evidence brought before them, are of the opinion that the crew of the lifeboat, City of Manchester, used their utmost efforts to launch the boat and proceed to the wreck with all speed, and the committee beg to tender them their thanks for their services on this occasion." The facts are simply these. The alarm bell was not heard at Ferryside until near eight o'clock on Thursday morning. Horses to drag the lifeboat to the water's edge were procured as soon as practicable; but owing to the soft state of the sand and mud the horses sank to their haunches and had to be extricated by ropes. In this way there was so much time lost, through no one's fault, that it was about half-past eight before the lifeboat was fairly launched. It will be remembered how, when the lifeboat was within a few hundred yards of the brigantine, the masts with six men clinging to them were seen to fall into the sea. Since then several bodies have been washed ashore at different points. On Friday a body was picked up at Ferryside, but was not identified. On the following day a second body was picked up near Ferryside and was identified as Timothy Morgan of Fishguard. A third body was found at Towyn on Sunday, but was not identified. On Monday a body was picked up at Laugharne, but was not identified; and on Wednesday another body was found at Laugharne, and was identified as the mate of the ill-fated Mary B. It is stated that the crew of a vessel coming towards Carmarthen bar, have reported that near the wreck buoy of the Sir. Henry Pottinger they have seen a vessel sunk in deep water. The vessel, they say, is square rigged, in an upright position, with sails set. And now, after the experience of the past week or two, it is evident that something ought immediately to be done to facilitate the launching of the lifeboat at Ferryside. It has often been said that it was a great mistake to place the boat in its present station; and its removal to a point near St. Ishmael's Church was suggested. To this it was objected that the boat would be so far from Ferryside that that it would be difficult to summon a crew. We this week heard a suggestion which would we think remove any such objection. If the lifeboat were stationed near the battery, a couple of miles south of Ferryside, on a signal of distress being seen the crew might be summoned by the firing of a gun, which would be heard for miles. The suggestion is a very good one, for there is no doubt that the crew would be at their post and the boat launched long before it could be taken from its present station. Besides, the men would be so much fresher for their work than they can possibly be at present, having to pull a distance of two miles through a heavy sea before reaching a point opposite the battery. This is a question that should be brought under the notice of the Lifeboat Institution without delay, for the lifeboat at Ferryside is of little use so long as it remains in its present position.

——◇——

DEADLY WAKES AND WASTEFUL FUNERALS

(*From the Builder.*)

An edict has at last gone forth against wakes and funerals, both in Ireland and England. Cardinal Cullen has felt it necessary not only to condemn the demoralising practice of nursing the dead but to threaten a sort of religious penalty that is likely to have some good effect with the members of his flock. It is many years now that the *Builder* first drew public attention to the pernicious and criminal custom of "waking the dead, and so killing the living" carried on in the homes of the London Irish.

An Irish Roman Catholic priest located at Camberwell has just made an announcement that the practice of "waking bodies is disgraceful." He cites what must be considered a terrible picture, that forty persons had sat in one room with the corpse, and that during the night fourteen gallons of beer were consumed.

To this painful picture might be added a little more colouring without the least exaggeration. Let us imagine that among these forty persons there were at least half of them females, the majority of them marriageable; and that besides the beer there were probably half a gallon of whisky drunk, and a quantity of tobacos smoked. The character of the songs and conversation that usually distinguish such gatherings can be imagined, and the moral degration and blunted feelings they superinduce. Having ourselves witnessed Irish wakes, not alone in Ireland, but in London, in the wynds and closes of Edinburgh, Glasgow, Newcastle-on-Tyne, Birmingham, Sheffield, Leeds, Liverpool and various other towns in the kingdom, we can form an estimate of their baneful effects.

We have known cases where deceased, when living, was only existing from hand to mouth; yet his death and wake were the signal of the most wasteful expenditure on the part of his friends and relatives.

Many thousands of the London Irish are members of burial societies, to which husbands and wives pay certain weekly subscriptions, amounting from twopence to perhaps fourpence, and even sixpence a week. In this the conduct of these poor people is most commendable. The sums paid at death average, perhaps, from 50s., for a child, and from £5 to £10 or £12 for and adult (husband or wife). Unfortunately this sum that should be economised by the survivor in the providing for the funeral and the grave, while bethinking of the future, is thoughtleesly squandered in nursing the corpse, and feasting jubilant mourners who come from miles around to drink with all due reverence, "The memory of the dead."

Then comes the solemn mockery of this poor man's funeral, or the poor woman's, as the case may be, and more money is wastefully spent. Certain of the East End undertakers, who specially provide Roman Catholic funerals, have in requisition, "a Catholic hearse" for the conveyance of the deceased London Irish, and this custom has become so recognised, that many of the Irish poor would resent as an insult any attempt to convey the remains of their relatives in any but the orthodox vehicle.

An Irish funeral of somewhat large dimensions may be seen any week in the year at the East-end of London, or in the Borough; but a bona fide Irish funeral *cortege* and procession, with all honours, is becoming a rather rare occurrence anywhere out of the Emerald Isle.

Once the body is consigned to the earth a few of the mourners may return straight home, but, unfortunately, a very large portion of the men who form the funeral procession will betake themselves to the public-houses in the vicinity, and night and drunkeness envelop the conclusion.

If the dignitaries of the Roman Catholic Church had begun their crusade a quarter of a century ago, how much disease and misery might have been prevented! Imagine, in the case of a man or woman dying, perhaps of some dangerous disease, the body being waked from Wednesday or Thursday till Sunday afternoon, the coffin, even if there be one, till the last moment unclosed.

The love for "the Sunday funeral" induces the people to nurse their dead for days, to the imminent peril of the health of the entire neighbourhood. We are not exaggerating in any particular. What we state we know.

We are free to admit that there are respectable families who permit wakes in connexion with their deceased relatives from feelings of reverence and the old ties of country and custom. Neither religious morality, public decency, nor public health can, however, sanction or permit the continuance of such a baneful custom. The practice is bad and reprehensible in all views, whether it takes place at home above the reach of want, or on the incomes of the working poor. If people could only be brought to realise the picture presented at these "wakes," in all their baneful, senseless folly and wickedness, their extinction might be looked for. There are probably very few writers or reformers of abuse who in reality know aught from personal observation of these doings. Many here in London, who view them in the mind's eye, through snatches of information from time to time in the newspapers, laugh at them, from their comical aspect. There are worse evils attending and arising from the practice of "wakes" than the drinking of beer and whisky; worse evils than the infection transmitted from the dead to the living. The corpse may be buried and the drunkard resume his daily labour, but in the home of the dead there may be more than one sad remembrance of virtue undermined, of young womanhood unsexed, and the dolorous sequence in the streets and the river.

Let the clergymen of all creeds side with the law, and let the law be not harshly but firmly enforced. It is sufficient to cope with the evils we have pointed out.

Serious Defalcations and Flight of a Swansea Income-Tax Collector. Swansea appears to be particularly unfortunate with respect to its Income Tax collectors. Within the past three years no less than three collectors have absconded, leaving heavy deficiencies in their accounts, which the surities or the town have to make good to the Government.

Scarcely had the town recovered from the surprise and excitement consequent upon the flight and defalcations of Messrs. John Jones and John Wilson with their respective liabilities, than the announcement was made that Mr. George Augustus Harry Potter, the collector of Income and Assessed Taxes for St. Thomas district, had absconded with a total deficiency in his accounts of no less than £682 4s. 3½d. In addition to the office of Income Tax collector, Mr. Potter was also the collector of poor rates for St. Thomas, was secretary of the Royal Swansea and South Wales Union Friendly Society, secretary to the Swansea Constitutional Association, publishing agent for the *Western Mail*, lessee of the Music Hall, auctioneer, commission agent &c. Connected with these various offices, several tradesmen have large sums against him, whilst there is a probability that there are considerable deficiencies in connection with the various accounts with which he was entrusted. Some three weeks since Mr. Potter stated that he was going out of town for a few days, directing his letters to be forwarded to Croydon, London, which was done; but no communication being received from him, a telegram was lately sent there, to which a reply was received to the effect that Mr. Potter had not been there, and all his letters remained untouched. Suspicions were aroused, which led to investigations, which resulted in the discovery of the deficiency in his Income-tax books to the amount named. Some what singular to state Mr. R. Rice Davies, as Surveyor of Income-tax for this district, had written to Mr. Potter (as also to the other collectors) requiring him to pay into the Bank all monies which he had collected, and within two or three days of his flight Potter actually paid into the Bank £603 on account of Income and Assessed Taxes. His books shew that he had collected a total of £1,285 4s. 3½d.; he paid into the Bank of this amount £603, leaving a deficiency unaccounted for of £682 4s. 3½d.

Why he paid so large a sum of money into the bank, on the eve of his leaving, is certainly a mystery. On Tuesday morning a special meeting of the Income Tax Commissioners for the Llangafelach district (the hamlet of St. Thomas being in that district) was held, when it was at once decided to issue a warrant for his apprehension, and also "to seize all property, freehold, copyheld, or personal whatever found or discovered." This warrant has been placed in the hands of the police, but there is little probability of its execution as doubtless the defaulter has long since left the country. We are credibly informed that no surities or bonds were given by Mr. Potter for the due execution of his office and the proper payments of the monies received by him in his capacity as collector. Strange to say that the most implicit faith was placed in him, and jumping suddenly into position, a confidence was reposed in him which men of twenty years' standing in the town might justly envy. We cannot pretend to give a legal opinion as to whose duty it was to see that Potter gave good and sufficient bail for the proper fullfilment of his duty, but we believe we are correct in stating that the ratepayers of the parish can insist upon the collector giving surities, and neglecting such (as in the present case), that the Crown will look to the ratepayers of the parish to refund any deficiency which may arise. – Investigations have, of course, taken place with respect to other offices held by Mr. Potter, and from the best information we can glean there is no reason to suppose that there is any serious deficiency in the accounts of the Royal Swansea and South Wales Union Friendly Society, nor with regard to the poor rates, but several tradesmen, both here and elsewhere have been "let in" for rather heavy amounts. What makes this affair the more serious and deplorable is that Mr. Potter has left behind him his wife and three children; and rumour has it that his flight is connected with the simultaneous disappearance of a young lady connected with one of the educational establishments in this town, of whose mysterious disappearance, three weeks since, there are no tidings, and who some short time since was presented with a gold watch and chain, "as a mark of the esteem in which she was held" by those who had the opportunity of witnessing the manner in which she carried on her scholastic duties.

A Careless Driver and its Consequences. – Morgan Rees, a carter in the employ of Mr. W. Davies of Ilston, Gower, was charged with driving at a furious rate and damaging property belonging to the Local Board. P.C. 24 said that about 3.15 p.m. on Saturday he was on duty in Walter Road when he saw the defendant, who was in a cart and was driving at a rapid rate. He attempted to stop him, when the defendant gave the horse a cut with the whip and it started on at a still more furious rate. After going about 200 yards the reins broke and the cart dashed against the iron railings surrounding one of the trees, breaking the railing, injuring the tree, and flinging the defendant out of the cart on to the ground. Witness went to the defendant and found him to be drunk and conveyed him to the police station. The defendant said that he had taken some beer upon an empty stomach which had "capsized" him. He was ordered to pay for damage, fine and costs, £1 8s. 6d. or in default to be imprisoned for 21 days.

The deaths of 4,155 persons in South Wales in the past quarter show an excess of 453 over the average of three years. They include 133 that happened in the workhouses, hospitals. &c.; 232 coroners cases were recorded, and in 172 instances death was due to violent means. Smallpox caused 213 deaths, measles 195, scarlet fever 181, and other fevers 166. Of 485 deaths in the union of Neath, 118 were by small pox. Merthyr Tydfil also furnished a heavy total under this head. Scarlet fever was principally fatal in the unions of Pontypridd, Merthyr, and Bridgend. Neath and also Llanelly suffered from fevers of various kinds, not including scarlet fever in this description. Cardiff, Pontypridd, Merthyr, Bridgend, Neath, Llanelly, Llandilofawr, Carmarthen, Narbeth and Aberystwith, are the districts of unions wherein the deaths are in excess of the respective averages.

Severn Commission. – At a committee meeting on Friday the Midland Railways Bill, containing provisions for vesting the Worcester and Birmingham Canal in the Midland Railway Co. was taken into consideration, and a resolution was unanimously passed to petition Parliament against such Bill. The several schemes for railways over the river Severn below Gloucester; and for a tunnel under the river, were also taken into consideration, and resolutions were passed to the effect that the Commisioners oppose some of those Bills, and will oppose others unless satisfactory provisions for the protection of the navigation be inserted therein. Several of the provisions proposed to be introduced into the Salmon Fisheries Bill, which has been prepared on behalf of the Boards of Conservators, with reference to weirs, were discussed, and the clerk was instructed to endeavour to obtain the consent of the promoters of such Bill to such modifications as will prevent injury to the navigation, to the weirs, or to the property of the Commision.

Fashions for February

There is but slight novelty to chronicle with regard to the fashions for the month, as it is seldom that any new colour or material is introduced towards the close of a season. There is a quiet luxury prevalent, shown more by the artistic adaptation of colours and style of trimmings employed than in richness of material. The fabrics to vogue are the same as those worn last month – cloth, double *cachemire,* silk *reps, poult de soie,* satin, *faille* and velvet, with a host of new materials which we do not enumerate, as their names vary so considerably as to be no guide to our readers. Many of these are comparatively inexpensive, but make very pretty and even elegant costumes. There is a slight difference in the manner of cutting skirts. Whether short or trained, this front breadth is, of course, gored; another breadth is gored half being placed at each side of the front; the whole of the remainder of the skirt is cut on the straight, and the fullness thrown towards the back. Of course a little more material is required than formerly, but this is amply compensated for by the fact that the pieces are of a much more useful shape and also for any agreed purposes. There are four distinct variety of bodices, high or low, and each capable of modification according to taste:– The round waist, with band or sash: this is very little worn except for young ladies with slight figures, to whom it is very becoming; the bodice *a basques,* of which there is a great diversity of shape, but always narrower at the sides; the *corsage a pointes,* very pretty for ball dresses; and the *corsage l'unique,* body and upper skirt cut in one. The first two have one, two, or even three front plaits, according to the figure of the wearer; the *corsage a basques* is cut either with plaits or two side bodice; the *corsage tunique* of course can only be cut with two side-bodies. The sleeves are much the same as those worn last month. The coat sleeve is too convenient and too becoming to be totally banished, though superseded by the open shapes for dress wear. The little coloured *Achus*so much worn this winter, for which China crepe is the favourite material, are now sometimes made with ends crossing in front and tying behind in a broad sash like "Marie Antoinette" *pelerines* so greatly in favour a few summers ago; they are also sometimes made in the form of a *Zouave* jacket, rounded off in front, and taken under the arms without crossing, tying loosely at the back.

These elegant little adjuncts to a toilette can also be made in plain crape, and have a very elegant effect; they are always edged with fringe or lace. We have also seen one made of alternate embroidered insertions and all muslin *bouillonnces*, a coloured ribbon run in the latter; this was intended for a dinner-dress for a young lady. The ribbon was cherry colour, and the dress white-foulard with cherry-coloured satin stripes. Ball dresses are a mass of ruches and *bouillonnces* with or without silk or satin tunics. One very elegant style is called the "Nuage," and, as it should be with such a nomenclature is excessively light and ethereal The under skirt is of tulle, gause or tarlatane, covered with ruches. Over this is a train of the same, with rounde apron front raised at each side. This is also a cloud of rouchings. The train skirt is generally made of rather coarse white set, on which the *ruches* are placed as thickly as possible, as it keeps in better shape than would be the case with any fragile material. Sometimes the *ruches* are all one colour, at others alternately white and coloured. For young unmarried ladies tiny bows of coloured ribbon are interspersed among the *ruches*; for young married ladies these are replaced by small flowers, such as heath, myosotis, rosebuds, very small convolvoli, or snow drops. Velvet and satin are still worn profusely trimmed with lace and curled feathers. Fur is not quite so much used being principally reserved for out door wear. There is really no alteration in the cloaks, either in shape or ornament. The *Algerienne* mantles are much worn as wraps; they are something in the form of a scarf, both ends thrown across the shoulders and hanging behind, with magnificent gold and coloured stripes on a black or coloured ground, black and *grosbleu* being the most *distingue* shades for the foundation; they have a very handsome parti-coloured fringe all round. The bonnets are very elegant *melanges* of *faille* and satin with flowers and feathers, or simply feathers fastened down by a *corarde* of lace and a Paris jet *nigrette.* The "Alsace" head dress is very much *a la mode*; it consists of a flat bow with short ends.It is made of broad ribbon, and placed flat on the top of the head. A flower is sometimes added for evening dress. – *La Follet.*

Correspondence.

^^^^^^^^^^^^^^^^^^^^^^^^^^^^^^^^^^^

GOOD NEWS FOR BOYS.

To the Editor of "The Cambrian."

Dear Sir, – I should feel much obliged to you if you would kindly let my school-fellows know that there is a large pond (or I might rather term it a beautiful lake) in the Mumbles-road near the gas works, where they might sail their boats on Wednesday and Saturday half-holidays, and have a regatta; but please manage to do it so that the Local Board should not hear of it, lest they might clear the roads and take the pools away.

I am, dear Sir, yours truly,

School-Boy.

P.S. – There is also another one forming in Rutland-street, which will soon be ready.

PORT AND HARBOUR OF NEATH,
In the County of Glamorgan.

PROPOSED BYE-LAWS.

Rules, Orders, Regulations, and Ordinances made and framed by the commissioners for Improving the Port and Harbour of Neath, for enforcing the provisions of "The Petroleum Act 1871," 34 and 35 Victoria, Cap. 105, entitled An Act for the safe Keeping of Petroleum and other substances of a like nature.

---

1. – IT is ordained that from and after the promulgation of these present Bye-laws, Rules, Regulations, and Ordinances no ship (which shall include every description of vessel used in navigation, whether propelled by oars or otherwise) carrying Petroleum (which shall include any Rock Oil, Rangoon Oil, Burmah Oil, Oil made from Petroleum, Coal, Schist, Shale, Peat or other Bituminous substances, and any products of Petroleum, or any of the before-mentioned Oils and the "Petroleum" to which the before-named Act applies, means such of the Petroleum so defined as when tested in a manner set forth in schedule 1 to this Act, gives off an inflammable vapour, at a temperature of less than one hundred degrees of Fahrenheit's thermometer.) shall be moored only at such place or places within the said Port or Harbour as shall be named or pointed out by the Harbour Master for the time being or his lawful deputy.

2. – It is ordained that owner or owners of such Petroleum shall give the notice in writing to the Harbour Master for the time being, that a Ship with Petroleum is chartered for the said Port or Harbour; and he shall also as the master of such ship, or some person duly authorised, give immediate notice to the Harbour Master of the arrival into port of each ship.

3. – It is ordained that such Ship shall discharge its cargo between the hours of half-past Ten o'clock in the morning and Twelve o'clock at noon, and also between the hours of Two o'clock in the afternoon and four in the evening on every day of the week except Sunday.

4. – It is ordained that such Petroleum as aforesaid shall be landed from the ship in such a manner as the said Harbour Master, or his lawful deputy shall direct, and be forthwith removed away by the owner or owners of such cargo.

5. – It is ordained that during the times and hours appointed for the discharge of such Petroleum no candle shall be lighted, no box or boxes of matches used, or be in the possession of any person employed in the discharge of such ship as aforesaid, nor shall any fire be lighted or contiuue in, on deck or below deck, or suspended in the rigging, during the time or times of such discharge, nor shall any person use or smoke any pipe, or cigar, or cigarette, or have any such in their possession or on board such ship during the discharge as aforesaid, nor shall any fire be lighted on the landing stage or wharf, or within one hundred yards thereof.

By the said Act it is provided – Where any ship or cargo is moored, landed, or otherwise dealt with in contravention of any Bye-Law for the time being in force under the said Act in any harbour, the owner and master of such ship, or the owner of such cargo, as the case may be, shall each incur a penalty not exceeding Fifty Pounds for each day during which such contravention continues, and it shall be lawful for the Harbour Master or any other person acting under the orders of the harbour authority of such harbour, to cause such ship or cargo to be removed at the expense of the owner thereof to such place as may be in conformity with the said Bye-Laws, and all expenses incurred in such removal may be recovered in the same manner in which penalties are by this Act made recoverable .

by order of the said Commissioners
(Signed) DAVID BEVAN,
Chairman.
(Signed) JAMES KEMPTHORNE,
Clerk.

6th. April 1874.

A FLYING VISIT TO
LLANGYFELACH FAIR.

Woe unto that nation which forgets or despises the heroes and saints, who in the far off past, laboured to elevate the race, to bring forth the rose and the myrtle of civilisation on the heretofore forbidden and barren tract of human nature, and who have succeeded so well as to leave the impress of their own individuality upon the character of their descendants! Such forgetfulness would indicate national ingratitude. But though Swansea, the mother city of Wales, is the seat of no Cambrian society, and though her denizens apear to "scorn to wear the leek upon St. Tavy's day," yet the patron saint cannot complain from the grim abode of his holiness that due honour is not done him by the observance of a commemorative festival. To the townsfolk of Swansea and to the inhabitants of the district within a very wide radius, Fig Fair is the occasion when the tribes go up through Caersalem (Jerusalem) to Cyfelach's Hill, with merry heart and "in merry trim" to hold the high festival of "Gwyl Dewi Sant." Remnant as it is of a civilisation less advanced than ours, and deservedly decried as it has been in many respects, one fee; Is that in order to appreciate it aright he must approach it in a very charitable spirit; and when once again the early days of March come round, he readily forgets all the evil he has heard of the fair, and, brimful of the healthy gaiety of the moment, he desires to mingle in the throng that wends its way thitherward. There are many things less pleasant than to suspend business at twelve noon on Wednesday, to get your pony harnessed the phaeton, and to drive to Llangyfelach in company with a few kindred spirits. As you speed through High-street, you gather from the glances flashing upon you on all sides that your position is envied by many a shopkeeper and assistant whose tether allows him to wander no further than his doorstep; and you naturally feel the pleasing elation incident to this situation. Gaining Greenhill, things begin to wear a more decided aspect. You fall in with crowds of the *genus homo,* of all conceivable sorts and sizes, and bedight in holiday attire, and every smiling face is directed and every foot hurrying fairwards. Here, also, begins the dawn upon the sight a varity of conveyances, from the meanest and most fragile donkey cart to the coal cart, the dray, the goods wagon, the handsome, the fly, and the imposing break with horses arranged tandem, all designed to assist the halt and ease-loving to fair. Nor is it possible to maintain a serious countenance as you journey along. The enjoyable relaxation from business, the exhilarating effects of the increased rarity of the air as you ascend the country-side, and the pleasantness of the weather are enough to induce good humour in the most dyspeptic; and when you add to these the overflowing mirth of each countenance you gaze into, the sportive twinks of each eye, and the unceasing banter and repartee indulged in by everybody, it is perfectly irresistible; you become fairly mastered by the spirit of the hour, and are ready for anything in the way of fun. The four or five miles of road are to the Swanseaite a local imitation of the highway to Epsom Downs on the Derby day, and you do not traverse it uneventfully. When your pony is toiling up the numerous declivities, you have to sustain a racy conversation with good-natured pedestrians who keep alongside, and when your animal again breaks into a trot you have to exchange hurried greetings with the hosts who lustily hail you as you pass. At length, Llangyfelach is in sight, with its square church tower clock crowned, and its booth-covered hillock top, and it is task requiring some patience to drive through the dense mass of people that fills the roadway. But somehow you do get through, and the next important getting is accommodation for your beast at the Penllegare Arms. That being settled you shake yourself and prepare for a ramble. Stalls for the sale of figs and ginger bread, and other eatables of a doubtful quality, together with toys, hardware, and nicknacks line the way on both sides, and the purport of the thousand and one invitations given you by voices of every degree of shrillness is to buy "figgish" and what not. You do not purchase ginger bread or figgish, but pass on towards the upper field, and find yourself in front of a booth wherein is practised "the noble art of self defence." Portraits of such notables as Tom Sayers and Jim Mace adorn the exterior, and at the doorway you have a good view of some highly developed pugilistic physiognomies. In the fulness of your heart you accede to the request of the money-taker to the "Derbyshire Slashers;" you pay your twopence and step inside, to the great discomfort of your olfactory sense. A couple of novices in the art are drawing the blood from each other's nose in a friendly way and when these have ended their "round" there steps into the ring a surly and muscular individual, who is described by one of the upholders of the establishment as "Shonnay Sherai, the Welsh veteran, and the finest Wales has ever produced." Shonnay is followed into the ring by "the Stranger from England," and they don the gloves, and practice a few "artful dodges" for the instruction of the spectators in the "wrinkles" of the noble art. You admire the dexterity of delivery and parry and take your leave of "Shonny" and the "Stranger" but not before they have tried to wheedle you of a few coppers for nationality's sake. Arrived once more in the open air you are refreshed by the afternoon's breeze and you pass in rapid review the closely packed public drinking booths, where a large business is doing; the Aunt Sallies, the spirometers, the various strength testers, the hawker who is always selling "the very last article" he has; and in that way you casually notice that the Good Templars have adapted the wise plan of proving refreshment in a good booth, and that the provision is greatly appreciated. It is not your intention to buy flannel, and after a little chaff with the weavers as to the proportion of cotton in the goods, you regain the scene of the shooting galleries, Marionette theatres, penny gaffs, swingboats and roundabouts. You are hilarious, the thoughts of younger days return, and but for your desire to preserve proper decorum you would indulge in a mad whirl on the back of a timber horse. The penny gaffs are full, and the performance proceeding, so that you cannot enter; but struck with the oddity of the occasion, and fearing that your little party may never meet again in like circumstances, and wishing for a momento of the visit, you turn aside into a photographer's to "have your likeness drawed" in a group. The photographer has many "clients," and you have to wait your turn, but ample amusement is found in making the lasses laugh out right, and distort their features at the critical moment. Your turn comes; you take your position at random, and before you are ready, indeed, while you are yet sore and unsteady from the continued laughing, you are "drawed." In a twinkling the likeness is ready; you pay the damage, 4s. and come away to laugh still more heartily at the personal peculiarities developed in the picture. You then look up at the neighbouring hostelries, of which, besides the Plough and Harrow and the Penllergare there are a large number of sign bearing facades, houses of only two rooms labelled "Farmers Arms" and so on. – and judging from the appearances at the window, every room is full to suffocation. You determine on a survey of the interior of the Penllergare, and so make your way from basement to attic, laboriously pushing through the crowded passages and up the narrow staircases. A peep into every one of the low-ceiled chambers reveals the same thing – men, women, and children, indistinct in the

The Lake, Brynmill Park.

Singleton, near the Swiss Chalet.

Cambrian Place.

Richmond Villas.

The Bush.

The Adam & Eve.

clouds of tobacco smoke, all huddled together, and in the best of spirits. If on passing you happen to step on the corns of a ferocious fumigating fellow, you may make the best of it by slapping him heartily on the back, giving his hand a vigorous squeeze and demanding concerning his health and enjoyment. You raise yourself quickly in the estimation of the victim of your clumsiness, and as quickly pass on. Approaching the last unexplored room, you open the door, when, O horror! you discover that it is a dormitory, and that a lady is arranging her toilet within. A hasty apology, an unabashed countenance, and a rapid retreat, conclude the episode. Another rapid glance around the fair, and you drive homeward, the drive being a repetition of the setting out. On the morrow, the happy reflection is that you have reaped all the benefits of Llangyfelach fair, in health and harmless enjoyment, without any of its evils.

———◇———

Brynhyfryd Board School.

It was resolved that the Board be recommended forthwith to complete the purchase of the site for the Brynhyfryd Board School and (in case the draft conveyance approved by the Board), to issue a cheque for £250, purchase money, and six month's interest at 5 per cent per annum, namely £6 5s. The foregoing recommendation of the committee was agreed to.

School Building Committee. – Danygraig Board School.

The following tenders have been received for the building of the Danygraig School:– Mr. Thomas Rees, £4750; D. Morgan. £4700; Mr. Thomas White, £4,435 – Mr. Thomas White's tender was accepted.

———◇———

LOCAL AND GENERAL NOTES.

The little conclave that rules the destinies of State elementary education in Swansea took some decisive steps in furtherance of their work at their last sitting on Tuesday afternoon. In another column will be found a detailed report of the work of the meeting, and it is our purpose hereto refer to the leading principles only. On the motion of the Vice-Chairman, seconded by the Chairman, and with the entire concurrence of the other members of the Board, it was decided to appoint a male children's officer to carry out, with the greatest possible efficiency, the compulsory powers now vested in the Board. The utmost satisfaction was expressed with the work performed by the female children's officer, and it was intimated that the Board had not the slightest intention of discontinuing her services, as upon her devolved duties which only a lady can perform effectively. At the same time it was felt that the filling of new schools about to be opened, and the proper supervision of the school attendance of the borough, absolutely necessitated the appointment of a male officer. A salary of less than £100 per annum was rightly deemed insufficient to attract an efficient officer. On the next question a larger amount of discussion arose. Mr. Trew moved, and Mr. Ellery seconded, a resolution to the effect that the bible be read daily in Board schools. Some remarks of a very pertinent nature were made by various speakers, tending to show that while the Board desired the moral culture of the children under their care, the simple reading of portions of Scripture uncommented upon, was a "mere sham" means to that end. The fear of sectarianism was evidently great, and once or twice a rupture of the harmony of the Board seemed imminent; but the good sense of the members prevailed, and the result was that the authoritative decision of the Board was recorded in confirmation of the principle now in vogue that the Bible be read daily in Board schools, it being understood that the discretion of the schoolmaster is to be used in putting such questions to the children as shall tend to the historical elucidation of the subject and the impressing it upon their minds, without in the slightest degree trenching upon the propagation of dogmas. While this decision can hardly fail to meet with the disapprobation of extremists, the Board have the satisfaction of knowing that they have chosen the much-lauded golden mean, by keeping true to which they may hope to win the approval and confidence of the majority.

———◇———

An increase of good philanthropic effort embodied in healthy institutions argues progress in the path of civilization, and cannot but be looked at as a gratifying indication of the times. To the long list of charitable organisations in the shire of Glamorgan we have to add one more, and though last it is not least among the beneficient agencies of the district. The long-contemplated Rest at Porthcawl is now becoming an accomplished fact. Long fostered as the scheme has been by the leading philanthropic spirits of the county, the advocacy of the claims of the incipient charity has been so successful as to evoke a very large amount of material assistance toward carrying into the effect the objects of the charity. We understand that the Lord Lieutenant of the county, besides giving the site at Porthcawl, is a donor of £1000 to the funds. Alexander Brogden, Esq., M.P. also gives £1000, and the Marquis of Bute a donor of £500. and these are not the only donations of a like magnitude. Now at length started under such good auspices, and not without time for mature deliberation on the part of the most prominent promoters, we hail the new institution as the fitting outcome of Glamorganshire's unexampled prosperity, and wish it may prove the means of alleviating human suffering, and of affording rest and comfort to many of the sick and weary toilers of busy Glamorgan.

———◇———

Dilapidated and Overcrowded Premises. – Ebenezer Davies, the medical officer of health, preferred a charge against both the owner and the occupier of the house No. 7 in Orchard-street – the charge against the owner being for allowing the premises to remain in a dilapidated condition, and that against the occupier being for overcrowding his house. Mr. Richard Birch, of Waterloo-street, who holds a lease on the premises under a Mr. Chapman, a pawnbroker, of Merthyr, said that he was not responsible for repairing the roof; and Mr. Mock, the occupier, professed his utter inability to eject his under-tenants, who threatened to knock his brains out when he mentioned the subject of their going. The prosecutor, Mr. Davies, said that the house was in a very damp and dilapidated state, in consequence of the damaged roof, and the house was totally unfit for human habitation. In the face of these facts, the premises were so crowded that seven persons occupied one room. The bench dilated upon the danger the town was in from contagion by the poisonous atmosphere generated in such foul habitations as this. The Stipendiary said he had been informed by Mr. Brock that fever was at the present moment prevalent in Swansea, and nothing was more conducive to the spread of typhoid and other fevers than the existence of such overcrowded and ruinous houses as the one complained of. They inflicted a fine of 20s. and costs upon the occupier Mock, and warned him to eject the superfluous dwellers in his house. The bench also ordered Birch to communicate with Chapman of Merthyr, and get the roof mended before the expiration of a fortnight, or he would be liable to a penalty of 10s. per day for every day the house remained unrepaired after the expiration of a fortnight.

Swansea Cricket Club. – The annual genral meeting of the above club was held at the Mackworth Arms Hotel, on the 18th. ult. There was a large attendance of members. From the secretary and treasurer's reports it appears that the club had a very successful season last year; out of their eight foreign first eleven matches, they won *seven* and lost *one* only. The funds are also in more satisfactory condition than they have ever been known before, and the numbers of playing members are continually increasing. The only drawback to their welfare is their inability to get a proper playing field. The one they have occupied for several seasons has been let for building purposes; and although they have secured it for this year, it will positively be the last, and next year they will be obliged to move somewhere else. It is to be hoped that such a sterling institution as the Cricket Club, which does so much to provide a noble and healthy recreation for the young men of the town and district, will not be allowed to be broken up for the want of a field. The Corporation, and all those who are interested in the welfare of the town, should take active steps to assist the Club in this dilemma. What is wanted is to secure a convenient piece of ground of a suitable size on a sufficiently long lease to enable the Club to lay out money in working and perfecting it, so that we might at least have as good a ground as our neighbours at Cardiff. We really hope that the matter will be taken up by those who are in a position to help the Club, and that they will not rest till a proper field be secured.

NEATH.

Neath – The River Floating Question, – Another meeting of the Harbour Commissioners to consider the best plan for improving Neath Harbour and making a floating dock, was held at the Town-hall, on Thursday. From reports which had been circulated it was expected that Lord Dynevor had withdrawn his opposition to the Bill, or at least that he had toned down his requirements to such an extent that the Commisioners would be able to consent to them. Such, however, does not appear to be the case, and the following resolution moved by Mr. Curtis, town clerk, and seconded by Mr. Charles, was carried, viz:– "That this meeting is decidedly of opinion that the requirements of Lord Dynevor (who, with his lessees are the persons to receive the greatest benefit by floating the river) are too onerous, and therefore the scheme of floating the river be abandoned; and that the Commissioners now consider the scheme for making a float across the Gnoll-marsh. That Mr. Brereton be instructed to prepare the necessary plans and an estimate to be laid before an adjourned meeting, to be held on 9th March next." The resolution was carried by 7 to 3.

Local Intelligence.

The Penllergare Hounds will meet on Monday, March 9, at Llandebie Station; on Saturday, March 14, at Trosarch – each day at half-past ten.

Football, – The return match between the Swansea Football Club and the Cowbridge School will be played on the Cricket Field at Bryn-y-mor, on Saturday (tomorrow) afternoon. Play will begin at a quarter to twelve, and a very close match is anticipated. As the admission to the field is free, we hope there will be a large attendance.

STREET STEAM ENGINES.

To the Editor of "The Cambrian."

Sir, – Can you enlighten us as to why we have steam engines continually passing and repassing our streets to the great obstruction of all other traffic. Trucks frequently get off the line, and other causes of stoppage often arise, which bring together and block up a crowd of vehicles unable to proceed about their business. The steam engine is also a source of fright to horses, and many persons have been in danger of being seriously hurt from this cause. On Monday night a poor fellow in crossing near the Quay got both legs smashed, which has unfortunately cost him his life; and many other escapes and serious annoyances have come come under my notice. When the matter was discussed by the Council a short time ago, I understand the feeling expressed was decidedly against street steam engines, and the decision arrived at was their discontinuance. Let us hope that the Council, at their next meeting, will look fully into this serious matter.

I am, Sir, yours faithfully,

Enquirer,

Swansea, March 4. 1874.

THE CORPORATION ACCOUNTS AND ITS LATE COLLECTOR.

To the Editor of "The Cambrian."

Sir, – Very severe and protracted personal and domestic affliction and bereavement have prevented me earlier addressing you on your report of the Finance Committee of the Swansea Town Council, in reference to my accounts. I hope, therefore, you will now allow me room to state:– 1st, That the books last mentioned, and reported upon by the accountant, have not been in my possession for the last two years, or in the office I used to occupy. 2nd, I was not asked for any explanation before the report was made public; in fact, I only became acquainted with the report by having it pointed out to me in the public papers. 3rd, I have never had or kept a private book for the accounts of the Corporation. 4th, I have never refused to give up any book to the Council. 5th, No book belonging to my accounts has come into their hands by accident. 6th, They have no book of mine relating to my accounts, but what they have had, or but what has been accessible to them in the office, from the beginning. 7th, I have never given a receipt for £10, or any other amount, to any ratepayer without entering the amount to the credit of the Corporation; nor held for two years moneys so received – and deny the statement made in the Council. Before I had completed my examination the Council refused me any further use of the books; I am therefore placed in a very disadvantageous position. 8th, I have never used nor spent Corporation money for the purpose of acquiring personal or private property. 9th, My freehold property came to me by the will of my first wife, who purchased it in 1849, before I entered the employment of the Corporation. The property in Rodney and Fleet Streets was obtained with the mortgage on it, £1820. My other property was purchased with legitimate savings out of my salary, and a mortgage of £1600. I may add that the Corporation have collected the rents from a part of my property for the last nine months; but I have not received any account of the money they have received, nor of the way it has been appropriated. If the Corporation should be making any arrangements for the sale of any of my property, privately, I caution any who may think of purchasing any of it, that I shall dispute their title to it; and all actionable statements made on this subject by whomsoever and wheresoever, I shall seek redress in the legal way. I hope that, while the ratepayers will approve of the care taken by the Corporation of their interests, they will wish the truth only to be spoken on the subject, and justice done all round.

I am Sir, yours respectfully,
Jno. R. Brenton.

Put Out a Bit. – A nervous lady, travelling by rail last week from Kensington to Croydon, found herself alone in a first-class compartment. Just as the train was leaving a wild-looking gentleman, with excited eyes jumped in. Presently he began talking aloud, lending emphasis to angry ejaculations by vehemently slapping his knees. The fog was dense, and as a matter of course, no lamp illumined the darkness. Naturally, the lady was much alarmed at the strange behaviour of her solitary companion, especially as she only that morning had been told that several lunatics are roving about England. What was to be done? For a moment or two she determined on changing carriages at the first station, but a fear of exciting the mad man's suspicion palsied the attempted movement. For a time this continued, the lunatic gesticulating and remonstrating vehemently with some imaginary person. Just when the tension on her nerves was absolutely in supportable, the train stopped, and to her intense relief the Bedlamite got out. Great was her surprise to see that his ticket was not demanded, whilst the officials touched their hats to him with the most obsequeous civility. Calling a guard, she inquired who the strange gentleman was, and why he seemed so excited. One of our directors ma'am, and he's put out a bit because the election's goin' against him.

——◇——

8th. April 1876.

The Welsh Calvinists indulge in eccentric names, borrowed from Scriptural words and titles, as largely as any body of religionists. A writer in the *Cornhill* says:– "We found at Bridgend a Mahershalalhashbaz. At Tremadoc we came across a Hosanna. There was a Sinai at Llanidau in Anglesea, and Selah near Monmouth. The oddities of old Testament nomenclature are clearly attractive to some for their own sakes. We have twins in the register named respectively Huz and Buz. But further the titles of the bad characters of the Bible are not infrequently selected and given to children. We have found in the registers an Absalom, a Cain, a Delilah, a Herod, and a Pharaoh.

WELSH NOMENCLATURE IN THE NEW DOMESDAY BOOK.

Some of the particulars to be gleaned from the Welsh counties are most amusing, especially to those who care for the study of local names. We investigated the county of Carmarthenshire, where 2,898 people own more than one acre a piece, the total population being 116,000. Now picture the confusion that must arise from the incorrect delivery of letters; the blunders which tax collectors must needs commit; the lawsuits that must miscaarry through serving notices on the wrong men, where whole villages are peopled by inhabitants of the same surname, many having also but one Christian name between them Out of those 2898 – which might fairly represent a country town – there is *one* name which no letter carrier could mistake Tacharia Christmas – man or woman we know not; then there are 23 Bowens, 292 Davies, including 52 David Davies; 193 Evans, including John Evans 20 times; 56 Griffiths; 40 Hughes; 314 Jones, among whom David Jones occurs 40 times and John Jones 47 times; 130 Lewis; 74 Morgans; 70 Phillips; 100 Rees; while as to the family of Thomas, there are only 286 landowners whose names begin with a T, and 271 of them inherit the surname of Thomas; yet either they hold that particular name in especial esteem, or from a total absence of fertility of invention, many of these Thomas's have also had Thomas bestowed on them as a Christian name, so that Thomas Thomas occurs 37 times. There are besides 270 persons whose names begin with a W, but they can only muster 25 different sorts of names amongst the lot; 214 of their number being members of the tribe of Williams. We once heard of a schoolboy who was fond of betting that he could write his name in full on a slate quicker than any one else. He always won, for he was called James James, and he used to write one name backwards, and the other forwards, with a slate pencil in each hand. He must have been a Welshman. – *Land and Water.*

STEAM TRAM-CARS.

The propulsion of tram-cars by some motive power other than that supplied by horses has long constituted a tempting subject for inventors. Many attempts have been made to get rid of horses, and, it must be confessed, with very little success. To the amateur it appears to be absurd to employ horses when a little engine not much bigger than a coffee pot ought to be able to do the required work; and besides it would be so much nicer to propel a car by steam or compressed air than by horses, who suffer very much in hot and very cold weather – things of which an engine would take no cognisance. Engineers see nothing peculiarly tempting in the propulsion of tram-cars by machinery. The question presents itself solely in the light of a speculation to them, and the very first point which demands their consideration is one which the amateur ignores altogether. Will it pay to use steam, or ammonia, or compressed air? On this point there happens to be no small diversity of opinion, and it must be admitted that the available stock of experience as to the working of tram-cars by steam is so small that it is difficult to say whether a saving may or may not be reasonably expected. A line of tram-way with cars, each drawn by one horse, requires a stud of about five horses per car to work say, thirteen hours a day. Each two horse tram-car requires about nine and a half horses, experience going to show that the proportion of horse-power per car is rather less than doubled by using two horses instead of one. Assuming that the horses cost on average £40 each, it follows that a double tram-car can be horsed for, say, £380. Of course it must be understood that this is no more than a rough estimate, the conditions of working and of buying horses are so different in different locations. It is extremely improbable that any machine can be constructed to take the place of horses for less than £100, but for the sake of argument we may admit that the cost of an engine and the cost of horses will be identical. The depreciation to the value of tram-car horses cannot be taken at less than 20 per cent, per annum – will the loss of value in the case of an engine be less? This remains to be seen. If a satisfactory motor, say a steam engine, can be produced which will be as durable as a railway locomotive, and if a sufficient number of these motors be employed to work a line properly, then a decided saving may be effected by their use as compared with the expense of horse labour. Whether such an engine can or cannot be produced will not be known until engineers have tried to produce one; and we are pleased that a fair prospect at last exists that the experiment will be made fully and fairly. In Copenhagen tram-cars have been worked for some time past with considerable success, and steam tram-cars are now running in Paris in a very satisfactory way. In this country the thing is being tested on an adequte scale with compressed air and also with steam. – *Engineer.*

——◇——

Football. – The following is a list of matches with the results, played by the Swansea Football Club during the season 1875-76:– Llandovery College at Swansea on 13th. November, was drawn; Llandovery College, at Llandovery, 4th. December, won by Llandovery by 1 goal; Glamorgan Football Club, at Cardiff on 11th December, won by Swansea by 1 try; Llandovery College at Swansea, 5th February, won by Swansea by 1 goal 1 try; Llanelly, at Llanelly, 5th. February, drawn; Glamorgan Football Club, at Swansea, 26th. February, won by Swansea by 3 goals, 13 tries; Llandovery College at Llandovery 4th. March, drawn; Llanelly, at Swansea, 7th. March, drawn; Newport, at Newport, 18th. March, won by Newport by 1 try.

——◇——

The Value of Property in Swansea. – Notwithstanding the temporary depression in the trade of this district, the value of house property, within an easy distance of the centre of the town, fully maintains its reputation and value as a safe means of investment. On Wednesday afternoon, Messrs Beynon and Hughes, auctioneers, submitted for sale by auction, at the Cameron Arms Hotel, a dwelling house in Northampton-place now in the occupation of Mr. J. Hughes. It is held on lease of 99 years, from 1850, at a ground rent of £4 17s. per annum. Some eight or ten years since, houses in the same row were sold at £450. On Wednesday the lot realised £700. A house and shop in Oxford-street, let on lease of 99 years from 1835, at a ground rent of £2 10s., sub let for a term of 14years from 1865, at a nominal rent of £16, was sold for £645. A small house in Edward-street sold for £194.

——◇——

The judicious outlay which the council has made, and is still making, for providing parks and recreation grounds for the people is becoming more and more appreciated, and in future years will prove a boon priceless in mere monetary value. Every day the worry and excitement of business becomes more intense, whilst once green fields and picturesque walks and nooks are being covered by the inexorable march of building. Hence the necessity for the means of relaxation, and the prescience of our corporation in securing eligible open spaces in our midst will be more and more recognised and valued If anyone should doubt the correctness of the motives which prompted our council to provide such recrearion grounds, let them pay a visit to the Brynmill reservoir grounds or the equally charming Uplands estate on fine Sundays or evenings, when he will see ample reason to justify the steps which have been taken. Hundreds of health and pleasure seekers visit each of these spots and enjoy and revel in the luxury of the recreation afforded them. More seats are urgently needed in the Brynmill grounds, for on fine afternoons not one can be obtained, and it is not always judicious to sit upon grass, however tempting a rest may be. We are sorry, too, that steps have not been taken to afford more direct access to these grounds. We had hoped that the gentlemen to whom the adjacent fields belong would have seen their way to respond to the request of the corporation on behalf of the public, and have afforded the right of way for a carriage and footpath, instead of the present long and tedious detour. With regard to the Uplands, we have heard complaints made as to the former rustic appearance being destroyed by the plan now being adopted of laying out the grounds. It is, however, too soon yet to judge of the effect, and when completed we think the whole spot will be one of the most charming and delightful in this part of the country, affording elevated views of the Mumbles headland and the whole adjacent picturesque scenery. Seats will, of course, be provided and we hope in no niggard spirit; and if a "maze" could be added it would add much to the attractions of the grounds. We hope our council will make another effort to secure a nearer and better approach to the Brynmill grounds, and that they will now push on the necessary work at Uplands, with energy, so that the public may have two eligible spots for their recreation and amusements.

Messiah Concert for the Benefit of the Hospital. – We have to remind our readers that Monday evening next, April 10th., is the date fixed for the performance of Handel's "Messiah," which is to be given at the Music Hall, Swansea, by the Swansea Choral Society for the benefit of the funds of the Swansea Hospital. As may be seen in detail in our advertising columns, the artistes engaged for the interpretation of the solos are – Soprano, Madame Barton-Edmonds; contralto, Miss Martha Harries, R.A.M.; tenor, Eos Morlais; and bass Mr. Thomas Brandon. Each of the quartett is so well known, and so deservedly popular in Swansea, that it would be superfluous to do more than mention his or her name. The band will be strong and will consist of well chosen performers, under the leadership of Mr. E. G.Woodward. The trumpet obligato will be undertaken by Mr. Lingwood, and Professor Fricker will preside as organist. The chorus will consist of upwards of 250 voices, under the able baton of Mr. Silas Evans. Since the unprecedently successful performance of this oratorio a couple of months ago, the members of the Choral Society have assiduously continued their careful rehearsals under the painstaking conduct of Messrs. Evans and Fricker, and the result will be, we expect, that the Handelian choruses will be rendered on Monday evening with a power and precision never yet equalled in Swansea. Having regard to the great disappointment experienced by hundreds in failing to get admission to the hall at the last performance we would advise an early application for tickets. The managing committee have this time taken their measures to prevent the overcrowding and inconvenience which were so complained of previously. The doors will be opened at 6.30. and the performance will commence at 7.30, but no money will be taken at the doors until 7 o'clock, so as to afford ticket holders the preference. It should be remembered that the proceeds of the performance are to be generously devoted to the funds of the hospital. We noticed last week that £45 had been handed over to the Deaf and Dumb Institution as the result of the last performance, and we trust a yet larger amount will accrue from this. Apart from the performance being in itself such a musical treat as is rarely accessible to Swansea, the effort ought to be warmly supported by the public as a recognition of the generous services of the leaders and members of Swansea Choral Society, and as a duty to so eminently useful and beneficent an institution as the Hospital, which in a quiet way, is accomplishing an incalculable amount of good, in relieving poor and suffering humanity.

Correspondence.

We do not hold ourselves responsible for the opinions and sentiments expressed by our Correspondents.

SWANSEA PROVIDENT SOCIETY.

To the Editor of "The Cambrian."

Sir, – It gave me great pleasure to see in your last issue that a Provident Dispensary is about to be established in Swansea. It has been a want of many years. Will you permit me to say a few words respecting such an institution?

In the first place, what I look upon as the most important feature of a dispensary is that it need not be elesmosynary, or only so to a very small extent. My belief is that through mistaken kindness a very great injury has been done, and is doing, to the working class of this country The sober working man and his family are no longer poor. It is an insult to call him a pauper, or to treat him as one. With the best intention the poor law of this country has done this signal injury, that so many look to it to provide for a future which they should trust to no other effort but their own. This is also the nature of every institution which offers gratuitous help to those who are well able by a little self-denial to pay.

The Provident Dispensary proposes to do this. I need not enter into detail. But I look upon this effort to enable the working man to provide against the day of trial as of far more importance than many a more pretentious scheme.

And further, I believe very few persons except those directly or indirectly connected with the medical profession are aware what a vast amount of medical help is given to the working class and no pay received. A medical man, if called upon night or day, must go to visit; for society will revenge itself somehow if he does not; and once in the house he gives his advice, and probably physic, and often money, without the faintest hope of any return. And why? Not because the family as a family are unable to pay, but because the father, and often, alas, now, the mother chose to spend perhaps 10s. to 70s. a week in the public house.

As a clergyman, I know that no class of men give practically more money's worth in temporal things than medical men do to the working class, and as is very usual when money is forced on the spur of the moment it goes to swell, in the long run, the enormous sums spent in spirits and beer. For the above reasons, and as one long interested in your Infirmary, I cannot approve of home visits being made by charity orders from the hospital. I believe it is done no where else. Out-door order oblige the the patient to go to the hospital. The dispensary will also issue to annual subscribers orders for home visits, which in cases of real need may be given to those too poor to pay for a sick entry.

I feel sure it is a positive injury to a

hospital for any of its officers to visit the sick in their houses. It must more or less bring the hospital in collision with the medical staff of the town, as all who are subscribers, were they ever so discreet, are liable to imposition. The dispensary pays the doctor for every case he attends. It may be a very small sum for each, but it is quite as good at the year's end as a host of small debts, many of which will never be paid.

It has been said that it will injure the hospital by loss of subscribers. I do not think this will be so, as all persons like to see their money well spent, and there is a growing feeling that for a man who has say £250 a year coming in from business or profession to subscribe to pay the doctor or the schooling, or rates, or income tax, to save families who are getting if they chose often £5 a man a week equal to £260 a year – is a process which nothing but the greatest ignorance of political economy could ever have brought into the repute it has in this country.

I am, sir, faithfully yours.
H. Knight Eaton.
Vicar of Christ Church Stafford.

E aster Monday, – Bank Holiday.

To The Editor of "The Cambrian."
Sir, – The Drapers' Assistants of Swansea, I am sure, will hail with great satisfaction and gratitude the announcement that it is the intention of all the leading drapers of the town to suspend business on the Bank Holiday, Easter Monday. Past experience shows, that Easter Monday, as a rule, is a very dull business day, and assistants only have to look at one another during the day without seeing a customer. In acknowledging the liberality of those employers who confer this boon on their employees, we can assure them that they will not be the losers by their kindness.

I am, Sir, yours obediently,
A Draper's Assistant.
Swansea, April 6, 1876.

Why have we not a Training Ship at Swansea?

To The Editor of "The Cambrian."
Sir, – In all large towns and cities a large portion of the population is devoted to misery and vice. The children of drunken, thoughtless parents naturally copy their example, until they grow up to manhood in drunkeness and crime Thus are our jails filled; thus are our work-houses burdened: and thus are let loose on society its terrors. Is there any remedy for this state of things? Can these outcasts, or some of them, be reclaimed and made useful members of society? Not in the tree, perhaps, but in the sapling it is possible. At the present time the Government are offering £25 per head to boys for the navy, and yet they cannot get them. This, perhaps, is because the boys do not have a fair opportunity of joining. Why have we not a training ship for Swansea? This populous port, with its 70,000 inhabitants, would be just the place for such an institution. It is the central point of a very large district, the Swansea and Neath valleys having a very large population to whom such an institution would be a great blessing. It may be argued that there is a training ship at Bristol, and I think another at Milford, but these ports are from 60 to 50 miles distant, and how could the poor lads of our streets get enough money to carry them to either? Say that we had such a ship and that she came into harbour occasionally from her anchorage in the Mumbles roads, and the boys dressed in their smart uniforms, would it not be an inducement for the poor neglected children of our streets to join and be equally cared for? Swansea, the largest ship-owning port of any in the Bristol Channel, is most interested in the training of good seamen. The expense of such a training-ship would be very little, as the present commander of coast guards could take the command, and his men help to man the vessel. The ship would also do for the annual training of the coast guard and naval reserve men, and save the present expense of sending them to Bristol or Milford, and also serve as a receiving ship for naval volunteers. The whole of the Welsh coast from Holyhead to Cardiff, is, with the exception of Milford entirely unprotected. Our ports deserve to be valued more highly, and to have at least one man o' war to serve as a training ship. This vessel need not be of very large size; one of the old 80-horse power gun boats would do very well, or even a small corvette, which could sail occasionally to afford the opportunity for necessary drill and seamnship.

Mr. Editor, I hope someone abler than myself will take up this question. There are many in our port whose talents and influence could soon bring the matter to a successful issue.

In conclusion I beg leave to say to the man who can accomplish this the community at large will be indebted.

I am, sir, yours truly
A Swansea Boy.

3rd. May 1878.

SHIPPING INTELLIGENCE

Corunna, April 24.— The Scotia, brig, of Swansea from Huclava, with minerals, foundered last night off Malpica; crew saved.

Noble Rescue of the Crew of a Swansea Vessel. – The coxwain of the "Out Pensioner" lifeboat of the National Lifeboat Institution stationed at Arklow, makes the following report of the circumstances attending the recent wreck of the barque "Broughton" of Swansea, on the Irish coast, and the rescue of her crew by that lifeboat:– "24th. April 1878, At 5 p.m., it was reported by the Arklow Coastguards that a vessel was on the Arklow Bank. The lifeboat was launched and taken through a very heavy sea over the bar, the wind being E.N.E., and the tide being ebb. She then proceeded to the Mizen Head where she was anchored about midnight. At about 1.30 a.m. got sail on the lifeboat, and proceeded to the Arklow Bank, where at daybreak the vessel was seen about two miles in leeward. The boat went outside the Bank to the barque and anchored under her port quarter, when a sea filled the lifeboat. The vessel's crew then veered out a cork-fender, but the line broke. A second fender was then veered out, to which a hawser was attached. The lifeboat then filled a second time. The boat then attempted to get close to the vessel, upon which she shipped a sea fore and aft, washing the coxwain overboard. He was not missed for a time, but happily, though with some difficulty, he was eventually rescued. The boat was afterwards again overwhelmed by the heavy seas, and the crew, believing it to be impossible for them to reach the vessel then, from the state of the sea and the long exposure and the severe trial they had undergone, it was considered best to return ashore and get a fresh crew. The boat reached Arklow at about 9.30 a.m., when a fresh crew immediately manned her, and proceeded under a double reefed foresail to Arklow Bank on the first of the flood tide, the wind still blowing very hard from the E.N.E. The boat was again filled twice in attempting to cross the Bank. Her head was then turned to the shore, and five tacks were made, and eventually she got through the Mizen Swash. She then ran before the wind to the vessel, and let go her anchor under the vessel's quarter. The boat was now filled twice, her crew being drenched; but they succeeded in taking on board the vessel's crew, consisting of 15 men, and safely landed them at Arklow at 6.15 p.m. – Richard Wadden, Coxwain of the Lifeboat." – The National Institution has granted the sum of £62 for these lifeboat services, being £2 10s. to each of the first crew of the lifeboat, and £1 10s. to each man forming the crew of the lifeboat on the second trip.

Wrecks and Casualties – During the month of April 191 wrecks and casualties were posted on Lloyd's book. In this number are included 35 steam vessels and 156 sailing vessels. Compared with the preceding month's return, there is a decrease this month of seven in the aggregate of marine accidents. These statistics include vessels of all flags – 116 were British, six United States, 13 French, five German, four Italian, three Spanish, one Belgian, seven Dutch, and two Greek. The remainder belonged principally to the northern countries of Europe. The most serious casualty that happened during the month was the wreck of the steamer Childwall Hall, whereby a portion of the crew and passengers lost their lives.

It is in the undoubted interest of the owners of house property to uphold the character for respectability of the streets in which they have a share, and especially so if these streets are of a purely residential character. In pursuance of this principle, an owner of residential property the other day, I hear dismissed one of his tenants because he was engaged in trade on the premises. But Walter-road is now studded with shops and public-houses, and the last move in the same direction is the opening of a public-house at the lower end of the hitherto select Mansel-street.

——◇——

The representative men of Swansea enjoy the sweets of office, the honours, and the emoluments, with but few drawbacks of a graver kind than adverse criticism or a chance epithet bandied about in the heat of debate; but in some parts of the world the amenities of municipal office are alloyed with such heavy responsibilities that the tinsel dignity they confer is more than counter-balanced by the attendant risks. Thus we learn that the unfortunate Burgomaster of Nieder Zwehren in Cassell has just been sentenced to 6 months' imprisonment in consequence of the sanitary supervision of flesh carried out under his authority having been so negligently performed that an outbreak of trichinosia resulted in the district. Possibly his sin was not altogether one of omission only, for it is stated that the public prosecutor demanded the more severe sentence of two year' imprisonment. Just imagine the chairman of Swansea Finance Committee going to gaol to expiate the recent defalcations, or the chairman of the Sanitary Committee made criminally resonsible for the spread of an epedemid disease! It would then need more heroic staff than mere ability to talk, to constitute a Town Councillor.

——◇——

Greenhill Mission Hall. – On Thursday evening an amusing and instructive entertainment was given in the above Mission Hall, the proceeds of which are to be devoted to the Pentre Iron Church debt fund. The choir was assisted by several amateurs of the town, and great praise is due to them for the manner in which they discharged their portion of the programme, and also to Mr. W. Griffiths conductor of the choir, for the successful manner in which the entertainment passed off. The hall was well filled. In the absence of Dr. Rawlings, Mr. F. J. Rayner was voted to the chair; when the following programme was gone through:– Glee "The Bells," Choir; recitation "Perseverance," Miss Elizabeth Emily Griffiths; song "The Better Day Coming," Master W. Owen; reading "The oiled feather," Mr. J. Griffiths; glee " Busy Town," Choir; recitation "Charity," Mrs. Dennes (encored); song "The shake of the hand," Mr. Evan Matthews; dialogue "Following Morning," Messrs. Ellery, Cornock and others; glee "Cloudland" Choir; reading "The opposed marriage," Mr. W. Griffiths; song "The honest heart," Mr. D. Matthews; reading "Tennyson's spaniel war," H. E. Fry, Esq; song "Poor old Kitty," Miss Elizabeth Emily Griffiths; recitation "The Soldier's Pardon," Mr. Dalton; duett and chorus "Our Mission," Choir. The usual vote of thanks having been accorded a most pleasanr evening's entertainment was brought to a close by singing the national anthem.

——◇——

The Stradivarius violin, dated 1794, known to connoisseurs as the "Betts Strad," has been purchased by Mr. Geo. Hart for the sum of 800 guineas. Some 70 years ago it was bought by John Betts, the violin maker, for a sovereign, and he declined all offer of sale, though the then unprecedented sum of £500 was tendered, but after his death it was disposed of to M. Vuillaume, of Paris, and afterwards to M. Willmote, of Antwerp, from whom the owner purchased it. – *Athanaeum.*

——◇——

Barnstaple has had the good fortune to have a prize fight unmolested by the police. It took place on Sunday last during church hours. The heroes were William Crooks, of Bristol, and William Porter of Barnstaple, and scores of – no doubt most intelligent – persons watched the progress of this very noble contest, chuckling all the while at how they had outwitted the Barnstaple police. The fight lasted half an hour, and Crooks had the worst of it throughout. Porter retired from the field the centre of an admiring crowd.

GOSSIP.

There is no more useful machine in Swansea than the steam-roller; it has done good work already, and will do more. Might it not be run a couple of times over the newly-laid stones in those by-streets that skirt Page, Nichol, George, Henrietta, and Russell-streets.

Poetry

THE SONG OF THE SHIP.

Sing, sing, ye all, of the joy of the ship,
With wide spreading sails and a pearly lip,
With a wake full of foam and showers of spray,
And a gallant crew to steer her way.

No billow too large to obstruct her prow –
There's no breeze too fresh for her piercing bow;
Anon in the clouds, and away in the strife,
On, onward she speeds like a thing of life.

In the tropical day, or the starlight night,
In the dark abyss, or the broad daylight,
Heedless of time, or of danger, or death,
She waits not, she rests not, not even for breath.

For away she hides with her teeming life,
Through tempests of wind, and oceans of strife;
Away to the South, where England's brave men
Seek a peaceful home and a lasting. Amen.

South Pacific Ocean, August, 1877.
I.A.C.

Correspondence.

CHEAP TRAINS
TO THE MUMBLES.

To the Editor of "The Cambrian."

Sir, – Could you kindly inform me, through the medium of your valuable paper, who is it who tries to prevent the working men having a cheap ride to the Mumbles? I see by today's papers that an application was made yesterday in one of the higher courts to prevent the Tramway Company from running their engines over the Oystermouth Tramway, saying that they were dangerous to the public, and that the road was consequently impassable. Surely a greater untruth than this was never told. I think that the neat little engines are a great improvement upon horses in more ways than one. I fail to see any steam or sparks issuing from them when running. At the time horses were used the fare to the Mumbles was one shilling, but now we are carried much more comfortably for fivepence, and I don't think the company could afford to carry with horses for this low figure. The return tickets used to be one shilling and sixpence, but now only eight pence. If it comes back to the old style we poor dabs will have to tramp it or stop at home.

Yours truly,
Leyshon Rees,
St. Helen's, Swansea, May 1st., 1878.

The Swansea Tramway Steam Cars. – The following statement has been issued in reply to a paragraph inserted in another column, which we copied from the *South Wales Daily News*:– "This morning a paragraph appears in the *South Wales Daily News* headed 'Action against the Swansea Tramway Company' calculated to mislead the public as to the true facts of the case. The solicitor of the company has been in Swansea for some days collecting evidence, and he is perfectly overwhelmed with statements from daily travellers on the line to the effect that the locomotives, emit little or no steam or smoke, and cause no more noise than an ordinary tram car as they pass over the rails. They run smoothly, and as a matter of fact do not frighten the horses These travellers have been, during the past two months, in the daily habit of observing the horses and vehicles passing the locomotives, and have not seen any cases of even shying. A very considerable proportion of the total passenger traffic between Swansea and the Mumbles is conveyed over the line in question, while the number of persons who drive their own vehicles is comparatively insignificant. The large majority of those who use the line would regard it as a matter of regret were the improved system inaugurated by the use of locomotives put an end to, and the cars drawn again by horses. By using locomotives the company has been enabled to carry at the the usual rate of fare the exceptional heavy holiday traffic during Easter week, amounting to upwards of 23,000 persons – a fact never before accomplished, the old system being to double the fare on these occasions and so preventing large numbers from enjoying a cheap trip to the Mumbles. Under these circumstances seeing that the daily travellers on the line are almost unanimous in their opinion that the the present system of traction by locomotives is infinitely preferable to the past system of traction by horses, and in view of the demands of the numbers who wish the enjoyment of a trip to the Mumbles on fine days and holidays, it would be a lamentable thing were the present conveniences of the general public curtailed in consequence of the protests of a few interested individuals, who driving their own carriages, are not in a position fairly to judge of the great inconvenience they will be causing the public if their action against the company proves successful.

Swansea and Devonshire Traffic. – We have often advocated the erection of a deep water pier at the Mumbles, as a means of not only affording the most direct communication between Swansea and the adjacent localities on the one hand, and the whole of Devonshire and the West of England on the other, but because we feel convinced that a traffic would soon spring up which would be most beneficial to both communities. Devonshire, Somersetshire, Gloucestershire, and the West of England are rich in agricultural produce, for which adequate markets cannot be found, whilst the dense aggregate population which exist in and around Swansea and throughout the Swansea and Neath Valleys are in daily want of those articles of consumption which our English friends have in such abundance to bestow. On this side of the channel there are many articles which would command a ready sale and large profits in the West. The one great obstacle to the interchange of commodities and an extensive trade, both passenger and general, is the want of a deep water pier at the Mumbles, allowing loading and onloading of steamers at all states of tide, and the establishment of regular time of train and steamer service. Such a service, once established, there would scarcely be a limit to the trade which would spring up. It would afford a direct route from the North of England to the west coast, Cornwall, &c., &c., &c., and the present long circuitous and inconvenient routes would be abandoned. The advantages of the direct communication between the two points we have have indicated, by means of a pier at the Mumbles, are so obvious that the wonder certainly is that the railway companies most directly interested therein have not long since carried out the scheme. But all large bodies move slowly, and we suppose we must wait patiently for the time when the railway companies will awake to their own interests and those of the public, and put into practical operation that which all admit, theoretically, to be a great boon. Even under present arrangements, imperfect though they be, every day experience fully proves the fact of the superiority of the Swansea and the Ilfracombe route over the present, and also the large trade which could be done did proper facilities exist. On Monday last Mr. J. W. Pockett's steamship Velindre made a voyage from Swansea to Ilfracombe and back (including the time for discharging and reloading of cargo) in five hours! She left the entrance of the South Dock, Swansea at 1.30 in the afternoon, with passengers and general cargo, discharged cargo, and reloaded and was back in Swansea at 6.45 the same evening. Now, if the pier existed at the Mumbles, so that steamers could arrive at any state of the tide, the regular service could be established, and passengers arriving in Swansea from the North of England would at once be forwarded to Ilfracombe, and arrive at the West of England and Cornwall on the same day, and thus time, money and great inconvenience saved. The railway trip from Swansea to Ilfracombe, via Bristol, takes 12 hours, so that the Velindre accomplished the trip to and fro in seven hours, less than the railway trip one way. We can only repeat that we hope the manifold advantages which must accrue from the erection of the deep water pier at the Mumbles and the coestablishment of direct communications with the west coast, will become so obvious that further delay will not be brooked, and that all interested in so beneficial a scheme will not rest satisfied until it is carried out.

SWANSEA SHIPPING INVESTMENTS.

To the Editor of "The Cambrian."

Sir, – A letter in your last week's issue, under the heading of "Swansea Shipping Investments," has but very mildly touched on what has been a problem that I have long since failed to solve. I invested nearly the little all I had saved by hard work, in a vessel belonging to and managed in Swansea, with a prospect of at least better returns than I would get if lent at five per cent; but what has been the result? My share cost me about eight hundred pounds. I have not received sufficient to pay the Insurance, but what I complain of is that the amounts are so made out that it is impossible to find out by them how the loss arises, or how much the manager profits by my misfortunes; and to crown all I find my property is reduced in value to about one-third. I don't understand much about shipping matters, but I hear there are many perquisites which amount to considerable sums which ships' managers consider belong to them, but which owners are not aware of, and which never appear in the accounts; such for instance as brokerages, commissions, and even discounts have been named. Now, if this is so, it is wrong in principle, as a proper charge should be made and arranged with the partners – but no pickings. My experience is that in my endeavours to be enlightened on these points, the result has not been satisfactory, as I have come away more mystified than ever. It would be a great boon if some of our practical men, in whom we have confidence would take this matter up and assist those, who like myself feel great dissatisfaction, but don't know how to seek a remedy, especially when I know many without other means have invested their all, and are depending on these ships for their living. Could not a general meeting of those interested in ships be called, and ask some practical man to attend who could assist us in these matters before it is all swallowed up? I would suggest Messrs. Bath or Messrs. Richardson firms, who have a knowledge of these matters . . .

Swansea, 1st. May 1878 A Sufferer.

4th. June 1880.

Aquatic and Foreshore Sports at the Mumbles. – It will be seen by a detailed advertisement in another column that a capital programme of water and shore sports will take place opposite the Mermaid Hotel, tomorrow (Saturday). The affair is got up by the distinguished visitors staying at the Mermaid Hotel, among which are Lady North, Sir W. H. Clayton, Bart., Capt. Barber, Morgan S. Williams, Esq., and others who have offered good prizes for the winners of the various contests. Besides some capital boat races, the programme contains such attractive features as "Bringing Ashore Dummy Man," tug of war, girls' boat race, greased pole &c., &c. There will be a band in attendance. Doubtless the sports will attract large numbers from Swansea if not from more distant places. If the good example of these ladies and gentlemen are more generally followed, the Mumbles would considerably benefit.

The Mumbles Visitors' List. – Mr. Thos. P. Syke, Glasbury, Radnorshire at

Brighton House; Mr. T. H. Green, Bath, at Rosehill Terrace; Miss Castle, Sydenham, at 3, Somerset Place; Miss Nankeen, Bristol, at Marine House; Rev. G. Williams and family from Abercamlais, at Singlewood, Caswell Bay; Mrs. and Miss Yeum, Hereford, at 3, Somerset Place; Mr. Jones, Gloucester, at Bath House; Major and Mrs. Ronsay and family, Bristol at Fairfield Villa; Mrs. Partridge, Tunbridge Wells, at Alexandra Terrace; Mr. and Mrs. J. N. Moore, Neath, at Caswell Bay Hotel; Mr. and Mrs. Hicks Beach, Cranheim Lodge, Painswick, at Caswell Bay; Mr. and Mrs. Williams, Aberpergwm, at Mermaid Hotel; Mr. and Mrs. A. Fulton, Cardiff, Upper Villa, at Langland Bay; Mrs. Sully, London, at Langland Hill House; Mr. and Mrs. Rux, Surbiton, at Castleton Cottage; Sir W. Clayton Bart, and Capt. Barber, at Mermaid Hotel; Miss Inkersole, Swansea, at Caswell Bay; Mr. Doggett, London, at Ship and Castle.

———<>———

The Doctor in the Kitchen. – The fourth and last of the drawing-room lectures under the auspices of the National Heath Society, given last week at the house of Mr. C. Matthews, 23, Hertford street, Mayfair, was by Mr. Ernest Hart, who presented to a large audience many facts regarding food, and a number of suggestions respecting its preparation. Mr. Hart altogether disapproved the usual diet in this country, especially what he described as its "meatiness," and the neglect of nitrogenous vegetables and fish food which characterises it. Touching upon fish food, he spoke of the great neglect of river fish by our population generally, and urged that the pike, the jack, the perch and other river fish might be advantageously included in the menu and would form a pleasing change in contrast to the unvaried roll of dishes now presented. The subject of waste in the kitchen was noticed by the lecturer, and he drew particular attention to the great amount of nutrition to be derived from what are now too often regarded as waste substances. He dwelt particularly on the extravagance of roasting, and urged that by the use of the ventilated, closed stove there would not only be a great saving in the food, but that the quantity of food saved would be enormous. He praised highly as a breakfast food the compound known but little in this country as hominy. The bread in England was excellent, and taken as a whole, the best in the world. French bread was over fermented and its crust was overbaked. The drawbacks in the "whole meal" bread were the hardness of its crust and its liability to turn sour, while the necessity for whole meal on account of the phosphates being removed from fine flour, was now removed by improvements introduced by Professor Hutsford, of Massachussetts. The lecture concluded with suggestions whereby the menu of of a dinner might be varied each day in each season of the year. These suggestions created much interest; and there were so many expressions of desire on the part of those present to attempt to vary the monotony of the general dinner, that the National Health Society was intrusted with the responsibility of making these suggestions more widely known. Cordial thanks were given to the lecturer and to Mr. Matthews.

———<>———

Musical Festival, – It will be seen by advertisement in another column that a Grand Musical Festival is to be held at the Music Hall, on Thursday next, when choirs from the town and neighbourhood will take part in a selection of Psalm tunes, Chants, Anthems &c. There will be three meetings in the course of the day, viz, in the forenoon, afternoon, and evening. The conductor will be the well known Mr. John Thomas (Llanwrtyd). This will be the third annual Festival held in connection with the above choirs, and we sincerely trust that it will (as in the past) be well attended. We may add that the singers on that day will number about 1200, the majority of whom have been in full practice for the past four months.

———<>———

MONSIEUR DE LESSEPS
IN SWANSEA.

Monsieur le Comte Ferdinand de Lesseps, the great French engineer, who at the invitation of the Mayor of Liverpool, had delivered an address in the Town Hall of that city on Monday last, honoured Swansea with a visit on Tuesday, when he was invited to a banquet at the Mackworth Hotel by the Mayor, Mr. J. J. Jenkins. We are indebted for this interesting visit to Mr. J. Messier, one of our leading merchants, who having been informed that it was the intention of Monsieur Lesseps to address the people of Liverpool on the subject of the proposed canal through the isthmus of Panama, thought it would be a good opportunity for securing to Swansea the advantages of listening to the views of so great a man upon so interesting a matter . . .

. . . Invitations were sent to many of the principal merchants of Cardiff, Newport, Neath and Aberavon, who gladly availed themselves of the oppotunity thus afforded them of meeting in the old capital of Wales one of the greatest engineers of the age.

. . . M. Lesseps accompanied by his little daughter, his Secretary General, M. H. Bionne (naval officer), and his private secretary, M. Daupart, alighted at the Mumbles Road Station of the London and North-Western Railway at 3.20 p.m. on Tuesday.

. . . the Chairman of the Harbour Board conveyed him to Sketty Hall, where refreshments had been kindly provided by Mr. Yeo, and the party at 4.30 left Sketty and drove through Walter Road, along the principal streets of the town to the South Docks, whence they returned to the Mackworth Arms Hotel, in front of which a large crowd had assembled to meet the distinguished visitor. Letters of apology for non attendance were received from the Lord Lieutenant (Mr. Talbot M.P.), Mr. H. H. Vivian, M.P., Mr. Dillwyn, M.P. . . . A letter from Dr. Siemens was as follows:–

3, Palace Houses,
Bayswater-road.
31st May,1880.

"My dear Sir, – Having been out of town on Saturday, I received your letter only this morning, asking me to meet

M. de Lesseps, and I telegraphed immediately to express my regret that my engagements made it impossible for me to avail myself of your kind invitation. I have the greatest admiration of your great countryman, and should gladly have met him under such favourable circumstances. Pray tell him that I once walked by his side in the great Exhibition of 1867 to receive the Grand Prize from the Emperor Napoleon's hands, and that I also had the honour of seconding his nomination for honorary membership of the Institute of Civil Engineers . . .

I am, Sir, yours very ruly,
C.WILLIAM SIEMENS.

"J.Messier, Esq."

. . . The banquet was a most sumptuous one, the menu being as follows:–

MENU,

SOUPS – Asparagus, Mock Turtle.
FISH – Salmon, Fillitted Soles, Turbot.
ENTREES – Lobster Patties, Stewed Kidneys, Rissoles, Calves Head.
JOINES – Sirloin Beef, Roast Lamb, Roast Chicken, Tongue, Ham, Ducklings and Green Peas.
SWEETS – Jellies, Blancmange, Trifle, Stewed Fruit, Custards, Tipsy Cake, Cherry Tart, &c.
DESSERT.
WINES – Campagne: Wachter Glealjer, and Perrier Jouet, Sherry Hock, Claret, Burgundy &c . . .

A Good Suggestion.– A correspondent says "I understand M. de Lesseps, the eminent French engineer, left Swansea after the banquet on Tuesday evening, about nine o'clock by special train, arriving in Gloucester in time to catch the train leaving that city at 12.20 for London. May I suggest that the evening 7.30 mail train from Swansea should be delayed until about nine o'clock, giving an hour and a half more time to answer letters and obviating the great inconvenience of waiting at Gloucester for a couple of hours, as is now the case before starting for town." If the facts are as stated by our correspondent we think the suggestion worthy the consideration of the railway authorities and the town generally.

It is estimated that not less than between 80,000 and 100,000 American tourists will visit Europe this summer, most of them landing first either at Queenstown or Liverpool. Anglo-American bankers, who are of course enabled to make reliable calculations on such matters, estimate that these tourists will bring with them eighteen millions of dollars to spend before they return.

The catches of mackerel on the south coast of England have been very large. One day last week West Bay Portland, was completely alive with fish. So large were the shoals that the fishermen's nets were too small to enclose them, and the boats were rowed through a sea of mackerel. Above 700,000 were taken on that occasion, and the other hauls have been unusually large.

As a temporary substitute for the proposed bridge across the Neath river at Briton Ferry, last week some gentlemen connected with the tramway scheme from the Burrows to Swansea came down from London, and we learn it has been decided to put on a steam ferry boat forthwith to ply between Briton Ferry and Ferry House Hotel. This will be a boon of no small value both for pleasure and business.

The Swansea Police Band will play the following selection of music at Cwmdonkin Park, on Thursday 10th. June, commencing at four p.m.:–
1. Grand March, "Far Away." 2. Valse, " Prairie Bird." 3. Scottische, "Romantic." 4. Selection, "Traviata." 5. Valse, "Prairie Bird." 6. Galop, "Kingston." "God save the Queen."

First Love. – How charming it is! The two young people meet at a picnic. There is much soft laughing and talking between the pair, and some exchange of eye language, more eloquent and thrilling than words. Who does not know that delicious sensation which is produced when glance meets glance for an instant, short as a flash, and when the girl lowers her eyes blushing? Then, comes the luncheon, and the pair sit side by side, and he contrives to squeeze her fingers in passing her the lobster salad. They meet several times again, after that, and their friendship ripens. They will walk together, questioning each other about their tastes, which they are surprised to find are just alike on all points. She likes rose-colour, so does he (she is wearing a pink ribbon when they discover this); she delights in poetry and music, as also does he. Then her brother invites him to come and spend a week at Christmas with Amanda's parents, and he comes. He waltzes and quadrilles with her; they sing out of the same hymn-book at Church; they exchange photographs; and there is some mysterious talk between them about a lock of hair, which, oft denied, is at length bestowed in that sweet, sad hour of parting, when young Harry, meeting Amanda in the garden by moonlight (just by accident) hugs her to his waistcoat, and calls her "My darling!" The next thing he hears of, some months afterwards, is that she is engaged to the wealthy son of a brewer; and he discovers that love's young dream is over.

SWANSEA POLICE COURT.

WEDNESDAY.
(Before Messrs. J. G. Hall, T. Ford and S. B. Power.)

Larcencies. – Samuel Talbot, a boy of 12, living in Sebastapol-street, was charged with stealing three packets of cigars, three packets of hard tobacco, a piece of cut tobacco, and two tobacco pouches from the shop of Georgina Pearson, 16, Wind-street. Prosecutrix said she found prisoner in the shop about one o'clock on Tuesday afternoon. She saw he had something bulky in his pockets, and made him pull out the articles in question. Prisoner pleaded guilty and was ordrered to receive 10 strokes with the birch.

7th. July 1882.

The Cambrian.

Swansea, July, 7. 1882

AN ART SOCIETY FOR SWANSEA.

At length it has been decided to establish in Swansea, what ought long ago to have been started here, a local Sketching Club and Society of Professional and Amateur Artists. Surely there are few districts in the kingdom, we had almost said, in the world, that can vie with the neighbourhood of Swansea and Gowerland in the breadth and variety of its scenic beauty. Here we have hill and dale, woodland and wold, farmlands and furzelands, with all the varied colour and effects of sand-stone, limestone, millstone, grit and other geological formations. Our coast lines are also of the most picturesque kinds, – long smooth sweeps of yellow sands, and bold cliffs of rugged limestone, now jutting out into frowning headlands, and anon indented into beautiful looking bays. There is river scenery, and estuarine shallows, and an almost incomparable Bay, and the ever shifting life and light that dance on the face of the channel waters. It cannot be doubted, therefore, that we have scope enough for the exercize of Pictorial Art on all hands, and even at our very doors. The determination to found this Sketching Club was arrived at by a meeting which was held on Friday evening last at the Swansea School of Art, Post Office Chambers. Mr. E. Seward, of Cardiff presided. A committee was struck, Mr. W. R. Thomas was chosen as secretary, and a draft of the constitution and rules was agreed to. It was further decided that application should be made to the local members of Parliament and other persons interested in Art for their patronage and support in this effort. We understand that it is decided to get up an exhibition in the early part of next year of the work of the members. In the meanwhile there will be sketching excursions in the neighbourhood. The members are expected to produce works of their own direct from nature and not mere copies from other pictures. They will probably be bound down, under the penalty of a small fine, to produce one or more pictures per month, so as to keep themselves thoroughly up to the practice of their art. Arrangements are intended to be made also for life classes at the School of Art during the winter. Mr. F. F. Hosford, the Head Master of the School of Art, lends this project his warm support, and, we believe the new Society will offer a great deal of pleasurable combined with profitable work.

THE "POLARIA" GERMAN EMIGRANT SHIP AT SWANSEA.

Swansea people have this week been brought face to face with the stern facts of emigration in an hitherto unprecedented fashion, by the visit to our port of the fine vessel "Polaria" on her voyage from Hamburg to New York. The attention of the townsfolk was especially awakened to this interesting fact by the crowds of foreign people who promenaded the streets early on Monday morning. From the appearance and language who first came ashore, it was thought that the whole of the emigrants were distressed Jews, from the troubled dominions of the Czar of Russia, and the Emperor of Germany, but a further acquaintance revealed the fact that the majority of them were Germans, from various areas of the newly constituted but not yet well consolidated Germanic Empire. The "Polaria" is a handsome new steamer, built at Newcastle-on-Tyne in the present year for the emigrant service between the ports of Hamburg and New York. She is of no less than 4,000 tons burthen. Her master is Captain Winekher, and her crew, all told, number 58, while she has on board 731 emigrants, men women and children, of several of the countries of Eastern Europe. The "Polaria" comes to Swansea as one of the new and admirable Cambrian line of Atlantic steamers, under the management of the Messrs Burgess and Co., of the Exchange Buildings, Swansea, who have already brought into our port so many fine steamships. We understand that the parties connected with the "Polaria" are under contract to carry from Hamburg to New York a total of 18,000 emigrants within the next six months. This is only the second voyage of the "Polaria," and it is expected that from henceforth she, and her sister ships engaged in the same trade will take in the emigrants and light goods at Hamburg and will call at Swansea on her way for her complement of dead-weight cargo and bunker coal. This will constitute an appreciable trade, which the Harbour Trust and our local shippers have have done well, hitherto, and will do well in the future, still further to foster. In the present instance, the "Polaria" takes from Swansea boxes of tin-plates of various brands, all from the works in the immediate neighbourhood. She also takes 800 tons of bunker coal from the Wenallt and Resolven collieries. The tin-plates were loaded from the large store sheds on the south side of the South Dock, and the bunker coal from the Great Western tips on the North side.

From the time when this fine vessel came in on Monday morning until she went out on Wednesday evening's tide about 9 o'clock, the ship herself and the large crew of strange people on board were the objects of the highest interest on the part of the local community. Not only have the emigrants been stared at as they walked along our streets, and joked about by the small minded and and the thoughtless idlers, but the South Dock has been visited by larger crowds than perhaps have ever gathered there before; and the ready permission granted by the courteous officers of the ship, has been taken advantage of by some thousands of persons to inspect the vessel from stem to stern, from cabin to steerage quarters . . .

The "Polaria" is a little town within herself, with a numerous and most diverse population. There are, first of all, nearly 200 Russian and Polish Jews, who are refugees from the lands where they have been so cruelly treated. Many of these are most miserably clad, and most wretched in appearance. Though they have distinct traces of Semitic type in their physiognomy, and though they manifest, in their dealings a great deal of that inimitable *savoir faire* which distinguishes the Israelite wherever and whenever found, yet these are of a very degraded standard. Their habillments, poor things, seem to be the refuse of the refuse of

"Petticoat-lane," and their faces and hands would be all the more seemly for a freer use of the soap and water which are so liberally supplied on board ship. They are confined as far as possible to one part of the ship, near the stern, and the odours that ascend from their quarters are not of the sweetest kind.

"They are evidently very poor," we say. "No doubt they have been stripped of all the little they once possessed."

"Ah!" says Captain Winckler, with a smile, "they certainly look poor enough, but you never know what money they have about them."

The passage money of all these refugees has been paid by the various international relief committees, including the proceeds of our English Mansion House fund, to which the people of Swansea have liberally contributed; and Mr. Goldberg, as the head of the Hebrew congregation here, and the representatives of these charitable committees, has attended to their wants, and supplied them with many little necessaries and comforts on their way to the new world. The fabled time for the restoration of the Jews in Palestine is evidently not yet fully come. Travellers tell us that the sacred land is wonderfully productive, and capable of yielding again the splendid harvests of cereals, olives and grapes which rewarded the cultivation of the ancient inhabitants; but, in spite of the cries of the devout in the "place of wailing" in Jerusalem, and in spite of some efforts at restoration of the race to their scriptural home, the matter is not warmly taken up, and the emigrant Jews prefer going into a new world to face the untried possibilities of the wide wild West.

So let them go, and may the blessing of their Jehovah rest upon them! May they be a blessing to themselves, and entail no curse upon the peoples among whom they may settle.

As they lounge on the deck of the "Polaria," their peculiar genius crops out, even amongst the youngsters, in petty bargaining, . . .

The remainder of the 731 emigrants are chiefly of Teutonic origin . . .

It is apparent that the mass of these German emigrants is of the respectable working class, clean in habits, if not showy in attire. They will make excellent colonists, taking things as they come in the rough, and making the best of them; not expecting more than they will get in the new land.

Their berths are arrayed in upper and lower tiers on the lower and the 'tween decks . . .We understand that there is no distinction of class aboard this ship, as in English emigrant vessels. There is no hard and fast division into saloon, fore cabin and steerage passengers. All are of one grade, and all pay the same fare; namely about £5 for the whole journey from Hamburg to New York. About 140 of them are holders of prepaid tickets, sent over to them by friends already settled in the States, so that these have a home ready made and awaiting them on their arrival . . .

Among the most curious sights on deck were the Russian peasants squatting on their haunches, reading their books of devotion, and the business of money changing, which was briskly carried on by some of our local Jewish tradesmen . . .

Since the " Polaria" came into the South Welsh waters, two births have taken place aboard. One child was born off the Mumbles head on Monday morning, and the second in the South Dock on Wednesday morning. Both mothers were accomodated in the light and airy hospital berths, and at the time when the ship left they were all doing well. A somewhat touching incident occurred while the ship was in port. Among the visitors allowed to go down to the hospital was a thorough Welsh woman in Welsh flannel bed-gown attire. Noticing that the mother of one of the newly-born babies looked weak and exhausted, the maternal instinct moved the woman to sympathy. Though she could not convey her meaning in words, she did so in looks. The mothers understood each other, and the warm hearted Welsh woman took up the little one and suckled it at her own breasts.

Captain Winckler contended that inasmuch as these youngsters, both boys, were born on board a German ship, they were subjects of the Empire, but he smilingly admitted that, since they were born within three miles of the shore, and since one had been suckled by a Welsh woman, some knotty points of international law were involved! But, perhaps, it is hardly likely that these youngsters will ever be drafted into the German armies . . .

The sight at the docks and the Pierhead on Wednesday night, when the "Polaria" went out from Swansea was an extaordinary one. Not less than 10,000 people of all classes of the community had congregated to see her off. The emigrants thronged the deck, and leaned over taffrails, and waved their hands and hats and shouted their outlandish farewells to the people of Swansea, who had manifested such an interest in them, and performed so many little kindnesses for them. And the crowds shouted in return, "Good bye! God help and bless you all."

It was a touching sight and sound, which will long be remembered here. Indeed so deeply had the thought of emigration, and the feeling of sympathy with these emigrants stirred the local community, that many of the poorer people in the crowd on the piers were heard to express the wish that they too, were off " to the west, to the land of the free!" And it is certain that no less than 30 poor men went to Capt. Winckler and begged him to allow them to work their passage out in his ship. This, of course, he was bound to refuse; . . .

When the ship got out into the Bay, it was found, on calling over the muster roll, that as many as fifty loafers and would-be stow-aways were aboard, and they were of course sent back in the steam tug.

Emigration as it is carried out here, is not grievous but agreeable. Whole families and small neighbourhoods go together, and so there is no severance of the old ties, no loneliness, no misery, save through the unavoidable accidents of life. The people carry with them the little home gods and homely affections into the new land, where they hope to pitch their tents in greater prosperity. This is the secret which should be brought to bear in Irish emigration. Don't divide families; but send them all together, and then there will be greater readiness to go, and no such sorrow as is now sometimes witnessed.

The "Polaria" like the "City of Lincoln," was towed in and out by the capable little screw tug the "Cruiser," which performed its duty thoroughly satisfactorily.

M. de Lesseps on the Suez Canal and Channel Tunnel. – At the banquet given at Dover on Friday evening to M.de Lesseps, that gentleman in replying to the toast of his health, said that the Channel Tunnel was now encountering the same opposition which the Suez Canal met with. The practicality of the tunnel having now been shown, the enterprise was sought to be kept back by prejudice. But England was above all a country where common sense reigned supreme, and common sense would fight the battle for Sir Edward Watkin as it had fought the battle for his own enterprise. He ridiculed the idea of an invasion of England by the French, and said that there was a much greater danger at this moment that the cordial relations between France and England might be disturbed by the Egyptian difficulties. He did not see that there was any danger for the Suez Canal. He fully recognised the immense importance it had for England, but he ventured to say that the Suez Canal was not so closely connected with Egyptian politics as was generally believed. The Canal did not run through Egypt, and he firmly believed that there was not the slightest danger of its perfect security. He who had originated and made it was entitled to be believed when he said that the fears which had so excited the public were exaggerated. He thought that the national movement in Egypt was a serious thing and should not be looked upon with contempt. He hoped that England and France would combine to give to Egypt fair scope for liberal development by which all parties would be benefited. M. de Lesseps concluded by expressing his conviction that the tunnel between England and France would be constructed, and that some day England and France would be equally desirous of it, seeing the benefit to both countries.

———◇———

MASONIC OUTING IN THE SWANSEA VALLEY.

The Caradoc Lodge of Freemasons, Swansea, had its summer outing on Thursday, 29th. ult. The place selected for it this year was the Swansea Valley, and the brethren were fortunate in having the experienced guidance of their Worshipful Grand Master, the Rev. Thomas Walters, D.D., Provincial Grand Chaplain, to direct them. His long residence in the Valley had, of necessity, made him thoroughly well acquainted with every nook and corner of it, and this enabled him to point out very advantageously the varied beauties and endless varieties of the picturesque scenery. The brethren residing in Swansea and the immediate neighbourhood assembled at the Masonic Hall, Caer-street at 10 a.m. They left Swansea in one of Mr. Rosser's well equipped four-in hand breaks and drove up the Valley, which at this season of the year appeared in its most charming aspect and to the best advantage. The drive was a lovely one, and the brethren enjoyed it to their hearts content. Passing through Clydach, Pontardawe, Ystalyfera, and Yniscedwyn, they eventually arrived at the Pontrhydarw Waterfalls, not far from Craig-y-Nos Castle. Here a very substantial cold collation was laid out on the rocks, near the Fall; and it was admitted by all that it would be difficult to conceive of a more charming spot – grand and beautiful beyond description. There was no need to coax the appetite with such choice viands as rabbit and veal pies, lobster salads, &c., which had been abundantly provided. The fine bracing air enabled the brethren to enjoy the more solid and substantial dishes of roast and boiled beef with a relish of the keenest and most enjoyable nature. After luncheon the Worshipful Master gave an open-air lecture on some peculiarly interesting points connected with the Valley. The following brief outline may serve to give an idea of the subject matter of the address; but we do not pretend to give a full report of it. He said that the scene of their outing that day was one of very great interest on many accounts. No doubt the whole of the valley was at one time submerged. The beds of sand, the smooth boulder or river stones found here and there, and the very cockle shells in the limestone rocks on the top of Cribbarth mountain yonder (to which he pointed) all tend to prove that the place whereon they then stood was at one time under water. Then the traditional or historical character of the place had an interest of a very important nature. In order the better to understand this it was necessary to go back to the very earliest ages of Christianity. Cynfelin was at one time king of Britain. He had a brother named Llyr, and Bran the Blessed (Bran Fendigaid) was son of Llyr and nephew of Cynfelin. Caradoc was the son of Bran and he had a daughter named Gwladys. Caradoc, or Caractacus, fought the Romans and beat them in nine pitched battles. He was however, at last betrayed and taken prisoner to Rome. His wife and his daughter Gwladys, his two brothers and his father Bran were fellow prisoners with him, and detained as hostages during the term of his imprisonment. Gwladys, daughter of Caradoc or Caractacus, married one Rufus Pudens, a general in the Roman army, and had four children, one of whom was called Pudentia, and there is a Church said to be dedicated to her at Rome, now called St. Pudentia. Gwladys had two brothers, called Cyllinus and Linus. He would show them how the former was traditionally said to be connected with that place which was called Ystrad Gynlais or Ystrad Cyllinus. In the year A.D. 56 St. Paul was imprisoned at Rome, and through his instrumentality it is said that Bran, Caradoc, and the rest of the British Royal Family were converted to Christianity. In the year A.D.50 Bran the Blessed, Caradoc his son, Gwladys daughter of of Caradoc and her husband Rufus Pudens, returned to Britain, and on their return established Christianity as the national religion. If traditional history and stymological rendering are to be relied upon, we may almost trace the landmarks which furnish evidences tending to prove the residence of the British Royalty in the Swansea Valley; for instance Briton Ferry is called in Welsh Llansawel, or Llan Saul, the British port where St. Paul is supposed to have landed. Then comes Ysciwen, now called Skewen, or Esgynfa-wen, the white or blessed ascent to Maesmelyn or Maes Cynfelin, the Royal Residence of the Ancient British King. Above that is Mynydd y Dryms, or Mynydd y Drenfa, the outlook or observatory. Bran, Glan Bran, and Gil-Fran, or Bran's retreat, Pen-yr-Ysfa, properly Pen-Arosfa (the Principal Station), Cwm Cyrnach, or Cwm-y-Cyrn – the Horn blowing Dingle, used as a telegraphic medium from Dremfa mountain to Cil-y-bebyll, the headquarters of Caradoc's. Hendre Gwladys, so called after Caradoc's daughter. Ystrad Cyllinus (Ystrad Gynlais) and Eglwys Caradoc, a small cave in the side of a rock, between Craig-y-Nos and Gwyn Arms, on the other side of the river Tawe. This is still in existence, and is probably the oldest Christian Church in the Kingdom. This list of names takes us back to the earliest ages of Christianity, and furnishes us with strong evidence that the distinguished personages referred to, lived at one time in the Swansea Valley. In 11 Timothy, iv, 21, we have these remarkable words – "Eubulus greeteth thee, and Pudens and Linnus, and Claudia, and all the brethren." They furnish us with a proof that Claudia or Gwladys, her husband Rufus Pudens, and her brother Linnus, were known to St. Paul and Timothy. This Epistle is said to have been written at the house of Claudia in Rome. If this be so, then it will appear evident, that God in his providence had so arranged it that Welsh people from the Swansea Valley, surrounded and comforted the aged Apostle in his last dying moments.

The foregoing address was listened to throughout with riveted attention, and at its conclusion was much applauded. A general request was made by all the brethren present that it be printed and published, and we have much pleasure in giving the foregoing outline of it, which comprises the more salient and substantial points of the address. After luncheon the brethren visited Craig-y Nos, Tanyrogof Cave, whence the Llynfell river flows and continues a short course of a few hundred yards, and then empties itself into the Tawe. Several interesting geological specimens and rare ferns indigenous to the district were collected by the brethren versed in those branches of study, and their nature and character explained. The weather was everything that could be desired, and the fresh mountain breezes were most invigorating, the beneficial effect of which could not fail to be enjoyed by gentlemen living at Swansea, the air of which the latter place is admittedly very relaxing. It was the unanimous opinion of all that an outing or excursion up the valley inland was of much greater advantage and benefit to the Swansea people than an outing down to the sea-side at Gower. It was agreed that residents at the sea-side should go to the mountain for fresh air, and that residents inland should should go to the sea-side for purposes of enjoying the full benefit to be derived from such a change. On the return journey the brethren, about thirty in number, sat down to a very sumptuous repast, laid out in quite an artistic manner, interspersed with rare specimens of plants, flowers, ferns &c. at the Ynyscedwyn Arms. The menu was on a *recherche* scale. The wines were of the choice and most approved brands, and the whole catering was served up by the host, Mr. Evans, in the best style. After dinner the usual loyal and Masonic toasts were given from the chair. Mr. Jenkins presided at the piano, and an excellent selection of songs was given by Mr. W. Davies of Ystradgynlais, and others. During the evening a young lad, of about 15 years of age, named Danny Prothero, of Ystradgynlais, sang "Gwymp Llewellyn," and afterwards other songs which so charmed and delighted the audience as to keep them quite spell-bound. He evidently is a most promising lad of rare musical powers and extraordinary ability. His talents, if properly trained and cultivated, would render him a star of great magnitude in the musical world. Before leaving he was called up to the Worshipful Master, by whom he was spoken to very kindly, and encouraged to write to him, giving full particulars as to age and attainments. A collection was made on the spot for the purpose of evincing the deep appreciation of his abilities and talents by the Brethren, who all seemed so struck with his voice and powers of singing. Young Prothero comes from a very musical family. He had the misfortune of losing his father when quite a child, and his mother's means are very straitened. The Brethren returned to Swansea in the evening delighted beyond measure with their day's outing, and hopefully looking forward to such another treat at no very distant period.

NOTES OF THE WEEK.

A question from a person at a great distance sometimes serves to throw light incidentally on matters of local history. Thus a gentleman, dating from Boston, U.S.A., May 18th, writes of a Swansea acquaintance as follows: "I am very desirous of obtaining information if possible (for historical and genealogical purposes) of my ancestor Robert Wheaton (or Whedon, or Wheadon, as he sometimes spelled it), and his wife Alice, who left your place between 1630 and 1640, and came to Salem, Massachusetts, finally settling at Rehoboth, Mass., 1644 and joining Elder John Myles, of the first Baptist church in Swansea Wales who fled from there with the records of that church about 1650, and organised a church and founded Swansea, Mass." It would be interesting to know more of these Pilgrim Fathers, who carried our name, as well as the Baptist Church records, across the sea. Perhaps the information here sought may be in the possession of some of our readers.

FAIRS FOR JULY.

Llangadog	10	Abergavenny	18
Nelson (Pontypridd)	10	Conwil-in-Elvet	19
Caerphilly	10	Caerleon	20
Talgarth	10	Tavernspite.	20
Carmarthen	10	Templeton	21
Pembroke	10	Canton (C'diff)	22
Little Newcastle	10	Llanddewibrefi	24
Haver-fordwest	11	Crymmych	25
Narbeth	12	Abergorlech	24&25
Boncath	12	Whitland	26
Newcastle Emlyn	13	Treslaw	26&27
Lansawel	15&17	Newport (Pem.)	27
Letterston	17	Neath	27
Llany-byther	17&21	Pandy	27
Reynoldstone	17		

Correspondence.

We do not hold ourselves responsible for the opinions and sentiments expressed by our Correspondents.

THE FOOTPATHS OF SWANSEA.

To The Editor of "The Cambrian."

Sir, – In your last issue a correspondent signing himself "Rambler," has asked you to make an effort to restore to the rising generation two footpaths. I beg to inform you that neither of the paths mentioned has been open to the public since the enclosure of the Town Hill.

The first stated, as going through Mr. Nott's garden and the field above to the upper road, has been used as a convenience among the neighbours, with a distinct understanding that each pay one shilling a year for going over the land.

The second, coming out by Hill House, Mr. Thomas informs me that it was made by him as a private path from Hill House to the Home Farm.

I have no doubt that "Rambler," like many others may have used that way, but whoever did so without permission committed a trespass. This plainly shows how careful occupiers and owners of land ought to be in not allowing ramblers to stray from the public highway.

When I took the land in question, I was requested to allow any footpaths to be made, and for the last five and twenty years my processor has locked the gates when the land has been under tillage, and I have the right to act in the same way, although hitherto I have not done so. Seeing the use and abuse of public footpaths one cannot but wonder at the efforts made to close them. –

Yours faithfully,
J. M. Harding.

Hill Farm, July 6th. 1882.

——◇——

1st. August 1884.

THE CHOLERA.

There is, we (*the Times*) believe, not the slightest reason to anticipate danger to any of our own towns from the present outbreak of Cholera on the Continent. But it is the duty of those in authority to be prepared even for very unlikely events; and it is never out of season to insist on the advantages of cleanliness, fresh air, and temperance. These are precautions against cholera more effective than all the fumigating apparatus in the world. If a case of cholera should unhappily appear among us, the safe and simple course is to isolate the patient, to keep a watchful eye on all persons who have come from dangerous neighbourhoods, and to abstain entirely from vexatious measures of detention, which tend only to increase the danger and to spread the panic. There is no reason to give way to excitement because cholera is in Europe, but there is always reason to be careful when one is living under unusual conditions. An eminent physician has declared that a large proportion of his patients visit him about the end of autumn to complain of ailments which they have contracted by eating strange food, sitting on dampstones, going out bareheaded after nightfall, and committing other imprudences which they fondly suppose will go unpunished because it happens to be holiday time. It is always wonderful to observe how persons of no great physical strength will imagine they can endure unlimited fatigue and worry because they are only travelling about and not making anything by it. It is to follies of this kind that we must attribute many cases of illness which are put down to the unhealthiness of foreign towns and hotels. While we do not wish to discourage those who meditate a Continental expedition for this autumn, we advise them to take caution as a travelling companion.

Protection against Cholera. – A Bill has been introduced by Mr. Gray M.P., with a view to making better provision against cholera and other epedemic diseases. The first clause is to apply whenever any part of England or Ireland appears to be threatened or affected by any formidable epedemic, endemic or infectious diseases, and the Local Government Board makes special regulations under the Public Health Act for the speedy burial of the dead, or for house to house visitation, or for the provision of medical aid and hospital accommodation, or for the promotion of seaming, cleansing, ventilation, and disinfection. Under these circumstances the Board is authorised by the Bill to require every medical practitioner within the district affected by the regulations to notify forthwith to the sanitary authority every case of such disease on which he is in attendance. For such notification a fee not exceeding half-a-crown is allowed. While the regulations are in existence, the Board is also empowered to issue orders for the prohibition or regulation of second-hand clothes and bedding. Another clause of the Bill allows sites for hospitals to be acquired by a sanitory authority outside its district, but "contiguous" to it.

——◇——

CLOUDY DAYS.

O days of cloud! O days of rain:
With face against the window pane
We watch the driving of the showers,
And count the long and dreary hours;
But wherefore murmur or complain?
We hope, now do we hope in vain,
The sun will soon shine forth again,
And waken into life the flowers —
O days of cloud!
Then if no shadow shall remain,
Nor shrouding mists hide hill or plain,
And birds sing in the leafy bowers,
And sapphire skies once more be ours
Peace lieth at the heart of pain,
O days of cloud!

——◇——

BOARD OF TRADE INQUIRIES AT SWANSEA.

The Court's Inquiry on the Stranding of the "Wimbledon" and the "Baines Hawkins"

The judge inquiring into the stranding of the above vessels, which were reported last week, came to a conclusion on Monday. The judge was Mr. J. C. Fowler, Stipendiary Magistrate, the assessors were Captain Castle and Captain Vaux. Mr. Edward Strick represented the Board of Trade, and Mr. Wyndham Lawrence represented the master, while Mr. H. Monger acted as clerk of the court.

The court found that the cause of the stranding was the fact that the ship did not make the courses set and steered; that no measures were taken to verify

Swansea Grammar School – built in 1853.

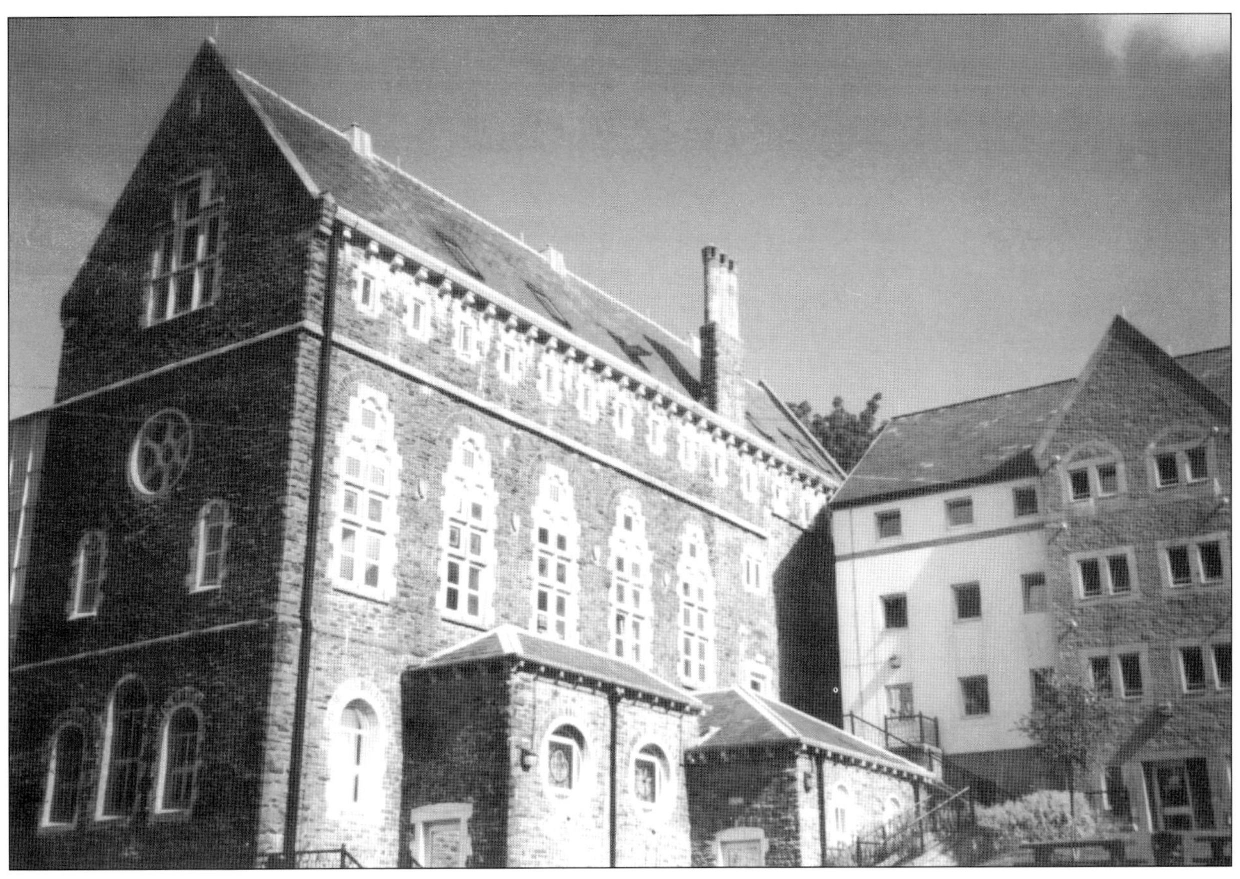

All that remains – 2003.

New Theatre – 19th century.

'New' Empire Theatre, erected in 1899.

the position of the vessel when off Bull Point, beyond taking the bearings of the light. The distance from it was measured by conjecture, but there was no means of taking cross-bearings at the time or afterwards, the light on Lundy being obscured by fog. Safe and proper courses were set and steered, and the Court were told that due allowance for tide was made, that the speed of the vessel was properly reduced when the fog came on, that a good and proper look-out was kept, that the alterations made in the course between 12.30 and 1.15 were judicious and proper, that if the lead had been kept constantly going it would have indicated danger prior to the actual stranding, though not so until the ship was very near that part of the island on which she struck. There are 23 fathoms within a quarter of a mile of the island on or very near to where she struck, and no great variation in depth over a large area of the channel; consequently the deep sea lead alone would have been of service in that part, though further to the N.E. there is a shallow bank with eight fathoms within a mile and a half of the island; but the ship did not go over that portion of the channel. The court thought the constant of the lead might have prevented the casualty, but the steamship was not sufficiently manned, there being only one officer and three able seamen in each watch. During the night it was necessary to have one man at the wheel and one on the look-out, and thus only one was left to heave the lead, trim lamps, or to do anything else that might be required; so the practical result was that without calling all hands on deck the master was unable to keep the deep sea lead going. That, with the exception of the omission to use the lead, the ship was navigated with proper and seamanlike care. That the master and mates were in default for leaving the port, bound to Madeira, without a patent log, but the court would not deal with their certificates, but censured them for the omission.

In addition to the answers which the court gave to the questions submitted by the Solicitor of the Board of Trade, the Stipendiary made the following remarks:– It seems hardly consistent with the duty of this local court to pass over a series of casualties within 30 miles of this port without making a few observations in addition to the short answers we have given. The case is probably unprecedented. In perfectly calm weather, with a smooth sea, no less than three valuable steamships were stranded on the same night, almost at the same time, on the same little island of Lundy, and within a short distance of each other. Lundy island lies like a great breakwater in the mouth of the Bristol Channel, separated from Hartland Point – the extreme north-west corner of Devonshire – by about nine miles of sea, and about twice that distance from Caldy Island in Pembrokeshire. The court has done all that lay in its power to ascertain the cause or causes of this extraordinary occurrence. We have not only examined the masters, officers and some of the engineers and seamen of the Wimbledon and Baines Hawkins but also two witnesses from the island – namely, the rocket signalman and the chief keeper of the light house. All these sources of information have been thoroughly exhausted. There has been no formal inquiry into the circumstances of the stranding of the third vessel, which might have thrown some fresh light on the subject. Certain it is, however, that she went ashore like the other two, about the same time and place, and probably got off the rocks without any such material damage as the others sustained. The first observation I wish to make is that the evidence taken and the whole circumstances of the case combined to shut out any idea of bad faith. There can be no doubt that these strandings were casualties in the true sense of the word – that is, strandings both unforeseen and unintended. As to the cause of these disasters, the master of the Wimbledon urged that the compass must have misled him and seduced him out of the course he had marked down on the chart. It is true that the agate in one of his compasses which we examined was not perfect, and if that had been the only guide of a single vessel on the night in question we might have attached some weight to that imperfection. But when three vessels come ashore on the island, each having three compasses on board, the imperfection of one agate is utterly inadequate to solve the difficulty. Therefore we reject the supposition that compasses were mechanically in fault, and also the contention that they were affected by the fog. I am advised that there is no foundation for the theory that mere fog affects them. Neither will the want of a log on board the Wimbledon afford an explanation of this event, for there was a log on board the Baines Dawkins, and though it was used it failed to avert the disaster. Again, we were told that the lead was not used by either vessel. But the omission to use the lead was reasonably accounted for by several circumstances. First (as stated in our answer), the masters knew that until the ships were close under the rocks of Lundy, the soundings would not have indicated their situation; secondly, they had not hands enough to execute the operation of heaving a deep sea lead continuously; and thirdly they had ample reason to believe that the Lundy fog rockets would be heard long before they even approached shallow water or rocks in that quarter.

Nevertheless we find the ships approaching Lundy bit by bit, on courses set and steered to take them at least four miles away from it, but actually moving under some influence of which the masters were not aware. For the explanation of all that happened afterwards we must look at the combined circumstances of the case. As to the courses set, no fault whatever can be found. The last object seen from both vessels was the Bull Point Light, the distance from which was estimated by conjecture. No cross-bearings could be taken, owing to the state of the atmosphere, and then the ships passed into the fog without any certain knowledge as to their distance from land on either side. It is not at all improbable that the distance from the Bull Light was erroneously estimated in all the ships, and that they were, really, farther from Bull Point. Further, the soundings off Bull Point would not indicate the exact position within a mile or two. Be that as it may, we suppose and believe (in the absence of any other probable cause) that the influence of any exceptionally strong ebb must have acted on the ships, and edged them gently but continuously towards the island, while their masters (deprived of the sight of all guiding objects, and unaware of the strength of the ebb on that night) were unable to correct, by the eye or otherwise, the lateral pressure which was slowly and imperceptibly affecting their courses. We come next to the peculiarities of Lundy Island. The lighthouse is lofty, and circulates a strong light for many miles all round. But on the morning of June 27th, the beacon might as well have been in America. The vessels were approaching the south end of the island, and we know that nothing can be more capricious than the local fogs. The island is narrow but lofty, and there are dense fogs on the side of the Atlantic, which do not extend to the eastern side and *vice versa.* But, strange to say, the signals are made on the Atlantic side only, and it was proved to our satisfaction that on the 27th they were, when made, inaudible on the east side of the island. The signalman who fires the explosive rockets informed us that his duties do not extend in any way whatever to the eastern cliffs. He never traverses the island, and repudiated all knowledge of what goes on except on the outer or western side. He has been ten years on the little island, but could not or would not even tell us what its breadth is. In the official sailing directions for the Bristol Channel it is stated "a sound rocket which explodes with a loud report on reaching the height of 600 feet will be discharged at intervals of ten minutes during thick and foggy weather from the west side of the island." Now this explanation is not sufficiently explicit. The masters were undoubtedly justified in expecting that no danger from fog was to be apprehended by the neighbourhood of Lundy without audible warning from the explosive rockets; but so local was the fog on the night in question, and so defective the knowledge of the signalman as to the condition of the east side of the island, that the rocks were approached without any indication of their close proximity. Considering that a very large proportion of the vessels leaving the Bristol Channel pass between Lundy and the Devonshire coast, and considering the enormous increase in the number of vessels annually taking that course, and the prevalence of local fogs in that neighbourhood, we beg leave to point out that the provision made years ago for averting danger on the western side should be now extended in some form to the eastern side. Mr Strick asked the court, inasmuch as the Wimbledon was undermanned, to order the owners to pay the costs of the inquiry; but the court decided to make no order, as it was not due to undermanning that the casualty occurred.

There seems to be quite a mania for coffee taverns in Swansea at the present moment. The vacant premises immediately opposite the upper entrance to the market have been taken by Messrs. Dan Davies and Jones and will be immediately converted into a spacious dining and coffee establishment. But this is not the point to which we wish to call attention. A few months since, one of our most enterprising tradesmen submitted plans to the Council for the entire demolition of these old premises, and the erection of a handsome edifice, which would have been a credit to the town, and a great improvement to the whole of the surrounding locality. He failed to get the plans passed, however, because it was proposed to build over some six feet more of the open space at the back. The whole scheme was thereupon abandoned, and an effectual stop put to anything like architectural improvement in one of the principal streets of the town. Now, however, the old premises are to remain, but a spacious room *covering the whole of the available space at the back,* to be erected. We understand the plans for this addition have been passed, the Council having no option in the matter. Under the old Act, plans for the erection of new premises must be sanctioned by the Urban Authority, but alterations and additions to old premises could be made without the licence of the authority. We think our readers will agree with us when we say there is neither justice or common sense in this, and it is satisfactory to find that the new bye-laws which now come into operation are more in accord with the requirements of modern times, and will mete out more justice to all classes.

Everyone who is at all alive to the interests and the future of Swansea town and port, must read with interest the Barry Dock and Railways evidence before the Select Committee of the House of Lords. In directing the attention of our readers to the evidence given by Sir J. J. Jenkins which appears in another column, we would especially refer to the serious charge made by Mr. D. Davies against the gentleman with regard to the application for the sole use of a tip for the shipment of 1000 tons of coal per day. The evidence by Sir John has since been corroborated by Mr. Robert Capper, who produced documentary evidence of the most satisfactory nature. The speech delivered by Mr. Riches at the banquet given by the Harbour Trust on the occasion of laying the foundation stone of the Prince of Wales Dock, by Sir H. H. Vivian Bart. conclusively proved that he had at that time every intention to carry out the proposal made by his firm. This quite exonerates the worthy M.P. for Carmarthen from the odium conveyed in the statement, if there was any doubt upon the subject, after straightforward statement made by him. The Counsel for the Promoters tried their utmost to throw obscurity over the statement, but the Chairman permitted the matter to be thoroughly thrashed out, which resulted in the satisfactory result of shewing that the dock accommodation at Swansea would have been in all respects good enough for our Cardiff friends if they had no ulterior object in view in promoting Barry Docks. It is expected that the evidence and speeches will be completed and the decision given today (Friday).

The Regatta of the year in Swansea Bay will take place on Monday next, on which occasion we doubt not, the Bank Holiday will be much appreciated by the thousands who will be enabled to flock to the Mumbles to watch the yachts and skiffs and to laugh at the long-shore sports. There is no lovelier sea range to be found than Swansea Bay, and, given a genial sky and lively breeze, there are few more enjoyable experiences than a cruise on the waters, or more interesting than to watch the sailing of the various craft from the shore. On Monday next the racing of all kinds is expected to be well contested, and, as for the shore sports, great preparations have been made. All the aquatic race-horses have arrived. The Club studs are in excellent condition, and under the care of Messrs Howell and Davies, the experienced trainers, promise to outstrip all previous performances. The jockeys have all got a new rig-out, and will look gorgeous when seated on the backs of their fiery no watery untamed steeds. Mr. George Gronow, the captain of the shore-line on regatta days, will again act as starter. Altogether the regatta promises to be a very enjoyable local holiday.

Correspondence

Sunday Band Playing

To The Editor of "The Cambrian."

Sir, – By accident I happened to see my old friend *The Cambrian* newspaper, and was very much surprised and pleased to read that the Corporation had decided to allow the Band to play in the Parks on Sundays.

On Sunday July 13, 1884, I took my family up to "Central Park," New York, at 4 p.m., to see and hear the same experiment tried for the second Sunday. After the first piece was played, a Welshman, (one of over 2000 Welshmen who were present on the ground) said to me, "Oh! the Bands play in the Swansea Parks on Sundays now." Seeing that I doubted the truth of this remark very much, he took a copy of *The Cambrian*, dated June 20th, out of his pocket, and said, "here read and believe." What could I say, only – "Well done Swansea." – Yours respectfully,

William Lewis,
Late Colliery Manager, Llanharry,
Glamorgan.

158, E.23rd.-street, New York, U.S.
July 15, 1884.

3rd. September 1886.

OPENING OF MESSRS. B. EVAN'S & CO'S NEW PREMISES, SWANSEA.

A stranger on entering Swansea is at once struck with the almost total absence of anything approaching to an architectural elevation in the public and private buildings of our town. Some advance, it is true, has been made in this direction within the last few years, but much yet remains to be done before Swansea architecture can compete with that of other towns of equal size and importance. With a few notable exceptions, our tradesmen appear to have failed in grasping the idea that in this day something more than an established reputation is needed for the complete success of any business, whatever its nature may be. Among those of our business firms which early appreciated the necessity of a change in the method of conducting a modern business, the most noteworthy example is that of Messrs. B. Evans and Co., the well known drapers and furnishers of Temple-street, who are tomorrow (Saturday) opening a further extensive addition to their already huge premises.

This firm, although it had at the time a large and flourishing business under the credit system, was about the first to adopt the cash principle in this town; and in spite of adverse criticism, they persevered in this policy, believing that it would be both to the advantage of their customers and themselves.

The premises which will be tomorrow opened for the first time for the transaction of business are situated in Lower Goat-street, and, as will be seen from our description of them are contiguous to, and practically in one with the old premises. On entering Goat-street from Temple-street, one is immediately struck with the large and imposing building on the left hand side of the street. Its proportions are such as to completely dwarf the surrounding houses, rising as it does to the height of 60 feet from the pavement level. The elevation attracts the eye at once as being something infinitely superior to the stucco work of which unfortunately we have so much in our streets. The idea produced in the mind of the beholder is that of dignity and solidity. From the massive stone pillars up to the free-stone gables it is evident that strength has been one of the primary objects which the architects have striven for. The front is carried upon six massive Portland stone pillars, and the same stone is used for the facia and cornice over the shop front. In the latter a spring sun blind has been ingeniously arranged for the purpose of shading the shop windows. The upper portion of the front is built of buff Ebbw Vale bricks, which are tastefully relieved with red brick hands and window arches. The key stones of the latter, as well as the various cornices and window sills, are of free-stone. The window openings are improved by the use of beaded brick. Brick pilasters are carried up in continuation of the Portland stone pillars, and terminate in nicely proportioned free stone peliments above the eaves level. The attention which has evidently been given to detail has not been in vain, for the general effect is extremely good, and the most critical observer would scarcely find a more pleasing *coup d' aile*. On entering the building from the street, the conclusion one arrives at is that the interior in no way belies the exterior. The constant striving to put the best side outermost pervades architecture as well as other things, but in this case we find just the reverse, and as much (if not more) care has been bestowed on the interior of the building as on the elevation.

The Ground Floor. – The entrance doors, and indeed the whole of the framing of the shop front, is moulded and polished teak, filled in with plate glass. The splendid shop, or rather range of shops, on this floor, which has until lately resounded with the stroke of the workman's hammer, is now filled with a vast selection of furniture of every conceivable description, ranging in value from a few shillings up to a small fortune, and the purchaser, whether for cottage or mansion, cannot fail to find here precisely what he requires.

The first shop one enters from the street is spacious and lofty, and admirably lighted, and the furniture arranged here makes a pleasing contrast with the French grey tint with which the match boarding of the walls is painted. At the back of this shop, and connected with it by a large and lofty opening, we arrive at a shop which, until lately has been used as a packing room, but which has now been converted into a valuable and handsome Show Room. From this room communication is obtained with the present fine Lace Shop by means of a well designed pitch pine staircase. Passing through this room again, and still farther to the rear, we arrive at the Long Show Rooms, in which the Fancy Bazaar was held last Christmas; but which has now been re-converted to its original use as an integral part of the furnishing department, and is at present fitted with a choice selection of brass and iron bedsteads. In the side wall of this room an opening has been made in order to give a direct access to the Carpet Shop in Caer-street, which has been rather disconnected hitherto. Thus we find one long range of Show Rooms extending from Goat-street to Castle-Bailey-street, the total depth being considerably over 200 feet. Again returning to the front shop in Goat street, we descend by a wide flight of stairs to the:

Basement. – This floor has been fitted up as a Packing Room and Receiving Room, and is amply large enough for this important branch of the business. The room is well lighted by means of Hayward's patent prismatic lights, fixed in the street pavement, and, although this was the only available means of obtaining light, yet we were astonished at the almost dazzling brightness which pervaded the whole room. The floor is boarded throughout, and the walls are covered with Portland cement. The goods for delivery are brought down from the Show Rooms in the large Lift. They are here packed up, and are then sent up by the same means to the loading platform in the Cartway, communicating with Goat-street. Bales and boxes of goods coming from the manufácturers are let down by a rolling way into the Receiving Room. They are there unpacked and sorted, and are then distributed by the lift to the various departments for which they are intended. Great attention and forethought must evidently have been given before such a convenient arrangement could have been devised for the quick and easy despatch of business. Returning again to the shop, we proceed by means of a handsome staircase of polished pitch pine to the

First Floor. – This floor is used entirely as a Show Room for Furniture, and is really a very fine room. It is lighted by eight large windows on the side fronting Goat-street. Communication is here again maintained with the old premises, for a very short flight of stairs brings us into the present Carpet Room. This staircase is arranged with a well hole looking down on to the ground floor, and, as there is a large lantern light immediately over the stairs, a flood of light is shed both on to the first floor and also through the well hole on to the ground floor. This staircase and the arrangement of the different levels is one of the prettiest and most effective features in the whole building. Standing on the first floor and looking through the large opening on to the floor below, one is able to form a considerable though inadequate idea of the extent of the present additions. The eye is carried down a long vista filled with every kind of valuable and choice goods, until distance alone seems to proclaim that the limit is reached. We learn the the floor space devoted to the furnishing department alone is now not far short of half an acre. Again proceeding on our upward journey, we arrive by means of a handsomely carpeted staircase at the

Second Floor. – The first room we enter is the refreshment room, and in close proximity are the Ladies's retiring rooms. The refreshment room is prettily and even luxuriously fitted up. The walls and ceiling are coloured a light cream tint, and the woodwork is painted a darker shade of cream, picked out with light blue. The chimney piece is very handsome, being of polished walnut, the overmantel having bevelled plate-glass panels. The room is served by a light dinner lift from the kitchen above, and ladies will here find a long felt want supplied, and will be able to vary the monotony of of a tedious day's shopping in a very pleasant manner. On the same floor (but approached by a separate staircase, which ascends from the cartway to the third floor) is the dining room for the use of the employees. This is a very large room, and, of necessity, it must be so, in order to provide for the numerous assistants employed on the premises. The walls and woodwork are coloured in a very pleasing terra cotta tint, picked out with a lighter shade of the same colour. The two fireplaces in the room are fitted with slow combustion stoves and massive chimney pieces. There is a general air of brightness about this room which gives us the impression that Messrs. B. Evans & Co. have done their utmost to study the comfort of those in their employ. But we must not linger. Our motto must be "Excelsior," so we proceed upwards until we arrive at the highest or

Fourth Story, – The first room we enter is the kitchen, and one glance is sufficient to show that this important branch, i.e. the commissariat department, has been amply provided for. The old idea of placing a kitchen at the lowest level of a house, has been exploded long ago, and the more sensible plan of placing it as high as possible is coming into general use. The object of this is, of course, that the effluvia from the cooking which, in large establishments, is particularly objectionable, may not permeate throughout the rest of the building, as in the case so often under the old arrangement. The kitchen at Messrs. B. Evans and Co's premises is fitted up with all the conveniences and accessories which are essential to the expeditious cooking for such a large number of people. The range is worthy of special attention. It is 14 feet long, half of it being heated by gas and the remainder by the ordinary coal fire. It comprises a gas oven, a steamer for cooking vegetables, a coal fire oven, and gas jets for boiling saucepans, &c. and at the back is a large boiler which supplies the steam. Besides this, there is another smaller range fixed against the opposite wall, which can be used when desirable in place of the larger ones. The large range, we may mention, is capable of cooking for 500 persons at ease. Splendid ventilation is assured for the kitchen by a large lantern light placed in the roof immediately over the range, and the air can thus be kept at an even temperature. Indeed, we noticed that the ventilation of the whole building had been carefully considered for Tobin's tubes for the inlet of fresh air are arranged on every floor, and extraction fans are placed in the walls just below the ceiling line. Passing through the kitchen and on the same level, we enter a passage with which communicate several servants' bedrooms, a housekeeper's room, store room, &c.&c. so that the mounting of wearisome flights of stairs is quite avoided. It will thus be seen that what may be called the administrative department is centrally situated, but so arranged as to be in no way detrimental to the business part of the premises; whilst at the same time communication is maintained with the rest of the building by the lifts which we have already mentioned. We have now traversed this huge block of buildings from its basement to the roof, but we feel that we have not been able to give our readers an adequate idea of the accommodation contained in it. We advise them to see for themselves, and we think they will arrive at the same conclusion to which we ourselves came, viz., that Messrs. B. Evans and Co. can claim to have one of the most extensive and complete furnishing and drapery establishments to be found in the Provinces. Great credit is due to the builders, Messrs Thomas, Watkins, and Jenkins.

——◇——

New Theatre, Swansea. – Mr. Melville has prepared for the Swansea public an unusual treat next week. As will be seen by an advertisement in our columns of this day, no less a personage than the celebrated Mrs. Weldon, of legal and musical fame will appear for six nights on the boards of the New Theatre, with her powerful drama, founded on the existing Lunacy Laws, entitled 'Not Alone,' the principal character of which she herself has alone appeared in. The third act of the drama is admirably arranged to enable Mrs. Weldon to introduce a selection of her popular songs, a fact initself sufficient to fill the house each night. Not long ago Mrs. Weldon – Georgina, an impudence delighted to call her – was the best and most abused woman in existence. But her indomitable courage, her untiring activity in a worthy cause, and her many excellent qualities of heart and brain have at length silenced the tongues of her calumiators. Mrs. Weldon deserves the gratitude of the nation for her persistent and ultimately successful attempts to ameliorate the state of Lunacy legislation in England; whilst the plucky stand she has taken in resisting oppression against difficulties that most people would have given way to, is especially worthy of admiration. "Not Alone," will initself be well worth seeing, as it gives a good insight into the chief events of Mrs. Weldon's life. We predict an overflowing audience throughout her visit, and advise our readers to secure seats as early as possible.

Grand Ball at Glanbrydan. – A grand ball was held at Glanbrydan Park (the residence of Mr. J. C. Richardson) on Friday night, when a very large gathering, comprising the *elite* of the county and others attended. The scene in the ball room was most brilliant and imposing, the effect being produced by costumes of rare and varierated description. The music was discoursed by Mr. Hulley's band. Appended is a list of the names of the ladies and gentlemen present with description of their respective apparel:– from Glanbrydan: Mrs. Richardson (rose queen), Mr. Richardson (uniform of 3rd. G.R.V.) Mr. Alfred Richardson (Charles Surface), Mr. Ernald Richardson (Eton volunteer), Master Eden Richardson (Prince Charming), Lieut.-Col Innes (Sir Peter Teazle), Mrs. Innes (Lady Teazle), Captain Penn (uniform Welsh Regiment), Mrs Penn (Unionists), Miss Mabel Pearce Serocold (Gipsy), Miss Violet Pearce Serocold (Vivandiere), Miss Margaret Pearce Serocold (Nasturtium), Mr. Prendergast (uniform R.E.), Mr. Warren (Windsor uniform), Mr. Eric Pearce Serocold (Eton boating costume). From Tregib: Mrs. Gwynne Hughes (Norwegian peasant), Mr. Gwynne Hughes (Norwegian peasant), Miss May Gwynne Hughes (Swiss peasant), Miss Maggie Gwynne Hughes (Incroyalde), Miss Maud Gwynne Hughes (Daffodil), Mrs Wodehouse (Midshipmite), Mr. Wodehouse (Egyptian runner), Capt. Percy Armitage (uniform 24th. Regiment), Mr. Macleod (uniform 79th. Highlanders, Mr. Cutbill (old hunting costume). From Abermarlais: Mrs. Thursby-Pelham (Madame Elizabeth), Major Thursby-Pelham, (hunt costume), Mrs. Jeffreys (George I, riding dress), Mr. Jeffreys (evening dress H.O.H.). Miss Croxton (Esmeralda). From Velindre: Mrs Jones (Pondree), Col. Jones (evening dress H.O.H.), Miss R. Jones (Worcester china), Miss M. Jones (French peasant), Miss Neville (Pondree), Mr Brenchley (Neapolitan sailor), Mr. G. B. Elkington (Penllergare hunt). From Hafodmeddin: Miss Beresford (Monte Carlo), Miss Lilian Beresford (Myrrha – a Greek girl), Mr. Aden Beresford (Windsor Uniform), Mrs Thomas Parkinson (white China), Mr. Thomas Parkinson (Venetian Gondolier), Miss Rosamund Peel (July), From Courthenry: Miss Ellen Saunders (my grandmother's bridesmaid), Mrs J. D. Lloyd (Pondree), Captain Lloyd (uniform 24th. Regiment), Captain Tower (uniform 24th. Regiment), Mr. J. H. Hartley (Mexican Ranchero), From Church House Llangadock: Mr. Meuric Lloyd (barrister-at-law), Mrs Neame (evening dress), Mr. Longley (evening dress), Mr. J. H. Longley (uniform 4th. East Surrey Regiment). From Glandulais: Mrs L'Estrange (Mother Hubbard), Miss L'Estrange (Grace Darling), Mr. E. W. L'Estrange (Albanian), Miss Clapham (Sophia Primrose). From Talley House: Mrs Long Price (evening dress). From Froodvale: Mrs Davies (lady of the eighteenth century), Miss Davies (hospital sister), Mr. O.W. Davies (Indian). Glansevin: Capt. Lloyd (uniform 1st. Royals), Mr. E. Lloyd (hunt costume). From Capel Lisa: Miss Lewis (French marquise), Miss Levett (Undine), Mr. Philip Scott (Zouave). From Alltyrodyn: Capt Stewart (uniform of the Horse Artillery), Miss Stewart (Lady Nithsdale), Miss M. Stewart (Vivandiere). From Blaenos: Mrs Jones (Di Vernon), Miss Fenton (shepherdess). From Llanon: Mr Goring Thomas (uniform D.L.), Miss Goring Thomas (Newhaven fishwife). From Aberglasney: Mrs Mansfield (Dresden china). From sundry places: Mr Hugh Nevill (hunt costume), Mrs Hugh Nevill (Pondree), Captain Mitford (mess uniform), Mrs Mitford (frost), Mr Newington (Windsor uniform), Miss Newington (Pondree), Mr W. Phillips (a bobby), Mr W. Picton Phillips (uniform 3rd. Middlesex), Mr. Hugh Phillips (French cook), Mr. W. Baillie (police inspector), Mrs Wyndham Lloyd (Corfu peasant), Mr. Curre

(Monmouthshire Hunt Club), Mr. de Winton (tennis dress), Miss Pryse (Welsh woman), Mr C.Vaughan Pryse (old Gogerddau Hunt Club), Miss Williams (Moorish lady), Miss Edwardes (Dolly Varden), and Mr E. Milner Jones (18th century).

——◇——

The Severn Tunnel – A noteworthy example of engineering skill and of commercial enterprise is afforded by the Severn Tunnel, which the Great Western Railway Company opened on Wednesday last, the 1st. inst., for goods and mineral traffic. The importance of this undertaking to a large portion of the trading community is evident, and on that ground alone the work is one upon which the contractors and the public alike are to be congratulated. From first to last this tunnel has been in progress nearly fourteen years, but by far the larger portion of the task has been carried out within the last five or six years, notwithstanding serious obstacles. In September last the first train was run through between South Wales and Gloucester carrying officials and visitors. A few months later an experimental goods train travelled from Wales to Southampton, demonstrating at once the great value of the new line when it should be made available for general service. It was at once hoped that this would be possible early in the present year, but warned by past experience, of the serious kind already described, Sir John Hawhshaw counselled some delay with a view to securing absolute safety, and to the better completion of the whole of the extensions in progress, and even now the new system will not be available for passengers for a few months to come, when no doubt the final opening will be celebrated in a fitting manner. Now, however, a service of goods trains will be established between South Wales and the southern part of England up to London; and looking back at the arduous and trying nature of the undertaking, the engineer and contractor may well receive the highest praise for their skill and indomitable perseverance. To traders and to travellers generally this new line will prove of the greatest value, dispensing, as it will, with the circuitous route which has hitherto been the only course for goods and minerals, and for passengers the only alternative to a journey partly by rail and partly by ferry across the Severn.

The journey from Swansea to London will be shortened by between 40 and 50 miles and at least an hour's time.

It is expected that the time occupied in passing through the tunnel will not exceed ten minutes, which, when travellers have become accustomed to the idea of being under water for the greater part of that period, will be no deterrent to the free use of the new line.

——◇——

5th. October 1888.

The Cambrian.

Swansea, Friday, October 5 1888.

SHALL SWANSEA REPLACE GAS BY OIL OR BY ELECTRICITY? – This is one of the important questions which are now agitating the minds of the men into whose hands are committed the governmental destinies of Swansea. Up to and including the present hour, our nightly darkness has been lightened by the inflammable vapour manufactured by the Swansea Gas Company, whose model works are such an addition to the sights of the Oystermouth-road. We need hardly say, however, that there have been cherished in Swansea, as in many cases elsewhere, two complaints against such companies, viz., that they are monopolists; that their illuminating power is too low, and their price too high. Often and often has it been declared that Swansea would put an end to the private monopoly, and, by the erection of new municipal gas works, or else by the purchase of the existing plant, reap some of the wonderful profits of gas-making, such as have been brought into the public exchequer of Birmingham and other large towns. Hitherto it must be admitted that we have had all cry and no wool. Now, however, a new series of circumstances has occurred, and a new departure seems to be imminent. We need not recapitulate the very modern history of the Gas Company's application to Parliament for power to raise more capital to extend their mains, and for other purposes. The evidence adduced at the inquiry in the Committee Rooms of the House, we have been publishing from week to week, and interesting information it must afford for local readers. The Corporation decided to oppose the measure for the purpose of safe-guarding the public interests. The result of the fight was an increase in illuminating power and a decrease of the maximum price which the Company is authorised to charge. On the other hand, the Gas Company secured the extended powers which they asked for. Since then the Company has given notice of an increase in the price to be charged for the gas supplied to the public lamps. This has not unaturally "riled" some members of the Corporation, whose feelings have been communicated to the whole body, and the result has been a determination to see what the Corporation itself can legally and profitably do to supply its own gas. In another column we give the text of the case submitted by the Town Clerk to counsel, and the legal opinion expressed thereupon. The expert declares that, in his opinion, the Corporation will be quite within its powers to in erecting gas works on its own lands, and in providing gas for its own consumption. The Corporation has gone further, and has got careful estimates from reliable sources for the lighting of the central area of the Borough with electricity and with oil lamps. The results of these enquiries are instructive, and they will probably awake in some of our readers, as they have awakened in some members of the Council, the hope that the town maybe better lighted by electricity or oil as cheaply, if not more cheaply, than by gas at present. For the purposes of the estimate a special area was taken – starting at Wind-street, passing along Castle-square, Castle Bailey-street, Temple-street, Castle-street, High-street, Alexandra-road, Cradock-street, Union-street, Oxford-street, and so back to about Temple-street. This may be said to include the best portion of the town. The various estimates for properly lighting this area were these: £452, £380, £452, £400, and £305. The last figure is the estimated annual cost of working, if the Corporation puts up its own installation. The former figures, we understand to be the contract price per annum, if the contractors put up installations of their own. These estimates are obtained from some of the leading electric lighting companies in the United Kingdom. Turning to oil, the estimates were £300 10s. and £220. 17s. 6d., the latter being with the Dufries lamp. To make clear the comparison we may say that the annual cost of lighting the same area with gas has been, up to the present – with gas at 2s.6d. per 1,000 feet, £370; but now that the price is advanced to 2s. 10d., the cost will be £400. There appears to be a disposition on the part of several influential members of the Corporation to try the experiment, in one form or another, of lighting the town by other means than by the present gas supply.

———◇———

NOTES AND COMMENTS.
THE GREENWAY BREAKWATER
TO BE TRIED AT SWANSEA.

We understand that the chairman and members of the Swansea Harbour Trust have fully considered the ingenious proposals of Mr. Greenway Thomas, the inventor of the floating Breakwater or Turn water system, and are so far favourably impressed with it as to consent to undertake an experiment under certain specified conditions. At a numerously attended meeting of the Executive Committee held on Wednesday, it was agreed to recommend for confirmation at the public monthly meeting on Monday next that the Trust do find £3,000 for the manufacture and mooring of 200 yards of steel buoys, provided Mr. Greenway Thomas or his friends find a similar sum, so as to complete 400 yards of floating breakwater buoys. This length of 400 yards, when completed is to be placed in Swansea Bay, at a suitable distance from the Mumbles Head, and is to remain there for twelve months so that the merits of the invention may be fairly tried in all weathers and under all circumstances of tide and storm. If this proposition be affirmed on Monday next, and if Mr. Greenway Thomas will accept the conditions imposed by the Trust, as we have no doubt will be the case, then we shall soon have the novel and important experiment tried. Should it prove successful – should the floating buoys prove effective in appreciably stilling the stormy waves so as to afford safe anchorage behind them – then the new system will certainly have an early and extensive application in other parts of the kingdom and of the world, and Swansea may hope to reap benefit not only from the credit of having carried the experiment to a successful issue, but also, we hope, the profit of manufacturing the buoys in our own district. We therefore wish the Greenway Breakwater and early and thorough success.

———◇———

A WORD TO THE WISE MEN
OF THE MUMBLES.

Now that the Mumbles is about to be made a fashionable health resort, and to enter into competition with a thousand and one other places on the British Coast, in seeking to attract profitable visitors, it will be well for the Oystermouth administrators to remember that the scientific schoolmaster is abroad, and that the health seeker is becoming better instructed and more exacting year by year. The *Sanitary Record* has just been pointing out to its readers some of the "Dangers of rising Health Resorts," in the course of which it says: People little reck of the dangers which they run in exchanging their own comfortable well-ordered house for stuffy seaside lodgings, where imperative economy requires that no more rooms shall be hired than are necessary. The sink and water-closet arrangements at all "rising" health resorts will be found almost uniformly bad. In the old days, when only a few stray visitors came, the sewage went into cess pools, and the water supply was obtained from wells. Now all the houses boast their closets, connected in more or less unscientific fashion with drains laid down in the streets and converging to a sewer discharging into the sea. The drains are usually put down piecemeal, and the levels are not right. The water supply is intermittent, and, as a consequence closet-pans get dry, and sewer gas pours up into the houses. Add to this the fact that the place has no building bye-laws, and that anyone may and does erect new houses, in his own fashion, and at any angle that he chooses to existing roads, and the dangers in the case of infectious diseases getting a foothold in the place will at once be manifest. The men of the Mumbles will be able to appreciate how far these disparaging remarks will apply to their own district, and they ought to be stimulated by it to do what they take in hand with greater thoroughness than ever. It may be said that "a little sanitation is a dangerous thing."

———◇———

Matthew Arnold's Daughter in Gower. – It is stated that the daughter of the late distinguished poet and critic, Matthew Arnold, is now on a visit to her aunt, Mrs. Benson at Fairy-hill, Gower. Some years ago, Matthew Arnold, while staying at the same place, attended Divine service one Sunday morning at the Calvanistic Methodist Chapel at Burry's Green, where he joined in the communion service as well.

———◇———

An Old Roman Plane Road. – in illustration and support of the theory of Rev. J. D. Davies, M.A., of Llanmadock, that the ancient paved way over Rhosilly Down is of Roman workmanship, it may be interesting to give the following particulars of the existence of a plank road of old world construction:– The Prussian Minister of Education, Von Gossler, having learnt that Professor F. Knoke had lately found traces of old Roman plank-roads on the moor between Menthols and Bragel, not far from Diephois, in lower Hanover, invited that gentleman to fully investigate the matter. He has just completed the task. He was able to trace the lines of two parallel plank roads, right across the moor, presenting all those distinctive features which are found in Roman works of this kind. One of them shows evident signs of having been demolished by force, the boards, which were originally fastened with pegs to the bearers, having been violently torn away and buried in the bog to the right and left of the track. The other road seems to have fallen into decay, but there are signs of repairs executed during the Roman period; for in places boards have been fastened over the original planks, the fashion of both being the same. Those repairs seem to have been carried out hastily, for in one place a mallet, employed probably to drive home the pegs, was found on the track, forgotten no doubt by the workmen. The local archaeologists feel assured that they have here the *pontes longi* which was used A.D.15 by the Roman commander, A. Caccina, in his retreat from Germany to the Ems.

——◇——

Concert at the Albert Hall. – Owing to the inclemency of the weather, the attendance at the ballad concert held on Monday night, in the Albert Hall, was exceedingly small, but those who did brave the elements enjoyed a musical treat, and testified their appreciaation by frequent and hearty applause. Subjoined is the programme:– Part I, – Quartette, "Queen of the Night," Madame Williams-Penn, Miss Lucy Clarke, Eos Wenallt, and Mr. John John; song, "Alone on the Raft," Miss Lucy Clark; song, " My Pretty Jane," Eos Wenallt; solo violin, "I Lombardi," Miss Meta Scott; song, "Love's Old Sweet Song," Madame Williams-Penn; song, "The Old Campaigner," Mr. John John; duet, "Over the Hawthorn Hedge," Madame Williams-Penn and Miss Lucy Clark; humorous sketch, "Cruise of the Cabar," Mr. Richard Elliot. Part II. – Duet, violin and pianoforte, Miss Meta Scott and Mr. J. F. Fricker; song, "Good Company," Eos Wenallt; song, "Father O'Flynn," Mr, John John; duet, "The Sailor's Sigh," Miss Lucy Clarke and Eos Wenallt; seranade with violin obligato, Madame Williams-Penn and Miss Meta Scott; song, "Angus Macdonald," Miss Lucy Clarke; solo violin, "Fantasia on a Welsh Air," Miss Meta Scott; humorous song, "Killaloo," Mr. Richard Elliot; quartette, "Good Night Beloved," Madame Williams-Penn, Miss Lucy Clark, Eos Wenallt, and Mr. John John; finale.

——◇——

Excursions. – The Great Western Railway Company advertise cheap trips to London for one, two, four or six days on Friday and Saturday next, leaving Llanelly at 11.30 p.m., calling at Swansea at 11.50, and intermediate stations. The periods at the disposal of those wishing to pay the Metropolis a visit are most convenient, and ought to be popularly patronised. The season is now drawing to a close, so that but few further opportunities will be offered. – The same company also intend to place facilities at the disposal of the working classes and others in the neighbourhood of Swansea of visiting Cardiff and Newport on Saturday afternoon the 13th. inst. This is a chance all too seldom given the toiling classes of visiting these great centres of industry and shipping, as the half holiday people have hitherto had it all their own way by the trips taking place on Thursday afternoons, which, in addition to the other expenses, means to the working man the loss of half a day, thus proving a deterrent in many instances. This objection is now removed, as the train leaves Swansea at 2.30 p.m., returning from Cardiff at 10.30 p.m., affording ample time for them to view the various exhibits, listen to the strains of classical music daily discoursed, and, if necessary, affording a few hours about the town and docks. The excursion to Cardiff promises to be well patronised as the Exhibition is now in full swing, and together with additional attraction of the Blue Hungarian Band, is bound to prove a popular rendezvous. Further particulars can be gleaned from our advertising columns and the small bills to be obtained at the stations named.

The Comptometer. – One of the most ingenious of recent American inventions is a calculating machine called "The Comptometer." It is the work of a resident of Chicago, and with its aid the most complicated mathematical computations can be made with great ease, accuracy and swiftness. The instrument is 14½ inches long, 7¼ inches wide, 6 inches high, and weighs 8lb. It can be placed upon an ordinary table. It differs from all other machines of this character, as it can be worked with a typewriter keyboard. This machine performs large multiplications in a second of time. It was recently tried by by the official experts at the Treasury at Washington. Various examples not previously known to the inventor were given to him for the testing of his apparatus as well as to experts detailed from the Treaury. The machine always surpassed the experts in speed, and was invariably correct. The inventor was given an example like the following:– "Suppose you bring £234 from England to New York, where the rate of exchange is 4.84½ dol., what is the American value of your money?" In one second of time this marvellous calculating machine recorded the correct answer l, 134,60¾ dol.

Correspondence.

WELSH-ENGLISH EISTEDDFODIC CANT.

To the Editor of "The Cambrian."

Sir. – I beg you to allow me to enter a public protest against the despicable twaddle to which we are being treated on the platform and in the press of Wales, about the so-called "glories" of Cymric lore and literature. Language of the most superlative degree is just now being made use of to laud wit and wisdom, the poetry and the preaching of Wales.

The irritating part of the matter is this: That all this fullsome flattery is indulged in not by men in whom ignorance or partiality might be well excused, but by men whose education or position ought to lift them above error or such venality.

Why is it done? Why do we find men who ought to, and who do, know better, pandering in Welsh to the vulgar vanity of the Welsh nation?

If Welshmen had only a little common sense – leave alone that literary and musical genius to which they so glibly lay claim – they would not be able to stand the fulsomely insulting talk to which they are treated by Saxons who unworthily wish to win their favour, or more often still, by wily Welshmen or Anglo-Welshmen who wish to win their suffrages and support.

In politics, the arrant lies which preacher and press pour forth in praise of Wales are such as would shock any modest and self-respecting community; yet Welshmen swallow all, and appear to like it. In this direction Welshmen are deep in the hopeless drunkeness of self-appreciation.

In literature and art, things are not much better. As an illustration of what I mean, let me quote a flagrant case. Last winter, Mr. Marchant Williams, barrister-at-law, delivered a lecture at the Royal Institution of South Wales, Swansea, on the beauties of Welsh poetry. Among the audience were some students who were ready to be instructed by this much advertised representative of the "London Welsh." The learned gentleman was certainly not wanting in manner. It soon became apparent to his hearers that he was a pupil of the great Turveydrop, to whose school, manner is more than matter, and tablecloth more than dinner.

Mr. Marchant Williams attempted to show that Wales had of old time a fine and valuable literature – that her poets were especially worthy of attention – and that, in special, Dafydd ap Gwilym was a bright particular star in the poetical firmament.

These statements he made in finely formed phrases and sounding sentences, but of proof of the validity of his assertions he produced none. So extravagant was the language he used in laudation of ancient Welsh literature, that one gentleman who occupied a front seat, and is no mean judge of an argument, scientific or literary, ostentatiously left the Theatre, half audibly ejaculating the expressive syllable "Bosh!" – a verdict which was assuredly endorsed by all present.

Whether the lecturer heard the commentary or not, he continued to the end of his discourse, which was nothing more than a tissue of exaggerations pitched in the key which is now so unhappily common – dishonest laudation of Wales and things Welsh. Judge of my surprise and indignation, sir, when I find this very lucubration published under the name of Mr. Marchant Williams in a special full report of the proceedings of the recent National Eisteddfod at Wrexham. Of course, Mr. Williams is said to be looking out for a Welsh constituency to return him to Parliament, and that explains the matter.

Oh, dear, but it is very, very sad. It has become the trade of the venal politician to pander to vulgar tastes, however degraded and harmful.

But really, the thinking men of Wales, especially those who are interested in cosmopolitan literature, ought to protest against the over praise of things Welsh. Wales has never yet produced a really great – a first class – hardly even a second or third class writer in prose or rhyme; and if ever Welshmen are to rise to a higher place in the world's literature or art, it will not be by over estimating and imitating old mediocrities, but by valuing them at their true worth and by following higher ideals. –

Yours faithfully, Ieuan Tawe.

A SWANSEA PICTURE FOR SALE.

To The Editor of "The Cambrian."

Sir, – In my wanderings I called in at Mr. Harvey's Auction-rooms, in Goat street, and there saw a picture of Mozart's Last Sonnet, singing his last requiem, painted by the late Mr. Jefferys Lewis. It will be sold in the course of a week or so, and I trust that this picture may be secured for the Fine Art Gallery at the Free Library, as it will be a sad loss to the town if so meritorious a work of art, by a native, is allowed to be lost to Swansea. – I am, yours, &c.

Oct. 3, 1888 Paul Pry.

Swansea Baths and Laundry Co. Limited.

NOTICE TO THE PUBLIC.

IT having been desired to keep the SWIMMING BATHS open during the Winter Months, arrangements will be made to do so if 100 Family Season Tickets of 10s. each can be sold.

These tickets may be used by any member of the family as often as desired, and will be available from November 1st, 1888, to March 31st. 1989.

The water will be kept at an equable temperature of 70 degrees.

FAMILY SEASON SLIPPER TICKETS MAY BE HAD FOR 10s. EACH.

Season Tickets may be obtained at the Ticket Office or of the General Manager, at the Baths, on or before the 25th inst. [4370

7th. November 1890.

THE BATH AND WEST OF ENGLAND SHOW IN SWANSEA, 1892.

HOW ABOUT SITE AND PRESIDENT?

There seems to be such a strong concensus of opinion in favour of holding the above show in Swansea the year after next, that the discussion as to site, &c., has become a topic of pretty general conversation in the town. As to site, there are several suggested, but all of them have some drawback or other.

I. The Victoria Park, with the adjacent Cricket field and Recreation Ground.

Objections: (1) Too small. Only 27 acres in all, whereas from 30 to 40 acres are needed. (2) Can't be spared by public and players so long as three months which would be necessary for preparation, &c.

II Top of Town Hill, with hill tramway (Permanent) leading to the summit.

Objections: (1) Cost of hill tramway. (2) Impossible to get machinery and heavy beasts up. (3) Public would not mount the steep hill in the hot month of June.

III. Clyne Valley, near Mr. Barron's farm, where the races used to be held.

Objections: (1) Too far from town. (2) No sufficient roads of approach. (3) Ground too soft. (4) In case of heavy rain, a swamp.

IV. On Manselton Race Course.

Objections: (1) Too far from town; people would not go to it.

V. Singleton Park, near the farm, approached from the Sketty Gate.

Doubts: (1) Whether Sir Hussey Vivian would grant it. (2) Whether the surface of the ground would be suitable.

The above is a summary of the suggestions with their *pros* and *cons*. There are some who undertake to say that Sir Hussey, who is an ardent and successful agriculturist, would grant the Park if properly approached, and further, that the Hon. Baronet might be induced to take the Mayoralty of Swansea for 1892, so as to uphold the dignity of the town during the memorable year. The Bath and West of England Show ranks next, and is in nothing inferior, to the

Royal, and its advent here would more than repay the town for the trouble and outlay. From all points of view, therefore, the matter should receive the most careful consideration.

——◇——

THE DISGRACEFUL STATE OF THE SWANSEA FORESHORE.

THE PIER APPROACHES NOW IMPASSABLE.

One of the chief points of interest to visitors, as well as to inhabitants of Swansea, is, of course, the fine western pier extension. On that grand promenade the healthful breezes of the sea may be inhaled, and the eye may be delighted by the fine sweep of the Bay and the grand amphitheatre of Swansea's environing hills, and of the town and the valley itself. When the tide is in and the ships are passing in and out, there is no spot more interesting or suggestive than the pier, and yet, while we have the incomparable health and pleasure place prepared for us, the townsfolk are almost unable to make use of it, because of the neglected, and worse than neglected, state of the approaches thereto. For the greater part of every day the outer gates of the South Dock basin are open for the ingress or egress of ships, and therefore no foot passenger, much less vehicle, can cross the seaward side. The only practicable means of approach therefore, to the pier is by means of the swing bridge near Gloucester-place. This bridge is itself very frequently open, and would be passengers are detained for longer periods than are comfortable, or perhaps proper, but once they have crossed the bridge they find themselves landed in a narrow lane, which cannot be called a roadway. The area is occupied by tram lines, on which engines and trucks are constantly passing to and fro day and night, to the serious danger of all passengers, young or old, who wish to get to the foreshore. Then, supposing one has reached the foreshore, there is nothing but a series of dismal swamps and mud sloughs to wade through. The ashpath which someone or other was good enough to lay down on the edge of the bank some twelve months ago, has now been cut up entirely by mud carts, ash-carts, and general refuse carts, which tip their vile contents on the foreshore. The process of making more land is certainly going on at a rapid pace, but meanwhile the whole foreshore is a wilderness of the most disgusting kind – disgusting to sight and to smell. The Inspectors of Nuisance of the Urban Sanitary Authority ought really to pay some attention to the condition of the place, and an arrangement ought to be come to by the Corporation, the Harbour Trustees, and the London North Western Railway Company, so as to provide a proper and a properly kept footpath, however narrow, for the townsfolk and for visitors to pass back and fore to the Pier. The cost of our Recreation Grounds and Open Spaces in Swansea is over £1,300 per annum. This money is spent ostensibly for the purpose of promoting the health and happiness of the people of Swansea; but here we have a magnificent marine parade, worth, in the opinion of some people half a dozen of our Open Spaces, and yet our local governing bodies have not the *naus* to provide the means of access to it. Will not some of our forty County Councillors, or our Harbour Trustees endeavour to remove this state of things, which is nothing less than a disgrace to the Borough.

——◇——

THREATENED DISCONTINUANCE OF THE MUMBLES SHIP-SIGNALLING STATION.

MERCHANTS AND SHIPOWNERS TO THE RESCUE!

It is to be hoped that the merchants and shippers of Swansea will not allow the useful and now world-known ship-signalling station at the Mumbles Head to fall into discontinuance for the want of a little – a very little – financial support. When the Swansea Harbour Trust entered into an arrangement with the General Post Office for the construction and maintenance of the telegraphic wire to the Head a few years ago, it was understood that some of our local merchants would help to defray the cost. But when calls were made upon them, very few were found willing to contribute. Under these circumstances the Trust have had to reconsider whether they were justified in keeping the station open entirely at their own cost, which meant up till now an expenditure of about £70. The General Post Office are now willing to make a substantial reduction, and it is to be hoped, therefore, that the necessary amount of outside support will be given to justify the Harbour Trust in keeping the signal station open

——◇——

LOCAL FIXTURES OF FORTHCOMING EVENTS.

FRIDAY, Nov. 7.

"The Gondoliers," at the New Theatre, Wind-street, and during the week.

SATURDAY, Nov. 8.

Excursion to Newport, per Great Western Railway.

SUNDAY, Nov. 9.

Sermons on behalf of the Swansea and East Gower Extension Fund, in the various churches of the neighbourhood.

MONDAY, Nov. 10.

The Vokes Family at the New Theatre, Wind-street, and during the week.

THURSDAY, Nov. 13.

Annual Tea and Concert at St. Jude's Schoolroom, Terrace-road.

Lecture in connection with the Gilchrist Educational Trust, at the Albert Hall, by R. D. Roberts, Esq., M.A., D.Sc., F.G.S., on "The Building of the Earth's Crust, with Special Reference to the Carboniferous Beds."

SATURDAY, Nov. 15.

First Popular Concert at the Drill Hall, Singleton-street.

WEDNESDAY AND THURSDAY, Nov. 19 & 20.

Grand Exhibition of Chrysanthemums, Orchids, Primulas &c. at the Drill Hall, Singleton-street.

THURSDAY, Nov. 20.

Miss Florence Fricker's Concert at the Albert Hall.

——◇——

IS FOOTBALL A VALUABLE ENTHUSIASM OR A DANGEROUS FRENZY?

HOW SWANSEA MEN DIFFER ABOUT IT.

OBSERVATIONS IN SWANSEA AND IN CARDIFF.

By Peter Clark.

On Saturday week last, there being a half-crown excursion to Cardiff on the occasion of an inter-town football match, I availed myself of the occasion to pay a visit to that place on other business bent. As I stood on the platform and watched the eager rushing procession of excursionists from the ticket office to the train, I was accosted by a friendly railway official, high up in the service.

"Hullo," said he, "are you touched with the general madness? Going to see the football match, I suppose? Look here, I consider it a most brutal game, and that it ought to be suppressed. I would prefer any day to see a prize-fight, low as that is, than I would look on at a football match."

And so with a friendly salutation, but no reply from me, he wended his way and disappeared.

The circumstances brought to mind what had occurred on the preceding Saturday afternoon, as I came up St. Helens-road, after witnessing the play of Swansea v Gloucester. One of our most refined and thoughtful doctors, a gentleman who always was, and still is an ardent yachtsman, met me in the middle of the town-coming crowd, and said:

"It is a pity to see so many people addicted to football. It is a rough and dangerous form of amusement. I thoroughly agree with *Punch* of this week, who has a capital cartoon. Pointing to a picture of trapezists and acrobats of all sorts, 'Talk of putting down dangerous amusements,' says he, 'deal with *that* first (pointing to a picture of a football scrimmage)'."

And so the doctor passed on.

My *vis-a-vis* in the not very clean or savoury railway carriage in which I had the pleasure of being squeezed and conveyed to Cardiff, was also a deprecator of the popular game, and he gave me from time to time on the way the benefit of his remarks.

As for myself, I am neutral. On this, as on some other more momentous questions, which my friends dogmatize pretty loudly about, I have not been able to make up my mind. (If I have any) so decisively on one side or the other, though I have thought a good deal about it. I feel somewhat like Lord Lushington in a similar dilemma when he ejaculated:

"I wish to heaven I could feel so cock-sure about anything as Tom (Lord) Macaulay feels about everything."

What strikes me – and strikes me more forcibly the longer I contemplate it, is this: that as regards football and many other popular fashions or fads, "there is a good deal to be said on both sides."

The company in the railway carriage fairly illustrated this position. Our compartment contained a young Swansea Town Councillor, a middle aged manufacturer, two clerks, two very bright and intelligent "operatives," a small boy, &c. &c. Football was naturally the subject of conversation from start to arrival. They all, especially the manufacturer, displayed remarkable knowledge of, the *technique* of the game, and of the personal qualifications of the players constituting the rival teams. Here are a few specimens of their remarks:–

"What a wonderful couple the two Jameses are."

"Yes, but only when they are together. They are always on the ball. But playing separately they are not up to much."

"Jerry Edwards is not in the team today."

"No, he is not hard yet – not in true football form."

"He couldn't do much last week."

"Couldn't he indeed! Didn't he kick-that drop goal against Glo'ster? A drop goal now and then counts up, I can tell you."

"Bancroft is a cool customer, isn't he?"

"Aye! See the way he walks to meet the ball; see how he dodges; how he rushes through the opposite forwards, and how he kicks when he gets a fair chance. "

In Cardiff the feeling was very high – so high that it issued in more than one free fight, and there were manifestations of some brutality towards a few of the Swansea players before they left the field. The learned Deputy Town Clerk of Cardiff, Mr. J. Davies Williams, who is a thoroughly loyal Cardiffian, told me that, if the victory were gained by Swansea, the disappointment and consequent anger of Cardiff would be great. And so it undoubtedly would have been. Happily such a terrible state of temper was averted, by the fact that the game ended in a draw.

The sight of the football visitors, as they wended their way to and from the field, as they promenaded the streets, as they invaded public-houses and restaurants, and as they gravitated back to the railway station, men and women, boys and girls together, was a suggestive one.

My friend took up his parable at once.

"Football," he declared, "is a species of mania. It is an epedemic. It leads to gambling, it promotes bad language, and it is made the occasion for drunkeness and debauchery. It is a brutal and brutalising passtime."

"I grant you," I replied, "that it is dangerous – dangerous not only to the players, but also to the onlookers. The players get hurt, sometimes killed, often injured for life. The onlookers take fatal colds in standing about the wet grass; they injure their stomachs by drinking vile spirits and beer in the excitement of the play; and they corrupt their minds and manners too often by listening to the foul language which streams forth from the mouths of the observers."

"Well, isn't that indictment enough against it?"

"No, I think not. That is only one side of the question. Look at the other side of the account."

"What other side?"

"Look at the good side of the popular game. It draws young fellows away from the public-house and from all sorts of deleterious indulgences of appetite in order that they may train themselves up to 'good form,' for play. It teaches endurance, it awakens pluck, it promotes friendly rivalry, it accustoms men to do their utmost to win, and yet to control their tempers when they inevitably fail."

"Go on; go on."

"The enthusiasm is a most healthy one, in as much as it gives a population a common interest, and a subject which is certainly not degrading, to talk and think about."

"Go on; go on."

"In the noblest epoch of our Christian Chivalry, the popular spectacular games were jousts and tournaments. They were dangerous games, if you like. The knight was nearly always knocked about, often wounded, and sometimes actually killed. Yet the nobles and the ladies of the land, as well as the populace, enjoyed these doughty doings, and they were as much talked about as football. The Olympic games of old Greece, too, demanded the same abstinence, the same endurance, the same pluck as our Football, and the Grecian games were taken part in by the flower of youth and beauty, their achievments were celebrated by the greatest poets, and their likenesses preserved by thr greatest sculptors the world has ever seen. Don't let us make any mistake about the matter. Let us decry and suppress the evil features and parasitic overgrowths of Football, if you like; but don't let us by any means discourage manliness, pluck, generous rivalry and endurance, which are among the finest and rarest qualities of human nature."

"How can you separate the good from the evil?"

"Tares grow with the wheat always."

Would it not be well for Swansea to take a leaf out of the book of Worcester. At Worcester the following notice has been issued:–

"Police Caution. – Nursemaids Beware. – After this notice the police will rigidly prosecute any person found obstructing or incommoding the free passage of any footpath by gossiping, loitering, or running two abreast thereon with perambulators or other carriages, with or without children therein. Penalty under City Act, £5.

A. E. Sommers, Chief Constable.

Here is good news for painters and purchasers of water-colour pictures in general, and for the members and patrons of the Swansea Sketching Club in particular:– Professor Hartley declares that we may expect water-colour drawings to last 400 years, provided they are protected from the influence of direct sunlight.

A statement has gone the round of our contemporaries to the effect that the horses of Swansea are suffering from an epedemic of influenza, or something of that kind. We are glad to be able to state, on the authority of Mr. T. C. Small, the vetinary Inspector for the borough, that there is no truth in this alarming statement. Mr. Small tells us that he never knew the town and district freer from horse disease than at the present moment. There is no epedemic at all, but there is a certain percentage suffering from slight colds, a circumstance which is normal at this time of the year.

WHERE ARE THE GHOSTS OF GOWER-LAND GONE?

To The Editor of "The Cambrian."

Sir, – I have always looked upon Gower, or little Fleming-land beyond Wales, as one of the most out-of-the-way, and consequently out-of-the-world places within easy reach of modern civilisation. It is certain that the late Mr. Talbot regarded it in that light, or he would never have dealt with his tenants there in the old world fashion which we have heard so much about. Another proof of the same thing is the fact that Mr. J. C. Fowler, the learned Stipendiary of Swansea, in a lecture on the Feudal System, pointed to the Gower Peninsula as the place where the old customs of feudality have ligered longer than in any other parts of the district.

This being so, I should have thought that, with old legal and social customs, old superstitions would be found lingering side by side. In the History of West Gower, by the learned Rector of Llanmadoc and Cheriton, in the fantastic and poetic "Wanderings" of "C.D.M." and in the interesting South-west Gower letters which appear in *The Cambrian* from time to time, I find allusions to old faiths that have fallen and old practices which are suppressed.

What I should like to know is this:– Do the Gower peasantry still retain any real belief in witchcraft, in charms, in demonic fairy deeds, in ghosts or apparitions? Does the corpse-candle still burn for them? Crows the cock still at midnight as an indication of a forthcoming funeral? Is the death-tick still heard in the house wall? Are illusory lights still seen on the shore before a fatal shipwreck?

I do not ask these questions idly, for the purpose of raising a laugh for those who fancy themselves more enlightened; in order to stir up again in simple minds fears which time may have allayed; but simply because I desire to gauge how far modern influences of science and sceptism may have invaded the secluded land of Gower.

Perhaps one of your many intelligent readers in Gower may be induced to take the matter up, and to tell us through your columns the real facts of the case. I fancy that the Devil and his Imps are as dead in Gowerland as elsewhere, and that Ghosts and Goblinsare gone the way of all flesh who long ago so strongly believed in them. – Yours faithfully,

Swansea, Nov. 1st. 1890 Faust.

THE REFORM OF NATIONAL EISTEDDFODIC ABUSES.

DO WELSHMEN REALLY STUDY THEIR OWN LANGUAGE AND LITERATURE?

To The Editor of "The Cambrian."

Sir, – Now that we are to have the National Eisteddfod held at Swansea, it is full time to consider what can be done by us to lessen the abuses and increase the benefits of the ancient and admirable institution.

From this point of view, I hail the sensible remarks made by "Delta" in *The Cambrian* of last week. The article was perhaps a somewhat wordy and windy one, and there was a certain affectation of fine diction about it that was indicative – and of much. But still the questions raised were healthy, and the general effect must be good.

As a student of Welsh, like Mr. C. H. Glascodine the barrister – all honour to him for his Cymric fervour! I have been shocked to find so few Welshmen – who really know their own language. Among our public men who affect to be Welshmen, in speech as well as soul, how many can address a meeting for two minutes in Welsh? They, for the most part, speak a gibberish, that is neither Welsh nor English, – neither flesh, fowl, nor good red herring.

Then look at our bards – even our bards of the Gorsedd – how much Welsh do they know? Just enough to enable them to make a few eliptical and eccentric englynion or turn some verse in the *Mesur Caeth*. But what about grammar? In the matter of rules of their own tongue, they are hopelessly at sea. Why? Because they do not study comparative grammar and comparative style in other languages, ancient and modern.

Then take their boasted literature. I have had the *advantage* of hearing in the Theatre of the Royal Institution of South Wales that great and burning eisteddfodic and Cymric light, Mr. Marchant Williams, on Dafydd ap Gwilym. I went to learn; I came away in lament – I could not laugh. I must not blame Mr. Williams. He has been trained in a bad bombastic school. He, like most other professed admirers of Welsh Literature, treats us to a great deal of rhodomontade about the greatness, and the genius of Welsh poets, but he gives us no specimens which we can compare with the utterances of poets of other races.

And so the whole serpentine length of unintelligent twaddle goes on – all talk and no thought, all supposition and no substance, all table-cloth and no dinner.

The fact of the matter is – Welshmen do not love their literature, or they would study it; do not believe in its greatness, or they would convince us by quoting specimens of it.

The only man who has had real insight into Celtic literature was an Englishman, Matthew Arnold, and, I suppose, not one professedly literary Welshman out of ten thousand has ever read what he said about it.

In these days of inductive science, the *comparative* is the only method of profitable, progressive study, and Welshmen, as a whole, and Eiseddfodic Welshmen in particular, are not educated enough to follow fearlessly in such a footpath.

For Heaven's sake, let Swansea Eisteddfodic Committee try to rise above the low, low levels of the past.

Yours faithfully,

Ffynonllwynygog.

November 4th, 1890.

——<>——

2nd. December 1892.

THE MUMBLES CLIFF ROAD.

When is it to be extended?

A question which many people interested in the welfare of the Mumbles, and who hold somewhat optimistic views regarding her future prospects, are asking just at present is. When is the Cliff road to be extended? This is a matter of importance, and it is generally agreed that the Local Board should not allow it to hang fire longer than is absolutely necessary. We know there were, a few years ago, certain difficulties in the way of extension, but we believe we are right in stating that they were overcome. If this is really the case, and if Sir Hussey Vivian Bart, M.P., Mr. Thos Penrice, J.P., Mr. Pendarves Vivian, and Mr. Nicholl Morgan, who own the land over which the road will have to be extended, have given their sanction to defray the cost of the work over their own particular ground, then we see no earthly reason why the matter should be allowed to remain in abeyance any longer. A road extending along the cliffs from South End to Langland Bay would almost be unsurpassable as a marine drive; it would open up some eligible sites, and would render the small bays and caves on this part of the Gower coast more accessible to the public, and, at the same time, materially reduce the parish rates and bring Bracelet, Limeslade, and Langland Bays, and the neighbourhood in general, into even greater popularity, than at present. The cliff road, in its present unfinished state, is a *cul de sac*, to which may well be attributed the cause of the disfavour with which it is viewed by summer visitors. There are few things more annoying to Mrs. Grundy than to find an abrupt and unnecessary termination to her constitutional recreations and exercise – when walking along a road, with a magnificent view of the sea and coast, land and town, to come to a sudden halt, without there being any cogent reason why that halt should be encountered so early in the pleasurable excusion. There was a time when the landowners declared to the public, "Thus far shalt thou go, and no farther." but now no such mandate exists; the landowners, like wise men, have seen at last that the extension of the road would not only benefit the Mumbles but also themselves. Indeed, they have gone so far as to declare that they are prepared to do their share of the work. Then who is to blame for all this delay? Plans have been prepared and submitted to, and approved of by the land-owners, while they have also agreed to defray the cost of the extension over their own respective properties. Such being the case, we think it is the duty of the Mumbles local Board to take the matter in hand at once, and thus take a step which, if properly carried out, would ultimately result in an incalculable amount of good to the Mumbles. If the road were extended to Langland Bay, we feel sure the Langland Bay Hotel Company would carry it on to Caswell Bay. It would be to their interests to do so, for it would open up their own property to the east of the bay, where there are some really excellent sites for villa residences. If the local Board does not set about this very desirable and important improvement at once, the members will be wanting in their duty to the ratepayers, and Mr. Nichol Morgan, the chairman will not be fulfilling the pledges he made some years ago when he was a candidate in opposition to Mr. Thos Penrice, J.P. for County Council honours. To see the extension of the cliff road and the completion of the Mumbles Railway and Pier "accomplished facts" in the same year, would be a striking epoch in the history of the district. Yet it is within the power of the local Board to bring this about, and the sooner they set about the work the better.

I must congratulate "Kitreb" on the very graphic description he gave in last week's *Cambrian* of his travels in Gowerland. In some things he has been wrongly informed, but that is not his fault. I can quite understand that it is a difficult matter for a stranger travelling about to get accurate information about everything – for even in Gower I must admit there are *some* big story-tellers, and what they don't know they will make up; and if a stranger should ask the way to a certain place, of some men in Gower, they would quite as likely direct him some miles out of his way as in the right direction. But I'm pleased to say such characters are few and far between.

——◇——

It was news to me that the old round levelling from Moor corner in the direction of Rhosilly is supposed to be a Roman road. I have never heard that before, and doubt it very much, but I would advise "Eitreb," when he next visits Gower, to go to Llangennith through Combe-lane, and there he will find a Roman road proper.

——◇——

EXTENSION OF THE MUMBLES RAILWAY.

Absurd and Unnecessary Grumbling by the Natives.

The average Mumbleonian is an ungrateful specimen of the *genus homo,* while his lethargy and supineness are only too well known. During the past few weeks they have referred in no uncomplimentary terms to the gentlemen who are responsible for the work of extending the Mumbles Railway, and are loud in denouncing the attempt which is being made, according to them of depriving them of their natural rights and priviliges. They complain that the Railway Company have deceived them, that land has been acquired which it was intended should never be given up, and that fishermen are now at their wits end to find places for their boats. Prognostications of the most pessimistic nature are being made about the future of the Mumbles, and the owners of property along the front of the village declare that their houses have depreciated considerably in value by what is now being done. Indeed, some go as far to submit that the extension of the railway will not in any way benefit, but rather injure, Mumbles, and to hint that the proposed pier will never be constructed. It was ever thus with the average Mumbleonian. Unable to take care of themselves, they always resent the action of those who come forward to help them, and darkly hint that they – the people – are being taken advantage of. It seems almost incredible that any one should think for a moment that the Mumbles Railway Company would go to the expense of extending their line to South End, without ultimately constructing a pier, and if they did not have expectations of there being a reasonable return in course of time for the money laid out. Any ultimate financial success which may accrue to the Company consequent upon this scheme, would naturally be beneficial to the Mumbles generally and would be material in reducing the rates. The Local Board, having obtained the sanction of the rate payers, granted to the Railway Company powers to utilise certain portions of the Promenade. There were of course, stipulations made as to provisions being found for the shelter of the fishermens' boats, and the construction of arches and crossways to enable people to get to the beach. We do not believe for a moment that the Railway Company would flagrantly break the agreement, or that they would unsrupulously trample upon the rights and provisions of the ratepayers. Yet it is asserted that this is now being done, and from what we can hear there is likely to be a storm shortly – between the Railway Company and certain ratepayers; but the work is not yet half completed; the Company have not been given time to see what they really intend to do, so we cannot but think that it would be a "Storm in a tea cup." There is no doubt that the Mumbles Railway Company have in view the ultimate construction of a pier – indeed, we have every reason for stating that the pier will be an accomplished fact within the next two years; and then, we feel sure, Mumbles will prosper and become an important trading station, and, at the same time, a popular health-resort. It ill becomes Mumbles people, or at least a section of them, to throw dirt at the Railway Company, or to place any obstacle in their way. The promoters deserve every commendation for their enterprise and public spirit. A policy of dilly-dallying and procrastination has been the curse of Mumbles long enough.

——◇——

As has already been hinted at, Swansea is going to be comparatively merry during this winter. The pleasures of the dance and of social gatherings are to be enjoyed to a larger extent than in recent years. The Hospital Ball will be held on January the 10th. The Charities Ball has been fixed for the first week in the sequent month of February, and there will be, in all likelihood, the annual soiree of the Royal Institution of South Wales, in the same place, the Albert Hall, in the last week of February or the first week of March. In addition to these more distinctively public events there will be a considerable number of semi-private invitation fixtures, including the very enjoyable reunions which are annually given under the direction of Miss Langdon on the one hand and Miss Craven on the other hand. Putting all things together, therefore, we may safely present a rather "jolly" season for the younger and more lighthearted members of the local community.

People go a long distance to see exhibitions, and yet what is more interesting as an exhibition than a studious walk along the pavement of a a well kept, well equipped town? Swansea has a good deal to recommend it in this respect. Some of our local shop-fronts are well worth looking at, and the insides are better still. It is interesting, it is educative, it is inspiring to take a walk through B. Evans & Co's establishment. When I was there last week I saw some charming tea gowns, and some gems of bonnets. Of course, they were expensive, but you only have to ask one of the young ladies belonging to the establishment, and she will tell you that they will make you one exactly the same with a less expensive material.

Mr. B. Evans is to be congratulated on the efficiency of his staff. This is the season for dancing and evening dresses. The show of these attractive "compositions" now at Temple-street should be seen to be appreciated.

———<>———

Miss Marion Evans in Bristol. – Miss Marion Evans, Swansea's popular young soprano, has been winning golden opinions at Bristol, where she has made herself quite a favourite. On Saturday last she took part in a popular concert. This is how *The Bristol Times and Mirror* refers to her:– Miss Evans achieved some of her greatest successes in Bristol, whose musical citizens were captivated by her pure, clear voice and manner, unadorned by artistic polish. Although the singer has now been for some time a student of the Royal Academy of Music, her freshness of voice, and simplicity of method have not disappeared, while her artistic appreciation and interpretation of pieces she sings have been improved. Her voice, however, still lacks power, which may come bye and bye. The pieces were given with taste, expression and clearance of utterance and phrasing, the pleasure of the audience being testified by torrents of applause, the singer being recalled."

———<>———

WELSH PLACE NAMES.

[By E. Roberts Metal Broker, Swansea.]

Some 170 years ago Cheland wrote a little book entitled, "*On the way to things by words, and to words by things*" and it treated of the origin of words. This mode of procedure is, I think, peculiarly applicable to etymological research of Welsh Nomenclature – which to so great extent are founded upon the the natural features and characteristics of the localities they represent; and in the list following these observations will be found some remarkable instances of Welsh word painting, and of the fidelity and exactness of the Welsh language to nature. Prominent in this respect are the following names: *Twmpath Diwlith and Bryn troedgam,* every syllable in each word clearly defining local features – and so it is in this case, more or less, with Welsh names in general. It will also be observed that certain vocables such as *Bryn, Troed, Cam, Pont, Rhyd and Nant,* are frequent factors in the names below; and these prefixes prevail, to a large extent, in Welsh names – over the principality of Wales in general. I hope to continue my remarks upon additional names in the Margam district in next week's *Cambrian.*

Twmpath Diwlith. – From *Twmpath,* a hillock, a tump, "Y Twmpath lle cleddid Rhys di wyr, a elwir *Bryn-y-beddau.*" – the place where Rhys and his men were buried is called the Hill of the Graves – Caradawg o bancarfan. *Di* a privative prefix meaning not or without and *Wlith Gwlith* – Dew, the whole name *Twmpath DIwlith,* meaning a hill or hillock not having dew on it. It is a *Cara* (a heap) on Margam Mountain. and is of considerable size, and is supposed to be the burying place of the slain after a battle; and according to tradition in the parish, it appears *Twmpath Diwlith* has never been known to be covered with dew, while the surrounding ground has been observed to be so – hence its name – a most perfect expression of such a circumstance.

Bryntroedgam. – The correct and original form of this was, most probably *Bryn-y-troed-gam,* from *Bryn* – a hill, *troed* – a turning and *gam – cam* – crooked – the hill of the crooked turning.

Pontrhydyfen. – I am inclined to think the original orthography was *Pont-rhyd-Afan* – from *Pont* a bridge. "*A fo pen bid pont*" that which would be a top, let it be a *bridge.* Adage: *rhyd* – a ford, a passage. "*Moled pawb y rhyd fel y Caffo.*" – let everybody praise the *ford,* as he finds it. Adage: and *fen,* a phonological corruption of *Afan* – the name of the river over which the bridge has been built – the bridge of the ford of the Afan (river).

Nantytewlaeth. – Literally *tewlaeth* means thick milk, which is obviously inapplicable to such a case as this. I am inclined to think the name is so called from the bell flower, which in Welsh is called *Llwyn tewlaeth,* which probably may abound in the dingle, through which the brook runs; or the original form of the name may have been *Nant y tew-wlith* – from *Nant* a brook, *tew-wlith* copious dew.

Nant y Gregen – Probably its original name was *Nant y crygen,* from *Nant* a brook, *y* the, and *crygen* harsh, hoarse or rough, the brook of harsh or noisy sound. Another conjecture is that it may have been a corruption, *Nant y gregyron,* the brook of the herons, which frequent this district, and which may be seen frequently in the brooks of the district.

Nantytrafael. From *Nant* a brook, y the, *Traf* an ancient Welsh word for scour, and *Aelmael* iron. The brook may be a rough scouring one, tearing up the ground, and thereby bringing to light some iron-stone from the ground or its bed.

Nantyfrwdwyllt. – From *Nant* a brook, *frwd* a flood, a torrent, *"A'i ffrwd difodd drosof"* and the *flood* overflowed me, Bible; and *wyllt-gwyllt* wild rushing – the brook of the wild rushing torrents or floods.

Llanfihangel-Ynys-Afan. – The ancient Welsh name of Michaelstone-super-Afan – from *Llan,* a church, *Fihangel,* St. Michael. *Ynys* here means adjacent, and *Afan,* the name of a river – The Church of St. Michael near the Afan.

Capel Anwes. – Most people, and especially Churchmen know what a Chapel of Ease is – but it is seldom its Welsh name is applied. In this case, however, the Welsh name has out lived to the present day all anglicising influences, and still retains its Celtic name. *Capel Anwes* is a literal translation of Chapel of Ease.

Tanygroes. – From *Tan,* under or beneath; *y,* the; and *groes* cross, a turn (as *croesffordd,* a cross road); also a cross – a crucifix.

Margam. – Originally called *Morgan* after *Morgan Mwynfawr.* Was founded about the tenth century. I have seen many old charters relating to *Margam,* and find the name invariably spelt Morgan or Maggan till 1542, when for the first time we find it spelt Margam, from which time it has retained the same form of spelling.

———<>———

Swansea is to go ahead presently. There has been serious depression, and there is not a little restriction as a consequence. But signs are not wanting of a better condition of things. We hear of several schemes of a new and cheering character, which if carried into effect, cannot fail to promote the general as well as the private interests of the district. It is being more and more felt that Swansea would be benefited if we had fewer mere talkers and dreamers in our local public life, and more workers and helpers in the work of buiding up the prosperity of the town and district. Let those who wish to rise in the world "go to work" honestly, and they will have a chance of succeeding. Dodging and chicanery and treachery seem to succeed for a time but such success has been found, by experiment, in the longer run to be unsound. Trickery, is in time found out and then the trickster has to change his jubilant tune. Swansea folk need more faith – more faith in themselves and above all things more faith in the results that follow pure motives and earnest work.

———◇———

One of the landmarks of the centre of Swansea is about to be moved. All the sportsmen who have been born and bred in the district, and all who have been in the habit for many years of visiting the neighbourhood for the purpose of sport, know the "Sporting Depot" in the narrowest part of Castle-Bailey-street. It has long since passed into the hands of B. Evans and Co., and has been conducted on the old established lines, but with newness of life and effect, by Mr. Crouch. With a view to facilitating matters for the commencement of the widening of the street, the Sports Depot, will in a week or two, be removed across the road to the shop long occupied by the late Mr. Moulding, the butcher, but for some years past rented by Mr. Margetts, as a seaman's outfitting shop. Mr. B. Evans finding that Mrs Margetts wished to retire from business, has taken the premises and stock off her hands, and is now offering the stock for sale on most advantageous terms, so as to clear out the place in readiness to receive the Sporting Depot business. It will be a comfort to all who have grown fond of the old associations of the town to learn that Mr. Evans will most piously remove the fine old figure of the Angler with his rod and a fish dangling therefrom to the opposite side as well as the business. Old sportsmen will therefore still recognise the old place by the old image, so lifelike and so suggestive, that has so long been indicated where all sorts of sporting requisites are to be procured.

———◇———

THE NEW CUT BRIDGE.

A Serious Stoppage of Traffic.

For the second time a serious disarrangement of traffic has been caused by a hitch in the working of the New Cut Bridge, leading to St. Thomas. Over this bridge is carried, perhaps more traffic than any other similar bridge in the entire district, and on Tuesday afternoon last, about one o' clock, at a time when the traffic, both pedestrian and vehicular, as is usual at this hour of the day, is the heaviest, the bridge was swung round for the purpose of allowing a vessel to pass up the Tawe. When, however, an attempt was made to shut the bridge again, it was found impossible to get into place, the result being that communication between the town and the eastern side of the water was cut off for almost an hour. During this time hundreds of vehicles and people innocently wended their way for the purpose of crossing over as usual, so that on either side a great block occurred. Ultimately, however, with the aid of a winch, and a chain which had been procured, the bridge was got into position again and a tremendous crush to get over ensued among the crowd on either side, while a considerable time elapsed before the vehicular traffic resumed its normal aspect. Men were employed to make a temporary hold fast for the chain to draw it back into position, next time it is opened, with as little delay as possible. The cause of the apparent breakdowns that have occurred of late is said to be the ineffective balance of the bridge.

Poetry.

ACROSTIC – " THE EDITOR."

Take a peep at the Editor's room,
where he's sitting.
(**H**is table piled up like St. Martin's-le-Grand).
Every courtesy showing, in manner befitting
Editorial magnate – he's patient and bland.
Do you ask his opinion? No matter what topic;
It may be Birds, Flowers, Sounds, Science, or Sight.
The range may be wide as the pole from the tropic,
Or differ as widely as Day does from Night,
Ready aid will he give – for his motto is * "Light."

Swansea. Rosabelle Joseph.

* Referring to a foot-note in a recent issue of *The Cambrian.*

———◇———

FOOTBALL AND GENERAL ATHLETIC NOTES.

By "Argus,"

(The Editor of *The Cambrian* has made arrangements to devote space in this column, recording the results of local football games during the forthcoming season, and will be glad to receive dates of fixtures and other information from secretaries of local clubs, to be addressed to "Argus," *Cambrian.*

To ensure insertion, scores of games and any other particulars must reach the *Cambrian* Office not later than Wednesday evening in each week.)

* * *

READ THIS YE FOOTBALLERS! PRIZES WHICH OUGHT TO BE FOUGHT FOR.

The Editor of *The Cambrian,* with the object of creating a spirited and healthy rivalry among the junior football clubs of Swansea and district offers prizes for the best club record, and for the largest number of tries and goals scored by an

Sole Agents
for Norton & White's
Silver and Electro-plated Novelties.

Heavy Silver
English Lever Watch,
£1 12 6.

Engagement Rings,
Wedding Rings and
Keepers a Speciality.

PRESENTATIONS
Special Terms Given.

105, Oxford St., Swansea.

(Bottom of Temple Street).

Businesses of the era.

F. C. Eddershaw & Son

Complete House Furnishers,
Cabinet Makers, Upholsterers,
Bedstead & Carpet Factors,
Removal Contractors,

OUR new Showrooms are very extensive, and the Stock has been selected with great care from the best markets in the various Departments.

National Telephone No. 94.

Telegrams: "Eddershaw. Swansea."

BEST POSSIBLE VALUE in...
Overmantels and Pier-Glasses,
Sideboards and Cabinets,
Bed-room
Drawing-room Suites.

Illustrated Catalogues and Estimates Free.

Cabinet Manufactory and Stores—ORCHARD STREET.

Nos. 19, 20 & 21, High Street, SWANSEA.

Swansea's oldest surviving business.

19th and 20th early century road transport.

individual player during the season 1892-3. The *club* entries must reach me on or before Tuesday, November 22, a coupon to be filled up and signed by the Captain, vice-Captain and Secretary.

FOOTBALL ON THE DOWN GRADE IN SWANSEA.

NEATH ROMP ROUND THE "ALL-WHITES."

A few seasons ago my football effusions were always about victory; they recorded the brilliant football exploits of the "All Whites;" How they fought and won battles which created surprise and admiration throughout the whole football world, and how they vanquished the renowned Blackheath combination, a feat which placed them on the top of the ladder. In these good old days, when sturdy Bill Bowen captained the team, Newport, Cardiff, Llanelly, Neath &c. were almost always knocked over, and in such a manner too, that astonished the supporters of the vanquished ones. Even up to last year, the "All Whites," kept well in front, Newport just succeeding in stealing the premiership from them. But now all that is changed, and unless a great effort is put forward by those in authority, it is very likely that the team will go from bad to worse. I do not for a moment pin my faith for this assertion upon last Saturday's game when the Neath boys gave us a thrashing, but upon certain information which has come to my knowledge during the past week. The cause of last week's defeat can hardly be explained away. First to over-indulgence on the part of the vanquished when in the Midlands; second the complete neglect of training during the week, and in under rating the strength of the Neath boys. Saturday's game may teach us a severe lesson. It ought to, and I hope players will benefit thereby. But apart from that there is disloyalty in the camp . . .

* * *

IS THIS TRUE?

I have had it from a somewhat reliable source this week that it is the intention of Mainwaring and R. G. Edwards to throw in their lot with Morriston. If this is really true, then the sooner they announce their determination to do this, the better, so that the Club may not find itself in an awkward position at the last moment. All I can say is, that these players would be adopting a very unwise procedure in acting thus, not only unwise but, meanly and shabbily. We should, no doubt, soon be able to find good substitutes, but at the same time chopping and changing is a very undesirable thing.

* * *

Since writing the above, I have ascertained that Dick Edwards and Mainwaring have decided to throw in their lot with Morriston . . . Teams are generally better off without players who take offence at the slightest thing. Edwards and Mainwaring are evidently annoyed because they have not been picked for the "Possibles" and " Probables" match tomorrow. They should remember that there are forwards their equals and superiors in Neath, Aberavon, Llanelly and Cardiff, not to say, Newport and Swansea, so how they can expect to get at the top of the ladder at once is more than I can understand. So far as Jere Edwards is concerned, we can well do without him. He will, of course, throw in his lot with his brother and Mainwaring. But there! Jere has never been consistent in his "love" for the teams he has joined.

* * *

Bancroft made a very poor show. If he does not look to his laurels at once, Billy will find that Tommy England, D.W. Evans, and Alun Morgan will be ahead of him. Bancroft should remember that a football player cannot live on his reputation; and, besides, he should recognise the importance of his position, and not trifle with it. I know that he was unwell, but then he ought not to have played.

Such exhibitions are bound to do him an incalculable amount of harm.

9th. March 1894.

Disaster at Sea. – The loss has been ascertained of the schooner H.E. of Llanelly, which left that port on February 2, coal laden for Faversham. She must have foundered off the coast, and her crew, six in number, were drowned. The body of the captain was washed ashore at Pendine, on Friday.

One Month for a Kiss. – George Youd, of Manchester, has paid dearly for a kiss. He met a girl on Ardwick-green and forcibly kissed her. He coolly told the Stipendiary that he was attracted to the girl by the way she was dressed; her hat, he said, especiaaly took his fancy. He was sent to gaol for a month.

ST. DAVID'S DAY IN LONDON.

On Thursday, March 1st. the Anniversary Dinner of The Most Honourable and Loyal Society of Antient Britons, took place at the Holborn Restaurant, under the Presidency of Stanley Leighton Esq., M.P., who was supported by many distinguished Welshmen and Welshwomen.

In proposing the toast of the Society, Mr. Stanley Leighton said that they were proud of their loyalty, and not unmindful of the prestige which their existence of 180 years conferred. They could look back on a lineal succession of benefactors, each generation renewing the liability of its predecessors, and they could look forward with confidence, because every year brought them new supporters. The cardinal idea of their Founders was to establish a Society, not for Wales but for the Welsh. Patriotism must not sink into Provincialism. Not only was Welsh Wales represented by their school, but Welsh England also. Where could they more appropriately meet than in the Capital of England and of Wales – in London. Their affection for the land of their Fathers did not evaporate in patriotic speeches, or in annual celebrations, or in trying to get others to do what they could and ought to do themselves. They were engaged in very practical work. Their school at Ashford had become the largest residential College for the Welsh in the world, and was indeed the only great school which was exclusively Welsh in its character. Their heart's desire was to place the children of the Welsh altogether on a level with the rest of the world, and to give them, in the competition of modern life, as good a chance as their English neighbours. The school was full – about a hundred and fifty girls in residence. Their Welsh children had done their Scholastic Home some credit, and they might be proud of the results. A large number of pupils had gained in the last year distinctions in public examinations. Miss Gertrude Thomas had gained a 1st. class at the Matriculation for the London University. They were gratified last year in having gained twenty-one, and of these six were Honour Certificates. Out of five Candidates who were placed equal for the first place in the 1st. class in the Junior Cambridge University Religious Examination, two were Ashford girls. For the South Kensington Science and Art Examination, ten Certificates for Mathematics and seven for drawing were awarded to Ashford. From Trinity College one senior and five juniors had obtained Certificates for Musical Proficiency; and their 46th Honour Certificate was for proficiency in Shorthand. Their School and their Scholars were well abreast of the times. They might fairly be thankful, but they knew not rest. He should like them to take another step forward. He should like them to be able to assist their promising pupils when they left Ashford, either to study languages abroad, or, if they had taken an Open Scholarship to avail themselves of the opportunity offered, by the Scholarship being supplemented out of Ashford funds. The zeal and admirable co-operation amongst the members of their Committee made him sanguine enough to believe that they would maintain the good name they had earned. He asked them to pay due honour to the toast of the Most Honourable and Loyal Society of Antient Britons and he hoped it would for ever remain in the future as it had been in the past – Honourable, and Loyal and Progressive. He coupled the toast with the name of the Treasurer, Thomas Wood Esq., of Gwernyfed, Breconshire.

During the evening, Welsh National Songs were sung by the Choir of the Welsh School, who were accompanied by their own excellent String Band. Miss M. Elaine Mills, a former pupil of the School sang several solos. The musical arrangements were under the direction of John Thomas, Esq., Pencerdd Gwalia, Harpist to the Queen.

THE LIGHTING OF THE SWANSEA PARISH CHURCH BY ELECTRICITY.

A SUSPECTED ADVERTISEMENT REMOVED AS SOON AS POSSIBLE.

On Sunday morning last, as the congregation of St. Mary's went into the Church, they saw with some surprise that electric lighting wires had been brought into the sacred edifice, and fixed in the great arched roof above the Nave. This only surprised a few, because there had been for sometime past talk of experimentally lighting the Church by electricity. What did surprise the congregation appears to have been three large glass globes, intending to include the arc lights, these globes bearing the legend "Studt and Son." The first sight of objects of this sort in the Church seems to have awakened the supposition that the Church was being taken advantage of for the purpose of a trade advertisement.

Consultation apears to have taken place in the vestry as soon as possible, and it was decided that these objectionable globes should be removed at once. This has since been done, we understand, and globes of a kind which cannot be suspected of the intent of advertising have been placed in position; so that on Sunday next the Parish Church will be lighted by electricity. In reply to enquiries we learn that this new departure arises out of an offer from Messrs Studt and Son, the well known purveyors of children's games and exercises in this part of the country, who have previously done the same kind of thing in Pembrokeshire, with the result, so it is said of substantially increased collections for Church causes. We are told that St. Mary's Church is to be illuminated by the electric light during the next four Sunday evenings. We understand that Messrs. Studt and Son have also offered to provide a fete and gala in the Victoria Park in June next with the object of raising a considerable sum of money for the benefit of Swansea Hospital. His Worship the Mayor will support this charity.

Mr. MELVILLE AND THE ACTRESS.

ALLEGED SERIOUS INJURY AT SWANSEA NEW THEATRE.

In the Queen's Bench Division of the High Court of Justice on Thursday, the case of Eden v. Melville came before Baron Pollock and a special jury. The plaintiff, Eva Eden, was described as an actress dancer and the defendant Andrew Melville as the proprietor of the New Theatre Swansea. The plaintiff's case was that in the month of February, 1893 she was engaged by Mr. Carles Goold to go on tour with the "Maid Marion" Provincial Company. Goold agreed with the defendant for the use of the new theatre at Swansea for the week ending February 11, 1893. One of the provisions between Goold and the defendant was that the defendant was to provide a stage, duly and properly arranged for the performance to be given by Mr. Goold's Company. The stage carpet was, however, so badly fixed that the plaintiff was thrown down, and was badly injured, besides receiving such bodily strain and such shock to her nervous system that she has not since been able to follow her profession. She claimed £750 damages. – The defence was a denial of the alleged terms of the agreement and a denial that the plaintiff had suffered the alleged injuries.

Defendant alleged that the effect of the agreement was to give Goold entire control control of the theatre and all the permanent staff, and it was Goold's duty to see that the stage was properly arranged. In the alternative defendant alleged that the accident to the plaintiff, if any, was not caused by the improper arrangement of the stage, but by the plaintiff's carelessness, and further that her illness was not due to an accident but to natural causes.

Mr. Lockwood Q.C., and Mr. Morton Smith appeared for the plaintiff, Mr. Darling, Q.C., and Mr. Pritchett for the defendant.

A member of Goold's Company, named Ida Butler, witnessed the accident, and saw that the carpet was loose and rumpled. The dance was a "Tarantella," a dance which was not necessarily a high kicking one. The stage was darkened when plaintiff came on.

Eva Eden, the plaintiff, who was brought in in an invalid chair, said she was 23 years of age and was engaged by Mr. Goold in the "Maid Marion" Company at £2 10s. a week, and travelling expenses and costume. She said she was dancing in the second act when she caught her foot in the carpet and fell. She resumed her dance as well as she could, and she continued to fill her part for eleven days, but on the 23rd of February she got so bad that she was obliged to give up. Mr. Darling: Is not the technical name for the dance you were engaged in high-kicking? – No, certainly not; I am not a high-kicker, (Laughter.) Mine was a skirt dance. – Mr. Darling: Oh, that is, a society dance. (Laughter.) – Yes; society took it from the stage. (Laughter.) – Mr. Lockwood: As it has taken many other things. (Laughter.)

Mr. Thomas William Nunn, surgeon, of London spoke to examining plaintiff on 23rd of Feb., and finding a swelling in the lower part of the body. He ordered her to at once cease dancing. He feared she would never again be able to follow her profession, but she might, under favourable conditions, be restored to fair health in the course of 18 months or two years. At this point the further hearing of the case was adjourned.

The hearing of the case was resumed on Friday, when Mr. Nunn the plaintiff's medical attendant was cross questioned by Mr. Darling as to the injuries from which the plaintiff suffered. Dr. Robert Boscall, a specialist for diseases of women, said he made an examination, using anaesthetics, and found that an operation was absolutely necessary. He performed the operation on 28th of October, assisted by Dr. Lakin. In his opinion, plaintiff's injuries were caused by the fall. In conclusion witness was asked as to his charges, and said they amounted to £179. – This concluded the plaintiff's evidence, and Mr. Darling proceeded to open the defendant's case. He said Mr. Melville was a gentleman of considerable experience in theatrical matters, and was in the habit of letting his theatres to travelling companies. He let his theatre at Swansea to Mr. Charles Goold for the week ending February 11th, 1893, and it was during that week the unfortunate accident took place, though he thought it would turn out that the accident did not occur on the 11th; but, however it occurred, there was no doubt the plaintiff suffered considerable pain, and must have the sympathy of everybody; but he hoped the jury would not allow their sympathy to work an injustice to the defendant, who really had nothing whatever to do with the management of the theatre during the week that it was let to Mr. Goold. – Mr. Andrew Melville, the defendant, gave evidence showing his agreement with Mr. Goold during in question. – Henry Chappell, defendant's resident manager at Swansea, attributed the accident to plaintiff trying to kick higher than she was able to reach with her toe. – Alfred Jones, defendants property man at the Swansea Theatre, held the same opinion as to the cause of the accident. – Mr. Clay, surgeon to the Orthopaedic Hospital, Birmingham, and Dr. Jossett, of the Cancer Hospital, London, were examined in support of the view that the condition of the plaintiff arose from natural causes, and were not attributable to the accident. – The Court then adjourned till Monday.

The action was resumed on Monday.

After some further medical evidence on behalf of the defendant, Richard Hopkins, scene shifter, was called, and said the dancing was of the high kicking order, and was, in his opinion somewhat reckless. (Laughter.) – His Lordship interposed with the remark that he was not aware a scene shifter constituted himself a *maitre de ballet.* (Laughter.) Thomas Tomlison, musical director at the Swansea Theatre, spoke to seeing the plaintiff dance. He thought she was rather clumsy, and appeared to be overtaxing her powers. – After further evidence Mr. Darling addressed the jury for the defence, contending that no negligence had been made out on the part of the defendant, and that the injuries from which the plaintiff suffered were not caused by the fall.

His Lordship summed up the case at great length, going into the details especially of the medical evidence, and the jury retired to consider their verdict. About a quarter to four o'clock, after an absence of two hours-and-a-half, the jury intimated that they were unable to agree, and were discharged.

A POLICE RETROSPECT OF SWANSEA IN 1893.

INTERESTING FACTS AND FIGURES.

The Head Constable of Swansea Captain Colquoun reports as follows for the year 1893:

To his Worship the Mayor and Watch Committee of the County Borough of Swansea.

Gentlemen I beg to lay before you my sixteenth annual report of Criminal Statistics for the year ending December 31st, 1893.

Police Establishment – The strength of the establishment remains the same as at the date of my last report, but during the year, one constable has been pensioned. The total cost of the establishment was £9509 9s. 9d.; of this sum tthe government will pay £4322 5s.6d. The total number of persons proceeded against was 4,390 being an increase of 153 compared with last year; the increase consisting chiefly of simple larceny, assault on police and cases under the Excise and Vagrancy Acts.

Indictable Offences, – There were 161 offences under this head, compared with 145 last year, being an increase of 16. For these offences 63 persons were arrested, 44 of whom were committed for trial at Assizes or Quarter Sessions, 2 bailed for further examination, 10 were discharged for want of evidence, 6 for want of prosecution, and one pending at the end of the year.

Offences Determined Summarily. – The number of persons proceeded against summarily was 2,211, in addition to 2,125, Poor Rate, Local Board of Health, bastardy summonses and cases under the Quasi-Criminal Proceedings which are excluded from this table. Of this number 597 were discharged, and 1,606 convicted; of the latter 210 were sentenced to various terms of imprisonment, 17 were sent to Reformatory School, 1,341 fined, and 18 were subjected to various other punishments.

Robberies Committed, – The total number of robberies which came to the knowledge of the police were 244, and the value stolen £340 2s. 2¾d. being a decrease of £152 12s. 1¾d. in value, and a decrease of 15 in number. The number of persons proceeded against for these robberies was 216, compared with 219 last year.

Drunkenness, – The number of persons proceeded against was 586, or a decrease of 14. There would have been a slight increase, but in consequence of instructions from the Home Secretary that, in the new Government Returns, when a person is charged with more than one offence the graver one only is to be entered against him. Such as drunk and assault on the police, the assault is recorded and not the drunkenness.

Sunday Drunkeness, – The number of persons proceeded against for Sunday drunkeness was 60 compared with 46 last year, an increase of 14.

Public and Beer-houses, – Proceedings were taken against the occupiers of 17 public and beerhouses, 8 of whom were convicted. Of the total number proceeded against, nine were charged with breaches of the Sunday Closing Act, two of whom were convicted.

Stone Throwing, – For this offence, which is a very prevalent one, 48 persons, principally youths, were proceeded against, 42 of whom were convicted, and in addition to this, cautions were sent by me to the parents of several boys who were too young to proceed against.

Brothels, – There are now five supported brothels, and 91 known prostitutes in the town.

Vagrancy, – Under this Act, 56 persons were arrested for begging, forty of whom were convicted; the figures for last year being 22 arrested and 14 convicted.

Adulteration; Food and Drugs Act, – During the year 300 samples were purchased by the Police under the provisions of this Act, and as will be seen by Table 5, proceedings were taken against 210 persons, 130 of whom were convicted.

Vagrants admitted to the Work-house, – The number of persons admitted to the Work-house by tickets issued by the Police was 2,937 against 2,329 last year, or an increase of 608, which I attribute to depression of trade.

Superannuation Fund, – The amount in the Fund on the 31st March last was £6,459 3s.10d. Of this amount £6,206 11s.8d. is invested in Corporation Bonds and £162 12s. 7d. in the hands of the Borough Treasurer.

Fires, – The number of fires that occurred during the past year was 57 against 39 last year, an increase of 19.

Lost Children, – Ninety-nine children were taken charge of and restored to their parents by the Police.

Inquests, – During the year 98 inquests were held in which inquiries were made by the police and verdicts returned as shown in table 11.

Prevention of Crimes Act, – Under the Prevention of Crimes Act, four persons have reported themselves to the police, one has been sent back to penal servitude, one has left the town, and two are still residing in the borough.

Defective Water-shoots, Pavements, Gratings, &c.— During the year, 197 defective water-shoots, pavements &c. have been reported by the police. In the case of water-shoots, notices were sent to the owners of the premises, and particulars of the pavements forwarded to the Borough Surveyor. Thirty-eight persons were cautioned by the police for having defective cellar gratings in front of their premises.

Waste of Water, – During the year, 51 cases of waste of water were reported by the police, and particulars of each case forwarded to the Borough Engineer.

Lamps, – The number of street lamps reported "out" by the police amounted to 1,732.

Insecure Premises, – During the year, 503 doors and 37 windows were found open by the police on night duty.

Dogs, – During the last nine months, ending December 31st., 100 dogs were taken possession of and detained by the police. Of this number, 23 were claimed by the owners within the required time, 13 were sold, and 69 destroyed. The sum of £5 1s.6d. was received in respect of their detention and sale, which has been paid over to the Borough Treasurer.

Inspection, – The Force was inspected by Capt Parry, one of H.M. Inspectors of Constabulary, on the 22nd. Septemer last.

I am, Gentlemen,
Your obedient servant,
I. Colquhoun, Chief Constable.

26th. June 1896.

Thoughts of Thinkers.

Good manners frequently conceal the absence of good nature, and ill manners frequently conceal the presence good nature.

Hast thou considered how the beginning of all thought worthy of the name is love; and the wise head never yet was, without first the generous heart? – *Carlyle.*

It is not what others think of you which signifies, but that which you think of yourself. It matters little whether the world regards you through rose-coloured glass, but much whether you look through rose-coloured glass at the world.

It is sweet on waking in the early morn to listen to the small bird singing on the tree. No sound of voice or flute is like to the bird's song; there is something in it distinct and separate from all other notes. The throat of a woman gives forth a more perfect music, and the organ is the glory of man's soul. The bird upon the tree utters the meaning of the wind – a voice of the grass and wild flower, words of the green leaf; they speak through that slender tone. Sweetness of dew and rifts of sunshine, the dark hawthorn touched with breadths of open bud, the odour of the air, the colour of the daffodil – all that is delicious and beloved of spring time are expressed in his song. Genius is nature, and his lay, like the sap in the bough from which he sings, rises without thought. Nor is it necessary that it should be a song; a few short notes in the sharp spring morning are sufficient to stir the heart. But yesterday the least of them all came to a bough by my window, and in his call I heard the sweet briar wind rushing over the young grass. – *Richard Jefferies.*

What is the good of carrying a million of people through the bowels of the earth, and at fifty miles an hour, if millions of working people are forced to live in dreary, bleak suburbs, miles and miles away from all the freshness of the country, and away miles and miles even from the life and intelligence of cities? What is the good of ships like moving towns, that cross the Atlantic in a week, and are as gorgeous within as palaces, if millions of our people find nothing but starvation at home? What is the use of electric lamps, and telegrams and telegraphs, newspapers by millions, letters by billions, if sempstresses stitching their fingers to the bone can hardly earn fourpence by making a shirt, and many a man and woman is glad of a shilling for twelve hours' work? And if we can make a shirt for a penny and a coat for sixpence, and bring bread from every market on the planet, what do we gain if they who make the coat and the shirt lead the lives of galley slaves, and eat their bread in tears and despair, disease and filth? – *Frederick Harrison.*

GOWER ECHOES.

AN ADVERTISING SCHEME – THE HEALTH BILL – THE FORTHCOMING JAPANESE BAZAAR.

See *The Cambrian* Visitor's List for Gower and Mumbles in another column. Complete and accurate. The necessary forms may be had on application to the office, 58, Wind-street, or to any of the Gower newsagents.

Mumbles' health sheet is quite clean. Not a single case of any epedemic disease; the death rate remarkably low; and some of the most eminent doctors declare that Mumbles is one of the best health resorts in the kingdom. According to the Registrar-General, Swansea is the healthiest town in Great Britain. Mumbles may claim the same distinction among the seaside health resorts.

Why is it that the natural attractions of Mumbles as a health resort are not more extensively advertised? Nothing succeeds like success; and it may truly be said that nothing succeeds like judicious advertising. It is absurd for any man to hide his light under a bushel; it is ruinous for any health resort to neglect to make its attractions known to the world. A few years ago an attempt was made to boom the Mumbles. Artistic photographs were prepared, well-written descriptions of the natural beauties printed, and the whole prettily framed and – put away in a storeroom, with the exception of a few, which were put up at some railway stations. Nothing further seems to have been done. This is to be regretted, for there can be no doubt that had the initiators of the scheme persisted in their efforts, Mumbles today would be much better off in more ways than one.

It is not too late in the day to again attempt advertising the Mumbles. The cost of it would be comparatively nominal. The only serious aspect of it would be the financial aspect. Advertising, however judicious it may be, is expensive; but this should not deter well-wishers of the place taking the matter in hand. We feel sure that if the hotel and lodging-house keepers were approached, and some feasible scheme laid before them, they would not hesitate to give the necessary support, financial and otherwise. The Langland Bay Hotel Company have done more than any one to circulate throughout the country Mumbles' claims as a health and pleasure resort; but their efforts have been somewhat hampered in that they have not received the cooperation and support of other hotel and lodging-house proprietors.

The present would be an opportune time for the initiation of an advertising scheme. The Swansea Bay Royal Regatta is shortly to be held, and already it is exciting the interest of all England. It is estimated that in addition to 70,000 to 80,000 day visitors to the town, the owners of the many yachts which will compete will be followed by numbers of wealthy friends. It is well known that where Royalty goes the smaller fry will follow in shoals. Accommodation will have to be provided for these people, many of whom will very probably stay in the district a few days, from Friday or Saturday to Monday, at least. Of course, Mumbles, and particularly Langland Bay, will be well patronised on the occasion. No better time, therefore, for booming the place could possibly be hoped for, and it would be to the interest of the residents to take advantage of it. What we suggest is that a meeting of a few of the leading hotel and lodging-house proprietors be at once canvassed to discuss ways and means.

The article in last week's *Cambrian* showing how the health of Swansea and Mumbles is often misrepresented in the Cardiff papers, seems to have aroused the ire of the *Mail.* It asks for proof of any single case of small-pox reported by it which had not previously appeared in an exaggerated form in the Swansea evening papers. Two blacks do not make a white; two wrongs do not make a right. Does the *Mail* remember publishing a half-column sensational article about scarlet fever at the Mumbles at the opening of the season? Does it know that that article, in its mis-representation of actual facts could not be beat by Baron Munchausen himself? It would take a column or more to particularise instances upon which the Cardiff Conservative organ has shown its enmity to this district. Take the Swansea Royal Regatta for instance. Although it is known that upwards of 20 to 30 yachts, including several of the leading craft of this island, will compete, the *Mail* on Tuesday sneeringly said:– "The Swansea Bay Regatta is getting on apace. Two yachts have already been secured."

On Sunday next the anniversary services of Paraclete Congregational Chapel, Newton, will take place, when the veteran pastor, Rev. J. C. Davies will officiate. Paraclete is not only one of the oldest places of worship in the district, but also one of the most interesting from an historical point of view. Mr. Davies has been in charge of the chapel for nearly 30 years, and although there are signs of physical enfeeblement, the rev. gentleman is almost as vivacious in the pulpit as he was ten years ago. He retains all his mental faculties. His sermons, if not quite so learned as they used to be, are more homely and effective, and suit the people of Newton admirably.

The ivy-clad and historical castle of Oystermouth will next month be transformed into a Japanese Bazaar.

It is admirably adapted for this purpose and the Church people of the parish are to be commended for their thoughtfulness and enterprise in choosing it. The object of the Bazaar is a most laudable one and should commend itself to all who desire to see the religious and educational work carried on as it ought to be. Arrangements on an expensive scale are being entered into; several local ladies have thrown their hearts into the work, determined to out-do each other in the scope and attractiveness of the various stalls. The Vicar and Curate are at the head of affairs, and have the cordial and active cooperation of the leading members of the church.

FLASHES FROM THE ASSIZE COURTS.

The Assizes are likely to last a full fortnight. The calendar is the filthiest on record – it blots and blurs the social life of our country to a shocking extent. In spite of the explanation of Mr. Justice Wright in his charge to the grand jury that the number of prisoners was increased by the Assizes taking over some of those who should have come up at the Quarter Sessions – excepting those on bail – the calendar is an ugly one. Glamorganshire is a great industrial county, comprising upwards of 700,000 inhabitants of every grade and nationality, among whom we must always expect to find men and women as brutish as the brutes. The strong arm of the law, however, should be brought to bear with the utmost vigour upon those miscreants who waylay defenceless women and innocent children., and who commit such moral atrocities as must send a thrill of pain and horror through the great majority of people. Cardiff, as usual, contributes a very large share of prisoners to the assizes. The calendar reveals the depravity of the Cardiff slums in a lurid light.

Mr. Justice Vaughan Williams, who presides over the Civil Court, is a Welshman, and is proud of the fact. He is painstaking, good humoured, and rapidly grasps the situation. It was Mr. Williams who investigated the affairs of the New Zealand Loan Company, by which he enhanced his reputation as an honest, fearless Judge. The interest he took in that company was in no ways extraordinary – it was quite characteristic of him. His lordship's zeal is disinterested and generous. He is one of the ablest judges on the bench. The only fault is to be found in his dilatoriness in preparing his judgments; but when given they are marked by splendid lucidity, closeness of reasoning, and terseness of language. Yet they are carelessly written on little scraps of paper, mostly the blank edges torn from newspapers.

When the first case was called on Tuesday, the well of the Crown Court was taken up by nearly forty barristers, among whom were several new and young-looking faces. Mr. Ernest Bowen Rowlands seemed to enjoy the compliments paid him upon his articles in the *Strand Magazine* on English Judges.

Justice Wright, who conducts the Criminal Court, is a kindly gentleman. His looks belie him. At first sight he gives the impression that he is querulous, pedantic, irritable, but quite the opposite is really the case. His Lordship is patience itself. He rarely loses his temper, although he has had occasion for it this week more than once, and while he is anxious that strict justice should be meted out, his interest in the welfare of the prisoners manifests itself at each turn of the cases. As one member of the Bar remarked on Wednesday, "The prisoners could not get a better defender than his Lordship."

The barristers seem to appreciate, to a very great extent, the natural attractions of Mumbles, and to have much faith in the health-giving properies of the air. Every evening dozens of them may be seen sauntering along the sands at Langland. For the time being they throw off their legal severity and intellectual poses, and join with much gusto in the little nothings that go to make our lives pleasant and light. For which, no doubt, they are better and happier men.

Mumbles was conspicuously represented upon the first jury empanelled at the Crown Court, Mr. R. I. Bevan, Mr. Stephen Davies, Mr. Beer, Mr. Colquhoun, and Mr. Burt were among the twelve "good men and true."

An interesting little incident was enacted on Tuesday. The actors were Mr. Justice Wright, Mr. Marchant Williams, the Hon. Stephen Coleridge, Mr. Vaughan Williams, son of Judge Vaughan Williams, and Mr. L. Stephens, son of Judge Stephens. A German sailor was charged with breaking and entering, and it was necessary to obtain the services of an interpreter. No interpreter was forthcoming, and the case was about to be adjourned until next day, when Mr. Marchant Williams, the Clerk of Arraigna pro. tem., asked if any gentleman in the Court could speak German. A flutter ran through the legal dove-cots; tell-tale eyes were cast towards Mr. L. Stephens, while Mr. Vaughan Williams was seen to make strenuous efforts to conceal himself behind the bulky form of a policeman. Mr. Stephens, upon being appealed to, blushingly admitted that he could speak German, and undertook to interpret. When he took the prisoner in hand, however, he found the task greater than he had expected, and the case was again stopped, and was about to be put off, when the Hon. Stephen Coleridge took his place at the table, and being acquainted with what was before the Court, told his Lordship that his friend, Mr. Vaughan Williams, was conversant with the German tongue. Mr. Williams then had to go through the ordeal of interpreting. This he did with some success. Mr. Stephens was somewhat surprised that he was displaced by his learned friend, especially as he had satisfactorily interpreted the prisoner's remarks. The incident was much enjoyed among the crowd of barristers present, especially Mr. Vaughan Williams.

On Tuesday afternoon, Justice Vaughan Williams announced that in all probability the Criminal Court would not sit on Saturday, for the public convenience. The convenience referred to was, of course, the visit of H.R.H. the Prince of Wales to Cardiff. This new arrangement, his Lordship explained, would not affect the sitting of the Nisi Prius Court. He proposed to sit on Saturday in any case. However, if it would be more convenient for some jurymen, who wished to be present at Cardiff, he would prefer that non jury cases should be taken.

FLOATING THE TAWE RIVER.

To the Editor of "The Cambrian."

Sir, As you remarked some time since, there have been various schemes for improving the entrances to the North and South Docks in Swansea, and to my mind the one the Harbour Trust is now obtaining powers for, is the weakest of them all.

A lot of money is to be spent in making a new entrance or lock at both docks, and that for the North Dock, is in order to be able to continue the traffic of the dock whilst the old cills are lowered some six feet.

The effect of this work would no doubt be a very great improvemnt to both docks, but sometimes one pays too dearly for one's whistle, and this seems to me one of those occasions, as the money spent must, of necessity, in a few years become so much money spent uselessly so soon as the river is floated, which will surely be done sooner or later.

Today, floating rivers is quite a common everyday affair. Engineers of the old school do not like it, because they do not grasp it, and do not see their way to work it.

The Manchester Canal has rivers running into it; Bristol is seeing about the Avon; Cardiff is talking of weiring the Taff for pleasure purposes; yet we in Swansea appear afraid to weir the Tawe, not half its size, and all because the late Mr. Abernethy many years ago said it was not possible.

Let us try and consider some of the so-called difficulties:–

Owners of property on the riverside would all be glad to have it done so that good-sized vessels could get alongside at any state of the tide; and, as the water would not be at any time higher than the highest spring tides, they would have no claims for flooding.

Silting up – What occurs above the present weir? Does not the river remain practically the same as before, except that the water is deeper? And if a weir of modern construction, with balanced sluices were built below the present South Dock entrance, with sufficient outlet for water without hindrance, either in the usual state or in flood time, would not the silt left in the dockised part of the river be all but nil, except in the dead waters outside any eddies? – and this could be readily lifted by a dredger.

Cost – Without going into any very serious calculation, one may assume that the lock at the side of the weir should not cost very much more than the new lock and lowering of the present cill at the North Dock, and the weir would not cost very much more than the new lock at the South Dock.

We have then to consider rights of Dry-dock owners and sewerage. The dry-docks in the river would require sluices to carry off the water when docking a vessel, and the sewers would have to be carried out below the entrance to the docks.

Now, the Corporation will be bound some day to carry the sewerage out to sea themselves. They would no doubt join with the Harbour Trust in making those outlets, and these would carry off the water from the dry-docks, and could carry also part of the water at flood time.

Floods – As soon as a freshet began, the lower sluices would be opened, and if the water rose, the balance sluices would come into action automatically before any damage would be done. The water could never rise very much, as the area over which the water could spread would extend from Morriston to Swansea in the River and over the three docks.

Scour of the dredged channel from the docks to the sea. – This would not be so materially affected as some have supposed. The water coming into the river from the sea at flood tide being salt, when it meets the fresh water, flows at the bottom, carries up some silt with it, and as the tide ebbs, the fresh water runs at the top over the salt water, until the tide has nearly approached the end of the ebb in the river. As the water in the sea gets lower than the bottom of the river – the scour really begins. This would be the same when the river was dockised, as the same amount of water would come out of the river as if not dockised, except the amount that would have got in by the flood tide, but this water, I say, has but little effect, if any, in scouring the river bottom of the dredged channel; and if the river were dockised, at low water time the sluices could be opened and a good scour very readily obtained, much more so than can be done now.

Before spending money on the dock entrances it is to be hoped that the Trustees will give their very best consideration to the floating of the river. – Yours truly J.R.Leaver.

Swansea, 23rd.June, 1896.

1st. April 1898.

SCIENTIFIC NOTES.

A New Antiseptic.

From Germany comes a new antiseptic called "protagol." It is a compound of silver and protein, for which the property is claimed that a 1 per cent solution of it will destroy the bacteria of anthrax and enteric fever.

Electricity and Animalcula.

The effect of electricity upon micro-organisms is remarkable. If a current of electricity pass across a bath in which a number of Paramecium aurelia (easily found in any stagnant pool) are swimmiong the micro-scope will detect the little organisms rushing towards the negative electrode. Other species prefer the positive electrode under like conditions. The result is particularly striking in the case of tadpoles. A mass of these will immediately form up into regular rows and point their heads towards the negative poles as long as a current of electricity flows through the vessel of water in which the tadpoles are swimming.

A Gun that Shoots Electricity.

One of America's latest inventions, or rumours of inventions, is a gun which shoots electricity. The inventor is Mr. John Hartman, who devised the carbon rocket, which has been used in the United States Army for sixteen years. He claims to have discovered "conditions by which the rays of a searchlight can be charged with electricity, the beam of light thus taking the place of an ordinary wire." The new gun has been tried upon rabbits, and the experiments, made with a current from a lamp of only 50 voltage, have resulted in several of these animals being killed at a distance of 50ft.

Colour-blindness in Japan and China.

The *Lancet* states that a surgeon in the United States Navy reports as the result of an examination in Japan the finding in that country, among 1,200 soldiers, some 1.58 per cent. who were red blind and 0.833 per cent, who were green blind; among three hundred and seventy-three boys, 1 per cent. were red blind, and among two hundred and seventy girls 0.4 per cent. Of five hundred and and ninety-six men in Kioto, 5.45 per cent. shewed defective colour sense. Dr. Fielde, of Swatow, China, examined 1,200 Chinese of both sexes, using Thompson's well known wool tests; among six hundred men were nineteen who were colour blind, but among six hundred women only one. It seems, therefore, that the percentage of colour blindness among Chinamen is about 3 per cent., and consequently does not vary greatly from that in Europeans. It was found, however, by Dr. Fielde that fully half the number who were tested mixed up blue and green, and according to this investigator, many of that race are quite blind to the perception of violet colours.

Singing Sands.

Still another theory is advanced – this time by a scientific writer in the *Boston Transcript* – in explanation of the singing sands, a phenonemon characterising certain shores and beaches. This theory is based upon results obtained by prolonged investigation on the spot, in all kinds of weather, and examination with a good microscope. This shewed that the particles of sand are nearly uniform in size, mostly quartz, every one exhibiting the sharp and hackled edges and the sub-concoidal fracture of the vitreous varieties, and as all the edges are extremely thin, it is assumed that the peculiar sound known as singing may be caused by the friction of myriads of corners and edges, and by the impinging of innumerable particles and the snapping and fracture of their frail, brittle edges when the sand is violently stirred. The fact, too, that when the sand is wet no sound comes forth is in accordance with the point made. viz., that when wet there is greater cohesiveness among the particles, just as between two wet sheets of glass: they are not free to move, tend to cling closer together when stepped upon rather than rebound, as when dry, and being surrounded with a cushion of water, they thus lose their elasticity.

TOWN AND PORT OF SWANSEA.

A PERTINENT SPEECH BY THE CHAIRMAN OF THE TRUST.

Mr. Griffith Thomas, Chairman of the Swansea Harbour Trust, addressed a gathering of the Cambrian Lodge of Odd-fellows on Monday evening, strongly advising the municipalisation of the tramways and gasworks, and saying it was better to buy at the price of today than the price of to-morrow. Continuing, he remarked that he would never be happy unless he saw Swansea on the main line. (Hear, hear.) At the present time the Great Western Railway Company were spending something like £40,000 in putting a place like Carmarthen on the main line, whereas if they would only put Swansea on the main line it would not only greatly benefit the town, but also the company to an extent which they could not expect from Carmarthen. He was certain that the day of Swansea was only dawning, and that in the immediate future they would have great works erected, which would develop the whole of the neighbourhood, but, on the other hand, what they had to guard against most were strikes of workmen. (Hear, hear.) There was a great movement in the Midlands to get their works removed to the sea board, and it behoved them to see that nothing was done to prevent such a movement, because to get up the rateable value of the town meant a reduction in the rates, and, therefore, they should do all they could to encourage people to come here.

"IS NONCONFORMITY AWAKENING?"

To The Editor of "The Cambrian."

Sir – I notice through an article in the last issue of the *Cambrian*, under the above title, that the Nonconformists of Swansea are alive to the falling off in the attendance at their churches, and the general decadence in the religious life of the period. Well, sir, I do not think this decadence is confined to the Nonconformist Churches. It prevails all round; but is less marked in the churches of the Establishment because they are supported by more attractive services and the prestige that surrounds and supports a national institution. The fact is that religion as taught has become a veiled hypocrisy – people no longer believe the absurd and monstrous assertions upon which it is based. Who now credits the story as told in the Bible of the creation of man; his residence in the garden of Eden; the temptation of the woman by the devil; man's subsequent "fall," and the curse that followed and enveloped the whole human race. And yet upon this the whole fabric of redemption – the "scheme of salvation" – is based. Who does not now know that man's first appearance on earth was that of a creature of the lowest organisation, but endowed with the attributes of progressive advancement? And who now credits the truth of that other "scheme of salvation," a universal flood, a few righteous persons being alone preserved, so as to renovate the whole human race? Can we conceive that the Great Creator would institute such a "scheme," and then suffer it to be absolutely abortive. Why, in the first place, there could not have been any universal flood, there is not the water to cause it, and the idea of the whole animal creation being preserved by the creatures going two and two into the ark, is simply ridiculous. Why, also, will the churches persist in making the Deity assert in the fourth commandment that the world was made in six days, and employ this false assertion as an argument for keeping the Sabbath day holy? And as regards the Great Founder of the Christian faith, the idea of the so-called "emaculate conception" is almost indecent, and then the account of Christ's resurrection in bodily form, eating and drinking as in the flesh, and then ascending through the clouds out of sight into the airless and inhospitable regions of space, is surely a great strain on the imagination, and affords no example or type of immortality as we understand it, and as described by Paul in that splendid chapter the 15th of Corinthians. Why will not the churches teach what common sense tells us, that the Bible is a collection of MSS. written at various times, and recording the ideas of the writers, some unequalled in their value and grandeur, others impregnated with the ignorance of the period and the imagination of their authors?

Now, the watch-word of Nonconformity is freedom from State control. Why, with one solitary section known as the Unitarian Church, do they not also assert freedom of thought? But in this respect they are, to a great extent, behind even the Established Church for within its orders there is the Broad Church struggling to be free. If Nonconformists seek for a revival, why not let it be a real one, on true, reasonable grounds? Why do they not copy Him they they call their Lord and Master? He taught no senseless creed. The prodigal son is received in his father's arms under no "scheme of salvation." The scheme of Christ is repentance and reform; of love and reverence and worship of Him He called His Father, and the Father of all; and to all he says "As ye would that men should do unto you do ye also unto them." If Nonconformists, and Churchmen, too, desire to prevent religion becoming simply an outward show, let them present it, not as a thing embodied in creeds and statements that affront the reason and shock the understanding, but as something that will inspire brighter and happier lives here, and prepare us for a higher existence hereafter. Your obedient servant, Free Thought.

Swansea, March 30th. 1898.

CONTEMPORARY CHAT.

It appears that in those towns where the proportion of the female population to be found in domestic service is largest infant mortality is smallest, says the *Hospital*. Thus in Brighton, Birkenhead and Bristol, where 13 per cent. of the female population over 10 years of age is so employed, the proportion of infant deaths is 153 per 1,000; while in such towns as Preston, Blackburn and Bradford, where servants are only in the proportion of 7 per cent. of the females over 10, the deaths of children rise to 193 per 1,000. The proportion of servants to the population of a town is a fair clue to the average circumstances of the inhabitants. To keep a servant implies a certain superfluity of means beyond that required for the maintenance of one's own family. Those who keep servants do not live in overcrowded nor, as a rule, insanitary localities; their children are well fed and well cared for. Occasional instances of servants being kept by those who cannot afford to do so, through vanity, are so few, proportionately, that the existence of them cannot be held to affect the rule.

Charles Dickens once wrote that he was frequently appealed to as an editor to insert some contributions on the score that he had been at school with the writer's brother-in-law, or even because he had lent his alpenstock to the writer's wife's nephew, or similar grounds. What he experienced as as an editor many of us experience in other walks, says the *Church Review*. For instance, a former Mayor of Scarborough was appealed to for assistance as follows:

A newspaper paragraph had described the Mayor as a Child of Fortune, and the writer begged for help as a child of Mrs. Fortune. An appeal has been issued this week to all persons of a certain name (let us say Jones) to help in rebuilding a Warwickshire church because many Joneses have lived in that parish. As far as we know this is an unworked vein of begging, and we make a present of it to all whom it may concern. Can we wonder that the poor have their peculiar appeals too? Clergy are appealed to for help to buy a ham for a funeral, for help towards a new boiler, and for help to get a watch out of pawn, for the man would lose his work if he did not know the time of morning. Even boards of guardians have their curiosities. The Scarborough Board, a short while since, received an application for relief for a couple who were living in their own freehold cottage. Relief was refused, but the couple had managed to get an order for half-a-crown's worth of groceries. A guardian inquired on what this had been expended, and found it had gone in sweets and tobacco. When upbraided with it the couple declared they wanted these additions to their comforts, and knew not how to get them save out of the ratepayers.

5th. October 1900.

The Cambrian.

FRIDAY, OCTOBER 5, 1900.

1115.

Swansea won a truly notable victory on Tuesday. Liberalism and Nonconformty achieved a triumph which is still the talk and wonder of the country. The mistake of 1895, when Sir John Llewellyn defeated Mr. R. D. Burnie by 441, has been rectified to the full. The fact that Swansea is a Liberal strong-hold has been demonstrated beyond all doubt; and it will remain so provided the Liberal Party be united and determined at the psychological moment.

Sir George Newnes has done Wales a great service – a service fraught with many and potent possibilities, not only in the Principality but to Swansea. He fought a good fight. He said or did nothing which can cause him even a passing regret. "Whatever the issue may be," he wrote in his election address, "I trust it will be faught without bitterness, without personalities, and only on political grounds." How well Sir George adhered to the high ground he selected for the fight may be ascertained among the Conservatives. Sir John Llewellyn needed no appeal for a fair and honourable campaign. He is a cultured and high-minded gentleman, who would scorn mean and petty subterfuges. The contest did not pass without some painful personalities, but for these neither Sir George nor Sir John was responsible. And now that the election in Swansea is over Liberals and Conservatives should put aside the political weapons of offence and defence, bitter animosities, unavoidable during a sharp fight, should be forgotten, and all sections of the community should join in promoting the good of the town as a whole.

A Liberal victory was confidently expected, but few dreamt of so decisive a swing of the pendulum. The Conservatives played a losing game from the start, and committed many tactical blunders. It is, however, neither dignified nor charitable to blame the Conservative agent. He did the best he could with the materials at his disposal. He was beset with many irritating difficulties, and he had to contend with the aftermath of the 1895 campaign. Mr. Crocker, the Liberal agent, deserves practical recognition of the work he has done, and we are glad that a testimonial to him has already been started. There are many reasons why Sir George Newnes scored so great a victory, but after all is said, we are confronted with one fact: Swansea is a Liberal stronghold. Sir George Newnes may be relied upon to keep it so. The *Western Mail* yesterday indulged in some fine sneers at the people of Swansea. We assure Sir George that the Swansea electors are neither worse nor better than the electors of other towns. This he will soon discover for himself. The public do not forget good service. They resent indifference in their material interests. So long as Sir George does his duty, so long will Swansea remain faithful to him.

ELECTION NOTES.

Mr. Winston Churchill must have found the attentions of some of the fair sex of Oldham as embarrassing as a certain Mr. Hobson found them some time ago. In his canvassing he has had occasion to visit factories and mills, and the factory lasses really had the audacity to throw glances and even kisses at the modest young man, until he is actually said to have blushed. And the grandson of a Duke, too! Such conduct!

Some of our Parliamentary candidates have hit upon somewhat original methods of canvassing during the election, but they must come far behind Judge John D. Holt, Democratic candidate for the Governership of West Virginia. The Judge is a versatile man, and all his talents he employs in his canvass. In the first place he is an excellent fiddler, and plays quadrilles, waltzes, reels and two-steps to the entire satisfaction of the young people in the country districts, where good fiddlers are scarce. Whenever Judge Holt therefore reaches a community on his canvassing tour, he is at once called upon to furnish the music for an impromptu ball.

But his talents do not end there. Judge Holt is, besides a good cook, and handy at all kinds of housework. When he goes to a house to canvass he takes care of the baby, and can soothe it even in its most tempestuous moments. At another place he is said to have made the best blackberry roll that ever was made in that part of the country. At still another place he peeled the potatoes while the housewife did the other necessary work, and again he swept the rooms while the lady of the house prepared the dinner. He has even been known to help in the family mending, and in a way that defied criticism from the envious and critical neighbours of the favoured housewife.

"NEVER WANT IT AGAIN."

A prison chaplain was once asked if his ministry were attended with success. "Not much," he replied, "I grieve to say. A short time ago I thought I had brought to a better state of mind a man who had attempted to murder a woman, and had been condemned to death. He showed great signs of contrition after the sentence was passed upon him, and I thought I could observe the dawning of grace in his soul. I gave him a Bible, and he was most assiduous in the study of it, frequently quoting passages from it which he said convinced him of the heinousness of his offence. The man gave altogether such promise of reformation that I exerted myself to the utmost, and obtained for him such a commutation of his sentence as would enable him to begin the world again, and, as I hoped, with a happier result. I called to inform him of my success. His gratitude knew no bounds; he said I was his preserver, his liberator. 'And here,' he added, as he grasped my hand, 'here is your Bible. I may as well return it to you, for I hope I shall never want it again.'"

MORRISTON.

'BUS FATALITY AT MORRISTON.

The Borough Coroner (Mr. J. Viner Leeder) held an inquest at the Police-station, Morriston, on Tuesday afternoon, touching the death of Gladys Violet Teague, aged two years, who was run over by one of the Swansea Tramway Company's 'buses on Monday afternoon, and was instantly killed. The Tramway Co. were represented by Mr. R. Lewis (Messrs Robinson, Smith and Lewis). Several witnesses were called, including the mother, a man named Edward Lloyd (who saw the accident), and the driver of the 'bus, James Lovering. They all exonerated the driver of the 'bus from blame. The little girl appears to have run out from an opening in a wall near the Cross at Morriston, where the road is extremely narrow, and at the time the 'bus was coming down the hill. Before the driver could pull up the child had fallen under the feet of the horses. The wheels did not pass over the body, but the child was kicked. The Coroner, in summing up, drew the attention of the mother to the danger of leaving little children play about the busy thoroughfare of the Cross. – A verdict of "Accidental death" was returned.

PORT TALBOT.

[By Our Own Correspondent.]

WEDDING.

Richards – Jones.

A pretty wedding took place on Wednesday, at St. Mary's, Aberavon, when Miss Olive Longdon Jones, daughter of Mr. Jones, Bryncaredig, Aberavon, was united to Mr. Richard T. Richards, of Porth. The officiating clergy were the Rev. H. Morris, curate, assisted by The Rev. J. S. Longdon cousin of the bride, and Rev. D. Mark. The bride who was given away by Mr. G. Longdon, (uncle), looked exceedingly well in a gown of ivory benagaline, trimmed with Brussells lace, chiffon, and orange blossom. She wore a tulle veil surmounted by a coronet of orange blossoms, and carried a choice bouquet. She was attended by four bridesmaids, the younger ones Miss Richards (sister of the bridegroom), and Miss Martin Jenkins, wearing empire gowns of Japanese silk, trimmed with lace and insertion, and large white drawn silk hats, with wreath of pink roses under brims. The elder bridesmaids, Miss G.Jones (sister of the bride), and Miss Griffiths of Cardiff, wore very pretty gowns of cream Japanese silk, trimmed with insertion, and coral pink chiffon sashes. Their large black picture hats were of velvet trimmed with sequin and plumes. Mr. Alfred Griffiths of Cardiif, was the best man. A reception given at the home of the bride, followed the ceremony, and later on, Mr. and Mrs. Richards left for London, *en route* for Paris, where the honeymoon will be spent. The bride's travelling dress was of Automobile cloth, trimmed with handsome lace and velvet, and hat to correspond. The entire *trousseaux* was supplied by Messrs. Ben Evans and Co. (Ltd.), Swansea.

THE BALL.

In honour of the event of the day a ball was given in the Public Hall, Aberavon, which was brilliantly decorated. There was a large company present, and dancing was kept up until a late hour.

LIST OF PRESENTS.

Bride to bridegroom, ruby and diamond pin and ring; bridegroom to bride, ruby and diamond ring; mother of bride, household linen, drawing and bed-room furniture, and cheque; mother and father of the bridegroom, dining-room furniture, gold links and studs, and cheque; Miss Jones, (sister of bride), standard lamp and shade and oil painting; Mr. and Mrs. George Longdon, silver tea and coffee service, set of Coalport china and cheque; the Rev. and Mrs. Griffiths, Cardiff, silver teaspoons and tongs; Mr. and Mrs. W. H. Jones, Porth, Coalport dessert service; Mr. and Mrs. J. P. Richards, Cardiff, pictures; Miss J. Langdon, case of table cutlery and brass bedstead; Messrs and Misses Griffiths, Cardiff, case of dessert knives and forks; Mrs and Miss Longdon, Clydach, carved spinning chair; Mr. R. C. Griffiths, Vice-Consul, Teneriffe, picture; Mr. Alfred Griffiths, Cardiff, case of silver salt cellars; Mr. and Mrs. T. L. Griffiths, Cardiff, reading stand and table; Mr. and Mrs. Phillips, Tonypandy, silver lamp; Rev. J. S. Longdon, Hirwain, two vols. of Kipling; Miss A. Longdon, Dresden centre piece; Mr. and Mrs. M. A. Jenkins, silver cake basket; Messrs. D. Jenkins and Sons, silver entree dish; children at Bronhaulog, silver cake knife; Miss Gerty Jenkins, silk cushion; Miss Aileen Jenkins, photos, and frame; Mrs. R. Thomas, Dafen, set of china, fire irons, and cheque.; Rev. D. L. and Mrs. Glanley, Ystradgynlais, case of silver salt cellars; Mr. and Mrs. F. C. Williams, Brierly Hill, siver sugar basket; Mr. and Mrs. W. M. Savours, Caerphilly, Drawing-room chair; Mr. and Mrs. Jackson, Swansea, Worcester vases; Miss Davis, Swansea, case of carvers; Miss Pentland, London, vol, Kipling; Mr. and Mrs. D. L. Griffiths, London, silver tea service and salver; Mrs. Young, Worcester and silver tea caddy; Mr. and Mrs. Oliver Adams, drawing room clock; Mr. and Mrs. J. E. Jones, Carlton and silver hot water jug; Mr. and Mrs. J. T. Jones, Porth, silver and cut glass jug; Mr. and Mrs. D. Jenkins, Porth, silver epergne; Dr. and Mrs. Treasure, Cardiff, silver flower pot; Miss Jenkins, Swansea, Worcester vase; Miss Cork, Swansea, Crown Derby china; Dr. and Mrs. Stevens, Cardiff, silver photo frame; Mr. and Mrs. Davies, Porth, silver breadfork; Mr. and Mrs. A.V. Williams, Cardiff, silver flower pot; Mr. and Mrs. T. M. Jones, silver serviette rings; Mr. and Mrs. W. D. Morgan, Pentre, Claret jug; Mr. and Mrs. Ben Lewis, Cardiff, butter dish; Mr. and Mrs. T. A. Burgess, silver afternoon spoons; Misses C. and E. Howells, silver hand mirror; Miss Edith Davies, clock; Dr. Boyd and Miss Davies, Cardiff, silver sugar basin and sifter; Miss E. John, butter dish; Mr. and Mrs. F. W. Page, silver sugar, cream sifter in case; Mr. and Mrs. E. Thomas, jam dish; Mr. and Mrs. J. R. Thomas, silver butter dish; Mr. and Mrs. M. Tennant, silver breakfast dish; Mr. C. Lovett, Cardiff, silver knife rests; Mrs. Painter, Monmouth, worked cushion and tea cosy; Mr. and Mrs. Perry, salt-cellars; Miss Jones, Coedparc, silver nut-crackers in case; Mr. and Mrs. Hayden, silver and glass fruit stand; the Misses Hayden, marmalade jar; Mr. and Mrs. R. Thomas, Cwmavon, silver and glass flower vases; Mr. and Misses Key, silver and horn knife rests; Mr. W. Lloyd, Africa, silver fruit spoon and grape cissors; Mr. T. G. Evans, America, Paraquay lace handkerchief; Mr. and Miss Williams, Porth, silver triple dish; Mr. and Mrs. D. E. Jones, pair Worcester vases; Miss Jeffereys, Briton Ferry, sugar basket; Mr. Hillier, silver photo frame; Mr. Davies, Cardiff, silver inkstand; Mr. Watkins, Cardiff, Worcester Biscuit Barrel; Mr. and Mrs. James, Porth, silver eggstand; Miss Connel, ivory covered prayer book; Messrs. Townsend and Richards, silver sugar and cream stand; the Misses Griffiths, silver and glass flower vases; Mr. D. Hugh, Porth, silver and cut-glass pickle stand; Mr. D. S. Smith, case of silver nut crackers; Mrs. and Miss Richards, Treherbert, claret jug; Dr. and Mrs. J. A. Jones, silver mounted crocodile purse; Mr. and Mrs. W. Thomas, Cwmavon, silver and glass sugar basin, Mr., Mrs. and Miss Davis, Porth, silver cake basket and knife; Mr. and Mrs. D. Blackie, Cardiff, silver sugar basket and sifter; Mr. W. Edwards, Cardiff, silver photo-frame; Rev. H. Morris, Bible; Rev. D. Mark, Lowell's poems; Mr. A. P. Jones, Aberdare, fish carvers in case; Mr. and Mrs. J. E. Griffiths, Worcester biscuit barrel; Mr. Crouch, Cardiff, silver and cut glass flower vases; Mr. G. B. Hill, antelope purse-bag; Mrs. Lander, jam dish; Mr. and Mrs. J. Key, panel photo frame; Mr. and Mrs. F. O. Card, Neath, Doulton, and silver butterdish; Mr. and Mrs. T.

Jenkins, sardine dish; Mr. and Mrs. Jacob, case of silver salt cellars; Mrs. Evans and Miss Phillips, salad bowl and servers; Mr. J. Davis, Pentre, case of fish knives and forks; Mr. and Mrs. D. G. Loveluck, ebony brush, comb and mirror in case; Miss A. G. Davies, silver knife rests; Mrs. Waite, silver butter knife; Mr. and Mrs. H. Jones, breadfork; Miss E. Walsh, pickle fork; Mrs. Morgan, London, Irish worked cushion cover; Mr. and Mrs. H. Walsh, pedestal; Miss Walsh, worked table centre, Messrs. Ben Evans and Co. Swansea, ebony cabinet; Mr. and Mrs. Lawson Jones, Cardiff, table centre; Mr. and Mrs. W. Williams, oak tray; Mr. J. H. Cound, silver butter dish; Messrs. E. and W. John, silver serviette rings; Mr. G. H. Burgess, Doulton vases; Mr. and Mrs. King, Cardiff, siver sugar tongs; Mr. and Mrs. J. John, case of silver salt cellars; Mrs. D. G. Thomas, jam and marmalade stand; Mr. H. J. Denner, Port Talbot, fruit dish; Mr. J. Jones, silver and porcelain tea tray; Mr. and Mrs. Llewellyn, Gorseinon, photo frames; Mr. and Mrs. Bond, silver and glass fruit stand; the Misses Burgess, Doulton flower pot; Miss Pugh, Clydach, fruit dish; Miss Kingdom, London, brass inkstand; Mr. Phillips, Cardiff, silver bread platter and sugar sifter; Mrs. Davies, Porth, breakfast cruet; Miss Wood, crystoleum; Mrs. T. Williams, fruit and butter dishes, sugar basin and cream jug; Mr. and Mrs. T. L. David, copper kettle; Miss A. Davies, Linen bed spread; Mr. and Mrs. J. M. Smith, salad bowl and servers; Mr. J. E. Thomas, Gong; Mrs. Curtis, Taibach, triple dish; Miss Lewis, set of jugs; Miss K. Lewis, hot water jug; Misses E. and H. Hooper, album; Mrs. M. Richards, case of fish carvers; Mr. J. M. Gibbs, silver toast rack, butter knife and dish; Mr. and Mrs. Thomas, silver butter dish; Mrs. J. E. May, case of perfume; Miss Adams, Port Talbot, double photo frame, Mrs Davis, quilt; Miss Davies, Wellfield, sofa rug; Mr. and Mrs. Lidyard, vases; Mr. Jeremiah, Porth, vases; Mrs. Richards, Hirwain, eggstand; Mr. and Mrs. T. Evans, Porth, silver jam dish; Mr. and Mrs. Matthews, Porth, epergne; Mr. and Mrs. Bevan, Porth, cheque; Rev. and Mrs. Roberts Barry, leather-work mirror; Dr. and Mrs. Ivor H. Davies, Porth, silver dinner gong; Mr. and Mrs. J. Olive, opal and silver ornaments; Miss M. Williams, work-basket; Dr. and Mrs. Pittard, table gong; Mr. T. Bevan, tea service.

28th. March 1902.

SWANSEA SOCIETY IN LONDON.

PROPOSED SOUTH WALIAN ORGANISATION.

The members of the Swansea Society met on Saturday last at the Haunch of Venison, Bell Yard, Fleet-street, for the purpose of discussing the proposed alteration in the name of the Society. The chair was taken by Mr. John J. Jacobs, treasurer; among those who supported him being Messrs. H. Morton Hedley, C. W. Bowles, W. W. Howell, Fred Morgan, A.W. Davies, Phil Evans, R. Lee, T. Lee, J. Walters, J. R. Long, Syd Jenkins, and others. Owing to slight indisposition Mr. T. Losson Thomas, the esteemed hon.sec., was unable to be present.

At an interval in the programme, the following resolution on the recommendation of the committee was submitted – "That the members of the Swansea Society (London) present at this meeting consent to the alteration of the title of their organisation to 'Glamorgan or South Walian Society.'"

The Chairman having read the resolution, said he thought it very desirable that the scope of the Society should be increased, but he was of the opinion that it would be best to enlarge it so as to include Glamorganshire. If they called it the "Glamorganshire" there would be no fear of its overlapping any other organisation. If, on the other hand, they called it the "South Walian" they might be the subject of serious adverse criticism. He then read a letter from Sir J. T. D. Llewellyn, who, while not being opposed to the alteration in the name, desired to remain neutral in the matter until he heard the opinions of the members.

Mr. Hedley proposed that the title of the Society be changed to "Glamorgan." He felt sure that if they took that step, they would never regret it. It was a bigger thing, but there could only be one result – ultimate success. If they remained the "Swansea Society" they would never have a permanent rendezvous, a building where they would be able to meet at any time of the day, and up to a certain time at night. Cardiff might be a little sore at first – (laughter) – but he was sure they soon come in and help to make it a great thing. He would like to propose that the alteration be made forthwith. (Loud applause.)

Mr. Fred Morgan seconded Mr. Hedley's resolution. Personally, he said, he was strongly in favour of the resolution, but he should like to hear, if possible, the opinion of everyone in the room on the subject.

Mr. Phil Evans supported the resolution. If the name was changed to "Glamorgan Society," he thought a good many Cardiff men would join, who would not care to join the "Swansea" Society. He believed there was a greater work before an organisation of that character. He had been told that 99 per cent. of the Welshmen who came to London managed to keep on top. He quite believed that, but they should take jolly good care that the other 1 per cent. did not go under. (Applause.)

Mr. A. W. Davies had been one of those who had at first thought that the Society should stick to its old name. Now, however, they had a large number of members and a good balance to hand, and he thought they were well advised in enlarging the Society to include Glamorganshire. He quite agreed with the previous speakers, that they would extend the Society and give it a wider scope as the "Glamorgan Society."

Mr. Bowledon asked whether the name "Glamorgan Society" would clash with any other organisation in London.

The Chairman replied that enquiries had been made, and they found that it would not clash in any way with another society.

The Chairman having suggested that that the Society be called the "Glamorganshire," the resolution was put in its amended form and carried unanimously, amid loud applause.

The Chairman then said he thought they had done the right thing, as they did not exist for amusement only, but to be a benefit to the Welshmen who came to reside in London. In his opinion all the necessary details might well be left in the hands of the Committee, and he would suggest that the co-operation of the mayors of Glamorgan be sought. The alteration would entail a lot of work, but he knew they would put their shoulder to the wheel. He thought they had to congratulate themselves on having formed such a useful Society. He then read a letter from Mr. Syd Webster containing the very excellent suggestion that certain districts of London be allotted to certain members, who would be responsible for the "whipping in" of all Welshmen in their respective districts. A letter was also read from Mr. Daniel Sugrae thanking the members of the Society for their vote of condolence passed at the previous meeting.

This part of the business having been concluded, Mr. Phil Evans proposed the following resolution: "That this meeting of the Swansea Society (London) strongly deplores the intention of the Housing of the Working Classes Committee of the Swansea County Council to erect dwelling-houses on Dyfatty Field, and respectfully request the Swansea County Council to maintain the resolution passed some years ago to convert Dyfatty Field into a recreation ground. Speaking to the resolution, Mr. Evans said his attention had been called to the action of the Housing Committee by a report he had seen that morning in the "Cambrian," He proceeded to give a history of the Dyfatty Field, and pleaded earnestly on behalf of the children in the neighbourhood, who, if this field were taken away from them, would be compelled to play in the streets. Since Mr. Thomas, of Lan, had become too old to champion the cause of open spaces, he said, no one seemed to care about it. A recreation ground in that part of the town was an absolute necessity, and he hoped if the Society passed the resolution, it would have some effect on the committee.

In seconding the resolution, the Chairman said, he thought the resolution gave practical evidence of the use of the Society.

On being put, the resolution was carried unanimously.

The Chairman next proposed that Mr. Hedley be elected as a member of the committee . . . Mr. Hedley was subsequently elected amid cheers, and the musical programme was continued.

Among those who contributed were Mr. Meurig James, R.A.M., who sang Lohr's "The Little Irish Songs" and an English song, "When dull care" in his excellent customary style, and responded to an encore with "Simon the Cellarer"; Mr. Cyril Davies, who, in splendid voice, gave "Nita Gitans," "The Sailor's Grave," and, as an encore, "The Honeysuckle and the Bee"; Mr. Ted Jenkins, who despite a severe cold, was heard to advantage in "True till Death"; Mr. Geo. Thomas, whose singing of Watson's "Samoa" and "The Toilers" was well received. Mr. W. H. Terril recited Leigh Hunt's "The Slave and the Lions" and " The Man with one Hair," and gave a humorous reading entitled "The Juggleton Scientific Club," his contribution coming in for a large share of the applause; Mr. Fred Morgan's recitation "Henry V's charge to his Soldiers" was also very well received; Mr. H. M. Hedley gave a laughable musical sketch, and Mr. Syd Jenkins sang a humorous song "Because I happened to be there." Mr. Will Kemp (Dan Leno, junior) gave "Will he" and "Bertie in love." Mr. Harry Young was responsible for a couple of good humorous songs, and Messrs Young and Livette gave a well executed banjo duet, "Maypole Polka." Mr. H. S. Jones (Ap Caeralaw) made a brilliant accompanist. The meeting terminated with the singing of "Hen Wlad fy Nhadau" and "God Save the King."

———◇———

A NEWSPAPER STORAGE AT HENDON.

The Trustees of the British Museum expect shortly to be provided with a depot for the storage of newspapers at Hendon, in respect of which a sum of £3,000 on account is set down in the estimates for the next ensuing financial year. Although negotiations have have been entered into for the gradual acquisition of the houses which now surround the British Museum on the north, west, and east sides, it is found that further and separate accommodation is needed to meet the influx of newspapers, amounting to an average of about 750 each weekday. The scheme contemplates the building of a storehouse at Hendon for a stock of the provincial, colonial, and other newspapers that are only occasionally required, and the establishment of a staff of messengers who will carry the bound voumes to and fro for readers at the Museum. It is stated that a site of six acres has been bought for the new buildings at the Hyde. – "Builder."

———◇———

ILLEGAL TRAWLINGS BY SWANSEA CAPTAINS.

IRISH BENCH IMPOSES HEAVY FINES.

At Dungarvan, County Waterford, Petty Sessions, Mr. J. Orr, R.M., presiding, Capt. Abbeys and Capt. Smith, skippers of the steam-trawlers Utopia and Vulture, of Swansea were prosecuted at the suit of the irish Department of Agriculture and Technical Instruction, for illegal trawling off the coast of Waterford on the 10th. ult. Mr. Tweedy, who conducted the prosecution, said the fine in cases of this kind had recently been increased from £10 to £100, and he mentioned that fact to show that Parliament had regarded the subject of illegal trawling off the Irish coast as a very serious matter for the offenders. In the absence of defendants, service of the summonses at Swansea on the owners of the trawlers Utopia and Vulture, was proved by Joseph Dunne of Dublin. – Capt. McAuley, of the Government ship Helga, employed cruising around the coast for the protection of the fishing industry, proved the offences. He detected the trawlers engaged in trawling illegally within the proscribed limits in Hallinacourty Bay, on the 10th ult. He boarded both vessels and seized their nets and fishing gear. Mr. Tweedy asked the Bench to have a substantial fine inflicted on the defendants. Mr. J. C. Curran, J.P., said he would be in favour of imposing the full penalty of £100 on each of the defendants, as this illegal trawling was most injurious to the fishing industry, on which so many Irish families were dependent. The court decided to inflict a penalty of £45 with £3 costs in each case; and that the nets and gear seized from the defendants be forfeited.

——◇——

"Would Old-age Pensions be Useless?" – The new edition of Mr. R. S. Rowntree's "Poverty: A Study of Town Life," is being published this week by Messrs Macmillan, and contains, among other fresh matter, and important chapter on "The Probable Effect of Old-age Pensions upon Poverty." Mr. Rowntree's conclusions on this subject will probably excite as much attention as did the more general aspects of his book when it appeared last November. By means of statistics drawn from an investigation of the economic conditions of many thousands of families, the author shows that poverty in general would only be relieved in an infinitesimal degree by the granting of universal pensions after, say, 65 years of age; and that it is upon the children, not the old folk, of the working classes that poverty falls most cruelly. This startling conclusion may be challenged; but, evidently, if established, it will seriously modify certain lines of social reform agitation.

——◇——

FASHION NOTES.

[By Messrs. Ben Evans and Co., Limited Swansea.]

We are not now-a-days so hopelessly dependent upon the fiat of our milliners, for it needs comparatively little experience, and only a reasonable amount of expense to enable us to evolve at home a smart piece of headgear. One can pick up really up-to-date shapes made of fanciful woven straw which need little trimming, and such garniture as as is necessary can be easily obtained, whether it be flowers, ribbons or feathers, ready to be lightly tacked to the hat or toque by a few frim stitches. There is a marked tendency in all departments of millinery to display a "cach-peigne" whether of velvet ribbon or lace. In the former instance the ribbon very often falls in long ends down the back. There is something rather unEnglish about this mode which will prevent it becoming universally popular we fancy, for it is given only to a few to wear such a style with complete success. It only requires a certain amount of originality for one to achieve a decided triumph in the world of millinery today, as in some of the greatest "salons" the somewhat exorbitant prices demanded are not for the value of the materials employed in the construction of the "creation" but because it evinces the perfection of good taste while exploiting the newest modes. Therefore, the girl possessed of clever fingers and observant eyes need never be otherwise than smartly hatted for quite a small outlay. It is always an easy matter for deft fingers with some faculty for millinery to produce a good replica of one of the spring model hats which greet and charm us on every side. There is a tendency to make our toilette from top to toe one harmony of colour, but there are some people who find a contrasting note necesary to the success of their "tout ensemble," while it undoubtedly strikes a chord of individuality which has a certain fascination all its own. The floral turban or marquise toques expressed in flowers or tinted foliage are expressly adapted to prove becoming to a petit lady, while the all-black picture hat of large dimensions is undoubtedly designed for the more stately damsels. A short, stout woman should never attempt one of these striking large hats, and the unwise who do so will only derive the poor satisfaction of knowing that they serve as an object lesson in the use and abuse of things. One of the prettiest fancies of the hour is a blouse composed of alternate strips of "chine" ribbon and insertion. The effect is extremely charming, and one of the advantages of this mode is that simplicity of style is necessary for its success, as any attempt at fussiness will detract rather than add to the elegance. In summer, we are told, some of the most fascinating gowns will be designed after this style, the ribbons being seamed in at the waist to give the desired slenderness, while the foot of the skirt consists of a deep, shaped, lace flounce. A toilette of this description requires, of course, a pretty under-dress, and therefore, owing to the difficulties of its construction in the graduating of the lace and ribbons and the consequent expense, the mode is certain to have a considerable amount of exclsiveness.

——◇——

HOSPITAL COLLECTIONS.

CARDIFF WANTS TO ADOPT SWANSEA'S SCHEME.

Cardiff, that is to say the authorities of the Cardiff Royal Infirmary, are contemplating adopting the scheme introduced in connection with the Swansea Hospital of a works' collection and to a representative of the "South Wales Daily News", the secretary (Mr. W. D. Hughes) has explained the Swansea scheme. He says that five or six years ago he took a course which has been eminently successful. At that time the contributions from works and collieries – that is to say, of the men engaged at the various works and collieries – were only about £450 a year. He thought he would try the effect of canvassing the works, and so he made a personal canvas of the works within about 15 miles, and induced the men of many to subscribe regularly on their pay days. He tried to get the men to subscribe through the works' offices, and some of the works now have a column in their pay sheets for the entry of such subscriptions as the men will voluntarily give. He continued the canvass for three years, and now this movement is on a firm basis, and the result may be gleaned from the fact that the income from this source has steadily grown from £450 to no less than £1,700 a year.

There are still some works which do not subscribe, but a fresh effort is to be made to get them into line. Mr. Hughes always finds that the workmen are quite willing to respond if they get someone to see to the collection and the despatch of the contributions. Sometimes, one of themselves undertakes the work, but generally it is the office, and there is an advantage in the office doing so, because although clerks or workmen may come and go, the office is a permanent institution. For use in small workshops is a specially-prepared card for recording subscriptions. As to the increased interest the adoption of these schemes has stimulated in the institution there can be no question. Any body of workmen contributing not less than £10 10s. annually may, while so contributing, nominate one of their body as a governor; any body of workmen contributing not less than £52 10s. annually may in addition, while so contributing, nominate one of their body as an ex officio member of the Board of Management, with the privileges of vice-president; while there is a privilige of recommending one indoor and six outdoor patients for every £4 subscribed. There are thus six representatives of the working men on the Board of Management and 30 governors. That the working men take full advantage of their representation is the best proof of the interest taken by them in the institution.

SWANSEA BOARD SCHOOLS

H.M. INSPECTOR'S REPORTS 1899-1900.

The following reports of H.M. Inspector were submitted at last week's meeting of the School Board:

ABERDYBERTHI-STREET SCHOOL.,

"The teaching, perhaps, is rather mechanical, and is not quite so thorough as might be desired. On the whole, however, the school is orderly and conducted in a conscietious and efficient manner. T. J. Huxworthy has obtained a 2nd Class Queen's Scholarship.

29th. January 1904.

"Thomas of Lan": 88th Birthday

"Many happy returns of the day." This is the familiar greeting that goes out from all Swansea and his wife today (Saturday) to Capt. William Thomas, of Lan, who was born on January 23rd. 1816. Though he has attained the ripe age of 88 years, the champion of open spaces in Swansea, still takes the keenest possible interest in the question of "open spaces," and any movement for adding to the number of Swansea parks or open spaces inevitably finds Mr. Thomas putting in a timely word in its favour. Thirty years ago it was that Mr. Thomas first took up what was destined to be his life's work, for on July 9, 1874, he delivered his first speech on the subject in the Swansea Council, and the older generations of Swansea know how from that time until he secured the St. Helen's Field (now Victoria Park), he spared neither, time, energy nor money in championing the cause, particularly on behalf of what he then characteristically described as "the gutter children." It was through Mr. Thomas of Lan, that the people of Landore and Morriston districts secured the gift of Llewellyn Park from the late Mr. J. D. Llewellyn, father of Sir John Llewellyn, consisting of 42 acres. This park was opened during Mr. Thomas's mayorality in 1878, and Victoria Park was secured and opened some ten years later, viz., June 1887. We may add that £150 raised by his friends – and they are legion, with the object of publicly recognising the efforts of Mr. Thomas of Lan, by placing a bust in some prominent place in Swansea, is now invested with the view of providing at some future time something more than a bust of the Welsh pioneer of open spaces. It is to be trusted that the old gentleman will be spared to see this recognition of his noble efforts promoted during his life time.

BRAKE COLLISION NEAR CLYDACH

Compensation Claim for £43

At the Swansea Court, on Tuesday, before Judge Gwilym Williams – Robert Hyman, Waunwen-road, Morriston, brought an action against Fred. Schumaker, haulier Llansamlet, to recover £43 6s. damages maintained by the plaintiff owing to the alleged negligence of the defendant. The claim was made up of depreciation in the value of a horse, charges of vetinary surgeon, and damage to a brake. Mr. I. M. Richards (instructed by Mr. Ed. Harris) appeared for the plaintiff, and Mr. D. Villiers Meager (instructed by Messrs. Andrews and Thompson) defended.

In opening, Mr. I. M. Richards said on Sept. 15, plaintiff, a coal haulier was driving a brake from Clydach Fair which was largely attended by Morriston people. It was between nine and ten at night, and on coming to Bwllfa, the plaintiff passed a brake driven by a man named Davie, back in the direction of Clydach. At the point he met Davies the road was 17 feet wide. Just after the defendant was seen driving the brake at a very rapid rate. Before the accident took place plaintiff had drawn up close to the side of the road, when defendant ran into him.

Thos. John Morgan, solicitor's clerk, Springfield-terrace, Morriston, said he was returning in plaintiff's brake. The animal was going slowly. Witness recounted how the defendant, who was driving 10 to 12 miles an hour, was shouted to before the accident occurred.

David Davies, brake proprietor, Llansamlet, spoke to passing the plaintiff's brake. Cross-examined, witness had passed plaintiff at the bend, and defendant was coming on after. Plaintiff's horse was struck in the breast. The value of the horse previously was £30, but it was not worth more than £10 now.

Other witnesses spoke as to the accident, and Mr. Stewart, vetinary surgeon, described the wound in the horse's breast, and the damage.

Defendant, who lives at 3, Bridge-street, Llansamlet, said he was going at the rate of about three miles an hour.

His Honour: You were going to get passengers at three miles an hour with competition besides. I am not one of the marines, you know.

Defendant said he shouted to to plaintiff and defendant pulled up on the side of the road when plaintiff's brake came into his. Defendant, in cross-examination, alleged that plaintiff deliberately drove into him.

After several witnesses had given evidence, Mr. Meager submitted there was no negligence.

His Honour found for the plaintiff, and awarded £31 15s. damages with costs.

MORRISTON MEMS.

The innovation was started at the monthly Communion service at Tabernacle Church, of playing and singing the "Dead March" should a member have passed away the previous month.

The funeral of young Harry Griffiths (22), the Morriston teacher and instrumentalist, which took place last Friday at Mynydd Bach Burial Ground, proved one of the most impressive ever seen at Morriston in recent times. It was in military style and the sight of the procession – 1st. G.A.V. Band and Police Band in front, followed by gunners of the 1st. G.A.V. and teachers with scholars from the school behind – was a most unusual one. The coffin, wrapped in a Union Jack, and covered with some beautiful floral tributes and the deceased's busby, was carried upon a gun-carriage. The burial scenes were very sorrowful, with the Welsh funeral hymns, funeral marche, and the Rev. W. Emlyn Jones' funeral prayer.

Who stole the magazine? is a query which most Morristonians would like decided, together with the punishment of the offender. It is not much of a library that Morriston has, and now someone or other takes advantage of the singular solitude which often enshrouds the room to whip off one of the most entertaining of the magazines – leather cover and all. Wanton mischief is evident here, and it is a great pity that the disgraceful deed cannot be brought home. As the Chairman of the Library's Committee stated, when the theft was related, it is a smirch upon the fair name of the town – as such an act hardly has a local precedent, and the action will be a stigma upon the young men who frequent the Library.

The Morriston Male Voice Party had a most encouraging attendance at their concert at the Hall on Thursday, the proceeds of which are to go towards the expenses of the visit to the Queen's Hall, London, in the middle of February to compete upon D. Jenkins "Son of God." By the rendering the party gave of the selection at the Hall – a magnificent one in every way – it will take a very fine party indeed to beat them. The party, led by Mr. W. Penfro Rowlands, also contributed successful items in the "The Destruction of Gaza," "Abide with me," and "On the Ramparts," they were admirably assisted by Misses Lizzie A. Jones and Rachel A. Davies, and Messrs, Willie Rees, T. J. Francis, W. E. Davies, Robert George and James Jones. Mr. T. D. Jones accompanying, with assistance fom Mr. Horace Samuel. Councillor David Matthews presided.

The endless battle of "Free Trade v. Protection" was fought out with much spirit at Libanus Guild last Thursday evening. Mr. Bertie Lewis, B.A. was chairman, and the champions of the respective sides were Mr. A. M. Squire for Free Trade, Dr. Chas. Kemp, M.A., for Protection. Both treated their subjects most thoroughly, and soon plunged into an overwhelming mass of statistics. It was becoming a most serious debate, when Mr. Trevor Williams stood up and treated the great topic in a bantering way. Mr. Chamberlain, he avowed, would never succeed as long as they were there. A telegram was then read from Mr. D. Brynmor Jones, in which, he regretted his inability to attend, was glad the cause of Free Trade was in good hands, and referred the members to the "all trade returns." Messrs. T. R. Williams, R. Buckland, and D. A. Jenkins afterwards stuck up for Free Trade, and Messrs, George Hughes and D. F. John for Protection. The figures had driven most of the audience home now, and after proposing a postponement of the debate, which proved futile, it was decided not to take a vote – just as well, too.

Several Swansea copper-ore men during the Civil War in America were numbered among the missing, and the last hope of the crew's sorrowing relatives was that the Alabama, being short of hands, had taken them, and they might return at the end of the war. But it was a wild and vain hope. Well, Mr. John Laird, grandfather of our future Swansea representative, Mr. C. W. Laird, was the builder of the famous Confederate commerce destroyer, and at an election at Birkenhead Mr. John Laird's opponent (Mr. Mather Jackson, afterwards a judge) thought to secure a bit from the fact. So at a large meeting of Mr. Jackson's held in Conway-street, the question was indignantly asked: "Who built the demon of the seas that preys on helpless merchantmen?" the speaker expecting the answer "Laird," with hisses, but to his surprise the whole meeting rose to their feet and roared out "We did: Laird did," and "Three times three for Laird," the same for Alabama and so on. The fact of the matter was, every man from designer down to rivet-boy, was proud, not ashamed of the bit he had done towards the terror of the Yankees, and every other public-house and mechanics cottage had a picture of her on the walls. The speaker did not seem to understand that Laird and Sons, turning out Alabama and blockade runners, meant bread and butter to his audience. Laird won hands down, like his descendant will at Swansea.

WATER DIVINER'S BILL,

Curious Case at Carmarthen.

At Carmarthen County Court on Thursday Mr. Hugh Stephens, Transmawr, sued Louis Evans, Pontycandy, Abernant, for three guineas for "locating water on Pontybigell Farm."

Plaintiff, who conducted his own case, said three guineas was his fee for advice – water or no water. After operating on the farm he asked Mr. Evans for his fee, and defendant said, "No water, no pay" – or words to that effect. He afterwards wrote to Mr. Evans, and he replied that he thought a sovereign liberal pay.

The Judge: If there was no water at all would you have the fee? Yes, it was simply for location. A doctor might give you advice as to your disease, and his advice might be absolutely wrong; but the doctor would have his fee just the same. (Loud Laughter.)

Mr. Louis Evans, defendant, said he told plaintiff about the trouble the tenant of the farm in question had as to water in the summer, and said he would pay him for his trouble if he found water there, adding that if no water was

Mackworth Arms Inn, Swansea

CAMBRIAN & GENERAL PICTON Coaches.

1818

GENERAL COACH OFFICE,
City Arms Hotel, Hereford.
NEW AND ELEGANT LIGHT POST-COACH,
From Hereford to Carmarthen,
Commenced on Wednesday, the 25th March, 1818.

1894

Varieties, &c.

1884

TRICKS OF THE TRADE.

MRS. BYKES: All the big gooseberries are at the top of this box, I suppose?

TOM CARTER: Oh, no, mum; some uv 'em are on top uv the other boxes.

The family tutor was invited to dinner, and surveyed with intense satisfaction the half-dozen wine-glasses arranged in front of his plate. The footman came round with the wine. The young man presented the smallest of the glasses.

"It is *vin ordinaire*," observed the waiter.

"Ah! precisely," replied our ascetic philosopher; "I am reserving the larger glasses for the finer sorts."

TOMMY: There's a girl at our school, mamma, they call Postscript. Can you guess why?

MAMMA: No, dear.

TOMMY: Because her name is Adaline Moore.

CONFUSION.

PATER (fuming): Don't look at me, sir, with—ah—in that tone of voice, sir!

FILIUS: I never uttered a——.

PATER (waxing): Then don't let me see—ah—another syllable, sir!

Grand Football Match.
SWANSEA CRICKET GROUND.
SATURDAY, MARCH 10TH, 1894.
SWANSEA 2nds
v.
BRIDGEND.
KICK OFF AT 3 O'CLOCK.
ADMISSION 3D. GRAND STAND 3D. EXTRA.

SWANSEA AND LIVERPOOL

1831

THE FIRST CLASS POWERFUL

Steam  Vessel.

TROUBADOUR,
JAMES BECKETT, COMMANDER.

1898

CHILD'S FROCK.

1824

MR. H. FAUNTLEROY.

1898

HAIR, HEAD, AND HAT.

A Soluble Soap Powder with which a powerful disinfectant and deodoriser has been incorporated.

Y-Z may be used in powder or solution. Sprinkle it about where a suspicious smell is detected-in lavatories, sickrooms, cesspools, sewers, &c.

Y-Z for disinfecting & washing bedclothes, bodylinen, bandages, &c. to guard against contagion.

Where Y-Z is used microbes die, and there is little chance of infection.

Y-Z combines a soap & germicide: it is no dearer than soap.

Y-Z to scrub floors, paintwork, linoleum, &c.- destroys vermin.

Y-Z in hospitals & public institutions: for disinfection.

Y-Z a soap, deodoriser, and disinfectant.

LEVERS Y-Z

1904

Lord Kelvin 1902

Cambrian images.

ALBERT HALL, SWANSEA

A

GRAND MORNING CONCERT,

ARRANGED BY

MADAME

ADELINA PATTI - NICOLINI,

ASSISTED BY

MISS GEORGINA GANZ, FRAULEIN KITTY BERGER,

SIGNOR NICOLINI,

SIGNOR BONETTI, SIGNOR TITO MATTEI,

HERR W. GANZ, & AUGUSTUS SPALDING, ESQ.,

WILL BE GIVEN ON

THURSDAY, OCTOBER 11TH, 1888,

AT 2.30 P.M.,

For the Benefit of the SWANSEA HOSPITAL and the POOR of the Neighbourhood of Craig-y-nos Castle.

RESERVED SEATS, 20s., 15s., 10s. & 5s.

TICKETS to be OBTAINED ONLY at Messrs. BRADER and SONS, Wind-street, Swansea. Special Railway Facilities will be Offered.

T. N. TALFOURD STRICK }
JOHN W. MORRIS } Hon. Secs.

Swansea, Sept. 1888. [4709

JOHN S. BROWN,

SOLE DISTRICT AGENT FOR ALL THE LARGEST CYCLE MANUFACTURERS IN THE UNITED KINGDOM.

LARGE STOCK OF GENTS' ROADSTERS & ROAD RACERS

Fitted with Pneumatic Tyres, from £8 10s. 0d. each.

Specially Selected Stock of Ladies' Cycles, from £10 10s. 0d.

Any Machine Supplied on the Deferred Payment System.

Singers, Premiers, Rapids, Raglans, Interchange-ables, Raleighs, Rudge-Whitworth, Roulettes, ETC.

Swifts, Humbers, Osmonds, Calcotts, Enfields, Wearwells, Hobarts, Peerless, ETC.

RIDING TAUGHT FREE TO PURCHASERS.

INTENDING CYCLE PURCHASERS WILL BE AMPLY REPAID BY VISITING MY CYCLE SHOWROOMS AND EXAMINING MACHINES IN STOCK.

Large Riding School open Daily, at Drill Hall, Singleton-street.

EXPERIENCED AND SKILFUL REPAIRERS KEPT, AND MACHINES PROMPTLY REPAIRED.

PRICE LISTS & ALL PARTICULARS FREE ON APPLICATION FROM

JOHN S. BROWN. OXFORD-ST., SWANSEA.

Ben. Evans'

GREAT DRAPERY AND FURNISHING WAREHOUSE.

100,000 FEET of FLOOR SPACE

AND

600 FEET of STREET FRONTAGE,

FOR THE

DISPLAY AND SALE

OF THE

NEWEST PRODUCTIONS

FOR

LADIES', GENTLEMEN'S & CHILDREN'S WEAR

AND

Complete House Furnishing.

The above illustration represents a portion only of the GREAT DRAPERY AND Furnishing Establishment of Ben Evans & Co., Ltd. } Swansea.

MOULE'S PATENT EARTH CLOSETS.

WHERE THE WATER SUPPLY IS UNCERTAIN, OR DRAINAGE DEFECTIVE,

MOULE'S PATENT EARTH CLOSETS ARE UNRIVALLED.

Where earth cannot be obtained, other dry, fine material may be used in them.

They are not only mechanically perfect, but the contents form a valuable manure. They are fitted either for Mansions, Cottages, Workshops, or Hospitals.

A PULL-UP-CLOSET.

PRICE LIST FORWARDED FREE BY

MOULE'S PATENT EARTH CLOSET CO., LTD.,

5a, GARRICK-ST., LONDON, W.C.

Mr. REGINALD DAVEY, Assoc. M. Inst. C.E., Engineer.

Contractors to the Admiralty, the War Office, etc.

Swansea Industrial Home for Orphan and Friendless Girls.

THE ANNUAL

Bazaar and Fancy Fair,

In aid of the Funds of this Institution, will be held in

THE ALBERT HALL, SWANSEA,

On THURSDAY, MARCH 29th, 1894.

LADY SWANSEA has kindly consented to Open the Bazaar at 3 o'clock.

Contributions, in money or kind, will be thankfully received by the Members of the Ladies' Committee; also by Miss Watkins, the Matron, at the Home.

THE Committee solicit the hearty co-operation of all classes of the community in augmenting the Funds of this Institution. The Home has been quite full during the past year, and a special appeal is now made for a larger amount of support of the ANNUAL BAZAAR than heretofore.

Mrs. CHAS. BATH,
Mrs. W. H. EMERY, } Hon. Secs.

Late 19th and early 20th century advertisements in 'The Cambrian'.

found there would be no payment. No stated sum was mentioned. Next day they met on the farm, and, after going through his wand performance, plaintiff indicated a spot where he said water would be found at a depth of fifteen feet. He afterwards altered the distance to sixteen feet, and at last said: "Well, anyhow, you will find it between fifteen and sixteen feet." A hole was dug at the place. Seven or eight feet feet of rain water accumulated in it. When the rain ceased the water was ladled out, and they dug down to a depth of twenty feet, but there was not a ghost of a sign of water. (Laughter.) The whole thing was as dry as the solicitor's table.

Judgment for the defendant.

Crushed to Death.

FAMOUS ANIMAL TRAINER KILLED BY AN ELEPHANT.

Mr. Geourge Lockhart, the famous trainer of elephants, was accidentally killed by one of his own animals at Walthamstow on Sunday. It was a singular illustration of the fact that elephants, even when kindly disposed are unaware of the power of their own weight and build. – a fact, of course, much relied upon in training them. Four of Mr. Lockhart's elephants had arrived at Hoe-street from Norwich, at about two o'clock and at a quarter to four Mr. Lockhart was superintending their removal from the cattle trucks in which they had travelled. Three of the elephants had made a deliberate exit from the train. The fourth elephant, a female, the largest, and at ordinary times the leader of the four, then stepped from the conveyance and seeing the exit of the goods yard made towards it. Plunging on she crushed her trainer between her bulky side and the wheel of the wagon. Mr. Lockhart fell broken and unconscious, and expired before anyone realised the tragedy.

Mr. Lockhart visited Swansea last in February 1903, fulfilling a week's engagement at the New Empire, under the Moss and Stoll management. His highly trained elephants were an appreciated item of the bill, and he was due to pay a return visit very shortly.

Messrs Vivian and Sons seem to be seriously concerned with the prospect of their tipping ground on the Neath-road being encroached upon by the G.W.R. Company, who purpose to bring their loop-line through it into Swansea. As is usual in these circumstances the company has scheduled considerably more land than it is likely to require, and as no other tipping ground is available to Messrs Vivian and Sons, the matter is serious. But may not a solution be found to these problems in the fact that probably all the slag tips in the neighbourhood – especially where easily accessible by rail – can be utilised in connection with the embankments etc., of the new dock?

By undertaking to remove the present tip, the G.W.R. Company might achieve three distinct purposes – (1) to cure the land required for the loop line; (2) increase instead of diminishing the tipping ground available to Messrs Vivian and Sons; and (3) supply the Harbour Trust with the ballasting necessary for the new dock.

There was quite a dramatic flavour about the special meeting of the Welsh University Court, convened at Shrewsbury, a week ago to consider the petition for improving the status of Swansea Technical College. Overnight it was understood that the Cardiff representative would offer strenuous opposition to the proposal that the Swansea Institution should be able to offer a complete course in science teaching to its students, and that practically the solid collegiate vote would be cast on the same side. Consequently the prospects for Swansea were seriously overcast. Evidence of the recognition of this might have been detected in the statement of Mr. Marchant Williams that the matter would not end with a refusal on the part of the court to concede the prayer for the Swansea Corporation were determined, if necessary, to appeal direct to the Privy Council. But the whole situation may be said to have changed with a most impressive appeal for a generous treatment of the Swansea College, made by Mr. Legard, H.M. Chief Inspector of Schools for Wales. He showed convincingly by the results obtained in the Midlands and elsewhere that no dissipation of energy or detrimental effect upon the the standard of higher education in Wales need be apprehended from adding to the number of constituent colleges by allowing Swansea to work out its manifest destiny in regard to Technical Education. After this the case for Swansea moved from one triumph to another, and in the result, even the opposition were glad to compromise on lines which allowed the Technical College all its needs, educationally, but deprived it of representation on the Senate and Court of the University.

14th. November 1914.

DR. T. D. GRIFFITHS

DISTINGUISHED SWANSEA SURGEON.

DIES AT BOURNEMOUTH: NOTABLE CAREER.

It is with great regret we record the death, which has taken place at Ferncombe, Bournemouth, where he went some time ago for the benefit of his health, of Dr. Thomas Druslwyn Griffiths, the distinguished Welsh surgeon, a past president of the British Medical Association, and who practised in Swansea practically all his life. For some considerable time he had been ailing, and eighteen months ago he gave up his practice. Some months ago he left with his wife, and an unmarried daughter, Miss Mabel Griffiths, for Bournemouth, where it was hoped he would derive great benefit from the change of air and surroundings.

The deceased gentleman, who was in his 76th. year, was a well known and popular figure in Swansea, the town of his adoption. His firm, erect and resolute figure, even after he had passed three score years and ten, coupled with a kindly disposition towards those who were brought in close contact with him, were traits of a distinctive character. He was throughout his life a great worker and it is admitted on all hands by his colleagues, that he was one of the greatest surgeons that Wales has ever produced. The profession which the late Dr. Griffiths so nobly adorned has suffered a great loss at his death, which, although coming as a shock, was not altogether unexpected by his closer and more intimate friends.

Biographical Sketch.

Dr. T. D. Griffiths, M.D. was born in Cardiganshire in 1837 and lived during his boyhood at Druslwyn, Carmarthenshire. He was educated at Carmarthen and at the Swansea Normal College. He served his medical apprenticeship under Dr. Michael, that man of many parts, whom was sometime Mayor of Swansea, and after forsaking the medical profession achieved further success as an advocate at the Bar. Under the influence of Dr. Michael's teaching Mr. Griffiths decided to adopt the medical profession and in due course proceeded to the University College and Hospital, London, where, in the course of an exceptionally brilliant career, he covered himself with honours. He took certificates of honour in many departments of his work, including the silver medal in medicine, pathological anatomy, and physiology and anatomy, the gold medal in comparative anatomy and natural history, the gold medal in botany, the Filliter exhibition in pathological anatomy, and the Atkinson-Morley scholarship of £40 per annum, tenable for three years. As a young man he displayed great talents. He was M.R.C.S. Eng. and U.S.A. In 1869, and three years later he graduated M.D., London, with honours in medicine, surgery and midwifery. In 1904 the University of Oxford conferred upon him the honorary D.Sc. degree. A breakdown in his health at the conclusion of five years' course of study in the numerous branches of the medical science in which he showed such proficiency, obliged Dr. Griffiths to leave London and he decided to setttle in Swansea In 1863 he was appointed to the positon of out-patients' physician at the Swansea General Hospital. But his

Zeal for the Work

in which he had achieved so much success was not to be confined within parochial limits. Dr. Griffiths soon became recognised as the foremost consulting medical practitioner in South Wales, where his surgical skill won him the well deserved admiration and confidence of all and life-long gratitude of a large circle of patients. The deceased gentleman did not often associate himself with municipal and political matters except in so far as his own private activities led him to do so. He, however, conferred a lasting benefit on the town by the assistance he gave in starting the Swansea Nursing Institute. He strongly advocated both by precept and practice the system of Lister and in other ways rendered valuable services to the nursing system of the town. To him also must be attributed the establishment of the Swansea Baths and Laundry, which involved a considerable financial outlay on the part of Dr. Griffiths. As a promoter and director of companies Dr. Griffiths did much to further the prosperity of the town, among his fosterlings being Weaver and Co's grain and flour industries. He was appointed a director of the Glamorgan Banking Company after his manful service in dealing with the difficulties arising in connection with the company in its earlier days. He was for years a director of the Swansea Gas Company.

With the management of the Swansea Hospital in his earlier days Dr. Griffiths was not exactly a favourite. He advocated reforms which were not appreciated by those responsible for the working of the institution, but happily a later generation has accepted many of the changes which he advocated.

British Medical Association President.

In 1903 the British Medical Association held its 71st. annual meetings at Swansea, and Dr. Griffiths was elected as the president.

On that occasion Dr. Griffiths delivered a notable presidential address, in the course of which he dealt with the question of the public health, and expressed the view that the application of modern knowledge to the improvemnet of the public health had not kept pace with the progress of medicine and surgery. While the rate of general mortality had decreased in the last 36 years, the mortality of children under one year had increased. This was largely due to preventible causes. Dr. Griffiths emphasised the point that even a moderate improvemnt in the sanitary law and administration would lead, at the lowest computation, to an annual saving of 60,000 lives. In the following year the Oxford University conferred the degree of Doctor of Science, Honoris Causa upon Dr. Griffiths. He was introduced to convocation by Professor Leve, who spoke in high praise of Dr. Griffiths' attainments. He had achieved great distinction as a physician. He was the author of numerous memoirs of great value, relating to medical subjects, and in Wales generally he was looked upon as a leader of the profession. Dr. Griffiths, in shaking hands with the Vice-Chancellor, was heartily cheered and warmly congratulated by his friends.

A Royal Visit Recalled.

On one occasion when the Prince and Princess of Wales (afterwards King Edward and Queen Alexandra) visited Swansea, Dr. Griffiths tried to persuade the Hospital Management Committee to invite their Royal guests to visit the institution. The committee rejected the proposal. However, the doctor persuaded their Royal Highnesses to pay the hospital an unofficial visit as they were returning from the opening of the Prince of Wales Dock, thus forcing the management of the hospital to accede to his request. On one occasion Dr. Griffiths offered a suite of salt baths to the hospital to cost £1,200 half the cost being promised him by friends, but the munincent offer was declined.

Dr. Griffiths was a devotee of healthy exercise and sport. When he was well on the way to his seventieth birthday it was noted that he cycled almost every morning before breakfast to Caswell or Langland to bathe in the sea, while in his younger days he was an experienced Alpine climber. Druslwyn, Dr. Griffiths' late residence at the foot of Mount Pleasant, called after the scene of his early life, was built in accordance with his ideas of health and usefulness, being thus another instance of his thorough going advocacy of the aims of his profession.

He was a learned contributor to the medical journals.

The Family.

The deceased gentleman's one son, Dr. Willie Griffiths became a prominent surgeon in Cape Town, but for some years now has been in practice at Uplands, Swansea. Of his three daughters one, Miss Gwennie Griffiths has acquired considerable note as an artist in London. Another daughter married Mr. Henry Bath. The deceased's widow was formerly a Miss Gabb, of Cheltenham.

The funeral took place on Monday at St. Stephen's Church, Bournemouth.

RADIUM FOR SWANSEA HOSPITAL.

The good fortune that attends the Swansea Hospital in virtue of the number and generosity of its supporters was again conspicuous on Wednesday, when an announcement was made indicating that most of the obstacles to the procuring of a supply of radium had been removed by the disinterested enterprise of Colonel Morgan, Dr. Elsworth, Messrs Brook and Aeron Thomas who offered to subscribe £400 towards the capital required for a company which, it is intended, shall purchase about £1,500 worth of the most precious substance. The institution is ultimately to donate the radium to the Hospital when the capital and a reasonable rate of interest have been recovered. Before the meeting of the Hospital Board had terminated, £800 had been promised towards this beneficent enterprise, which may result in the hospital becoming possessed absolutely of a sufficient quantity within ten years. The gentlemen named above and the others who so promptly supported them have laid under a heavy debt of gratitude the many people in Swansea who are stricken with diseases so painful and lingering that in comparison consumption is less to be dreaded. A cancer map published in the "Times" a few days ago revealed the curious fact that Cardiganshire in Wales and Huntingdon in England are to a wholly abnormal degree afflicted with cancer; large areas, including Glamorganshire in South Wales, are much less grievously affected. Though cancer still defies the skill and patience of the numerous devoted men who are searching for a cure, radium has proved of signal efficacy in its treatment, as well as in that of other malignant diseases, and it is no dim or little ray of hope that this marvellous, inexhaustible source of energy has cut into the gloom of a dark world of pain and despair. The pity is that the supply is still so pitifully scarce, the process of extraction so arduous, the quantities recovered so minute, and the quantities of pitch blend confined as yet in Cornwall and Bohemia. But fraction upon fraction of grain is being recovered by laborious effort, and humanity is steadily enriching its armoury of weapons against diseases that seem to be perturbingly upon the increase. At a Royal Institution lecture a few years ago a tiny quantity of radium was exhibited to the public. Seen against a dark background the energy it transmitted, which it has the power of pouring forth interminably without appreciable dimunition of substance appeared as a shower of luminous phosphorescent sparks scintillating in the blackness like shooting stars upon a clear, moonless light. At that time its medical uses had hardly been more than guessed at; since then their efficacy has been firmly established, and Madame Curie, the discoverer, a gifted Pole settled in Paris, has added her name to those of the very few women who have won lasting distinctionin scientiic research.

DIFFERENT MEN

SOME SPECIMENS OF LOUGHOR ENGLISH.

Wm. Edwards, who appeared at Swansea Crown Court on Saturday on a charge of using indecent language at Loughor denied it, and was discharged with a caution. But not before he had worked off some curious language. Speaking in a high-pitched voice of intensely dramatic tone, he questioned P.C. Lewis, who had given evidence, as to whether the latter had asked him if he wasn't "Bill Edwards." The officer denied doing so.

"Then it's another man who is in the box from him what saw me that evening!" declared defendant.

"Didn't you call me a ——, and 'shifle' me about?" continued the defendant.

The constable denied any "shiffling."

"Then I'm another man from what you spoke to that evening," avowed defendant.

He went on to describe the "shiffling." He admitted "my tongue went a little bit temper" but afterwards that the officer might have left the mark of his "fivers" (fingers) on his body. The Bench, as stated, gave him a chance.

"1812" at the Mumbles Pier.

Herr Simon Wurm's Hungarian Band still continues to attract at Mumbles Pier and on Thursday night a very large audience thoroughly enjoyed the splendid programme, which was mainly composed of descriptive pieces. On Friday evening all the items performed will be by special request of the many admirers of the band, and on Saturday evening the celebrated overture "1812" (Tschaikowsky) will be given, with fireworks effects.

At Pontardawe Council on Thursday, an appeal was received from Sir John Williams, Aberystwyth, for funds on behalf of the Welsh National Library. No action was taken.

CHEERS FOR " B.P."

What the Movement Really Means.

Over 500 people cheered Sir Robert Baden Powell and Lady Powell as they left the High-street Station Yard after arriving by the 12.48 train. At the Metropole the Scouts lined up in the foyer and saluted the general, who wore his several medals.

Sir Robert told a "Post" reporter that the movement was for the rising generation of all classes, and that they were particularly anxious to get the children of the poor.

"We give the boys," he said, "a certain amount of technical training, and we give them health and education too. We know no politics, no class, no creed. I want to see the movement on a sound financial basis, and that is why I am appealing for funds, because then we can extend, the usefulness of the movement."

MAYOR'S BLESSING FOR THE MOVEMENT.

Sir Robert Baden Powell emphasised at a meeting of business men at the Royal Institution, Swansea, on Monday afternoon, the aims and aspirations of the Boy Scout movement, dealing with four main objects:–

(1) The inculcation of character.
(2) Handicraft training.
(3) Health and physical development.
(4) Duty to one's neighbour.

Incidentally he mentioned as showing the importance of health point of view that he believed 50 per cent. of our enormous losses in the South African War was due to the fact of the men not knowing how to look after themselves. They had never been taught to look after themselves. Men would fall in many ways from preventible causes, and in many cases lives were lost from ignorance . . .

DISAPPOINTING.

SWANSEA'S SHIPPING RETURNS AT LOW-EBB.

Swansea, Monday, – The Easter holidays, in conjunction with the condition of the coal trade, which has shown no improvement, brought the trade of the port to last week to a very low figure, and compared with the corresponding week last year a decrease is shown of no less than 80,000 tons. The imports were about the average, and the shipment of tinplates very satisfactory. The coal and patent trades, however, were extremely inactive. The entries of shipping, which for some time were limited, now display improvement.

The shipments of coal and patent fuel amount to 54,440 tons.

Imports, foreign, include – Sweden, 150 tons general; Holland and Belgium, 600 tons iron pyrites, 320 tons scrap steel, and 2,450 tons general; France, 3,060 tons pit-wood; Algeria, 1.004 tons calamine; Chile, 537 tons copper ore, etc., etc., and 100 tons copper bars; Singapore, 45 tons block tin; Australia, 2,513 tons zinc concentrate.

Coal shipments – Sweden, 1,360 tons; Norway, 1,090 tons; Germany, 2,530 tons; France, 22,690 tons; Italy, 9,400 tons; Cuba, 2,500 tons; New York (bunkers), 1,600 tons; and home ports 9,090 tons. Patent fuel – France, 1,170 tons; Spain 880 tons; and Italy, 650 tons.

Imports, 19,709 tons; exports, 61,990 tons; and total trade, compared with 98,827 tons the preceeding week, and 161,895 tons the corresponding week last year.

Shipments of coal 51,740 tons; patent fuel, 2,700 tons; and tinplates and general goods 7,550 tons. The latter for – Norway, Denmark, Germany, Holland, Belgium, France, Spain, Texas (U.S.A.), Brazil and home ports.

Shipments of tinplate 148,562 boxes and receipts from the works 88,961 boxes. Stocks in the dock warehouses and vans 296,594 boxes compared with 356,195 boxes last week and 491,307 boxes at this date last year.

The following vessels are due to load cargo this week:– Resoy (Stavanger), Rainfos (Odde), Milo and Pluto (Amsterdam), Demetian (Marseilles, etc.), New Pioneer (Rouen), Cuba, Njaal, and Tagus, (Portugese ports), Veria and Fabian (Mediterranean ports), Hathor (Alexandria), and Yangstze (Chinese ports).

Vessels in dock on Saturday:–
Steam, 50; sail 42 – total 92.

THE "MAJESTIC,"

COMING TO SWANSEA.

FAMOUS LINER'S LAST VOYAGE.

The White Star liner Majestic, which is now lying at Southampton Dock, has been sold to Messrs. Thomas Ward, Ltd. for the sum of £25,000, and will be broken up at Swansea.

The Majestic is a twin-screwliner of 10,147 tons gross register, and was built for the White Star line in 1889 at Belfast by Messrs. Harland and Wolff.

Her hull dimensions are 565 ft. 8in. by 57ft. 8in by 39ft. 3in, and she is fitted with all modern appliances such as refrigerating machinery, electric light, submarine signalling, and wireless telegraphy.

For many years the Majestic sailed between Liverpool and New York, and in her day was

THE SWIFTEST LINER AFLOAT,

being capable of crossing the Atlantic on an average speed of 20 knots.

Lately she has been running in the Southampton and New York service of the White Star line, and during the Transvaal War was employed to convey troops to the Cape.

SUFFRAGETTES AGAIN.

PIER PAVILION GUTTED AT YARMOUTH.

The handsome pavilion on the Britannia Pier at Yarmouth was completely destroyed by fire on Friday morning. A night watchman discovered the flames in the new tea-room being erected at the rear of the pavilion and by the time he could give the alarm the pavilion, which was built four years ago at a cost of £9,000, was ablaze from one end to the other. How the outbreak occurred is not known, but the watchman states he heard a loud report like a gun prior to seeing the flames. A post-card was picked up the beach marked on one side, "Votes for women," and on the other side printed in capitals, "Kenna has nearly killed Pankhurst. We cannot show any mercy until women are enfranchised." This card was quite clean and bore no traces of fire or smoke.

A watchman who discovered the outbreak says there were no strangers on the pier at the time as he had a dog with him.

With the increasing conversion of the road surfaces from friable macadam to asphalte and wood and tar macadam, the task of street cleansing is being greatly facilitated, and increased attention can be diverted to other routes. Motor traffic possesses, for one of the "qualities of its defects," the reduction of the refuse that encumbered streets where horse traffic used to predominate, but it is to a much greater extent a disperser of dust with the draught of its progress, as well as a creator of it by the pulverising effect on road surfaces of the heavy motor lorry of from two tons of weight upwards. The very rapid extension of motor driven traffic in the district, through the formation of lines for passenger services, as well as the abolition of the horse driven traffic of the highways, opens up a serious problem for public authorities, not only in respect to the maintenance or reconstruction of roads that were never built to meet such strains, but in regard to public health.

To some extent the disease is providing its own remedy, or palliative, as the intolerable nature of the dust nuisance, as well as the breaking up of the roads, compel public bodies to lay down more durable road surfaces, but every dust cloud that whirls into the air like smoke behind one of these swift passing or cumbrous vehicles, with its millions of germs, is a reminder that the many-sided progress of science creates new dangers, besides abolishing old ones.

LEGION OF HONOUR.

STRIKING CEREMONY

SWANSEA'S FOUR NEW FREEMEN.

"SYMBOL OF PUBLIC AFFECTION."

IMPRESSIVE ADDRESSES

The honorary freedom of Swansea was, in the presence of a large and representative gathering assembled at the Albert Hall on Thursday afternoon last, conferred upon Sir J. T. Llewelyn, Bart, Mr. David Davies M.P., (Llandinam), Mr. Roger Beck, and Mr. John Dyer J.P., in recognition of benificent services rendered.

The scrolls setting forth the Council resolution conferring the honour, were contained in solid silver caskets of Celtic design.

The Mayor, having duly explained the object of the meeting, then made the presentations in a few, well chosen words, in which he wished the new freemen many years of happiness and prosperity . . .

SOME OF THE PRINCIPAL DRESSES.

Lady Llewellyn, who accompanied Sir John, was becomingly attired in a gown of black brocade and a coat of black satin with sables furs, and a toque of black with crown of white broche veiled in black tulle and finished with a white ostrich mount.

The Hon. Mrs. Odo Vivian wore a costume of biege cloth with Oriental silk facings and a white ostrich feather boa. Her hat was of black pedal straw upturned and had a crown of violet broche trimmed with a pink mount of wings.

The Hon. Elaine Jenkins came in a tailored costume of grey velour with white fox furs and a hat of grey pedal straw turned up at the side and trimmed with a blue bow and wreath of pink roses.

Mrs. Corker (Mayoress) was wearing a costume of blue with a collar of Oriental velvet and a becoming hat of rose Bengaline with a mount to match at the side finished with a posie of flowers.

Mrs. Llewellyn Williams chose an embroidered gown of rose with a long black velvet coat with a collar of skunk and a small hat of black moire turned up with an osprey at the side.

Mrs. Aeron Thomas was attired in a costume of grey charmeuse and a velvet hat to match adorned with an ostrich shaded feather of pink and grey.

Mrs. David Matthews was becomingly dressed in a costume of biscuit cloth with a brocaded velvet collar and necklett of ermine and a black velvet hat adorned with ermine and a pink rose.

Mrs. David Williams (Ex-Mayoress) chose a costume of grey cloth and a black hat with a swathe and mount of white merve ribbon.

Mrs. Fred Bradford wore a gown of black with touches of blue and a lace vest and a short wrap of biscuit cloth faced with Oriental silk. Her dome crown hat was of black tulle, banded with velvet, and finished with a La France rose and bow of velvet.

Mrs. Roper Wright was attired in a costume of black with rolled collar of sulphur moire and ermine furs. Her hat was of jet embroidered net with a smart feather mount.

Mrs. Charles Wright was dressed in a costume of pastel cloth with ermine furs and a small hat of straw moire with a half surround of pink feathers.

Miss Dingley wore a gown of green cashmere de soie and a mantle of black silk and a becoming bonnet of violets with cream crown and trimmed with an ostrich mount.

Mrs. P. Molyneux was smartly costumed in blue serge with an ermine necklett and a small blue hat trimmed with a swathe of rose ribbon and mercury wings.

Mrs. Lang Coath wore a belted costume of navy cloth with a collar of Oriental brocade and a small black satinhat with tam crown and a swathe of black tulle.

Mrs. Ben Jones was attired in a costume of black with a hat of black crinoline trimmed with a mount of black and white.

Mrs. Lee chose a costume of violet with a collar of pastel and a violet velvet hat with a swathe and mount of Oriental ribbon.

Mrs. G. Isaac was wearing a costume of violet with mole furs and a lime satin hat upturned at side and trimmed with floral ribbon.

Mrs. Waddington chose a costume of black bengaline and a small black satin hat with osprey mount of black and white and an ermine necklett.

Miss Corker came in a smart costume of tan frieze and a new sailor hat of rose colour with band and bow trimming.

"JOAN."

FROM FAR & NEAR.

Bishop's Boots.

"It is quite true that on one occasion I ate my boots," said the Bishop of Yukon (Dr. Stringer), speaking at Cardiff. He said that some people ridiculed his designation as "the bishop who ate his boots," but he was once making an episcopal tour in North America of about 5,000 miles, and when he was trying to cross the Rocky Mountains with a companion by a short cut to his home in Dawson City provisions ran out. Winter came on a fortnight earlier than usual, and they found themselves frozen in a remote part of the country. "Then the episcopal boots came in," said the bishop. "They were of sealskin and walrus hide and we boiled them, and toasted them to a certain turn. They gave us enough strength to reach an Indian encampment."

SWANS' EX-MANAGER

SUGGESTS HE IS "SCAPEGOAT."

PEEP BEHIND THE SCENES

Criticism of the Directors.

The announcement that the Swansea Town directors have decided not to retain the services of Mr. Walter Whittaker has caused much discussion throughout the town (writes "Ajax.") Although this has been confirmed by Mr. Whittaker himself, the directors have not yet made an official announcement, and Mr. Frank Newcombe has refused to say anything on the matter at all. Mr. Harry Behenna has announced his intention of resigning from the directorate as a protest against his colleagues' action, and I learn that Mr. Percy Molyneux and another director are also resigning. Mr. Molyneux, however, informed me on Monday morning that he is resigning entirely because he was unable in consequence of his private and public engagements to give that time he should like to give.

Bob Crone, the trainer, also has not been re-engaged, and I learn that the directors are going to advertise for a trainer-manager, whose sole business will be to have charge of the team. The negotiations for players will be left to Mr. Sam Williams, the secretary and the directors themselves. Except Brown and Bulcock no players had, at the time of writing, been fixed up for next season. Now that the list of the players the directors intend to re-engage has been published, it is not unlikely that there will be trouble in negotiating with them. If the terms asked, by the players are not satisfactory to the directors they will be allowed to go and vice versa, and I am informed that it is probable that some of the players not mentioned in the published list are likely to be re-engaged.

THE MANAGER VERY SORE.

Seen on Saturday morning, Mr. Whittaker was naturally very sore at the action of directors, and, in addition, he was very troubled by a serious illness of his wife, who is about to undergo a critical operation.

Asked about his intentions for the future, Mr. Whittaker said that he did not intend leaving the Queen's Hotel. "I have made many friends in town," he said. "and I shall be staying here for a while."

"How about managing another club?" he was asked.

"I can't exactly discuss that at the present," was the reply.

"What reasons have been given for the directors' decision?"

"They are

TRYING TO MAKE ME THE SCAPEGOAT

for not getting promotion, but they cannot do that. One director objects to me having two businesses, and another director has told me that he did not vote for my re-engagement because the terms they wished to impose would have made mine a 'dog's life.' Another reason given out is that there has been slackness. Yes, but whose fault is that? Why, the directors themselves. How do they expect the players to have confidence in themselves when the directors have no confidence in them? They have been chopping and changing the team about because there is no harmony among them, and they are continually

FALLING OUT AND QUIBBLING ONE WITH ANOTHER.

They cannot blame players; they have been true, faithful and loyal to the club."

In regard to criticisms of some players' conduct off the field, Mr. Whittaker observed:

"I say of the players as a whole that they will never have a finer, cleaner living lot connected with football."

With regard to the decision of the directors to engage certain players, Mr. Whittaker said that he could not express an opinion until an official list was published, because he was not present when they were selected.

"I can tell you candidly, however," he said "that they will

NEVER BE ABLE TO REPLACE

men like Duffy, Coleman, Swarbrick, Hamilton, and others – men who have stuck by the club and made it what it is today.

There have been rumours going round regarding the salary I have been reeiving from the Swansea Town Football Club," he added. "I cannot at the present time discuss what it is, but I intend to do so, and I am sure it will astonish many. It is just a mere acknowledgment of my services. I have it on excellent authority that several large shareholders of the club are going to resent this action in a manner which will surprise the directors."

THE OFFICIAL REASON.

I understand that the official reason given to Mr. Whittaker for not retaining him is that they intend adopting a new method of management. Although only four directors, outside those who have announced their intention of resigning, retire this season, there is a strong feeling amongst the supporters that the whole board should offer themselves for re-election.

Both Croydon and Luton have now completed their programmes (in the Second Division) . . . The league positions are as follows:–

	P.	W.	L.	D.	F.	A.	Pts.
Luton	30	24	3	3	92	22	51
Croydon	30	23	2	5	76	14	51
Brentford	29	19	6	4	75	17	42
Swansea	28	18	6	4	64	25	40

FIFTY MINISTERS.

IN "NONCON" PROTEST AGAINST CHURCH BILL.

A smashing blow has been dealt to the Welsh Church Bill. Over one hundred thousand Welsh Nonconformists have signed the Protest against Disendowment.

This is the resounding message which Welsh Nonconformists send to the House of Commons when it resumes consideration of the Bill on Monday.

The following shows the number of signatures secured:–

St. Asaph Diocese 15,321
Bangor Diocese 18,197
South Wales & Mon 69,706

103,224

The pretence that the demand for Disendowment was made by the united body of Welsh Nonconformity is now finally and formerly disposed of by the fact that over 100,000 signatures of Nonconformists, men and women over the age of 21, have been attached to the Nonconformist Protest.

It is significant of the true state of opinion among Welsh Nonconformity that in those districts where the "chapel screw" was not applied the promoters of the Protest found the people willing and anxious to sign it. They were constantly welcomed with the words: "Though we are Nonconformists we do not wish any harm to the church: we shrink from the crime of disendowment." Many deacons and other officials of Nonconformity had previously taken part in the Church Defence movement, and no fewer than 790 deacons have now signed the protest, besides 53 ministers or preachers, and 160 other office bearers:

THE SIGNATORIES.

The protest has been signed so far by 69,706 Nonconformists over 21 years of age, resident in South Wales and Monmouthshire, belonging to the following denominations:–

Baptists 20,919
Calvanistic Methodists 11,413
Congregationalists 19,603
Wesleyans 9,155
Other Denominations 6,846

In addition to these there are:–

Roman Catholic 1,661
Jews 100

LOCAL SIFTINGS.

Messrs. Beynon Bros. Bitton Farm Rhosily, sustained a severe loss last week, when their valuable gray mare, known throughout the peninsula as "Gower Princess." for which they recently refused an offer of 120 guineas, died in foaling. Last year she carried all before her taking upwards of a dozen first prizes, and at Gower Agricultural Show, first, special and cup. She was insured for a 100 guineas, and was entered for the coming Bath and West of England Show. The foal only lived a day . . .

1st. August 1924.

BIG MOTOR CONTRACT.

£40,000 Order Secured by Swansea Firm.

CHASSIS FOR 'BUSES.

The "Daily Post" is informed that Messrs Jeffery and Co., Ltd., the well known engineers, brass founders etc., of Wassail-square, Swansea, have placed an extensive order with W. and O. Du Cros, Ltd., for quite a number of chassis for saloon 'buses and charabancs, and commercial vehicles.

The contract runs into an expenditure of £40,000.

It is of interest to add, as showing the growing nature of the motor traffic in Swansea and West Wales, that since Easter the firm have already acquired no less than twenty chassis for commercial and other vehicles.

THE POST BAG.

Mentioned in dispatches: Rowe Harding, for the game he played out in Rhodesia.

We have two supreme riddles to answer – the riddle of Imperial cooperation and the riddle of manufacturing efficiency. Until Europe is settled down steadily and upon a comprehensible plan we can only approach the solution of the latter which is vital to the very earning of our bread and butter, as if groping with hesitation and bewilderment in a thick fog.

The Mother of Ten.

Problem of Preparing Them All for School.

Had a Penygroes mother carried out her intention on Monday very probably the interior of the Ammanford Police Court would have resembled a fully fledged nursery or schoolroom. Summoned for neglecting to send one of her children to school, she told the Bench that had it been a fine day the whole of her ten children would have been brought into court and placed in a seat facing him.

The chairman replied that he would have been very pleased to see them.

The mother added that the child in respect to whom she was summoned was the eldest of ten, and it meant no little labour to prepare the others for school.

The Chairman: You have our sympathy, but we cannot do more for you. Why don't you go down to Mr. Nicholas, who is a very nice and willing man? He might be able to get you an exemption.

The mother: I have tried to get an exemption, but the authorities won't listen to me. They seem to delight in bringing me down here and fining me when I cannot really afford to get boots for the children.

The defendant was let off on payment of the costs.

Another defendant, similarly summoned, was reported to have created a record so far as the Amman Valley is concerned. This was the twenty-third appearance on a similar charge. An order was made.

SWANSEA SNUBBED.

Deputation to Post-Master General On Removal Of Telephone Exchange.

MR. GRENFELL, M.P.'S, FIRM STAND.

The Swansea Parliamentary Committee at a special meeting on Saturday, met Mr. David Williams, M.P., and Mr. D. R. Grenfell, M.P., on the question of the transfer of the Telephone Exchange Offices from Swansea to Cardiff – a subject which has caused much soreness among business men.

After hearing statements from the two M.P.'s, the Committee decided to send a deputation to meet the Postmaster General, but Mr. Grenfell said that if a deputation was to be on the grounds that Swansea was not being treated with due consideration, he was not going to be on it.

Another motion was passed to take steps to defer the proposed removal of the Board of Trade Offices to Pier-street, and generally get first hand information of any departmental changes.

FEVER IN THE VALLEY.

The sanitary inspector of the Pontardawe Rural District Council reported at Thursday's meeting that during the last fortnight there were ten cases of scarlet fever and one of diphtheria, eight of which had been removed to the Isolation Hospital at Gellineudd. The report went on to state that the greater number of cases came from Ynisymond, Glais, which is in the Swansea area. The schools in Glais were closed owing to the epedemic.

Coun. Jenkins, Clydach, said that all epedemics of disease appeared to break out in the Glais area, and he put it down to lack of drainage, and this was supported by the clerk (Mr. Wyndham Lewis) and other members.

Mr. Edmunds, the sanitary inspector was asked to make further investigations.

"SPEEDING" AT NEATH.

David Henry Jones, of Treharris, was fined £5 5s. at Neath County Police Court on Friday for driving a heavy motor lorry at an excessive speed. P.C.White spoke to timing defendant over a measured stretch of road at Glyn-Neath on July 5th. His speed was 18 m.p.h., while the limit was 12 m.p.h. When spoken to defendant replied: "I am sure I was not going as fast as that."

"Why do not Mumbles and Gower appear in the daily weather reports of health resorts?" enquired a visitor to Swansea this week. And, why, indeed?

Few people are aware that just below Kilvrough, at the blacksmith's shop, is to be found one of the greatest authorities on the history of Gower. The advancing tide of modernism is touched even in Parkmill, and anvils, hammers, tongs and horseshoes have given way to petrol tins and spanners. But the charm of folk-lore and song still hangs about the place, and such as will can spend a very pleasant half hour with the blacksmith.

Sir Walford Davies, who has been invited to accept the vacant post of Gresham Professor of Music, would be a worthy successor to the late Sir Frederick Bridge, who held the appointment for over thirty years, and made the Gresham lectures more popular than they had ever been since Sir Thomas Gresham founded them in 1597. At one time the sure passport to a Gresham professorship was to be a member of the Gresham Committee. That was how a man named Griffin became Music Professor in 1763. He knew nothing of music, being a barber, but he kept the job for eight years.

Fifty Years To-day, July 26. 1874 –
The Last of an Old-fashioned Welsh Chapel, – Tynycoed Chapel, in the Swansea Valley, has stood the heat of fifty summers and the cold blast of fifty winters. It is one of the few remaining Welsh chapels and the reverse of comfortable to sit in. It was here that the Rev. James Williams officiated for thirty-nine years and after him the Rev. R. Lewis for fourteen years, and now the Rev. Lewis Jones is the minister. It is intended that the inside of the chapel shall be renewed, and one evening last week the wood and timber of the chapel were sold by auction, and keen was the competition to obtain a relic of "yr hen gapel". The alterations about to be carried out are greatly approved, although a few of the old members were very loth to move in the matter.

The Worm Turns.

Ammanford Council Answers Ratepayers Critics.

A protest against the interference of the Ammanford Ratepayers' Association was made by the Ammanford Council on Wednesday. One complaint was a request to know why the clerk had not replied to a letter protesting against an increase in salary.

The Clerk said he had not replied as he was the servant of the District Council and not of the Ratepayers' Association.

As one of the oldest members of the Council, Mr. Evans said it was fully conversant with with the needs of the place. Other complaints of the Association referred to the sewerage systems and certain improvements. These, said the chairman, had already been considered.

Mr. T. Lake said that since the electricity works had been taken over by the Council, a member of the Association had openly stated that councillors had been securing their light free of charge. They as members of the Council were repeatedly being approached by members of this Association regarding one thing or the other, and it was true that they were made to substantiate some of their statements.

It had so happened that his (Mr. Lake's) brother-in-law, who was the manager of the Electric Light works, had been staying with him, but he could produce a receipt for every quarter since electric light had been installed at this house.

Personally, he felt very strongly on the matter, and thought it unfair that these people should make such accusations. The sooner the better they were brought into line.

No further action was taken.

ELECTRICITY WORKS FUTURE.

The question of the Council scrapping the electricity works (recently acquired at a cost of £17,400) was raised by Mr. W. Evans, who suggested that they should go in for the supply in bulk from the Llanelly & District Electric Lighting Co. This was agreed to.

MOTOR FIRM SUED.

Titled Lady Sues for Recovery of £850.

A SWANSEA PURCHASE.

In the King's Bench Division on Tuesday, before Mr. Justice Swift, Lady Henrietta Yule, Hamsted House, Bricket Woods, Herts., was plaintiff in an action in which she sought to recover from Messrs R. E. Jones, Ltd., High-street Swansea, the sum of £850 alleged to have been paid by her through misrepresentation in connection with the sale of a D.F.P Coupe motor car. The defendants denied misrepresentation.

Mr. Thorne Drury, K.C., for plaintiff, said Lady Yule in 1920 desired to purchase a car for use in France, and went to the defendants' showrooms in Bond-street, where she saw a Mr. Pullen, who was in charge of the defendants' sales department.

She was shown a D.F.P Coupe car. She informed this gentleman that the car was for use in France, and asked if duty would have to be paid on it. Mr. Pullen assured her it would not.

SENT TO CANNES.

In these circumstances she eventually agreed to purchase the car, which was to be delivered at Cannes at Christmas 1920, at a price of £1,125.

It was eventually found that if this car had been introduced into France the duty would have been £418, which would so have increased the the price that the lady would not have bought it. Subsequently in August the defendants wrote stating that the chassis was ready and stating that the price was £850, which was considerably more than the agreed figure. This was paid however. There were then delays with regard to the body of the car.

Lady Yule was in America, and her husband, Sir David Yule, had gone to India.

DECLINED TO TAKE THE CAR.

Eventually the defendants wrote to Sir David's firm and, difficulties arising as to the question of duty for introduction into France, and a request for an additional 10 per cent on the chassis owing to the rise in prices, Lady Yule declined to take the car, and was seeking to recover the sum paid for the chassis.

Mr. Roy Bingley Pullen, former salesman with the defendant's firm stated that he had no recollection of any discussion with Lady Yule upon the question of duty. Had it been a condition of sale, it would have been entered in the order form.

Judgment was given for Lady Yule for the return of her money with costs.

Lorry Falls in Garden.

Narrow Escape of Driver and Children at Bynea.

A curious motor accident took place on Bynea Bridge on Monday afternoon.

Workmen had opened the road at a narrow point near the bridge, and about 4 o'clock in the afternoon, whilst a South Wales Transport 'bus (C.Y. 4216) was proceeding from Llanelly to Swansea, a lorry, laden with coal, belonging to Mr. F. Drury, of Loughor, was travelling in the opposite direction. To avoid a collision, the coal lorry drove to the right, and being unable to stop crashed through some railings and pitched down into a garden some considerable distance below the road.

Several local inhabitants rendered assistance and with the aid of ropes from the New Bynea Colliery, and a steam wagon which happened to be passing, the lorry was towed out, and was able to proceed under its own power.

It was remarkable that serious results were avoided, for, in addition to the drivers and passengers of the 'bus, there were a number of children at the spot, owing to the fact that the accident happened at school-leaving time.

HIS BETTER HALF.

Husband Who "Would Not Dare" To Get Drunk Often.

An Ammanford police officer found Stephen Phillips, Pengarn-road, Tycroes, with his arm around a wooden post and his head resting on his other arm at 11 o'clock at night. At the local court on Monday his wife appeared on his behalf to answer a charge of drunkeness.

Asked by the chairman of the Bench whether her husband usually got drunk, the wife replied: "No, he wouldn't dare to; I will see that he does not get drunk in future."

The Chairman: "Very well, but don't be too stringent with him." (Laughter.)

A small fine was imposed.

FUMES AT LLANSAMLET.

Ministry of Health Open an Enquiry at Swansea.

TOWN CLERK AND WORKS CLOSING.

The Government enquiry into the smoke fumes complaints at Llansamlet opened on Wednesday.

The Town Clerk summarised the complaints of the effect of the fumes upon people's health, the garden crops, and animals, but intimated that he did not know whether the Corporation would go to the length of closing down certain works, as he had been told would be the case if certain steps were taken.

"Rather beyond the limit," was the verdict of the Swansea M.O.H. on the fumes.

NUISANCE SINCE 1880

Effects on Inhabitants and on Horses and Crops.

. . . The nuisance was a very serious one and was so bad that the crops in the district were seriously affected, and in many instances garden produce withered.

It was further alleged that horses had been poisoned as a result of the deposit from the fumes, but cattle did not seem to be affected in the same way . . . Dr. Rees Lewis declared that respiratory diseases were excessive in the district, and this he put down to smoke.

The greatest offenders were the Swansea Vale Works.

Mr. Trevor Hunter asked Dr. Lewis whether it was his dream to turn Swansea Valley into an agricultural paradise once more or whether he recognised that it was now an industrial district and must remain so. No reply was given . . .

CASE FOR THE COMPANIES.

After evidence on behalf of farmers and allotment holders Mr. Trevor Hunter addressed the Inspector for the four companies he represented, and said that all the disadvantages arising from an industrial district were apparently laid at the door of spelter, which was such a precarious industry that if it had to buy its ore in the open market, it could not carry on.

In the four works he represented, 850 men were paid £140,000 a year in wages. The works consumed 100,000 tons of coal a year, and 45,000 tons of raw material. Thus the colliers, railwaymen and dockers were affected.

He submitted that no case had been made out against the industry, and that the agitation had been stirred up by people who had not long been resident in the district, and found its amenities were not so good as they might be.

The Town Clerk asked Mr. Cocks (Vivian's): "Have you anything to suggest as a remedy?" "None whatever." "If an order is made by the Government to abate the nuisance, would you have to close down?" Mr. Cocks: "Absolutely. I make that a definite statement."

The inquiry closed.

LORD OF THE MANOR.

The Borough Electrical Engineer's Purchase.

A £10,455 SALE.

The properties, farms and pasture land comprising Sir Lancelot Aubrey-Fletcher's freehold Llanmadoc estate, were offered for sale by Messrs. John M. Leeder at the Hotel Metropole on Tuesday, when twenty-three lots were sold for an aggregate sum of £10,455.

A freehold bungalow with out-buildings known as St. Madoc, situated close to the village of Llanmadoc, was sold to Mr. J. W. Burr, the Swansea Corporation electrical engineer for £1,400. The home has an extensive view of Broughton Bay and the Channel, and has pleasure and kitchen gardens extending to an area of over an acre. Mr. Burr also obtained in his purchase "The Manor or Lordship of the Parish of Llanmadoc," comprising a total of 1,514 acres, which include 190 acres of Lanmadoc Hill, together with the manorial rights, royalties, fines, and wastes appertaining thereto." He also purchased four freehold fields, totalling over 7 acres for £325.

Mrs Councillor H. D. Williams of Morriston, bought a freehold building site adjoining St. Madoc's Church for £40.

Cwm Ivy Marsh and Whiteford Burrows, comprising 656 acres, went to Mr. Shaw, stock broker, for £2,300.

A two-acre woodland adjoining Pill House was purchased by Mr. David Harry for £55.

Fir Tree Cottage went to the tenant, Mr. David Thomas for £300.

Hill House also went to the tenant, Mr. Robert Williams for £300.

Eight freehold enclosures on the road leading to Broughton Bay sold to the tenant, John Lewis for £900. Big House was sold for £1,350 to Mr. Thomas Taylor, Gower. There were only four lots withdrawn.

14th. March 1930.

SWANSEA TECHNICAL COLLEGE

Dispute With the Pharmaceutical Society.

The differences between the Swansea Education Authority and the Pharmaceutical Society are likely to come before Parliament.

It will be recalled that the Society attempted to dictate the amount of salary to be paid the head of the Pharmacy Department at the Swnsea Technical College, and the matter was reported to the Board of Education. A rather sharp letter followed to the Society, which then intimated that unless the salary suggested was paid the Society would withdraw its recognition for the Society's diploma.

The subject came up at Monday's meeting of the Swansea Education Committee in the form of the following recommendation of the Higher Education Sub-Committee:–

"The Director reported how matters now stand in respect of the Department of Pharmacy at the Swansea Technical College.

"Resolve (1) that the local members of Parliament be advised of the present situation and (2) that the Director of Education be authorised to give the necessary notice to the lecturers in pharmacy terminating their engagements at the end of the summer term 1930."

TO DOG OWNERS.

The Chief Constable of Swansea desires to inform dog owners that the police will shortly be making enquiries regarding unlicensed dogs. There has been a mistaken impression in the past that dog licences last for a year from the date on which they were taken out. They are only valid to December 31st. of each year.

£20,000 SPENT ON POWER STATION SITE.

Mr. T. Mainwaring Hughes Attack's Swansea Council's "Mad Finance"

LOSS OF £20,000 PER ANNUM ON ASYLUM HEATING.

FIGHTING SPEECH IN ST. HELEN'S

OPENING his election campaign in St. Helen's on Wednesday night, Mr. T. Mainwaring Hughes attacked the Corporation's "mad finance" and orgy of

spending, and decclared that practically £20,000 had been spent on the super power station site, which had been turned down.

Criticising the proposal to heat the asylum with electricity, Mr. Hughes said it would mean a loss to the town of £20,000.

"Mad finance" and Corporation spending was strongly attacked by Mr. Mainwaring Hughes, the Independent candidate in the St. Helen's Ward (Swansea) by-election, in a fighting speech at St. Gabriel's Hall on Wednesday evening.

There was a representative attendance. The chair was taken by Mr. W. Astley Samuel, who was supported by the candidate and Mr. Arthur Parkes, (manager Prince of Wales Dry Dock).

Opening, the chairman said it was time the town stirred and stopped "this mad spending of money" by the Corporation, and unless it was stopped he could see no outlook for the unemployed who were walking the streets. Ratepayers groused, but did not take the trouble to vote, and yet they would have to pay, pay, pay for the road schemes and the heavy cost of education.

SQUANDERMANIA.

In 1912-13 education cost about £4 per child; today it was £13. But were the children any better educated today than in 1913? ("No"). Moreover there were 111,000 less children in the country last year than in the year before. What were they building new schools for? He characterised it as squandermania. (Hear, hear.) . . .

Last month the council approved of an expenditure amounting to practically a million pounds. Some £280,000 it was proposed is for a superannuation scheme for the benefit of the municipal employees. That was a first instalment to level up the older employees, who were nearer the pensionable age. Then the Council propose to make a contribution equivalent to five per cent, on the wages bill. He did not object to superannuation and wished it could be general, but could the town afford it to a section of employees who were comparatively well paid and in sheltered occupations when the money had to be found at the expense of others, many of whom were not only unemployed, but had to struggle to make two ends meet? . . .

FINANCE GONE MAD

Then they had the "small item" of £580,000 passed in one afternoon with very little consideration by the Education Committee on a schools programme. Could they understand the mentality of men who passed expenditure like that? It was finance gone mad! (Hear, hear).

And they could hardly wonder thet this same Committee also passed an item of £800 for a hockey pitch and £600 for a tennis court "for the dears" who could not take the trouble to walk to the park and pay for their tennis the same as other players had to do. One wondered whether there was any limit to it?

ASYLUM HEATING.

Then there was the joint asylum, for which Swansea was paying its share and lending Merthyr the money to pay for theirs. Under that scheme the Electricity Committee proposed for some unaccountable reason to light and heat the Institution with electricity for ¼d. per unit that actually cost ¾d. to produce. That meant a loss of £20,000 per annum which should go to the reduction of the rates.

There was another side to it. The ¼d. per unit was at least four times more than the cost of central heating by ordinary coal. He had been twitted that he was biased because he was in the coal trade. Just so, and being in the coal trade he had access to the facts and knew something about heating values. Everywhere else heating by electricity had been condemned by heating engineers, but Swansea was to be the first to try it . . .

£20,000 ON SUPER STATION

Then in regard to the electricity power station site, when he told them that up to date practically £20,000 had been paid out they would be astonished.

And that was the fact, and of course the scheme had been turned down . . . and we have not finished paying for it yet. There are men in Swansea who have collected £6,000 from the Corporation for finding that site, and when I tell you further that the official who had the matter in hand made the arrangements, I understand, without a scrap of paper between himself and the people employed you think it is a matter for further investigation, won't you? (Hear, hear) . . .

HIS PROGRAMME:

"(1) That we absolutely refrain from any more non-essential schemes involving capital expenditure until the town is in a sounder financial state; (2) that we examine those schemes to which the town is already committed with a view of curtailing or abandoning them altogether, and (3) that an Axe Committee be appointed to thoroughly examine the spending departments of the Corporation to see what savings can possibly be effcted." . . .

Mr. Bert Evans proposed a vote of confidence in Mr. Hughes candidature and recalled the advent of the Municipal Reform Party in 1907 when it swept the town.

UP-TO-DATE SHOPS OF SWANSEA.

Appreciation of a Famous Actress.

THE LURE OF GOWERLAND.

"When my friends heard that my tour was to include Swansea, my friends sympathised with me, qualifying their remarks with, 'Frowsy sort of a place, you know; positively dirty,' but I have found it really a delightful city," said Miss Gwen Wyndham the vivacious little lady, who is playing the lead in the Walter Hackett comedy, "Sorry You've Been Troubled," at the Grand Theatre this week, in an interview on Monday evening.

"Every woman judges a town by its shops, and Swansea is indoubtedly one of the most up-to-date cities in this respect that I have visited she added. I am a particularly enthusiastic motorist, and I cannot help basing my opinion of a city on its traffic arrangements. Now, Swansea has the finest automatic signalling apparatus I have ever seen. Leeds has something like it, but not half as good.

"I have only one objection, and that is they are not easily seen in the nighttime. Imagine the difficulty of a stranger who comes to town knowing nothing of the arrangement. He is suddenly confronted by an automatic signal and forced to pull up very suddenly. However that is not much to cavil about. "I want to go out into your wonderful Gowerland. Everybody has told me about that. It must be really beautiful.

Miss Wyndham asked many questions about the mechanical arrangements of a modern newspaper office, and inquired if she might visit the new "Daily Post" offices in Worcester-place. "Everything mechanical interests me awfully," she said.

"When I am quite old and unable to play, I shall keep a garage and be nice and oily and wear old overalls and tinker with the works of motor cars."

Discussing her part, Miss Wyndham said that it was played much faster than in the West End. "Provincial audiences have a keener perception," she said.

A tap on the door and a very insistent, "Your call, madam," ended what had been a very pleasant conversation.

'POST'S' BIGGEST WAR SCOOP.

Stoker and the Battleship's Log Book.

STILL A MYSTERY.

To publish an account of the battle of Jutland extracted from the log book of – H.M.S. Irresponsible, shall we call her? – is a real scoop forsooth. Battleships' log books in wartime are not as a rule available by "open access," as Free Librarians say. Yet we did it.

One evening in June 1916, a stoker lurched into our offices about 6.30 in the evening, produced several grimy sheets written upon on both sides, and announced them as "a little account" of the battle he had jotted down." Right oh; leave them with me and I'll have a look at them," said the editor on duty.

Ten seconds after glancing at them the sub was thinking hard. "No stoker would write this; the style has official log book all over it – terse, staccato, and as replete with human interest and heart throbs as an ironmonger's catalogue. But it was unthinkable it could have been copied from any official narratives," he ruminated; and, with a few omissions – such as the reference to the cracking of the inner tube of a big gun, and details of the disabling havoc of an enemy projectile – the stoker's story was copied, sent up to the Naval Press Censor, returned, amended, and eventually published.

Then a human typhoon blew into the office one fine day a little later. He was not so much a breezy old salt as a hurricany old salt; and he was very salt indeed. "What did we mean by publishing extracts from the log book of H.M.S. Irresponsible? How did we get hold of it, etc." He was a morbid-minded old fellow, whose thoughts at the start ran on gruesome themes, like court martials and early rising to keep appointments with firing parties in the Tower and graves, and worms, and forgetfulness.

He was turned over to Mr. Davies. The latter, perfectly accomplished in the art of the soft answer that turneth away wrath, had the old sea-dog feeding out of his hand in a few minutes. Our defence was, complete innocence; the offence seemed unthinkable. And there was the Naval Censor's endorsement to boot.

So the Ancient Mariner went off presently to shoot albatrosses, or kick the cat, or otherwise vent his wrath.

Explosions later took place at Scapa Flow, we heard. Dim rumours floated out that the hapless stoker had had his pay, his liberty, and his grog stopped. But to this day we have never heard how the log book narrative got into his hands!

G.W.R. SCHEMES IN SOUTH WALES.

Government Approval of Company's Plans.

SPEEDING-UP IDEAS.

("Daily Post" Correspondent).

LONDON, Wednesday.

The Government has approved the Great Western Railway improvements scheme for South Wales docks, which are to be carried out at a cost of £3,000,000.

The schemes include the additional locks entrance to Swansea docks, extensions at Port Talbot, the improvement of trains, and the substitution of appliances for dealing with 20-ton wagons at Newport, Cardiff, Barry and Penarth.

It is understood that the Swansea scheme is to cost between £1,000,000 and £1,500,000.

The schemes will speed up the handling of general cargo at all the the Welsh and Bristol Channel ports, and will complete the docks equipment for dealing with the shipment of coal in 20-ton trucks.

SPEEDING UP.

The new lock entrance will expedite the entrance and exit of vessels at Swansea, which is now dependent upon one entrance, and it will enable vessels of larger tonnage to use Port Talbot Docks at all tides. It is not yet possible to ascertain the dates upon which the new schemes will commence, but probably a start will be made within the next two or three months. During the last nine years many improvement schemes have been carried out in the South Wales docks, and Swansea has had a good share of them. Among the most important were the installation of nine 5-ton hydraulic cranes at No. 4 Quay; 3-ton electric cranes opposite No 1. Emergency Shed, King's Dock; and three electric cranes at No. 1 Quay, King's Dock.

The G.W.R. has spent large sums of money in the adaptation of the South Wales Docks for the handling of general merchandise, and they provide the route between the Midland and overseas and the natural ports for an area with a population of 30 million people.

RECORD INTERNATIONAL CROWD.

G.W.R. Transport Over 30,000 People.

A record crowd of 30,000 people was brought into Swansea by the Great Western Railway Company for the international rugby match on Saturday last.

It is a very creditable performance to transport such a large number of people with every degree of comfort, and safety, and it is a matter for congratulation that the arrangements made by the company's local divisional superintendent. Mr. John Lea, worked so well.

The majority of the Irish supporters travelled by the G.W.R.'s route via Rosslare and Fishguard, between which ports an additional special steamer was run, and an express service consisting of four special trains, was arranged for the journey from Fishguard Harbour to Swansea and back.

Fast excursion trains were also run from London, Bristol, Gloucester, Pontypool, Pontypridd, Newport, Cardiff, Aberystwyth, Milford Haven, Pembroke Dock, Carmarthen, Llanelly, etc., at various times on Saturday morning, and were all well patronised, the influx of people into Swansea being the largest recorded.

OUR POST BAG.

Swansea Journalists' dream of their life is about to be realised. They are going to get room for everyhing that they would like to have put in, in the new "Daily Post and Leader". It will be like moving into a mansion after dwelling in furnished apartments

KIDNAPPED TO IRELAND!

Swansea Hosts on Lady Munster.

ROGER BECK TO THE RESCUE.

"Take me back to dear old Blighty!"

There are at least half a dozen Swansea men who will not readily forget the Ireland v. Wales match on Saturday.

They are members of the Swansea branch of the British Legion, but – no names, no pack drill. One thing is certain, that the adventure that befell them will live long in their memory.

The story is this. After an enjoyable smoking concert at the institute, and both teams and old comrades from the Irish branches (who were the principal guests as well as Welsh members) had been toasted in a proper army style, these six good soldiers went down to the Glasgow Wharf, at the South Dock, to bid their pals goodbye. They went on board the good ship Munster, and, during the wait to heave anchor a good sing-song was indulged in and this was followed by a severe shock, for, happening to look around, one of the six saw the boat had left the dock and was merrily sailing out past the piers. Naturally there followed a good deal of confusion and the position of the Swansea party was explained to the captain. Swansea was eventually communicated with and the tug, Roger Beck, was at once despatched to bring back the "troops" who had left their wives, mothers, sweethearts and sisters without a chance of saying good bye!

To get on board the Roger Beck was no easy task, but after much difficulty, the "troops" embarked and were landed safely back in Blighty without any casualties being reported, but, "Oh, what a night!"

SWANSEA FILM STAR.

Adolphe Menjou or Perhaps a Valentino.

Swansea has been nursing in its bosom a potential Adolphe Menjou, or perhaps a Valentino. He is Major Jack Rutherford, the son of Mr. Rutherford, the well-known Swansea docksman and member of the Chamber of Commerce. While at Hollywood he played many small parts, including a part with Pola Negri in "Hotel Imperial," and with Greta Garbo in "The Temptress." He was to have a leading part with Adolphe Menjou in "Paris," but his resemblance to the star made it impossible. He was therefore made an assistant director. Mr. Rutherford, who is now in England making several pictures, was educated at the Swansea Grammar School, and lived at the Mumbles.

PENLLEGAER HUNT'S GOOD RUNS.

Lady Follower Bogged at Tylydu Meet.

Penllergaer and Llandebie Hounds Hunt Club is still going strong, and there are many good runs recorded, but, unfortunately for local farmers, there have been no kills within the present month.

Foxes were reported to be plentiful and active in the neighbourhood of Tylydu, Penllergaer and Velindre, and there were three meetings recently and excellent sport. Three foxes were raised at these meetings, but were run to ground. One of the lady followers from Gower got into a bog at Tylydu meet. There were no other mishaps.

NEW "POST AND LEADER"

Majestic Hall of Giant Machines.

OUR NEW HOME.

High above the Strand in a great lofty, airy hall of yellow brick and glass, looking over the sun-bathed slopes of 'Kilvey', the long massive range of Weaver's buildings, and the waters of the North Dock, linotype machines are clacking and and clashing in the composing room of the office whence on Monday next the new "Daily Post and Leader" will issue to Swansea and South West Wales. In a few days the swift transferrance and reassembly of the mechanical equipment from the old "Daily Post" offices will be complete, and what is claimed to be the most spacious single composing room in South Wales will resound with the activity of rank upon rank of linotypes, filling the columns of a journal that will set a new standard of newspaper value for the town.

THE STERN BEAUTY OF MACHINERY.

Below in a hall of equal magnitude tower like small cathedrals the two superb new "Goss" machines, thrice a man's height, from which the "Daily

Post and Leader," will pour in torrents at the rate of scores of thousands of copies every hour. Alongside them a ridiculous "baby" of a printing machine, by comparison, is flicking off the contents bills at a faster rate than many an old time, full-size printing machine. These new printing presses will become one of the spectacles of Swansea, splendidly set off by the great hall in whose centre they rise, striking into the mind a Cyclopaen impression of solidity and bulk. Yet so perfectly controlled are they that a child's finger pressed on one or other of a row of pushes in a little control board that a handkerchief could cover, would stop them dead in the midst of their most furious career, turn them by inches, slow them gently down, or accelerate until in a roar and frenzy of labour the shining, oily seel cylinders, wheels and pinions revolve and whirl in fullest spate, reels of paper, thick as giant tree trunks, iron hard in their solidity melting away at one end, sheaves of papers pouring out at the other. The printing room of the "Daily Post and Leader" is going to make a fine subject for an artist – now that Art has discovered the beauty as well as the dignity of Labour; and MacAndrews hymn has chanted the saga of machinery.

"Lord Thou hast made this world beneath.
The shadow of a dream."

Upstairs are the rooms with brand new machines for moulding in a span of time measurable by seconds the curved leaden plates from the moulds, filled with liquid lead, that have been pressed from the pages of type; plates and pages passed in and out through a hatch like a serving hatch in a modern dining hall. Higher still are the spacious rooms dedicated to the delicate mysteries of the reproduction of the "Daily Post and Leader." Press photographers' work in metal blocks each made up, when you come to look at them closely, of myriads of tiny dots of metal, whose varying densities yield the contours and shadings that make up a picture.

Here, however, you will find the inconsolable man. He is deprived for ever and a day of the joy of deluging the room beneath with the spray of acid drops that used to radiate down upon the long suffering editorial staff of the old "Daily Post."

The editorial and sub editorial rooms are still to undergo renovations. Besides them, off a passage, lurks the Creed room whence the telegraphic news arrives on hundreds of yards of coils of paper.

A SUMPTUOUS OFFICE.

Behind the main entrance under the graceful tower in Worcester-place are the commercial, clerical and managerial rooms – another immense lofty apartment, sub-divided, coloured in soothing whites and creams and browns, where the soft light of the electric globes glows upon oak, mahogany, and rich carpeting – embellishments worthy of the dignity of the new paper that is to be given to Swansea. On the wall hangs a picture of Lord Northcliffe the creator of the modern British Press a latter day fashion that has no peer in the world.

DARKNESS AND LIGHT.

Romance of a grim and forbidding order clings to some parts of the new "Daily Post and Leader" offices. Girdled on one side by the beautiful delicate arches of the ancient castle, ivy greened, even with a plot of grass cresting the walls at a dizzy height, there are to be found below sombre vaults, low roofed and dim, stone walled a yard thick, with old, old doors, dry with age, studded with rusted iron bolts, and inset with tiny barred gridlings that a man's hand would cover.

There hangs about these vaults a dank, heavy smell of decay and depression. These were the old castle prisons; and, if the romance of grey stone wall and white archway and creeping ivy above appeals to the eye with its beauty and history, in these dark cold cells innured in dense stonework and thick iron grating, there is the terrible side of medieval life laid bare. Even as the Press has flooded with light the dark jungles of ignorance and superstition, in the mind, so now are these dungeons being penetrated with the wholesomeness of modern activities – marble electrical switchboards with green and red signal lamps, soft red copper wire and gleaming steel; racks of the latest and finest type for the most decorative and effective display of advertisements, stores and fresh white woodwork counters of the new publishing rooms. But a man who viewed the barred dungeons thought they could be turned even now to good account. His mind reverted to guilty eyed office boys, slinking furtively down passages "dodging the column." And the old phrase of the sergeant-major recurred to him (some say "Good old sergeant-major," others say, "Heaven bless him"); "I'll put you where I can find you."

NOTICE

To Our Readers and Advertisers

On MARCH 22

THE
"CAMBRIAN,"
"WEEKLY POST,"
"MID-GLAMORGAN HERALD,"
AND
"HERALD OF WALES"
will be merged into one paper
and produced under the title of

Herald of Wales

And Cambrian.

The New Paper will be published
on FRIDAY as before.

APPENDIX 1

THE CAMBRIAN NEWSPAPER PRINTERS AND PROPRIETORS

On 27 September 1851 William Mansel, a young errand boy, the son of a mariner, was apprenticed to the *Cambrian* – the first newspaper in Wales. This involvement with the printing industry which began when he was 14 years of age was to continue for the remainder of the century, during which time this young apprentice was to become editor and eventually part-proprietor of this important newspaper. The William Mansel Collection, deposited with the County Archive Service, contains documents appertaining to various printers and proprietors of the *Cambrian* allowing an insight into the early history of the paper and the later struggle to maintain its viability.

William Mansel, 1837-1926

A copy of the baptismal certificate of Thomas Jenkins, the first printer, reveals that he was born in Holborn, London in 1771. His apprenticeship to Archibald Hamilton, a stationer, was financed by King Street chapel school as is shown on the original apprenticeship indenture of 1786. An interesting document in its own right, it indicates the severe restrictions placed on apprentices – no gambling, theatre-going or the frequenting of taverns. Six pounds was paid by the trustees of the school for his apprenticeship. Whether he left London immediately following the completion of his apprenticeship is not known but a discharge certificate from the militia for 1797 shows him to be a printer in Worcester at that date. An agreement dated 15 July 1803 indicates that he was to become the printer, publisher and editor of a new newspaper shortly to be established in Swansea – the *Cambrian*. Among the co-partners in this venture were George Haynes, John Jeffreys, Thomas Lynch, Robert Nelson Thomas and John Voss who saw the need for a local paper relevant to the needs of the growing, sophisticated business community. Adverse weather conditions delayed the shipping of the printing presses from Bristol causing the postponement of the first edition until 28 January 1804.

In the early 1820s the need for an experienced printer meant that David Rees was induced to leave the *Carmarthen Journal* (a rival newspaper, serving the conservative, rural communities of West Wales, where the *Cambrian* was regarded as alarmingly *avant-garde*) to join the staff at Swansea. In a letter to an unknown person at the *Cambrian* offices, R. Philipps, the first editor of the *Journal*, feared, erroneously, that the departure of Rees could lead to the paper's demise. From this undated letter it is impossible to state whether Rees was to assist Thomas Jenkins or to be responsible for printing after Jenkins' death but certainly by June 1822 his name is given in the *Cambrian* as one of its printers.

An intriguing item in the collection is a lottery ticket, issued by Hazard in 1823. Popular at the time, tickets were expensive often costing as much as £20, although part shares in tickets were available. Lottery tickets were on sale from local agents and prizes were considerable. The obituary of Howel Walters Williams which appeared in the *Cambrian* of 4 March 1892 states that his father, John Williams, had purchased shares in the newspaper in 1823, with monies won on a lottery – possibly explaining the presence of this ticket. From its inception John Williams had been a frequent contributor to the columns of the *Cambrian*, and his interests lay in the content of the paper rather than its physical production.

The collapse of an ambitious but unwise local coal-mining venture in which John Williams had invested forced him to flee the country and take up residence in France for several years leaving his young, inexperienced son, Howel Walters Williams, in "nominal control of the business". This "young man-about-town" although artistically gifted showed little aptitude for business, and by 1879 his extravagant lifestyle had drained the family's monetary resources putting the future of the *Cambrian* at risk. After the death of his father, he had mortgaged the *Cambrian* on several occasions for substantial sums, and had borrowed heavily from a relative, James Walters of Penlan. This desperate financial situation forced him to relinquish his sole control of the *Cambrian*. William Mansel seized the opportunity to purchase a quarter share of the paper which, it would appear, he had managed single-handed for a number of years.

By 1885 Howel Walters Williams' control of the *Cambrian* was weakening. James Henry Jenkins and Samuel Clearstone Gamwell, both of whom were printers and journalists, became junior partners. (Gamwell was a man of considerable literary talent, many of his poems appearing in the *Cambrian* under the pseudonym Pierre Claire.) Mansel's influence was in the ascendancy, he alone controlled the finances of the paper and he was to be given first refusal of any shares offered for sale in the future.

Some of the letters written to Mansel in his capacity as editor survive: complaints about the tardy cancellation of advertisements; compliments about the timely obituaries of local dignatories; a request from a famous tenor seeking help to "educate" audiences; an invitation to the launch of Mr Vivian's yacht – all offering a glimpse of life in Victorian Swansea and the place of a provincial newspaper editor within that society.

We, the undersigned, in behalf of ourselves and others in a certain memorandum of agreement named, having agreed to become Copartners in a Weekly Newspaper to be entitled The Cambrian, and to be published at Swansea, in the County of Glamorgan, do hereby authorise Thomas Jenkins of the City of Worcester, printer, appointed Editor, Printer and Publisher of the said Newspaper, immediately to order all requisite materials and to make such arrangements as he shall deem proper for carrying on the same; and we bind ourselves to make good all charges so arising, in proportion to the shares we respectively agree to hold in the Concern

Dated this 15th day of July 1803

Geo. Haynes.
Jn. Jeffreys.
Thos. Lynch for self & Partners
Robt. Nelson Thomas
John Voss

Document relating to the founding of a newspaper at Swansea, 15 July 1803.

All of Mansel's working life had been spent with the *Cambrian* and in his will he stipulated that his memorial stone, in Oystermouth cemetery, was to bear the inscription:

William Mansel
Born March 29th 1837
In the town of Swansea
Apprenticed to the
Cambrian Newspaper Office
September 27th 1851
Died October 3rd 1926

Glenys Bridges and Sandra Thomas

APPENDIX 2

An extract from R. D. Rees' 'Glamorgan Newspapers under the Stamp Acts', Morgannwg III *(1959), pp. 61-94.*

"Nineteen publications which may be called newspapers are known to have appeared in Glamorgan before the Newspaper Stamp Tax was repealed in 1855. There may have been more. It was a time when interest in public affairs grew rapidly, and when men turned readily to the printing press to aid their cause. There were almost as many reasons for the appearance, conduct, survival or failure of these papers as there were papers themselves. A brief history of each paper has been given in preference to generalisations, with some reference to the contemporary background in each case. In the account of the *Cambrian*, the difficulties which faced them all have been outlined.

The best source of information about these newspapers is their surviving files. An attempt has been made, based on a reading of these files, to give an indication of their principal characteristics. A complete reading of the files, however, would give a very full social history of the times; the accounts are, therefore, highly selective, and cannot pretend to analyse all aspects of the papers. After 1855 many more papers came out, and daily papers began. A large amount of material remains undescribed.

The Cambrian, and, General Weekly Advertiser for the Principality of Wales

The *Cambrian* was the first periodical printed and published in Wales which began and continued as a newspaper, though some earlier magazines and treasuries, such as *Cylchgrawn Cymraeg neu Drysorfa Gwybodaeth*, had included items of news among their general contents, and, had they survived, might have developed as newspapers. The *Cambrian* was printed in the English language, and was brought into the country as a part of the development of Welsh resources by English capital and English enterprise. Its two most active promoters, George Haynes and Lewis Weston Dillwyn, were both English immigrants, Haynes from Warwickshire some time after 1784, and Dillwyn from London in 1802 or 1803.[1] Hayne's favourite name, *Cambrian*, the name he gave to his pottery and his brewery, was adopted as the title of the paper.[2] They led a proprietary of Swansea business men to raise the necessary capital in one hundred £25 shares.[3] The small printing offices at work in Swansea at the time were not employed. Instead, following an advertisement in the *Gloucester Journal,* as general manager and editor they appointed Thomas Jenkins, who had not set up a press in Swansea or Wales before.[4] The prospectus, said to have been written by Walter Savage Landor, was sent to J. Tymbs

1. *Cambrian,* 20, 27 April 1822 (obit. Thomas Jenkins); *ibid.*, 9 January 1830 (obit. George Haynes); *ibid.*, 7 September 1855 (obit. L. W. Dillwyn).
2. E. M. Nance, *The Pottery and Porcelain of Swansea and Nantgarw* (London, 1942), pp 34-6.
3. *Cambrian,* 15 July 1870 (obit. Miss Georgina Haynes Jenkins).
4. Z. B. Morris, *The Swansea Guide* (Swansea 1802); Ifano Jones, *Printing and Printers in Wales and Monmouthshire* (Cardiff, 1925).

of Worcester to be printed as a handbill.[5] An announcement was made in *St. James' Chronicle*, and types and press ordered in England. Offices were engaged in Wind Street, Swansea, and preparations made for the paper to appear on 7 January 1804.

Despite the encouragement of an expanding economy and a growing population in the area, it was in many ways a difficult time in which to start a newspaper. The effect of poor communications was felt at once. The *Cambrian* did not appear on 7 January, as announced, but on Saturday, 28 January. The sloop *Phoenix*, carrying the new press and type, was weeks overdue; at first held in Bristol by headwinds, and then, driven down-Channel by winter gales, forced to seek refuge in Milford Haven.[6] For most of his material, especially national news, the editor relied on what was brought by the incoming mails each day, sending extracts as soon as possible to the hand-compositors, so that they might have sufficient time to get the pages ready for press by the end of the week. During the winter months, storms at the Severn Passage, and snow and floods inland so delayed the running of the mails that the paper had to be put to press without belated news and advertisements, its columns filled out with general articles and paragraphs which the editor kept ready set in type for this purpose. Local news was difficult to obtain at first, since the paper could not afford to maintain regular paid correspondents, and since the editor could not travel very far afield himself in search of it. He relied on gratuituosly-sent paragraphs, and so had to be on his guard not to be hoaxed by false news, which, whether the product of error, frivolity or malice, could give serious offence to subscribers. Distributing the paper was also a difficult task. The stamp tax, which all newspapers had to pay, entitled them to free carriage by the mails along the roads on which they ran. Some other way had to be found to send the paper to outlying places, usually ill-served by cross roads. Papers left for collection at farms, inns and sub-post offices were not infrequently defaced or lost. When distant subscribers failed to settle their accounts, the paper had to pay the cost in wages, food and lodgings of a man on horseback sent out to collect them.

Heavy taxation and the suspicion or hostility of the ruling class also made the early years of the *Cambrian* particularly difficult ones. Newspapers could be printed only on single sheets, limited in size, and subject to a stamp duty. In 1804 the stamp duty for each sheet stood at 3½d.;[7] in 1815, it was raised to 4d., and remained at this high level until 1836, when it was reduced to1d. Other regulations governing the collection of the stamp duty also, in effect, determined the prices which could be charged for newspapers; for, provided the price did not exceed 6d. a copy (in 1804), 6½d. (in 1809), and 7d. (in 1815) purchases of £10, or more, of stamps entitled purchasers to claim a discount.[8] Paper itself was also taxed, each sheet costing about 1d.; little of the 6d., 6½d, or 7d., which were charged for the *Cambrian*, remained to the paper itself. These very high prices could be afforded only by the relatively well-to-do. In its early years, the weekly sales of the *Cambrian* seldom exceeded 500 copies, and so, after tax, about £5 or £6 remained to meet wages and other costs. To pay its way, therefore, it had to attract

5. Royal Institution of South Wales, Swansea, G. G. Francis collection.
6. *Cambrian*, 28 January 1804. Complete holdings of the *Cambrian* are at R.I.S.W., and a microfilm copy is at Swansea Public Library.
7. In 1797, the duty was increased to 3½d., and 16 *per cent.* discount allowed on purchases of £10, or more, of stamps, if the price charged for the paper did not exceed 6d., if it did, 4 *per cent.* only was allowed (*Cobbett's Parliamentary History, xxxiii*, 434). In 1809, an increase of ½d. per copy was allowed (49 George III, c. 50).
8. In 1815, the stamp duty was raised to 4d., the discount to 20 *per cent*, and the maximum price to 7d. (55 George III, c. 185).

advertisers. Advertisements were taxed as well, and the *Cambrian*'s scale of charges was raised by the amount of the tax.[9] Nevertheless, as an advertiser, it succeeded from 1805 onwards, being always able to fill between 35 and 40 *per cent* of its column space with them. Each column of advertisements, after tax had been deducted, earned from £2 to £2.5s., and a further £15 or so was added to the weekly income. There was always the danger of loss through subscribers or advertisers not paying what they owed. Since all taxes had to be paid promptly, this meant that the paper lost not only the cost of materials and labour, but the amount already paid in tax as well.

Believing that the security of the realm would be endangered by the spread of Jacobinical and other treasonable and seditious ideas, the Government added to its legal powers of suppression and increased its vigilance. the Attorney-General could file informations for libel *ex officio* against obnoxious newspapers, and the mere filing of an information in this way, even when no trial followed, involved the newspaper in heavy expense. From 1801 to 1807 14, and from 1807 to 1810 42 *ex officio* informations were filed.[10] There were countless ultra-loyal self-appointed watchers scattered throughout the country, many of them unable to see any difference between sedition and criticism of ministerial policy, who would send the Home Office copies of offensive papers for any necessary action to be taken. Inadvertence was no defence, nor, as has been said, need the paper be brought to trial; journalists had to be most careful when making up their columns. The *Cambrian* was itself reported by an anonymous informant two weeks before its first number appeared; his suspicions had been aroused by its prospectus which said that the paper would be filed at George's Coffee House, known by him to be Jacobinical.[11] No action was taken against the paper, but the incident shows how careful an editor had to be. Hostile criticism of the magistrates was similarly unwise as John Lewis Brigstoke, printer and publisher of the *Welshman*, discovered later.[12]

The *Cambrian*, having no cause to advance except the general cause of commercial improvement, took no direct part in public controversy while Thomas Jenkins was editor. Dillwyn left the paper about 1817, Jenkins retired in 1822, and Haynes and his son, George Haynes junior became its principal proprietors, with John Roby as editor. William Courtenay Murray and David Rees succeeded Jenkins as printers.[13] In 1826, Haynes became a bankrupt, and John Williams, formerly of Llanelly, joined Murray and Rees as principal proprietor, later purchasing their shares to become sole owner.[14] During Roby's brief editorship in 1822, the *Cambrian* declared itself Tory in support of Huskisson and Free Trade. When he left, later in 1822, it returned to its former neutrality in party matters until 1828, when it began to offer editorial comment in favour of reform. It approved of the abolition of the Test and Corporation Acts, the abolition of the Welsh judicature, the removal of Catholic disabilities, and, above all, the reform of Parliament itself. During the months of anxious struggle, when the fate of the Reform Bill was uncertain, the *Cambrian* Offices at 58 Wind Street provided local reformers with

9. In 1789, the duty on each advertisement, irrespective of length, was raised to 3s. (29 George III, c. 50); it was raised to 3s.6d. in 1815; it was reduced to 1s.6d. in 1833 (3 & 4 William IV, c. 23).
10. A. Aspinall, *Politics and the Press* (London, 1949), pp. 38-60.
11. Public Record Office, H.O. 42/75, dated 12 January 1804.
12. Between 1833 and 1839, five times charged with libel, fined and twice imprisoned.
13. *Cambrian*, 5 January 1822 (change of ownership); 20 April 1822 (obit. T. Jenkins); 9 March to 7 September 1822 (Roby editor).
14. *ibid.*, 24 December 1825 (Haynes' bank stops payment); 22 July 1870 (obit. John Williams). Murray died 1844; Rees retired 1852.

a rallying point, and it was here that Captain Edwards of the Bristol Steam Packet at once brought news of the victory, soon confirmed by shouts from the mail coach as it turned into Wind Street. In 1832, John Williams, "Proprietor of the *Cambrian*", was toasted for his work in the cause of Reform during a dinner given in honour of the election of L. W. Dillwyn and C. R. M. Talbot for the County.[15] Williams was a great admirer of Lord John Russell and his paper during the 1830s was strongly Whig. By the 1840s, its reforming zeal was largely spent, especially in local matters. Two other papers, the Peelite *Swansea Journal* (q.v.), and the liberal *Swansea Herald* (q.v.), were started to supply the *Cambrian's* deficiencies, but the *Cambrian*, though losing some readers, withstood their competition, and, as "the Old Lady of Wind Street", passed into the second half of the century as a successful advertiser, and a repository of safe and cautious news and views.

John Williams and his sons, John Walters Williams and Howell Walters Williams, owned, controlled or neglected the paper, according to their fashion, for many years. In 1881, H. W. Williams, having led, at great expense, "a life of masterly inactivity", took a partner, two more in 1885, and sold out to the *Cambrian Newspaper Company* in 1891. In 1902, David Davies bought it for the South Wales Post Newspaper Co. Ltd.[16]

The fortunes of the *Cambrian* up to the mid-century are reflected in its typographical changes, and its weekly sales. It began as a single sheet, folded to form four small pages, each 20" by 14½", with five columns to the page. It was slightly enlarged in 1828 to make room for more news and advertisements. Despite its high price, 7d. since 1815, its weekly sales were nearly 1,000 copies in 1831. In 1835, it was further enlarged to 24½" by 18", with six columns, and in 1836, following the reduction of the newspaper stamp duty, it lowered its price to 4d.[17] Its sales grew to 1,500 by 1840, though by 1850 the competition of other papers had reduced them to 1,200.[18] In 1845, to suit the new mail times, it was published on Friday. Still four pages, it was enlarged again in 1844, and, in 1852, reached the unwieldy size of 28½" by 19½". In 1853, it came out with eight pages, reduced to 25½" by 18", and, a little later in the same year, announced that it was now being printed on a Cowper steam press.[19] It had grown into a substantial local paper, in total superficies more than three times its original size."

15. *Cambrian*, 29 December 1832.
16. *ibid.*, 4 March 1892 (obit. H. W. Williams); National Library of Wales MS. 2985 E (papers re. management and sale of *The Cambrian*, 1881-92); Ifano Jones, *Printing and Printers*, p. 188.
17. *Cambrian*, 7 February 1835 (enlargement); *ibid.*, 17 September 1836 (price 4d.).
18. Somerset House (Inland Revenue Department), newspaper stamp ledgers from 1831.
19. *Cambrian*, 12 September1845 (published Friday); *ibid.*, 28 September 1844, and 13 February 1852 (enlargements), 6 May 1853 (eight pages), and 28 October 1853 (printed by steam power).

APPENDIX 3

1. 'Cambrian' Synopses

The following synopses are intended to give an indication of the *Cambrian*'s content at various times in its history.

28.01.1804.

Local news in the first edition was very sparse and except for the leading article 'To the Public', the front page was taken up by advertisements; these also appeared to a lesser extent on two other pages. Collieries and an Estate on the Burry Estuary were up for sale or letting, "very considerably below their real value"; a Mansion in Birchgrove and "commodious" houses in Wind-street, Swansea were also on the market.

The Marquis of Bute informed readers that the King had approved the provision of defences, for Swansea Harbour and the adjacent coast, against the threat of invasion by the French. A list of Subscribers to date was printed including £30 each from Harford and Co; Birmingham Mining Copper Company, Messrs Williams and Grenfell and Capt. R. Jones, officers and men of the sea fencibles. There were over sixty other contributions recorded ranging from ten guineas to two shillings and sixpence.

Treatments for mouth hygiene seemed to be money spinners. Newton's warranted tooth brushes and restorative tooth powder, it was claimed, would ensure beauty, health and a good set of teeth. Royal Sweet-Scented Lupin Soap preserved beautiful skin, prevented chapping in winter and cured sunburn in summer. As a sideline, T. Jenkins, printer of *The Cambrian*, advertised a competitive remedy, Amboyna and a cure for coughs, colds and asthma.

Several advertisements referred to books including *The Evangelical Magazine*, headed "Hottentots"; Dr. Turton's "A Medical Glossary", "General System of Nature" and "A Treatise on Cold and Hot Baths" and Thomas Rodd's "The History of the Civil Wars of Granada". Text books on Arithmetic, Book-keeping, Elements of English Grammar and Economics were also advertised as well as tourist guides on the beauties of Wales and France.

The "London" column contained articles and letters about national and international political and economic affairs. There were pieces about settlement day at the stock exchange and a list of stocks. New Jersey was proposing the gradual abolition of slavery and the Queen's birthday was celebrated. Letters had been received from Lord Nelson's fleet blockading Toulon in unprecedented atrocious weather conditions, which also caused havoc at home. The activities of French privateers and the threat of invasion, which was also referred to on the back page, were causing very serious concern.

The current involvement of the USA in foreign fields is not new. The differences between the U.S. and the King of Morocco "have been fully adjusted". Four American Frigates were moored before Tangier in case peace was not achieved.

There was a serious dispute between the 3rd. Company of the Southwark Loyal Volunteers and their Lieut. Colonel Tierney about the filling of vacancies among officers. The Company had elected their Serjeant-Major to the Second Lieutenancy but this was refused by Mr. Tierney who had appointed a stranger.

Under the heading of *A Violent Outrage,* there was a lengthy account of a sex scandal and trial involving a Mrs. Lee's abduction from her house in London's Piccadilly by the Rev. Lockhart Gordon and his brother.

A column headed *SHIP NEWS* announced arrivals and departures from Swansea, Cardiff, Carmarthen, Tenby, Haverfordwest, and Bristol. Notices of Marriages and Deaths of the elite were recorded along with details of Country and London Agricultural markets and high water at Swansea Bar. These items were featured regularly.

Poems entitled "Ode for the New Year" by H. J. Pye, Poet Laureat and "The Curate – a Fragment", by the Rev. Thos. Penrose were also published. The importance of developing London Docks and the Grand Junction Canal was described and there was a summary of the most prominent Political Occurrences of the year 1803. Details were given of Bankruptcies, Dividends, Certificates and the *Cambrian*'s agents throughout Wales, Monmouthshire, Herefordshire and many other parts of England.

——<>——

05.05.1854.

The inclusion of local news in the *Cambrian* had increased but there was still a significant emphasis on wider issues.

Advertisements continued to dominate the front page including those placed by Jones and Eaton, Drapers, of Temple-street; Fuller of High-street, wholesale and retail upholstery, cabinet and general furniture dealers; and the sponsors of the Cheltenham Great Exhibition.

There were advertisements for an excursion on the South Wales and Vale of Neath Railways and Beetham's Capillary Fluid which claimed to prevent greyness and baldness Several advertisements featured small illustrations of railway trains, ships, a Coat of Arms for the Swansea Dock Co. and "Elastic Ligament", artificial legs by James Ashman. Tea, Coffee and Hyam's "Tailors, Clothiers, Hatters and Outfitters, 37 Castle-street" were also advertised. Half a page was devoted to various prophylactic medicines and professed cures for many ailments including mental illness and cholera. Roper's Royal Bath Plasters, it was claimed, superseded the use of "Inward Medicine" for Coughs, Asthma, Hoarsness, Indigestion, Palpitations of the Heart, Croup, Whooping Cough, Influenza, Chronic Strains, Bruises, Lumbago, Pains in the Back, Spinal and Rheumatic Infections, Diseases of the Chest and Local Pains. Holloway's Ointment was said to be "The All-Healing Remedy". Land and Property, the "Fast sailing Pleasure Yacht SIKH", Alexander Murray's & Co.'s Constitutional Pills, Timber and Life Assurance were also advertised.

There were pieces about the Baltic, Russia, America, Mr. Cobden, The Emperor of Austria's Marriage, clerical obituaries and the proceedings of "Imperial Parliament". An "exciting chase" by the frigate Fury in the Black Sea was also featured.

Court news was included as well as a treatment for hydrophobia, a controversy about local rates and a leader entitled "A Glance at the Armed Neutrals" which criticised Austria's and Prussia's lack of resolve in assisting France and Britain to combat the threat of Russian interests.

Letters to the Editor, Births and Deaths of the elite and a report on the "Trade of the Port of Cardiff" appeared along with local news from Neath, Briton-Ferry, Bridgend, Merthyr, Aberdare and Llanelly. Other features included "Literature &c" and the poems "May" and "Old England" – the latter by Gerald Massey.

A lengthy report of the Parliamentary Committee as well as Swansea Police and Petty Sessions hearings, were covered. There were lists of Bankrupts, references to the Admiralty and markets and two columns on "Agriculture and Trade" A similar amount of space was devoted to Russia. The heading "General Intelligence" included pieces about official appointments, commercial speculation, the death of the poet James Montgomery, extensive forgeries by a shoe manufacturer, a reduction of wages in Blackburn and the death of the Marquis of Anglesey.

A "great public meeting" was reported; it was organised by the local Board of Health and dealt, in part, with 'poor book-keeping.' Three columns were taken to describe the scene in the Council Chamber of the Swansea Local Board during a discussion about the maintenance, at public expense, of a well on Mount Pleasant, on land owned by the mayor but used by the public.

——<>——

29. 02 1904.

In 1904 items were mainly of local interest. There was a very brief reference in this edition to the *Cambrian*'s one hundreth anniversary. The relevant extract has been included in the Introduction to this book.

Although the first page was still full of advertisements, the format had changed. As well as the usual columns for Public, Musical, Educational and Trade Notices, over seventy Situations Vacant advertisements were included. Some had been inserted by the up and coming residents of Carlton-terrace, Richmond Villas, and Rhondda-street for cooks, kitchen maids, house and parlourmaids, nurses and 'generals'. The Miscellaneous Situations included opportunities for apprentices, dressmakers, grocery assistants, local commercial representatives, hairdressers and a lather boy for evenings and Saturdays. The Manager of the Glendower Hotel in Torquay offered 30/- weekly for someone "of either sex who can write". Another advertisement claimed that "**Five Pound Notes** would be offered to anyone in exchange for half an hour's work. Clerks, foremen, and others employed in factories, workshops, collieries etc., should send a stamped addressed envelope for particulars of this extraordinary offer – Address Box 16, "Daily Post" Swansea."

There was a feature entitled, "Echoes of the Past. – Interesting Extracts from *The Cambrian* of 1805". Swansea man at Trafalgar. Lieut. Roteley's account of the "Great Battle." Two columns covered the "Endless Crisis" involving the Russians, Japanese and Chinese; and there was a mixture of other national and local news.

"Ladies Gossip" by "Vere" covered the play "Zaza", at The Grand Theatre; and "Football Notes", by "Old Athlete", featured, "Swansea Avenge the Lost Record. –

Decisive and Conclusive Defeat of Newport. – Brilliant Work by Jowett. – Great Game at Llanelly. – Cardiff Just Scrape Home: Nicholls Injured." There was a large advertisement for Lever's Royal Disinfectant Soap Powder and small advertisements for Bovril and Blair's Gout Pills.

Reports on local court cases and other miscellaneous news were included along with news of Morriston and Pontardulais; and the speech made by Akers Douglas, the Home Secretary, at Swansea was reported

"Swansea Jottings" featured reports on a big theft of Sheffield cutlery, the Swansea Jewish and Law Societies and the annual report of Dillwyn and Co. Ltd. "In Lighter Vein" was a column of light hearted snippets. "Neath Notes" commented on "The Scramble for J.P's. – What a Tibetan Spook Overhears. – Lord Chancellor Manifests Interest in Castell Nedd and – A Funny Remark at the Education Committee." Other local news items referred to a farewell banquet to Augustus Lewis, H.M. Inspector of Factories, Glynn Vivian's gift of Dore paintings and a Welsh – American Tinplate agreement.

Under the caption "District News" there were pieces from Swansea, Neath, Llandilo and Llandovery. A large display advertisement promised that, "Prosperity awaits every Willing Worker" in Canada. "G. K. Chesterton's article "Does Europe Exist?" was printed along with narratives about Mabon lecturing in America, a Llanelly boiler explosion, Thomas of Lan's 85th birthday and Gower ponies.

On the back page there were advertisements for Ben Evan's Sale, "Bibby's" Cake and Meals for cattle, an Eisteddfod at Cilycwm, near Llandovery and Oscar Snelling's Gospel meeting at the Albert Hall. Most of the page was devoted to "Notes on Men and Things". Bishop Owen referred to, "This important and growing town – Pontardulais"; and Dr. Jones of the Mumbles stated that, "there are four fifths of a man to each acre of land in this country."

——<>——

01.08.1924.

By 1924 the *Cambrian* was mainly a local newspaper. Its general format had changed; prominent headlines were used and the inclusion of advertisements on the front page had ended. This page now included items about a large motor body manufacturing contract won by Jeffreys and Co. Ltd. Swansea, a fatal collision between a car and a train at the King's Dock and the execution of a Swansea man-Abraham Goldenberg. Smaller pieces dealt with complaints about rival 'buses racing each other in Llanelly and the marriage of the late Dr. T. D. Griffiths' daughter in Switzerland.

There was coverage of a Ministry of Health Enquiry about the effects of fumes at Llansamlet, a child killed at play in Morriston, a Gorseinon man's death by falling into a vat of acid, prosecutions for running illegal 'bus services from Gower, a double bathing tragedy at Porthcawl, the sale of the Birchgrove steel-works for £19892 and a bolting horse tragedy.

Reports referred to a presentation banquet given by colleagues in the tinplate industry for H. C. Bond J.P., a Swansea bankruptcy, the suing of a Swansea motor firm by a member of the aristocracy, and the gassing of a Fforestfach woman. Three small advertisements appeared for Pluvex roofing felt, Foster Clark's Cream Custard and Archer's "Golden Returns Tobacco – the 145 Year's favourite"

Under the heading *The Cambrian* there was a minimal reference to business and political issues affecting the French and German economies and a plea for British industry to improve its efficiency. The 'Post Bag' was a mixture of gossip, humour and news of personalities. For example, Swansea rugby supporters were concerned as to whether Joe Jones' football destiny was with Leeds; and a visitor to Swansea enquired, "Why do not Mumbles and Gower appear in the daily weather reports of health resorts?" "And why indeed?"

Other items referred to a Pwlldu drowning tragedy, the Bowls Cup Final at Llandrindod Wells and a speeding fine of £5.5s. for driving a heavy motor vehicle at 18mph within a 12mph restriction.

——<>——

14.03.1930.

At this time *The Cambrian* was essentially a local paper and its final edition, number 6,204, was published on Friday, March 14th. 1930. At a price of one penny, it was printed and published by the South Wales Post Newspaper Co. Ltd. High-steet, Swansea. The next edition would be incorporated in the *Herald of Wales*.

The use of varying sizes of headlines was now firmly established. There were reports on Drinking Clubs, the future of Palmers' Dry Dock, and a forthcoming local election, including a vitriolic attack on "Swansea Council's 'Mad Finance'," by T. Mainwaring Hughes.

Coverage included the trial of a Swansea G.P.O. Clerk, the decrease in the number of women employed by the tinplate industry, a proposed new dock entrance at Swansea and the deaths of Mrs. Philip Ace of Sketty and Charles Brown, a Neath Bank Manager, who was to be cremated at Pontypridd. Small advertisements appeared for "The Sunday Dispatch", Merryweathers' Hosepipes, Bullins' Motor Cabs, P. Molyneux Fish Merchant, Pluvex Roof Felt and an appeal for the Free Cancer Hospital in London's Fulham-road.

There were 54 nominations for the new Llwchwr District Council listed and reports were given on a violent hailstorm in Swansea, weights and measures discrepancies in Neath, the scandalous quality and cost of furnished "digs", uproar in Swansea Refreshment Houses, Educational Lectures on Food and Drink and a widening scheme for Town-hill-road.

Under the caption of "The Cambrian", United Kingdom politicians' were criticized for their ineptitude and there were references to issues in South Africa and India. "OUR POSTBAG", contained a series of short flippant and sometimes humourous items. Pieces about "Penllergaer Hunt's Good Runs", and the forthcoming visit of the Prince of Wales to Swansea were also included as well as references to a gun accident at Burry Port and a tribute to W. R. Alban of *The Daily Post*. This was significant in that Swansea's *Daily Post* and *Daily Leader* were also merging.

Items also dealt with a fatal lorry crash, Gŵyl Dewi festivities in England, the Diamond Wedding anniversary of Mr. and Mrs. Davies, Channel View, Summer-lane Newton, Mumbles and the award of a D.Sc. to D. Glyn John of Clydach. Local motoring mishaps, a stone quarry worker's death, rugby international revels and the arrival of the s.s. Cambridge "the finest ship that has sailed into the port of Swansea".

One headline referred to a "St. Thomas Girl in Flames" and there were articles on Claude Hirst, a brilliant Swansea scholar, the initial meetings of District Councils, the exorbitant cost of land for Manselton's Infants School, the new *Post and Leader* offices and "Roger Beck to the Rescue."

The edition contained several accounts of local fatal and other serious accidents, the final meeting of the "Cottage Homes", the Drapers' Dance, music in schools, the *Post*'s biggest War Scoop, GWR development schemes in Wales and a "record" international crowd.

Most advertisements had been transferred to the *Herald of Wales*. There was, however one very large advertisement for the "Sunday Pictorial", featuring Mickey Mouse and pieces about Swansea's roads, an allegation that Llanelly's schools are "twenty-years behind the times" and criticism of car costs amounting to £491, incurred by Swansea's Borough Engineer.

——<>——

2. *Statement by 'Cambria Daily Leader' – 24th May 1861*

This statement was made following the objection of *The Cambrian*'s proprietors to the title of the new daily newspaper's title – *The Cambrian Daily Leader.*

"The world is a vast monopoly. There are large monopolies and there are small monopolies. The former differ from the latter only by degrees of magnitude, and magnitude engenders dignity. The large monopolist will play at marbles with mountains and make his bow with the dignity of a spectre of the Hartz; while the small monopolist will indulge in the same game in a pettifogging manner with mole-hills and make his obesience with the plebian jerk of a hackney cad. The world we repeat is a vast monopoly of large and small monopolies and Wales possesses a fair sample of both of them. There is a very small monopoly at Swansea and the little bubble has just risen prettily to the surface and broken under our very nose. A letter signed by a Mr. H. W. Williams professing to be the proprietor of a paper called the *CAMBRIAN* of which periodical some of our readers may have heard, has been laid before the proprietor of the *Daily Leader*. The writer considers that, to use the word "Cambrian" either as a noun or an adjective in connexion with the title of a newspaper is a monopoly and a privilige reserved for him and him alone, and threatens the conductors and the proprietors ot the *Leader* with the severe penalties of the law, in the event of the Principality being any longer used as the arena for the exploits of a weekly newspaper possessing the title of "Cambrian" as a substantive, as in Mr. Williams case and a Daily Newspaper luxuriating in the same title as an adjective as in ours. In using the title which we had assumed, we were sheltered in our position by law, by equity and by common sense, and at the moment of its selection, we were almost unaware of the existence of Mr. Williams' paper. However as we are busily intent on making the *Leader* worthy of the thousands of our countrymen whom we represent and as there are more words than one which will answer our original purpose of desiring to identify the *Daily Leader* with the Welsh nation we have little time and less inclination to contend for a disputed adjective, and this day magnanimously surrender to our friends the sole monopoly of that word, which we in our innocence had thought was free alike to all. Should any of our readers have entertained the faintest shadow of an idea that the *CAMBRIAN* or its people had anything to do with the *Daily Leader* we beg to observe his error forthwith and ask him in justice to give honour to whom honour is due. We have not started on our long course with the intention of trading upon the reputation of that which we were not aware had any reputation to help us, or of resting our claims to national notice upon a journal whose voice as we have discovered is but feebly heard at the circumference of the Borough in which it is published. In deference however to that newspaper and its belongings a consonant has been taken from the adjective "Cambrian" in our title and we press forward in the race as the *Cambria Daily Leader*, none the worse for the attention and being our friends none the better for this their public exhibition of a very small monopoly."

Index

The Cambrian, Friday, March 14, 1930

The Cambrian

AND WEEKLY GENERAL ADVERTISER FOR SWANSEA AND THE PRINCIPALITY OF WALES

ESTABLISHED JANUARY, 1804—THE FIRST NEWSPAPER PUBLISHED IN WALES.

6,204 | REGISTERED AT THE POST OFFICE AS A NEWSPAPER IN THE UNITED KINGDOM. | FRIDAY, MARCH 14, 1930. | Printed and Published by the South Wales Post Newspaper Co. Ltd. at 21, High-street, Swansea. | ONE PENNY

£20,000 SPENT ON POWER STATION SITE.

Mr. T. Mainwaring Hughes Attacks Swansea Council's "Mad Finance"

LOSS OF £20,000 PER ANNUM ON ASYLUM HEATING.

FIGHTING SPEECH IN ST. HELEN'S.

OPENING his election campaign in St. Helen's on Wednesday night, Mr. T. Mainwaring Hughes attacked the Corporation's "mad finance" and orgy of spending, and declared that practically £20,000 had been spent on the super-power station site, which had been turned down.

Criticising the proposal to heat the asylum with electricity, Mr. Hughes said it would mean a loss to the town of £20,000 per annum.

"MAD finance" and Corporation spending was strongly attacked by Mr. Mainwaring Hughes, the Independent candidate in the St. Helen's Ward (Swansea) by-election, in a fighting speech at St. Gabriel's Hall on Wednesday evening.

There was a representative attendance. The chair was taken by Mr. W. Astley Samuel, who was supported by the candidate, and Mr. Arthur Parkes (manager Prince of Wales Dry Dock).

Opening, the chairman said it was time the town stirred and stopped "this mad spending of money" by the Corporation, and unless it was stopped he could see no outlook for the unemployed who were walking the streets. Ratepayers groused, but did not take the trouble to vote, and yet they would have to pay, pay, pay for the road schemes and the heavy cost of education.

SQUANDERMANIA.

In 1912-13 education cost about £4 per child; to-day it was £13. But were the children any better educated to-day than in 1913? ("No"). Moreover there were 111,000 less children in the country last year than the year before. What were they building new schools for? He characterised it as squandermania. (Hear, hear).

Mr. Hughes, the candidate, recalled an admission made at a recent dinner by the Mayor that the present day public expenditure compared with eight or nine years ago was staggering, and that possibly it was due to schemes that should have been undertaken years ago. The candidate proceeded to examine the position.

Last month the Council approved of an expenditure amounting to practically a million pounds. Some £280,000 it was proposed is for a superannuation scheme for the benefit of the municipal employees. That was a first instalment to level up the older employees, who were near the pensionable age. Then the Council propose to make a contribution equivalent to five per cent. on the wages bill. He did not object to superannuation and wished it could be general, but could the town afford it to a section of employees who were comparatively well paid and in sheltered occupations when the money had to be found at the expense of others, many of whom were not only unemployed, but had to struggle to make two ends meet?

He thought it was a most grossly unfair thing for the Corporation to do at the present time. (Hear, hear).

FINANCE GONE MAD.

Then they had the "small item" of £280,000 passed in one afternoon with very little consideration by the Education Committee on a schools programme. Could they understand the mentality of men who passed expenditure like that? It seemed to him it was finance gone mad! (Hear, hear).

And they could hardly wonder that the same Committee also passed an item of £800 for a hockey pitch and £600 for a tennis court "for the dears" who could not take the trouble to walk to the park and pay for their tennis the same as other players had to do. (Hear, hear). One wondered whether there was any limit to it?

ASYLUM HEATING.

Then there was the joint asylum, for which Swansea was paying its share and lending Merthyr the money to pay for theirs.

Under that scheme the Electricity Committee for some unaccountable reason proposed to light and heat the Institution with electricity for ½d. per unit that actually cost ⅞d. to produce. That meant a loss of £20,000 per annum which should go to the reduction of the rates.

There was another side to it. The ½d. per unit was at least four times more than the cost of central heating by ordinary coal. He had been twitted that he was biassed because he was in the coal trade. Just so, and being in the coal trade he had access to the facts and knew something about heating values. Everywhere else heating by electricity had been condemned by heating engineers, but Swansea was to be the first place to try it. That was the attitude of the Swansea Electricity Committee. If his figures were wrong they at least should be told, but they could get no answer to it.

£20,000 ON SUPER STATION.

Then in regard to the electricity super station site, when he told them that up to date practically £20,000 had been paid out they would be astonished.

And that was the fact, and of course the scheme had been turned down. "The site has been turned down," Mr. Hughes said, "and we have not yet finished paying for it yet. There are men in Swansea who have collected £6,000 from the Corporation towards finding that site, and when I tell you further that the official who had that matter in hand made the arrangements, I understand, without a scrap of paper between himself and the people employed you will think it is a matter for further investigation, won't you (Hear, hear.)

VERY LAX.

"You will think that somebody has been very lax in this matter, and wonder why we put men on the Council to form themselves into committees and shelve their responsibilities in that disgraceful manner. And that is what is going on to-day." (Hear, hear). The candidate wondered if the Mayor would still suggest that the money the Council was wasting was for work which should have been started years ago.

He did not propose to harrow them with those things, but such expenditure had to be stopped and, without any frills, he stood absolutely for ruthless economy. (Applause).

HIS PROGRAMME.

His programme, if returned, was:

"(1) That we absolutely refrain from any more non-essential schemes involving capital expenditure until the town is in a sounder financial state; (2) that we examine those schemes to which the town is already committed with a view of curtailing or abandoning them altogether, and (3) that an Axe Committee be appointed to thoroughly examine the spending departments of the Corporation to see what savings can possibly be effected."

"PITIFUL, DISGRACEFUL."

He was not so foolish as to suggest that that could be achieved at once, or that one man was going to do it, but there was a small coterie on the Council who were in earnest and desirous of effecting economy. It was pitiful, disgraceful.

He remembered in that very hall hearing Mr. David Davies, who did the same fighting in those days, saying that "what St. Helen's does to-day the rest of Swansea will do to-morrow." (Hear, hear). And they could depend upon it that if the ratepayers of St. Helen's voiced their feeling in the matter on Tuesday next, their example would be followed very soon by all the other wards of the borough. (Applause).

Mr. Bert Evans proposed a vote of confidence in Mr. Hughes' candidature, and recalled the advent of the Municipal Reform Party in 1907, when it swept the town.

BLAENNANTDDU.

Touching upon the "moral victory over the Blaennantddu litigation," he asked if there was a single member of the Council who was prepared to stand up and say that the reservoir should be filled? (Hear, hear.)

Let them send Mr. Hughes to the Council, and he would ask that it be done. (Hear, hear.)

Mr. Dan Evans seconded.

Mr. W. Morgan (an ex-president of the Chamber of Commerce) supported, and said that industry simply could not carry this board of expenditure on its back. In his opinion, the rates of Swansea with its big Corporation estate, should not exceed 10s. in the £.

Mr. Arthur Parkes, also supporting, declared that the expenditure of the Council was appalling, and if it were allowed to continue, what was Swansea going to achieve by the support the G.W.R. was giving to the port? (Hear, hear.)

The resolution was carried unanimously, and a vote of thanks to the chairman for presiding concluded the meeting.

It was announced that Mr. Mainwaring Hughes would address another meeting at Rhyddings Schoolroom on Monday next.

HOW CLUBS GET RID OF THEIR PROFITS.

Mr. H. Rogers' Evidence Before Commission.

SUNDAY OPENING PROTESTS.

The matter of clubs giving bottles of whisky as presents to the members was raised when Mr. Harry Rogers, of Swansea, on behalf of the Licensed Victuallers' Defence League of England and Wales, continued his evidence at to-day's session of the Licensing Commission in London.

The Rev. Henry Carter asked if at Christmas time clubs had given out bottles of whisky to their members as presents? Mr. Rogers explained that clubs got rid of surplus profits by giving Christmas presents to members, and by running summertime outings at cheap rates.

Mr. Carter asked if the Christmas bottle of whisky was a rare thing or a widespread habit?

"WOULD BE DISAPPOINTED."

"Members would be very disappointed if they did not get their presents," replied Mr. Rogers.

Mr. Carter: Are you referring to a widespread practice in the mining districts of South Wales?

Mr. Rogers: Where clubs are rich enough—most of them are—this is a general practice.

Questions about tied houses followed, and then Mr. Carter referred to Sunday opening and Mr. Rogers' statement at the last meeting of the Commission.

Mr. Rogers said there had been a report in the local paper of protests against his statement for Sunday opening.

Mr. Carter: The Commission has received protests.

Mr. Rogers: I spoke then as a representative of the licensed victuallers and as a Swansea citizen.

PROTESTS FROM CHURCHES.

Mr. Carter stated that 58 churches of two denominations and local brotherhoods and sisterhoods in Swansea had protested to the Commission, saying that so far as they were concerned Swansea was just as strongly against Sunday opening as ever it were.

"I don't agree with that," declared Mr. Rogers. "I should like to know the number of people at the meeting, and I regard them somewhat in the manner of the nine tailors of Tooley-street."

He added that he was fairly religious himself and he knew many churchmen who would vote for Sunday opening.

Continuing, he said that had he taken a resolution in his own establishment after the big match in Swansea, last Saturday, there would have been an unanimous vote for Sunday opening.

The subject of workmen trying to get away from the blast furnaces ten minutes before work finished in order to get a drink was mentioned, and he used the phrase that "the men were dying for a drink."

The Chief Constable, thought Mr. Rogers, was in favour of the extension of hours as it would help the police.

SUGGESTED HOURS.

He suggested that the hour for opening in Swansea should be from 10.30 a.m. to 10.30 p.m.

Swansea was more anxious to please the general public than the rest of Wales. He measured the public demand by various reports made to him.

Mr. Rogers said that the churches and chapels had a greater hold on the public fifty years ago, than now. They pulled political strings then more successfully than now. They had political power then.

BARMAIDS' DRINKS.

Mrs. Symon, one of the three women members of the Commission, tackled Mr. Rogers on the subject of barmaids, and, in answer to her, Mr. Rogers stated that he did not think they worked longer than barmen.

Questioned by Mrs. Symon about the suggestion that barmaids are entitled to five free alcoholic drinks, he said that he would be very sorry to see any ladies drinking during the day.

"I don't allow barmaids to drink with customers unless under special circumstances, when they are allowed to have port wine."

REDUCED ESTIMATES.

Expenditure on Highways at Swansea.

Reductions in estimates were decided upon by the Swansea Highways Committee this afternoon as follows:

£1,000 due to electric lighting costs; £2,370 capital charges; £984 contingencies, making a total of £4,354.

Set off against this was an increase of £4,500 for road maintenance, which left a net increase of £146.

G.W.R. AND PALMER'S DOCK.

"We Shall Not Do Away With It."

PURCHASE POSSIBILITIES.

There is no doubt about the taking in hand of the second entrance to the main Swansea Docks. The Great Western Railway, owner of the world's largest dock system, covering a total water area of 1,300 acres, announced on Wednesday that the Government had approved the schemes, involving an expenditure of £3,000,000, for further improvements to its docks.

The schemes include:

Additional lock entrance to Swansea Docks.

Extension of piers at Port Talbot.

Improvement of cranes at Newport, Cardiff, Barry, and Penarth (making it possible to deal with 20-ton instead of 10-ton wagons).

At Wednesday's Parliamentary enquiry Mr. C. S. Page, docks manager of the Great Western Railway, stated that Swansea was the main centre for the export of anthracite coal. It was, in his opinion, absolutely necessary to have another entrance lock.

In cross-examination the witness was asked if, in case his company purchased Palmer's Dry Dock, would ships have to go abroad or elsewhere for repairs, and he replied "No, we shall not do away with the dry dock."

SIR BENFRO.

Officers Elected of the Swansea Society.

The third annual meeting of the Swansea and District Pembrokeshire Society was held at the Baltic Lounge. The chairman, the Rev. L. H. James, presided. The balance-sheet, given by the treasurer (Mr. Price Jones) showed that the balance in hand had increased from £13 to £38.

Mr. Griffiths, the secretary, in making his report, stated that the membership was now nearly 500.

The chairman was elected for another year, at least, and the pleasure this gave everybody was shown by the hearty manner in which his re-election was received. Mr. Ivor Gwynne was re-elected as vice-chairman. The treasurer, Mr. Price Jones, and the secretary, Mr. E. H. Griffiths, who were cordially thanked for the services they had rendered to the society, were re-elected. Sir E. Marlay Samson, K.C., was re-elected president for 1930. The annual outing was fixed for July 10, when a tour of South Pembrokeshire, including Pembroke, Manorbier and Carew Castles, Stack Rocks and Bosherston Pools, will be made.

AMMANFORD ELECTION CANDIDATES.

Possibility of Communists Standing.

The Trades and Labour organisations in Ammanford have decided to contest all the five seats on the Ammanford Urban District Council, which are to be filled at the election on April 7th.

At a ward meeting on Wednesday night the following Labour nominees were selected: Messrs. Thomas Davies (retiring councillor), John Harries, Haydn Lewis, Evan J. Thomas and Mrs. E. A. Lewis.

The councillors who retire besides Mr. Thomas Davies are: Rev. John Morgan, Mr. Evan Davies (present chairman of the Council), and Mr. W. Comery, B.Sc., and it is anticipated that they, too, will seek re-election and may be joined by several new candidates on the Independent side.

Another possibility is that the Communist Party will bring out a candidate

(Continued from preceding column.)

TALKING IN THE DARK!

Finance Committee and Chamber of Trade.

"WE ALL AGREE."

Swansea Finance Committee, on Wednesday, decided to reply "in suitable terms" to the Swansea Chamber of Trade's resolution "viewing with serious alarm the proposed enormous capital outlay in connection with the various corporation departments," and urging, in view of the present depression in trade, the necessity of not embarking on any capital outlay not absolutely essential to the health and well being of the community.

Mr. Bevan (when the resolution was read): We all agree to that.

Mrs. H. D. Williams: There is an impression abroad that we have no thought for the ratepayers.

Mr. Percy Morris complained of "ill-informed criticism from responsible bodies." If they were disposed to criticise, he added, they ought to do so constructively.

Mr. W. A. Jenkins: There is nothing at all in that of a critical nature. It is simply a very nice letter from a responsible body.

Mr. Morris: The impression is abroad that the Chamber of Trade and the Chamber of Commerce are the only people concerned with the rates. Of course, it is not so; we are equally concerned.

He added that if these bodies could help with constructive criticism it would be welcomed.

Mrs. H. D. Williams: They don't know how we go into the matters inside. We don't spend this money injudiciously; we are as much concerned about it as the people on the outside.

Mr. Miles: A good deal of the trouble in the world was caused by misunderstanding.

THE LIGHT THAT FAILED.

Mr. Owen: I notice that since we have been discussing this the lights have gone out!

The chairman (Mr. W. H. Miles): That is evidence of economy. (Laughter.)

THOSE DEPUTATIONS!

Neath R.D.C. Complaint of Substitution.

Once again reference was made at the Neath Rural District Council, on Wednesday, to the place of a member on a deputation being taken by another, to the surprise of the appointed man.

At the last meeting of the council Mr. Protheroe had pointed out that Mr. Jones' place had been taken by another member, and it was then said that it was not the first time such a substitution had been made.

Mr. Protheroe now said that when he made allegations in December he was asked two months later to withdraw. He did not intend to do so, and he would make some more allegations at the next council. He now wanted proof of the allegations by another member.

Mr. William Jones said that it was clearly understood that he was one appointed to go on the deputation to Cardiff.

Mr. Ogley L. David, the chairman, said that it was a misunderstanding that Mr. Jones did not go.

The matter dropped.

SWANSEA CHOIR'S BIG SUCCESS.

Legion Women Cup Winners in London.

The members of the Swansea British Legion (Women's Section) Choir acquitted themselves with credit at the annual singing contest held at Kensington, London, on Wednesday. Miss Mabel Chamberlain was the adjudicator and 13 choirs competed. In presenting the Essie Harris Cup to Swansea, Miss Chamberlain congratulated the choir upon their team work.

The Swansea ladies also won the Emily Daymond Cup, securing 475 marks out of a possible 500. Miss Irene Walters won the soprano solo certificate of merit, first-class, and Madame Bessie Griffiths a similar award, in the contralto solo competition. Miss M. Blain, the accompanist, and Mr. W. Norwood, the conductor, also received praise for their excellent work with the choir.

The Pontardawe Choir were successful in winning the Minnie McKenzie Cup.

Rev. J. Gimblett, Brynhyfryd, lectured on "Foundations of our Christian Faith" at Tabernacle Baptist Church, Carmarthen-road, Swansea, on Wednesday evening. Mr. A. J. Carver presided over an appreciative attendance.

The final edition.